Psychology Revivals

Experimenting with Personal Construct Psychology

Originally published in 1988, *Experimenting with Personal Construct Psychology* provided an up-to-date account of the state of personal construct psychology revealing the diversity of its application and its exciting developments at the time. It had been thirty years since George Kelly published his *The Psychology of Personal Constructs* and his ideas and methodology had become widely known internationally and acknowledged as significant contributions to the theory and practice of psychology as the science of human experience and behaviour. Kelly's ideas had been elaborated, the range of convenience of the theory had been greatly extended, and this was the focus for the congress on which this volume is based. It is divided into eight parts: Theory, Education, Children, Clinical, Methodology, Industrial Settings, Attitudes and Beliefs and The Arts. The contributors reflect the international reach of the theory.

This book is a re-issue originally published in 1988. The language used and views portrayed are a reflection of its era and no offence is meant by the Publishers to any reader by this re-publication.

Experimenting with Personal Construct Psychology

Edited by
Fay Fransella and Laurie Thomas

Routledge
Taylor & Francis Group
LONDON AND NEW YORK

First published in 1988
by Routledge & Kegan Paul

This edition first published in 2026 by Routledge
4 Park Square, Milton Park, Abingdon, Oxon, OX14 4RN

and by Routledge
605 Third Avenue, New York, NY 10158

Routledge is an imprint of the Taylor & Francis Group, an informa business

Publisher's Note
The publisher has gone to great lengths to ensure the quality of this reprint but points out that some imperfections in the original copies may be apparent.

Disclaimer
The publisher has made every effort to trace copyright holders and welcomes correspondence from those they have been unable to contact.

For Product Safety Concerns and Information please contact our EU representative GPSR@taylorandfrancis.com. Taylor & Francis Verlag GmbH, Kaufingerstraße 24, 80331 München, Germany

A Library of Congress record exists under ISBN: 9780710210623

ISBN: 978-1-041-29412-2 (hbk)
ISBN: 978-1-003-76939-2 (ebk)
ISBN: 978-1-041-29417-7 (pbk)

Book DOI 10.4324/9781003769392

Experimenting with Personal Construct Psychology

Edited by

Fay Fransella
Director
Centre for Personal Construct Psychology
London

Laurie Thomas
Director
Centre for the Study of Human Learning
Brunel University
Uxbridge
Middlesex

ROUTLEDGE & KEGAN PAUL
London and New York

This collection first published in 1988 by
Routledge & Kegan Paul Ltd
11 New Fetter Lane, London EC4P 4EE

Published in the USA by
Routledge & Kegan Paul Inc.
in association with Methuen Inc.
29 West 35th Street, New York, NY 10001

Set in Garamond 12/13
by Input Typesetting Ltd, London
Printed and bound in Great Britain by
Butler & Tanner Ltd, Frome and London

Library of Congress Cataloging in Publication Data

Experimenting with Personal Construct Psychology

Proceedings of the Sixth International Congress
Held at Churchill College, Cambridge, England, Aug. 5–9,
1985.
Includes Index.
1. Personal Construct Theory—Congresses.
I. Fransella, Fay. II. Thomas, Laurie F. (DNLM:
1. Learning—Congresses. 2. Models, Psychological—
Congresses. 3. Psychology, Applied—Congresses.
BF 636 E96 1985)
BF698.9.047E96 1987 155.2 87–12736

British Library CIP Data also available
ISBN 0–7102–1062–0

This book is dedicated to

DON BANNISTER

who died in Ilkley, West Yorkshire, UK,
in July 1986

Don Bannister has been a central figure in personal construct psychology for nearly thirty years. Friend and disciple of George Kelly, he became chief advocate for this vision of what psychology might become. Don was mightily involved in each international congress of PCP – from Nebraska, USA (1975), to Cambridge, England (1985), when he was chairman of the organizing committee and president of the congress. This book of papers from what was sadly to prove his last congress is therefore offered as a direct tribute to Don's lively mind and organizing abilities. He will be remembered with love and gratitude by many, not only within his clinical homeground but much more widely. He will be sorely missed by all those whom he encouraged and supported in their endeavours to apply PCP to an increasingly wide range of human activities, and to develop and extend its ideas into the vision as well as the words of George Kelly. We believe that this book of readings illustrates the success of the PCP community in moving in both these directions. We know that Don was much encouraged in his last year by the progress which continues to be made. Many of us have lost a friend, but whilst PCP continues to flourish, Don's constructively combative spirit is still out there with us. Perhaps he is even now arguing again with George. They are in our hearts. Long may their humanizing influence on psychology endure and grow.

Contents

Contributors

Don Bannister, deceased *Enquiries to*: Sharon Jackson High Royds Hospital Menston Ilkley West Yorkshire LS29 6AQ England

Miriam Ben-Peretz University of Haifa Mount Carmel Haifa 31 999 Israel

Stephen Black Massey University Palmerston North New Zealand

Philip Boxer Director, Boxer Research Ltd 8 Sutherland Road London W4 2QR England

Cathleen A. Brown 414 Yale Avenue Claremont California 91711

Eric Button Department of Psychiatry University of Southampton South Hants Hospital Graham Road Southampton 509 4PE England

John Cary School of Agriculture and Forestry University of Melbourne Parkville Australia

Sylvia Chard College of St Paul and St Mary The Park Cheltenham Gloucestershire GL50 2RH England and Associate of the Centre for the Study of Human Learning Brunel University Uxbridge Middlesex UB8 3PH England

Li Chin-Keung Clinical Psychologist St Clement's Hospital Foxhall Road Ipswich IP3 8LS England

Graham Crosby Hampshire Education Authority and Associate of the Centre for the Study of Human Learning Brunel University Uxbridge Middlesex UB8 3PH England

Peggy Dalton Consultant Clinician Centre for Personal Construct Psychology 132 Warwick Way London SW1V 4JD England

Charles J. Detoy Vice President Training and Development Coldwell Banker Commercial Group 533 Fremont Avenue Los Angeles California 90071

Patrick Diamond Queensland Education Department University of Queensland St Lucia Queensland Australia 4067

Auriol Drew Speech Therapist Speech Therapy Department Thornton House General Hospital Nottingham England

Gavin Dunnett MRC Psycho. Consultant Psychiatrist, Redcliffe Centre for Community Psychiatry 51 Hatton Park Road Wellingborough Northants England

Peter du Preez Department of Psychology University of Cape Town Rondebosch Cape 7700 South Africa

Anne Edwards Principal Lecturer in Primary Education West Glamorgan Institute of Higher Education Wales

Marie Luisa Figueroa Faculty of Humanities Universidad Aubonoma Metropolitana Azcapotzalco Mexico and c/o Centre for the Study of Human Learning Brunel University Uxbridge Middlesex UB8 3PH England

Robert Foley Rehabilitation Institute Roslyn Park Sandymount Dublin 4 Ireland

Fay Fransella Director Centre for Personal Construct Psychology 132 Warwick Way London SW1V 4JD England

Georgianna Gardner Centro Psicoterapia Cognitiva Via Degli Scipione 245 00192 Rome Italy

Alison Gold Hall Department of Psychology University of Florida Gainesville 32611 USA

E. Sheila Harri-Augstein Centre for the Study of Human Learning Brunel University Uxbridge Middlesex UB8 3PH England

Rosemarie Hayhow Lecturer in Speech Therapy Central School of Speech and Drama London England

Elizabeth Ann Hill (E. A. Rix) Education Consultant 37 Devonshire Drive Bramalea Ontario Canada L6T 3G5

James Horley Research Department Mental Health Centre P.O. Box 698 Penetanguishene Ontario Canada LOK IPO

Annabel Jackson Marketing Manager London Industrial plc England

Sharon Jackson Senior Research Staff Medical Research Council Project Grant High Royds Hospital Menston Ilkley West Yorkshire LS29 6AQ England

Professor Marie Jahoda Emeritus Professor of Social Psychology University of Sussex Falmer Sussex England

Helen Jones Independent Management Consultant and Counsellor 2 St George's House 23 Castlegate York YO1 1RN England

Devorah Kalekin-Fishman University of Haifa Mount Carmel Haifa 31 999 Israel

Vincent J. Kenny Institute of Constructivist Psychotherapy 21 Summerhill Dun Laoire Dublin Eire

John Kirkland Massey University Palmerston North New Zealand

Robert Lambourne Massey University Palmerston North New Zealand

Richard Lansdown Chief Psychologist Department of Psychological Medicine Hospital for Sick Children Great Ormond Street London WC1N 3JH England

Larry M. Leitner Department of Psychology Miami University Oxford Ohio 45056 USA

Roberto Lorenzini Psychiatrist and psychotherapist Centro di Psicoterapia Cognitiva Via Degli Scipioni 237 00192 Rome Italy

Spencer A. McWilliams Psychology Department Winthrop College South Carolina 29733 USA

Jenny Maddick Principal Educational Psychologist Child Guidance Centre Tanner Street Winchester Hampshire England

Francesco Mancini Centro Psicoterapia Cognitiva/Associazione Italiana per la Psicologia dei Construtti Personali Via Degli Scipioni 245 00192 Rome Italy

James C. Mancuso Professor of Psychology University at Albany – State University of New York Albany New York 12222 USA

Michael F. Mascolo Assistant Professor of Psychology Merrimack College North Andover Massachusetts 01845 USA

David Miall College of St Paul and St Mary The Park Cheltenham Gloucestershire GL50 2RH England and Associate of the Centre for the Study of Human Learning Brunel University Uxbridge Middlesex UB8 3PH England

Adrian Needs Senior Psychologist HM Prison Love Lane Wakefield Yorkshire WF2 9AG England

Greg J. Neimeyer Associate Professor, Department of Psychology University of Florida Gainesville Glorida 32611 USA

Rosamond Nutting Queensland Education Department University of Queensland St Lucia Queensland Australia 4067

Bernadette O'Sullivan Institute of Constructivist Psychotherapy 21 Summerhill Dun Laoghaire Dublin Ireland

Maurice Randall Department Head, Business Development Trustee Savings Bank, York Region 310 Tadcaster Road York and Centre for the Study of Human Learning Brunel University Uxbridge Middlesex UB8 3PH England

Tom Ravenette Principal Educational Psychologist London Borough of Newham Child Guidance Clinic West Ham Lane London E15 England

Sandra Sassaroli Psychiatrist and psychotherapist Centro Psicoterapia Cognitiva Via Degli Scipioni 237 00192 Rome Italy

Antonio Semerari Centro Psicoterapia Cognitiva/Associazione Italiana per la Psicologia dei Construtti Personali Via Degli Scipioni 237 00192 Rome Italy

Peter Stringer Policy Research Institute Queen's University of Belfast and University of Ulster Belfast Northern Ireland

Laurie F. Thomas Centre for the Study of Human Learning Brunel University Uxbridge Middlesex UB8 3PH England

Norman Todd Parish priest/Spiritual director and consultant The Vicarage, Rolleston Newark Notts NG23 5SE England

Linda Viney Department of Psychology University of Wollongong P.O. Box 1144 (Northfields Avenue) Wollongong New South Wales 2500 Australia

Joyce Watson 94a Clyde Road Croydon Surrey CR0 6SW

David Winter Principal Clinical Psychologist Napsbury Hospital London Colney St Albans Hertfordshire AL2 1AA England

Mantz Yorke Centre for Educational Development and Training Manchester Polytechnic Hathersage Road Manchester M13 0JA England

Preface

Thirty years have now elapsed since George Kelly published his *The Psychology of Personal Constructs*. Following the highly successful 1975 Nebraska Symposium on Kelly's work and ideas, there have been a series of biennial international congresses. The sixth, most recent and best attended took place at Churchill College, Cambridge, England, 5–9 August 1985.

From a slow start, Kelly's ideas and methodology have become widely known internationally and acknowledged as significant contributions to the theory and practice of psychology as the science of human experience and behaviour. Its place among the leading psychological theories of today is now much more clearly defined. Kelly's ideas have been elaborated and the range of convenience of the theory has been greatly extended.

It is on this issue of range of convenience that Professor Marie Jahoda chose to focus attention in her invited address at the start of the Sixth International Congress. The rest of this book contains a selection of papers from the over 150 presented there. Choosing the papers has been very difficult, since the overall standard was high. We decided to select those which appeared to attract more interest from fellow participants, which seemed fairly representative of the range of topics, ideas and methods covered and which will introduce readers to relatively new areas of work. In short, selection was never solely upon academic merit. The book also obviously reflects our own interests, values and judgments.

Following on from Marie Jahoda's invited address, the papers have been divided into eight parts. As proponents of personal construct psychology will appreciate, the divisions are of necessity somewhat arbitrary since elements never fall completely and easily into the cells of somebody else's category system. However, our part headings did emerge from successive reordering of the topics and themes of the papers.

There is a healthy crop of items which we have grouped under Part A, 'Theory'. These link personal construct psychology with some of its scientific and philosophical antecedents and point towards its possible future. Radical reflections upon how Bartlett, Popper, Maturana and Bateson relate to Kelly and to therapy, neo-cybernetics, human learning and computers, encourage us to expand our range of alternative constructions.

Parts B and C are on 'Education' and 'Children' respectively. Personal construct psychology ideas and methods in education are being applied to the encouragement of personal learning in polytechnics, primary education and universities as well as to teacher and technical training. While not new, reports of work with children and parents is still sparse. We are therefore pleased to be able to include five papers covering a variety of topics from parent-role construing to trying to construe the construction processes of children to a mother's very personal account of the role personal construct psychology ideas played in helping her deal with the dying of her child.

Kelly's ideas continue to thrive and grow in its 'clinical' birthplace. Chapters in Part D, 'Clinical', are concerned with building theoretical alternatives to concepts previously subsumed under the medical model; studies of interpersonal perceptions and conflicts; the elderly; and a personal-construct view of social-skills training.

Much work described in the previous and following parts use some form of repertory grid. Part E, 'Methodology', is therefore included for the many who are interested primarily in developing these methods and exploring their limitations.

The final three parts are more varied and cover relatively new areas of interest. The first concerns work within industrial settings. The second is, perhaps, the most heterogeneous grouping, containing as it does feminism, politics, religious belief and a psychological investigation of offending behaviour. The best we could do here was to name it 'Attitudes and Beliefs'.

The last part is on The Arts. The artist demands to be accepted in his or her own terms. Society sometimes finds this difficult to appreciate. The Arts – novels, music, poetry and personal biography – are therefore ideally suited to a personal construct psychology approach. The papers in this last section indicate how well this is proceeding.

We feel particularly encouraged to have been able to present work by authors from Israel, Italy and Mexico as well as Australia, USA, Canada and Britain. We hope that this up-to-date presentation of the state of personal construct psychology is informative, stimulating and supportive for those already operating with these ideas and methods as well as attractive, interesting and 'moreish' to those who are coming to them for the first time.

Fay Fransella
Laurie Thomas
1986

Opening address:

The range of convenience of personal construct psychology – an outsider's view

Marie Jahoda

Given my admiration for George Kelly as a psychologist, why have I remained an outsider to this Kelly community and never used his theory in my own work? Whatever my own shortcomings, there is hidden in this personal question a general issue: the range of convenience of PCT.

It was twenty-five years ago that Neil Warren – whose tragic death has deprived the Kelly community, as it has his other friends – first made me realise that there was more to PCT than my vague acquaintance with it had led me to suppose. At Neil's initiative we organised at Brunel, where we both worked, a series of Kelly seminars. They became memorable because Kelly, asked to advise on a suitable speaker, came himself and spent four days with us. Some of you may be familiar with the documentation of these seminars which Neil edited.[1] There it emerged that there was more to Kelly than the grid, more even than PCT, and I do not mean his gentle and passionate personality, impressive though this was, but his general approach to psychology.

To spell out what I mean by this will be the first point in this presentation. In the light of this I will then discuss the claim that Kelly's work has a range of convenience beyond personality theory[2] from the point of view of a social psychologist.

Personal construct theory: approach or theory

First, then, an appreciation of Kelly's achievements. Kelly began to go his own original way at a time when American academic psychology was still in the grip of a behaviourism that recognised only external, not psychological reality. Two factors, one experiential and the other intellectual, were particularly significant in his development. First, he was a practising psychologist, deeply involved with people in distress and committed to helping them. Second, he came to terms with Freud, whom he had first read as a student and totally rejected, then under the impact of his practical work rediscovered as a kindred spirit, becoming first a 'good' Freudian and finally adopting some psychoanalytic terms and insights while rejecting others in the process of gradually developing his own ideas.

The Kellian body of thought is as a rule referred to as a theory. He himself was highly ambivalent about this designation. In his 'brief introduction to personal construct theory'[3] he uses three different terms about his contribution. First, he rejects the term 'theory' because 'it does not say what has or will be found, but proposes rather how we might go about looking for it' (p. 1). A few pages later (p. 8) he talks none the less of his 'theory', and almost immediately afterwards (p. 9) he agrees to call it a 'meta-theory', that is 'a theory about a theory'.

At the Brunel seminars there was a rather heated debate, this one unfortunately without Kelly, about whether he had provided a theory or an approach. With due respect to all the participants I find on rereading the arguments that we got it all wrong; certainly I did. It is not an either/or issue as I then thought; Kelly had both, an approach and a theory.

To make this more than a quibble about words, I shall spell out what I mean by an approach and then describe Kelly's. An approach is a relatively content-free point of view about how best to proceed in studying people. It is based on extra-scientific assumptions and often incorporates personal values. It contains the fundamental question to which a psychologist seeks answers. In contrast to theories, an approach can therefore neither be verified nor falsified: you can only take it or leave it. If, for example, Skinner's concern is with the impact of the environment on organisms, or Eysenck's with the biological foundations of psychological phenomena, this is – as it were – their affair; they too have their place in the many-splendoured mansion of psychology. Only to the extent that they deny the legitimacy of other approaches (as they both are inclined to do) or that their theories or research data can be attacked on their own ground are such enterprises questionable.

Cognitivism

What then is Kelly's approach? Above all Kelly is a cognitivist, in the modern sense of this term. In the dim past when I first studied psychology, the term 'cognitive' was, following Aristotle, understood as one of the three basic faculties of the soul, the other two being conative and emotive. At present, the use of the term is confused and confusing. While some cognitivists still adhere to the old distinction, the broader view that Kelly had in mind is gradually gaining ground. 'PCT', he said, 'is built on the intellectual model but is not intended to be limited to what is called cognitive'.[4] Kelly, and modern cognitivism in general, increasingly tend to embrace all three faculties. This modern concept is best understood in contrast to behaviourism, that relegates all internal events and processes to the 'black box', by definition outside its concerns. Modern cognitivism, however, makes the entire content of the black box its exclusive concern in the recognition that all psychological phenomena rest on symbolic representations in the mind, including not only perceiving, learning, thinking and remembering but also desire and feeling because they too are tied to cognitions. You cannot perceive, learn, think, remember, desire or feel without an internal representation of an object to which these psychological processes refer. In artificial intelligence, the newest branch of the cognitive sciences, it has become commonplace to speak of computing systems as being goal-directed, and there is even talk of emotional states in such systems. Sloman, for example, writes, 'not every intelligent robot will be emotional, only . . . have the ability [to be emotional] – and abilities are not always exercised'.[5] I hasten to add that I use this example only to indicate the range of modern cognitivism in its broad conception, not as an endorsement of all AI claims.

Long before modern cognitivsm became the dominant pattern, Kelly's central question was: how does a person, consciously or unconsciously, construe the world? This is, of course, one of the basic questions that Freud and all psychodynamic schools ask. The concern with the content of the black box is, however, much wider spread than this suggests, as Anthony Ryle has recently pointed out;[6] he is not alone in the belief that the language of cognitivism, with its emphasis on the processes of internal representations and its freedom from reification, has the power of clarifying psychological thought.

In this aspect of his approach Kelly is, then, not – or at least no longer – a lone wolf, notwithstanding various calls in the recent post-Kellyan literature on constructivism for 'apostles' to spread the word.[7] I agree it is both surprising and annoying that Kelly's approach is not more widely recognised. In a recent symposium on cognitivism, for example, not even his name is mentioned.[8] But the reaction to this neglect is, perhaps, more a matter of personal loyalty to the memory of an outstanding psychologist than an issue for the discipline. Cognitivism is, after all, carrying the day anyhow.

There are further aspects to Kelly's approach. He deals with persons, not with variables. Indeed, it is his commitment to the whole person that forced him to broaden the concept of cognition. What is more, he emphasises the uniqueness of every individual while not finding this a handicap in arriving at general statements about human beings.

Persons not variables

No psychologist can deny that every human being is indeed unique, for genetic as well as life-history reasons, but all too many regard this undeniable fact as a nuisance which has somehow to be eliminated from serious research, as a rule by random assignment to experimental conditions and reporting results as averages – a procedure which disguises as much as it reveals; some consider case study presentations to be the only way of dealing with uniqueness. Kelly found a way to a quantifiable description of individual uniqueness. Instead of eliminating it by the straightjacket of experimental controls, he goes out to discover it. In this context I have always treasured his remark that while most psychological experiments had the subject guessing what the experimenter was after, he preferred to have the experimenter guessing what the subjects were thinking.[9]

Two more aspects of Kelly's approach should be identified.

First, his advice to psychologists not to start their work with theories, but with involvement in the life situation of the people whom they wish to study; to go where the action is in order to be able to draw on one's own experience, which is richer than the constructs provided by available theories or those that are easily verbalisable in the rarefied atmosphere of one's study; theories come later.

The second aspect is the famous metaphor of man as a scientist testing his constructs against events. Provided a realistic picture of scientists is intended, including their extra-scientific assumptions and their frequent obstinacy in relinquishing favoured hypotheses, never mind some apparent disconfirmation, this metaphor is a powerful image, implying once again Kelly's deep respect for the dignity of every human being.

These, then, I take to be the major features of Kelly's approach to psychological research, easier to admire than to emulate: as a cognitivist he deals with psychological realities; with persons, not with variables; with uniqueness in a systematic fashion; quantifying where appropriate; respecting individuals by not imposing on them the investigator's frame of reference and by recognising their full human competence; and requiring the psychologist's experiential involvement with the topic of his choice prior to theoretical formulations.

The theory

What then about his specific theory? Its systematic exposition is contained, by and large, in about the first hundred pages of the 1,200 in his *magnum opus*. It consists of the Fundamental Postulate and the corollaries, which even so committed a Kellyite as Fay Fransella regards as 'statements of faith',[10] as a model from which systematic hypotheses can be derived. I will resist the temptation to engage in an epistemological discussion of the distinction between a model and a theory and take the model plus the hypotheses as Kelly's theory. The first thing to be said about it is that Kelly presents it much more modestly than some of his followers; 'expendable, at best an interim theory', he says.[11] The second, that it leads him to a marvellous optimism, as rare in psychology as elsewhere, about what psychology can achieve. To the extent, he says, that one is able to construe one's circumstances, one can find for oneself freedom from their domination.[12] The very word 'anticipate' in the Fundamental Postulate reveals that his psychology is that of a young, forward-looking man. Katz has recently expressed some hesitation about the term 'anticipate',[13] which I share. While I admire Kelly's future-orientation and optimism, I can for obvious reasons not share it. The processes of construing one's past, of wondering about the eternal unanswerable questions of existence, of moments of ecstasy as much as of deep depression in the here and now, are not future-oriented. They are psychological phenomena; constructions, to be sure, but not anticipations. Perhaps 'man as scientist' continuously engaged in prediction and control is too limited a metaphor for the human condition – it is suitable for understanding action in the world but not being in the world. Nothing of Kelly's thought beyond the all-embracingness of the metaphorical expression is lost by replacing 'anticipating' with 'construing'.

I recognise, of course, that Kelly's emphasis on being actively engaged in anticipating events from the inside out was at the time most important in the struggle against the then dominant notion of complete determination from the outside in. But that battle is won; perhaps it is time to abandon the either/or position here too and recognise that while we have the ability to shape our lives to some extent, we are also shaped by events and processes outside our control. More of this later.

The corollaries of the Postulate have proved their value in much substantive and methodological research. Kelly is almost unique among psychologists in the explicitness of his formulations. This great virtue encourages critical development of his theory. Several suggestions have been made in the literature to add to the corollaries in the effort to include further psychological concepts and processes with explicit definitions within the theory. So Thomas has suggested a self-awareness Corollary,[14] Katz an Emotion Corollary.[15] Both meet an earlier criticism of Kelly that he had nothing to say about the acquisition of the earliest constructs, by suggesting that primitive, biologically rooted constructs are available to human beings from birth. Both these additional corollaries seem to me to be useful and in the spirit of Kelly's thought.

This is not the place to discuss the implications of all the corollaries. Others have deduced systematic hypotheses from them and Kelly-inspired work has led to some impressive achievements as, for example, Bannister's work with schizophrenics,[16] Fransella's with stutterers[17] or Thomas's with learners.[18] The claims for the theory go, however, beyond such remarkable achievements. PCT is presented as a paradigm for all psychology.

The repertory grid

Before examining this claim, however, an appreciation of Kelly requires some comments on the repertory grid as a research tool, this methodological implementation of the Dichotomy Corollary. I had better confess straight away that I found the administration of the grid in its pristine form quite difficult in self-administration. The grid tends to evoke adjectives connoting stable personality attributes. What I learned from self-administration was that people whom I knew intimately, whom I had experienced in a large variety of situations, could be both gentle and aggressive, vulnerable and tough, cheerful and depressed. Of course, every one of them was more frequently on one pole than on the other, but frequency may only refer to everyday life; in a clinical situation the most frequent pole may no longer fit. To nail them down, as it were, on the more frequent pole felt in any case like violating their full humanity, denying the large repertoire of stances and emotions of which they were capable and which I had experienced. When the elements were relatively distant acquaintances, this resistance to commit myself to one construct diminished; and disappeared completely when I sorted various psychological theories[19] where not only the elements but also the constructs were less personal. I do not know, but I would like to, whether other outsiders to your community have had similar experiences with self-administration. I cannot believe that people whom I happen to know intimately are more situation-dependent than others; but it is possible that my wish for a critical understanding of the grid experience made me too self-conscious and was an altogether inappropriate motivation. Having recently read Laurie Thomas's account of his conversational method of grid elicitation,[20] I begin to understand that under his guidance even I might have been able to complete a grid whose elements were significant others.

Apart from this exercise in introspection, however, the grid is by now a well-established diagnostic and research tool. Neimeyer reports that 95 per cent of the 800 studies referring to Kelly that he surveyed, used the grid.[21] Some difficulties in its administration have been noted by others too[22] and have led to various changes from its original form. A major issue here is the use of elicited versus provided constructs. With some people – for example, young children and some mental patients – elicitation is very difficult and time-consuming, particularly on the dissimilarity pole, which may be reduced to a content-free negation of the first construct. But Kelly insisted rightly that the content specification of similarities was as revealing as that of differences. The reason for this difficulty was recognised by him: he realised that constructs can be unconscious or unverbalised, even though still effective. In such cases constructs known to be frequently used or of particular interest are often provided. In investigating adolescents' identity issues, Peter Weinreich has used an ingenious combination of elicitation and provision: before administering the grid he asked the youngsters to tell him their life history and noted the constructs they used spontaneously in their description of people.[23] Later he provided these same constructs for a systematic grid administration. Sophisticated statistical analyses of grid data are now available and have made it possible to link the grid data to corollaries of the theory that have to do with the organisation of cognitive space. In many studies, however, the application of the grid is linked neither to Kelly's theory nor to his approach; it has become a free-standing research tool. This, however, has the danger of ignoring Kelly's thought and falling into the trap of method-fetishisms, a trap in which so much of academic psychology has landed. The grid is often used together with other methods of inquiry, thus establishing a link with other psychological approaches.

A universal paradigm

This brings me to the second point of this presentation: the claim expressed by several Kellyites[24] that his system of thought could and should become the universal paradigm in psychology. I do not think that this claim has a chance of becoming reality; nor that the very desirable aim of spreading the knowledge of Kelly's contribution is advanced by the repetition of this claim. Whenever a new and important idea appears in psychology, those whose minds are open enough to recognise its newness and importance tend, it seems to me, to go overboard and extend its focus of convenience beyond the original intent. This happened to Freud, and Skinner did it himself with the result that the original achievement is exposed to attack or becomes watered down, sometimes beyond recognition in its wider applications, leading in the end to an underestimate of the original contribution when it is inappropriately applied to questions that it was not designed to tackle. I fear that this may happen to Kelly's contribution. Kelly's is a theory of individual personality. No more, but also no less.

As I have hinted before, there are legitimate questions in psychology that are outside Kelly's province, both outside his approach and his theory – neuropsychology, for example, or behaviourism. My major concern, however, is with the suitability – or otherwise – of Kelly's thought for social psychology. There is, after all, a Sociality Corollary, and nobody who has read Kelly's essay on social inheritance,[25] written at the age of twenty-five, and is familiar with his general approach, could doubt his deep personal concern with social reality. Yet, his formal theory is fundamentally a theory of individual personality only. As Duck has rightly pointed out, for Kelly the social in social psychology is the social knowledge of an individual.[26]

Duck is motivated by the wish to demonstrate that Kellyan thought has a contribution to make to social psychological issues beyond translating one terminology into another. In his constructive critique of the sociality corollary as Kelly formulated it, there are two major points. First, he says, that Kelly fails to distinguish between central and peripheral areas of a construct system, but central areas (e.g. the construct of the self) are more important than others in understanding a person. In other words, he points to the fact that Kelly is concerned with formal processes to the exclusion of content.

Duck wants to extend Kelly's structural theory into a theory of content. Structural theories such as Kelly's, or system theory for that matter, are tools for thinking; content theories are tools for enlarging knowledge. To talk in the language of AI, Kelly specifies computational inference processes, never mind their data base, while Duck is concerned with that base. It speaks for Kelly's formalism that Duck finds no difficulty in combining the structural processes with specific content, just as computer simulation must do.

In social psychology there is a plenitude of content theories – more or less useful ones – but no structural theory, at least none as fully developed as Kelly's for individual processes. All we have are a few statements on structure, such as Marx's dictum that social being determines consciousness (which, incidentally, is the opposite of Kelly's belief that constructions shape one's fate) or Kurt Lewin's famous formula that B = f(P,E). If one wished, however, to extend such statements into a fully developed structural theory in social psychology, one turns in vain to Kelly's system of thought for help. There the social remains unconceptualised. Now, it is one thing to say that the social is outside the range of convenience of what is essentially a psychological theory of individuals. It is quite another matter, and I believe an unacceptable one, to deny ontological reality to the external world, to regard it as construction only. My friend and mentor in questions of philosophy, Margaret Boden, tells me that it is indeed difficult to disprove this position logically, but she agrees with me that we must all live with the attitude of naïve realism about the ontological status of both, the inner and the outer world. Kelly himself never doubted this, but in his theoretical formulations he left the external world alone, recognising its ontological reality, but refraining from conceptualising it. Constructivism taken to the extreme is in danger of calling persecuted people paranoid; of turning 'into an unhappy and unacceptable *solipsism*'.[27] After all, a construct system is as much a construction as a social system, with no less and no more 'reality'.

In any case, social psychology, concerned as it is with construing the interaction between people and the world outside, requires conceptualisations on both levels. This brings me to the second point in Duck's argument. He distinguishes six levels of sociality, ranging from the perception and judgment of persons to the definition of the self through contact with others *à la* interactionism. His demand for an extension of Kelly aims at making all six amenable to the developing theory. While this would certainly include some traditional areas of social psychology, it remains – like these areas – restricted in its conceptualisations to individual processes and experiences in interpersonal relations, often limited to dyads. These are important areas for thought and research, of course. The social, however, is more than face-to-face contact. A recent programmatic statement for social psychology maintains that the discipline 'can and must include in its theoretical and research preoccupations a direct concern with the relationship between human psychological functioning and the large-scale social processes and events which shape this functioning and are shaped by it'.[28] Kelly's theory does not even have a vocabulary with which these large-scale events and processes could be described. I do not believe that the addition of corollaries would extend the theory's range of convenience, for by definition they must be inferences from the Fundamental Postulate which stipulates an individual process.

Given that, ontologically speaking, individual and social processes are inextricably intertwined – there is no individual construction outside a social context, no social context outside construing minds – given that the Individual and the Social are therefore conceptual artifacts, social psychology has the difficult task of dealing with what Kurt Lewin called 'circular causality';[29] from the individual to the social and vice versa. There are all too obvious limits within which constructions shape experiences, let alone one's fate. To take a trivial example: however varied your constructions of this lecture may be, nobody, I hope, can construe it as a series of jokes, nor will anybody fail to anticipate its forthcoming end. The point is that it is the structure and the content of the situation, not your construction systems, that permit me to make these statements with confidence.

Roger Barker, another psychologist whose original work has received less attention than it deserves, has coined the term 'behaviour setting' to indicate the power of the social situation to limit the degrees of freedom that individual constructions can have.[30] Another concept, transcending individual processes, is Moscovici's revival of Durkheim's *répresentations sociales*,[31] by which is meant the values, ideas, and practices which are not of our making but into which we are born; they change, but in a rhythm independent of an individual's constructions, and must be assumed to affect them. There are a few other social psychologists who have made a beginning in conceptualising the social in its own right. In an effort to understand why unemployment is largely experienced as a curse rather than a liberation from boring jobs, I have tried to analyse the social structure of employment, independent of whatever personal constructions are put on a particular job.[32] But I will not spell out here the promise that such a broader social psychology holds, nor the conceptual and methodological difficulties it confronts, for I hope I have made the major point relevant to an appreciation of Kelly: he produced a theory of individual processes whose range of convenience does not include social psychology.

Perhaps it is in order to add that nothing I have said should be construed as an argument against the usefulness or validity of the study of interpersonal encounters, only against the idea that the social is adequately defined by adding up individual processes and dividing them by *n*.

I have come to the end of my remarks – almost. Let me summarise the stance I have arrived at. I am happy to see Kelly's approach gaining ground in psychology and I believe this to be an increasing trend. I regret that his pioneering work is not sufficiently recognised in these new developments, but I believe that this is also gradually changing. He himself would not have minded this relative neglect quite as much as some of you do. What mattered to him was what can be done with his theory. 'A theory, in order to maintain its respectability', he said, 'ought to be good for something'.[33] It is indeed good for many things. I have already indicated that one of the great virtues of Kelly's formulations is that they can be developed and extended without violating the spirit of his intellectual enterprise. Their range of convenience should, however, in my opinion, remain limited to the study and therapy of individuals. Whether or not you regard Kelly's as a personality theory that can replace all others depends in my view on how seriously you take two basic psychoanalytic notions that Kelly discarded: repression and the unconscious. It is true, he talked about unconscious constructs, but he had nothing to say about unconscious dynamics. I recognise that the application of Kelly's ideas can bring preconscious constructs into awareness and that doing so has great therapeutic potential not only for those we call patients but also for those we call normal. He himself never claimed to have all the answers to questions about personality; perhaps he did not have answers at all; rather, he has created a way of thinking about human beings whose great promise still awaits full implementation.

Notes and references

1 Warren, Neil (ed.) (1964). *The Theory and Methodology of George Kelly.* London: Brunel University.
2 Several such claims have been made in the relevant literature; the most recent in L. F. Thomas and E. S. Harri-Augstein (1985), *Self-organised Learning*, London: Routledge & Kegan Paul, p. xxvii.
3 Kelly, George A. A brief introduction to personal construct theory. In D. Bannister (ed.) (1970), *Perspectives in Personal Construct Theory.* London: Academic Press.
4 Kelly, G. A. (1955). *The Psychology of Personal Constructs.* New York: Norton, p. 130.
5 Sloman, A. Towards a computational theory of mind. In M. Yazdani and A. Narayanan (eds.) (1984), *Artificial Intelligence.* Chichester: Ellis Horwood, p. 180.
6 Ryle, A. (1985). Cognitive theory and object relations. *The British Journal of Medical Psychology* 58, 1–7.
7 For example, Steve Duck has used the term 'apostle' in several of his articles, as in his chapter in J. Mancuso and J. R. Adams-Webber (eds.) (1982), *The Construing Person.* New York: Praeger, p. 230.
8 Royce, J. R. and Mos, L. P. (eds) (1984). *Annals of Theoretical Psychology.* London: Plenum Press. The first five chapters deal with cognitivism.
9 Kelly, *The Psychology of Personal Constructs*, p. 77.
10 Fransella, F. (1980). Man as scientist. In A. J. Chapman and D. M. Jones (eds), *Models of Man.* Leicester: British Psychological Society.
11 Kelly, *The Psychology of Personal Constructs*, p. 14.
12 *Ibid.*, p. 21.
13 Katz, J. O. (1984). Personal Construct Theory and the emotions: an interpretation of primitive constructs. *British Journal of Psychology* 75, 315–27.
14 Thomas, L. F. (1979). Construct, reflect and converse: the conversational reconstruction of social realities. In P. Stringer and D. Bannister (eds.), *Constructs of Sociality and Individuality.* London: Academic Press.
16 Bannister, D. (1965). The genesis of schizophrenic thought disorder; re-test of the serial invalidation hypothesis. *British Journal of Psychiatry* III, 977–82 (and many other articles).
17 Fransella, F. (1979). What sort of person is the person-as-scientist? in J. R. Adams-Webber (ed.), *Personal Construct Theory.* Chichester: Wiley.

18 Thomas, L. F. and Harri-Augstein, E. S. (1985). *Self-Organised Learning*. London: Routledge & Kegan Paul.
19 This has, of course, been done before. See Veness, Th. (1964), The Conceptual Basis of Personal Construct Theory. In N. Warren (ed.), *The Theory and Methodology of George Kelly*. London: Brunel University.
20 Thomas and Harri-Augstein, *Self-organised Learning*.
21 Neimeyer, R. A. (1983). The development of personal construct psychology: some sociohistorical observations. In J. R. Adams-Webber and J. C. Mancuso (eds), *Applications of Personal Construct Theory*. London: Academic Press.
22 For example, Rathod, P. (1983). Metaphors for the construction of interpersonal relationships. In J. R. Adams-Webber and J. C. Mancuso, (eds), *Applications of Personal Construct Theory*. London: Academic Press.
23 Weinreich, P. (1979). Ethnicity and adolescent identity conflict. In V. Saifullan Khan (ed.), *Minority Families in Britain*. London: Macmillan.
24 Thomas and Harri-Augstein, *Self-organised Learning*. See also, among others, F. Tschudi and R. Rommetveit in J. R. Adams-Webber (ed.) (1979), *Personal Construct Theory*, Chichester: Wiley.
25 Kelly, G. (1979). Social inheritance. Reprinted 1979 in P. Stringer and D. Bannister (eds), *Constructs of Sociality and Individuality*. London: Academic Press.
26 Duck, S. (1983). Sociality and cognition in Personal Construct Theory. In J. R. Adams-Webber and J. C. Mancuso (eds), *Applications of Personal Construct Theory*. London: Academic Press.
27 Gergen, K. J. (1985). The social constructionist movement in modern psychology. *American Psychologist* 40(3), 270.
28 Tajfel, H., Jaspars, M. F. J. and Fraser, C. (1984) (eds.). *The Social Dimension*. Cambridge: Cambridge University Press.
29 Lewin, K. (1951). Problems of research in social psychology. In D. Cartwright (ed.), *Kurt Lewin: Field Theory in Social Science*. New York: Harpers.
30 Barker, R. and Wright, H. F. (1955). *Midwest and Its Children: The Psychological Ecology of an American Town*. New York: Harpers.
31 Moscovici, S. (1983). Social representation. In R. Harré and R. Lamb (eds.), *The Encyclopedic Dictionary of Psychology*. Oxford: Blackwell.
32 Jahoda, M. (1982). *Employment and Unemployment*. Cambridge: Cambridge University Press.
33 Kelly, *The Psychology of Personal Constructs*, p. 559.

A

Theory

Chapter 1
On becoming a personal anarchist

Spencer A. McWilliams

The term 'anarchy' is typically used in the political context, in relation to a philosophy espousing the abolition of all established governments. The word elicits images of bombs, violence, disorder and chaos, but etymologically it simply means 'without ruler.' Thus 'anarchy' may refer to a system which functions without reliance on established rules or patterns.

The anarchist insight

Anarchist philosophy (Read, 1971) is based on the role of freedom and equality as factors which facilitate human progress, measured by the degree of articulation and differentiation among the individuals within a society. This notion of progress is similar to Kelly's (1979a) proposition that human evolution continues to accelerate and that humans participate in it through elaboration of construction systems for understanding the universe. Elaboration and differentiation of constructs enables a person to more greatly appreciate the significance of human life and be a productive participant in human progress. The social group may function as an aid to this evolution, but progress only comes through individual differentiation from the group.

As personal consciousness evolves, a natural tendency of the person is to attempt to discover the patterns of nature and live in harmony with them. Anarchist philosophy suggests that when this principle is followed, and constructs are revised to correspond more closely to events, human social conduct will naturally be 'moral' and cooperative. In contrast, when construing fails to adapt to the nature of events, conflict and 'immoral' behavior toward others, such as hostility (Kelly, 1979b), occurs.

The natural sense of proper conduct becomes distorted when it is codified into moral laws which become institutionalized into religious, legal, and political organizations. The natural tendency is deformed when it is rigidly defined, and it is ultimately inhibited by the weight of the structure. Sarason (1976) summarized the central insight of anarchism. First, once an institution is developed it inevitably becomes a power hostile to the interests of its members by reducing their sense of personal independence and autonomy. Second, as the institution becomes more powerful its members tend to see it as a major source of assistance and initiative, which reduces their sense of responsibility and community. An implication of this insight is that any form which evolves to serve a human need must be entirely *ad hoc* in nature and must never be allowed to develop into an 'institution.' This notion is reflected in the position of those personal construct psychologists who have resisted the formation of a formal PCP organization, suggesting that it would come to have institutional qualities that would impede the natural evolution of the theory.

Science and anarchy

Although the concept of anarchy has most frequently been applied to political settings, its central insight that human progress is impeded by reliance on rules or forms may be extended more broadly to the context of science. Several philosophers and historians of science have criticized emphasis on adherence to strict rules regarding how scientific knowledge is to be accepted as valid. Kuhn (1970) described the nature of change in scientific disciplines and proposed the concept of a 'paradigm' as representing the global world view which characterized a scientific discipline, including rules by which the science is to be conducted and examples of 'appropriate' problems and methodology. Polanyi (1958), however, proposed that there is no way to specify beforehand rules by which knowledge might be discovered. Discovery is rooted in the scientist's personal awareness of coherence among what have previously been seen as unrelated events. It is the scientist's deeply held belief of being in personal contact with a yet unknown but potentially real entity which drives scientific discovery, and there is no way to anticipate the evidence which will eventually justify and support a new idea. Feyerabend (1978) suggested that the scientific practice of relying on rules of methodology and proof often hinders scientific progress and does not reflect the way it has actually proceeded throughout history. His research found no support for the idea that science proceeds according to 'a method that contains firm, unchanging, and absolutely binding principles (p. 23).' Any such rules that have been proposed have been violated at one time or another, often in ways which were responsible for the growth of knowledge. He proposed a philosophy of knowledge, called 'epistemological anarchy,' which argues that since it is impossible to determine any rules by which scientific conduct can be guided, 'the only rule that does not inhibit progress is *anything goes*' (p. 23).

The tendency to follow rules for scientific research has been a particularly acute problem for psychology. Kelly (1970) discussed psychology's self-conscious concern with scientific respectability and the emphasis on appearing scientifically rigorous. He proposed that psychologists would be more effective if they abandoned *a priori* rules of methodology which emulate the procedures of the physical sciences, and use whatever methods they might invent to pursue their inquiry. He suggested that if psychologists were successful in this endeavor, the scientific community would be most prompt in acknowledging their findings as scientific.

Bakan (1973) developed this theme more fully. He likened the relationship between 'real science' and psychological investigation to that between 'real cowboys' and children playing at being cowboys. By concentrating on following particular rules and models of scientific methodology, psychologists imitate the behavior of scientists without doing the most important thing that real scientists do, which is to confront their subject directly and creatively. Bakan characterized psychology's approach to research as 'methodolatry,' a practice akin to idolatry in religion. For Bakan, idolatry occurs when a particular form which evolves in the human quest for deeper understanding of the universe comes to be seen as an end in itself. It is this sense of idolatry that the anarchist position seeks to abolish by refusing to worship any particular form.

Personal anarchy

The preceding discussion has touched briefly on ways in which the construct of anarchy may be applied in political and scientific arenas, but this discussion has been intended primarily to set the ground for drawing a metaphor from the social to the personal. Kelly (1955) used the 'personal scientist' metaphor, which suggests that people in general may be usefully understood as behaving similarly to scientists, as the basis for the psychology of personal constructs. In analogous fashion, the 'personal anarchist' metaphor proposes that 'institutionalization' of our personal constructs may come to impede, rather than enhance, ability to differentiate and elaborate the perceptual field. Relying on personal constructs as 'rules' or 'codes' may lead to personal difficulties, distortions, and rigidities analogous to those discussed in political and scientific settings.

Development of 'self'

The process through which constructs become an institution is rooted in the sense of self that evolves with the construing process. The initial purpose of construing is to make the world more understandable and to anticipate events effectively. Kelly (1955) emphasized that the construing process was a practical one that exists for this applied purpose. Central to this process is Kelly's philosophical and epistemological assumption, *constructive alternativism*, which proposes that ideas are never to be 'institutionalized' but always open to revision or replacement, easily abandoned to make way for a new order. This tentative, *ad hoc* nature of constructs clearly parallels the similar anarchist conception.

In order to anticipate future events, the person must have the ability to imagine that future and a possible personal role in it. This requires a concept, or construct, of the self who will experience this future. Kelly (1955) described the self as the core structure, a set of constructs which exist for the purpose of anticipating personal maintenance processes. There are two central elements to this conception of the self: (1) the self is a portion of the person's processes but not their totality, and (2) the 'self' requires personal awareness; to have a self construct is to be conscious of the self as the subject of experience.

Jaynes (1976) proposed that awareness of the self, as a conscious agent responsible for making choices and guiding actions, appeared rather recently in human evolution, perhaps no more than 3,000 years ago. One of the central points to Jaynes's theory of the origin of consciousness is that it developed subsequent to the use of language. He presented a persuasive argument that human beings could have existed with language, thought, reason, and learning, yet with no sense of self-consciousness or awareness of an 'I' which was responsible for the actions. Wilber (1980, 1981) also suggested that the self is a social artifact that evolves in parallel with language. As a child develops the ability to use verbal symbols, particularly those relating to the self, an exclusive identification with the socially determined mental ego also develops, serving as a constant reminder of identity.

This emerging identity as a mental self enhances ability to anticipate the future, since it creates a fixed, permanent entity which will experience future events. Without this sense of self humans would be unable to transcend immediate needs to make choices or anticipate events in the distant future. The development of this self-consciousness was a major evolutionary step in increasing human ability to survive effectively in a wide range of environmental circumstances.

Self as 'institution'

This sense of self consciousness, however, is a double-edged sword. In addition to its utility, there are potential hazards to *exclusive* identification with the self that can impede, rather than enhance, ability to deal effectively with the ever-changing universe. Angyal (1982) described the tendency of the self to attempt to control and manage the total personality organization:

> The conscious self which is only a part, namely the conscious or symbolized part of the biological subject, tends to establish its own autonomous government. What we call 'will' represents autonomous determination, the self-government of this narrow conscious or symbolic self. The symbolic self becomes a state within a state. Thus a split is created within the subject organization. This split is greatly aggravated by the fact that the symbolic self tends toward hegemony, tends to take over the

> government of the total personality, a task for which it is not equipped. (pp. 35–6)

Up to this point, the self structure has been described as the conscious, verbally labelled portion of the person. Much of this self structure, however, is not accessible to awareness. Kelly (1955) described a number of ways in which 'covert construction' can occur. Pre-verbal constructs are those associated with experiences that occurred prior to the development of language and continue to be used in spite of the lack of consistent word symbols. Suspended constructs developed overtly at one point in the person's life but are incompatible with the current self organization. Although the person may not have awareness of these experiences, they continue to exert an influence on psychological processes and may represent unconscious 'rules' that are followed automatically. Another type of covert construction is the 'embedded unconscious' (Wilber, 1983), the 'rules' that govern the operation of the core structure but are not available to self-awareness because of the complete identification of the self with those structures.

> The self [cannot] see those structures because the self [*is*] those structures. . . . One uses the structures of that level as something with which to perceive and translate the world – but one cannot perceive and translate those structures *themselves*. (Wilber, 1983, p. 112)

Thus, in both conscious and unconscious ways, the self, originally a servant of the person, becomes an 'institution', that has lost its natural tendencies and now consists of a set of rules or models that are followed regardless of whether they are an appropriate match to the events with which the person is confronted. The task of personal anarchy is to destroy this institution so that the person may continue the process of evolution.

Fomenting personal insurrection

Anarchist philosophy draws a distinction between revolution and insurrection (Read, 1971). Revolution refers to the replacement of one form of governmental structure with another, while insurrection is an action against *all* forms of state structure. In discussing various methods through which human consciousness evolves to higher forms, Wilber (1983) drew a similar distinction between changes of form within the same level of consciousness ('translation') and evolution to a higher level ('transformation'). For genuine transformation to occur, there must be a 'personal insurrection' in which all forms of self structure at that level of organization are 'overthrown' in order to be transcended.

Before a self structure can be transcended, however, a functioning self organization must exist, just as political insurrection would not occur in the absence of an existing state structure. The self structure can thus be seen as a universal stage in personal evolution, developing to serve useful and necessary purposes, but eventually becoming an empty form that hinders the evolutionary function. This stage or level of evolution cannot be avoided, and personal insurrection must follow the development of an effective, functioning self organization.

Given the existence of a functional self structure, the concept of personal insurrection may be applied to the weakening or dissolution of exclusive identification with the symbolized core structure, and its covert components. In a sense, personal insurrection is a personal application of constructive alternativism, for it represents an intentionally aggressive approach to following Kelly's assumption that constructs are revisable and replaceable. The goal is not to destroy the ability to deal effectively with the real world, but to facilitate continuing differentiation and elaboration of personal functioning, to remain fresh and open, perennially ready to deal with moment-to-moment reality in new and effective ways without rigid reliance on pre-existing rules.

There are many possible approaches to this process. Their common core is an emphasis on self-knowledge for the purpose of self-transcendence. This goal may be differentiated from that of personal improvement. Although many techniques and practices may be used for both purposes, the goal of self-improvement is to make the self 'better', while the goal of self-transcendence is to study the self, to see its basic structure so that it ceases to have the governing role in life. Personal anarchy may be approached through the vehicle of psychotherapy. Although it is typically used to assist a person in developing a strong, effective self structure and to overcome maladaptive patterns which inhibit healthy functioning, psychotherapy may also be used to assist the personal anarchist to develop self-knowledge that can weaken the hold that the self structure has on the entire personality. Meditation practices, derived from Eastern perspectives on psychology, represent another tool for gaining the self-knowledge necessary to personal anarchy. Zen meditation, for example, is a study of the 'self' to observe its ever-changing nature and the transparent quality of dualistic construing. Through this process, the 'self' is 'forgotten,' allowing expression of a more basic nature through living in harmony with ordinary daily life (Aitken, 1982).

From the perspective of personal construct psychology, anarchist self-knowledge may be approached through the use of techniques oriented toward making covert construction overt. Many repertory grid techniques (Fransella and Bannister, 1977) may be applied to the anarchist end. Construct-elicitation, laddering of superordinate constructs, and grid-analysis methods, that display the 'meta-structure' of the construct system, may be used to assist greater awareness of the covert 'rules' and 'organization' that control the construction of events. Boxer's (1979, 1980) approach to 'reflexive learning' represents one method by which repertory grid techniques can be directed toward studying the *process*, rather than the *content*, of construing.

A closing comment

To be used to its best advantage, a metaphor should be taken lightly and quickly, for it is at best an incomplete and only suggestive construction. The personal-anarchist metaphor proposes some alternative ways of construing the human situation. A few specific techniques have been briefly mentioned, but in keeping with the anarchist insight it must be remembered that there can be no rules governing how to be a personal anarchist.

References

Aitken, R. (1982). *Taking the Path of Zen*. San Francisco: North Point Press.

Angyal, A. (1982). *Neurosis and Treatment: A Holistic Theory.* New York: Da Capo.
Bakan, D. (1973). *On Method: Toward a Reconstruction of Psychological Investigation.* San Francisco: Jossey-Bass.
Boxer, P. J. (1979). Reflective analysis. *International Journal of Man-machine Studies* 11, 547–84.
Boxer, P. J. (1980). Supporting reflective learning: towards a reflexive theory of form. *Human Relations* 33(1), 1–22.
Feyerabend, P. (1978). *Against Method: Outline of an Anarchistic Theory of Knowledge.* London: Verso.
Fransella, F. and Bannister, D. (1977). *A Manual of Repertory Grid Technique.* New York: Academic Press.
Jaynes, J. (1976). *The Origin of Consciousness in the Breakdown of the Bicameral Mind.* Boston: Houghton Mifflin.
Kelly, G. A. (1955). *The Psychology of Personal Constructs,* Vols. I and II. New York: Norton.
Kelly, G. A. (1970). Behaviour is an experiment. In D. Bannister (ed.), *Perspectives in Personal Construct Theory.* New York: Academic Press.
Kelly, G. A. (1979a). Ontological acceleration. In B. Maher (ed.), *Clinical Psychology and Personality: The Selected Papers of George Kelly.* Huntington, NY: Krieger.
Kelly, G. A. (1979b). Hostility. In B. Maher (ed.), *Clinical Psychology and Personality: The Selected Papers of George Kelly.* Huntington, NY: Krieger.
Kuhn, T. S. (1970). *The Structure of Scientific Revolutions.* 2nd edn. Chicago: University of Chicago Press.
Polanyi, M. (1958). *Personal Knowledge.* Chicago: University of Chicago Press.
Read, H. (1971). *Anarchy and Order: Essays in Politics.* Boston: Beacon Press.
Sarason, S. B. (1976). Community psychology and the anarchist insight. *American Journal of Community Psychology* 4(3), 246–59.
Wilber, K. (1980). *The Atman Project: A Transpersonal View of Human Development.* Wheaton, Ill.: Quest.
Wilber, K. (1981). *Up from Eden: A Transpersonal View of Human Evolution.* New York: Doubleday.
Wilber, K. (1983). *Eye to Eye: The Quest for the New Paradigm.* Garden City, NY: Anchor Doubleday.

Chapter 2
PCT: still radical thirty years on?

Fay Fransella

The radical nature of the theory in 1955

Some say that Kelly's work produced a considerable effect in the USA when it was published (e.g. Neimeyer, 1985a) and, in certain respects, I am sure this was so. But in relation to psychology as a whole, my impression is that the two weighty volumes did not severely disturb the psychological waters in 1955, even though there were some very favourable reviews. One of the most influential, by Jerome Bruner, starts:

> These excellent, original, and infuriatingly prolix two volumes easily nominate themselves for the distinction of being the single greatest contribution of the past decade to the theory of personality functioning. Professor Kelly has written a major work. (Bruner, 1956, p. 355)

Brendan Maher was one of the inner circle of students with whom Kelly discussed his ideas and tells a fascinating story about this major work. Kelly never really believed that the two volumes would ever be published, but felt he should test the validity of that belief. So he had twenty copies of the 1,200-page manuscript prepared. These twenty boxed manuscripts were put into a van and one delivered to each of twenty publishers. To Kelly's apparent amazement, eight publishers offered him a contract. Maher thinks that Kelly never really got over that invalidation. In fact, in a taped interview I had with him in 1965, he talks of the five books he had written, only one of which had been published, and says, 'and that I think was probably a mistake'.

After publication George Kelly became sought after as a speaker and teacher, but little lasting excitement was generated by the theory. One reason to account for its restrained reception, apart from the sheer weight of the two volumes and the complexity of the theory, could well have been its very radical nature. What follows does not attempt to be a definitive account, nor is it the first to look at Kelly's work in the broader context of psychology (see e.g. Holland, 1970; Davisson, 1978). This is the personal view of someone who has identified herself professionally and personally with Kelly's ideas for over twenty years.

Unusual presentation of the theory

1 The psychology is presented in an extremely precise and detailed manner. It has been likened to an engineer's blueprint. It starts out with the Fundamental Postulate, which is then elaborated by eleven corollaries, each word being defined. Then comes a whole range of constructs about how we, as individual human beings, may go about trying to make sense of their world.

2 There is no extensive bibliography showing just where Kelly got his ideas from. Some of the basic philosophy does seem to be remarkably similar to that generated by physics. This is not surprising when one considers that Kelly did his physics and mathematics degree about the time that Einstein was revolutionising that discipline (Fransella, 1983).

Unusual features of the theory

1 Psychology was largely an empirical discipline used to notions or small theories with clearly limited *ranges of convenience* and one which distrusted theoretical systems. Here was a theoretical system with potentially a vast range of convenience.

2 It is pitched at a very *high level of abstraction* – in my view a major problem for those wishing to grasp its full meaning. Superficially, it is common sense; deeper understanding requires effort. It is much easier to deal with specifics, such as ids, egos and superegos; extraversions, introversions and psychoticisms;

fixed and variable ratios and fixed and variable interval schedules of reinforcement.

3 It is a *reflexive theory*. Strangely at odds with Freudian and behaviourist theories.

4 Kelly's ideas on *motivation* were controversial. Psychologists at that time conceptualised the person as a passive being whose behaviour was governed *either* by unconscious urges and conflicts (Freud) *or* by our schedules of reinforcements (Skinner) or by some system of psychological needs and drives. Kelly suggested instead that we look at ourselves as if we are alive and kicking and that a feature of living creatures is that they get up and do things. No special explanation has to be given to account for why they are active.

5 He *challenged the current adherence of psychologists to the Newtonian form of science*. This must surely have been one of the most revolutionary statements prevailing in psychology. All those psychologists in the 1950s happily accumulating those golden fragments of truth, supposed to represent 'reality', suddenly told by Kelly that all they had was support for their best notions at that time – a jumping off point for asking new and better questions. This also suggests that the controlled experiment, so much loved by psychologists, is not the way to study human beings. His suggestion that psychologists give up 'accumulative fragmentalism' and take up 'constructive alternativism' was not likely to endear him to his colleagues. They had fought long and hard to be recognised as 'proper' scientists and here was some relatively unknown, unpublished psychologist telling them they were wasting their time!

6 But there was worse to come. Kelly was also saying that psychology should be an idiographic and not a nomothetic discipline; that *the person* should be the focus of their concern and they should stop trying to establish laws about large numbers of people; equally, that psychologists should be regarded as human beings who interact with the actual experiment they are trying so hard to keep under careful control. In essence, the scientific thrust of personal construct theory to the 1955 psychologist was that the person is:

(a) no longer passive but active
(b) not only active but a 'scientist' as well
(c) not only an active *personal* scientist at the centre of his own concerns, but one who carries out *experiments*.

By making behaviour the active person's scientific experiment to test their own construing, Kelly removed *power* from the hands of the psychologist (the expert on behaviour) and gave it to all individuals.

7 A further potentially unacceptable feature of personal construct theory in 1955 was its insistence on viewing the person as a total, indivisible entity. There was no familiar separation of the person into motivations, learning, emotions or perceptions. However, the one aspect of the total, integrated human being that most people focused on was the denial of a distinction between thinking and feeling. Descartes' dualism is deeply entrenched in most of our minds. An early criticism of the theory stemming from this was that it did not deal well with the emotions. In his review Bruner says, 'The book fails signally, I think, in dealing convincingly with the human passions' (Bruner, 1956).

Presented with the problem of what category to put the theory in – and so assuage their anxiety of the unconstruable – psychologists in 1955 tried hard to squeeze it into a 'cognitive' pigeonhole. Bruner again led the way by saying that 'The book succeeds, I think, in raising to a proper level of dignity and importance the press that man feels toward cognitive control of the world' (Bruner, 1956).

With all that stacked against it, I am amazed that anyone wonders why it caused few ripples on the establishment waters of psychology in the mid-1950s.

The theory's status thirty years later

Unusual presentation of the theory

How many theories today can be likened to blueprints with their fundamental postulates and corollaries set out in such a way that each can be tested? How many theories do not have pages of references at the back of the book? How many spell out their philosophy? Not many that I have come across.

Unusual features of the theory

1 *Range of convenience*. The range of application of the theory is continually being extended. Kelly says a theory should be fertile. I certainly think he would have been pleased at just how fertile his theory is. Marie Jahoda focuses on this issue in her address (Introduction of this volume) and points to some limitations of its range of convenience. I am sure all welcome this, because there could have been a danger that its range was just *too* wide. But it is certainly wider than most other theories in psychology.

2 *Its high level of abstraction*. This clearly relates to the degree of its fertility. But this also is still one of its most difficult features as far as potential users are concerned.

3 *Its reflexivity*. Here there does seem to have been some movement. The humanistic psychologists have played a leading role in bringing to the fore the importance of theories being reflexive. One indication of this change in emphasis is the comment of Helson and Mitchell in the *Annual Revue of Psychology* (1978) that the study of personality has been through decades of depression and that 'one of the sprouting seeds may be a growing awareness of the subjectivity of theory in psychology'.

4 *The person as active rather than passive*. There has been much movement here also, and this is no longer an unusual feature in a psychological theory.

5 *Its challenge to the Newtonian view of science*. At the present time there are two distinct groups in scientific psychology. One is represented by the accumulators of fragments, who claim that 'the others' are not proper scientists and therefore not psychologists (Fransella, 1980). These 'others' are largely the 'humanists', many of whom do not care for the science game at all.

Few personal construct psychologists have tried to examine the full implications of constructive alternativism as a scientific model. I think many people use repertory grids (and I include myself here) as a type of 'security blanket'. It makes us feel more a part of the establishment scientific world. As such, it prevents an in-depth examination of Kelly's revolutionary view of science.

6 *Its focus on 'the person'*. There has been increasing recognition of the importance of the idiographic approach in psychology. But viewing the person 'as if' each were a scientist is still unique and radical with its implications that all behaviour is an experiment.

This has, for instance, profound implications for behaviour

therapy. It was not by chance that Kelly took this as the example for his paper 'Behaviour is an Experiment' (1985). Many behaviour therapists acknowledge that they no longer have a theory, particularly the cognitive behaviour therapists. At the present time they are following the trend of attempting to subsume personal construct theory under some such heading as 'cognitive behavioural therapy'. I would argue that it should be the other way round – personal construct theory subsumes behaviour therapy leaving a very useful set of techniques. This can be illustrated by the following examples.

(a) Primacy. Behaviour therapy is caught up in a dualistic debate about which takes precedence over the other: feelings or thoughts (e.g. Rachman, 1984; Greenberg and Safran, 1984a, 1984b). Historically, it was thus: first there was classical behaviourism, with behaviour at its centre – changes in behaviour lead to changes in thinking. Then came the cognitive and social psychologists saying that it was changes in thinking that lead to changes in behaviour. A third view came from psychoanalysis and the more recent humanistic groups, such as gestalt, saying that it is the *emotionally laden* memories, beliefs, and so on, which have to be 'worked through' and transformed in order to achieve meaningful and enduring personal change. This is a non-issue for the personal construct psychologist. With the person viewed as an integrated process, 'primacy' makes no sense.

(b) Systematic desensitisation. The hierarchy of feared situations is a very useful device for encouraging the client to conduct small, well-designed, behavioural experiments. The agoraphobic person systematically reconstrues as she goes up the steps in her ladder of fear.

There is a current argument going on in behaviour therapy circles about whether *in vivo* (live) experiences obtain better results than going up hierarchies in fantasy. But this is not an issue for the personal construct therapist. It is axiomatic that no lasting change is likely to occur until we have conducted our behavioural experiments *to test out those thoughts or fantasies.*

(c) Implosion. There is plenty of evidence to show that this works with some clients. The obsessional person, for instance, is *forced* to test out his construing by being *made* to handle dirt.

(d) Operant procedures. The man in the psychiatric ward may respond well to being given a token (with which he can buy the necessities of life) for doing up his trouser zip. He is 'being reinforced for target behaviour'. But what does *he* think he is doing? Perhaps he is testing out the hypothesis that 'every time I do up my zip the nurse gives me a token so I can buy more cigarettes'. In which case no one should be surprised that he stops doing up his zip when the treatment programme stops. His behavioural experiments are producing invalidation. No attempt has been made to give his behaviour personal meaning – no attempt made to help him construe himself and his zip-doing-up as part of wider 'social' construing at a more superordinate level.

Perhaps we should start 'personal construct behaviour therapy'. We have a very workable theory, and they have very workable techniques.

7 *The total, indivisible human being.* The struggle continues to maintain the dualistic way of understanding the person. It is here that psychology is becoming hostile in its effort to 'prove' that personal construct theory is no different from other theories. It *is* classifiable. Over twenty years ago Kelly started writing a book to be called 'The Human Feeling', aimed at combating psychologists' denial that personal construct theory is a theory about the emotional and experiencing person as well as the 'thinking' person.

Today some are attempting to combat this trend from within. Neimeyer (1985b), for instance, has a chapter on 'Personal Constructs in Clinical Practice' in a book on *Advances in Cognitive-Behavioral Research and Therapy* (Kendall, 1985) and another in *Cognitive Behavioral Approaches to Psychotherapy* (Dryden and Golden, 1986). Indicating the extent of the move to subsume Kelly's ideas within cognitive psychology, Neimeyer (1986) starts his chapter with this quote:

> Virtually every point of George Kelly's theorizing of the 1950's . . . proved to be a prophetic preface for the psychology of the 1970's – and, it seems safe to predict now – for many years to come. Long before 'cognitive psychology' existed, Kelly created a truly cognitive theory of personality, a theory in which how people construe is at the core. . . . There is reason to hope that the current moves toward a hyphenated cognitive-behavioral approach will help fill in the grand outlines that Kelly sketched years before anyone else even realized the need. (Mischel, 1980)

I believe these pressures to integrate personal construct theory under the cognitive label are potentially most destructive. I take note of Marie Jahoda's distinction between cognitive and cognitivism (see pp. 1–14 in this volume), but when I talk to people in the 'cognitive' world they seem to be using it in the old way. And I would predict that the majority of psychologists reading that quote from Mischel would construe that personal construct theory was to do with thinking rather than with feeling or experiencing.

Construing is experiencing: new paths to understanding

Where does it get us if we follow Kelly in suggesting that it may be useful to see all experiencing as construing? At a simple level there is no problem with issues such as primacy – it just depends what is going on at the time. But it goes much further. If all experience is seen as construing, we can extend our interest and study of things like meditation. This could be seen as experiencing within a different personal perspective – one in which self and time are suspended. We are in another sub-system of construing.

We may be able to get access to the nature of hypnosis. We all know about those experiments in which the person under hypnosis is told that a lighted cigarette is put on their skin and a blister erupts. Again, could this be understood from a personal construct perspective as the person having suspended his 'everyday' sub-system of construing (experiencing) the world and having entered another sub-system in which body and mind are at one?

It leads to our looking at psychosomatic problems differently. For instance, stomach pains that are shown to be connected with enlarged veins can be eliminated by progressive relaxation. Both stomach pains and enlarged veins disappear.

The personal construct theorist, who views all experience as construing, has a part to play in the treatment of cancer. By 'getting into' one's own cellular construing it is at least theoretically possible to see how this could lead to cellular reconstruing. I do not believe this is as far-fetched as it seems when put into words.

In my view, personal construct theory is indeed still a radical theory in 1985.

References

Bruner, J. S. (1956). A cognitive theory of personality. *Contemporary Psychology* 1, 355–6.

Davisson, A. (1978). George Kelly and the American mind (or why has he been obscure for so long in the USA and whence the new interest?). In F. Fransella (ed.) *Personal Construct Psychology 1977*. London: Academic Press.

Fransella, F. (1980). Man-as-scientist. In A. J. Chapman and D. M. Jones (eds.), *Models of Man*. Leicester: The British Psychological Society.

Fransella, F. (1983). What sort of scientist is the person-as-scientist? In J. Adams-Webber and J. C. Mancuso (eds.), *Applications of Personal Construct Theory*. Ontario: Academic Press.

Greenberg, L. S. and Safran, J. D. (1984a). Integrating affect and cognition: a perspective on the process of therapeutic change. *Cog. Ther. Res.* 8, 559–78.

Greenberg, L. S. and Safran, J. D. (1984b). Hot cognition – emotion coming in from the cold: a reply to Rachman and Mahoney. *Cog. Ther. Res.* 8, 591–8.

Helson, R. and Mitchell, V. (1978). Personality. *Annual Review of Psychology* 29, 555–85.

Holland, R. (1970). George Kelly: constructive innocent and reluctant existentialist. In D. Bannister (ed.), *Perspectives in Personal Construct Psychology*. London: Academic Press.

Kelly, G. A. (1985). *Behaviour Is an Experiment*. London: Centre for Personal Construct Psychology.

Kendall, P. (ed.) (1985). *Advances in Cognitive Behavioural Research and Therapy*, Vol. 4. New York: Academic Press.

Mischel, W. (1980). George Kelly's anticipation of psychology: a personal tribute. In M. J. Mahoney (ed.), *Psychotherapy Process*. New York: Plenum.

Neimeyer, R. A. (1985a). *The Development of Personal Construct Psychology*. Lincoln: Nebraska Press.

Neimeyer, R. A. (1985b). Personal constructs in clinical practice. In P. Kendall (ed.), *Advances in Cognitive Behavioural Research and Therapy*, Vol. 4. New York: Academic Press.

Neimeyer, R. A. (1986). Personal construct therapy. In W. Dryden and W. Golden (eds.), *Cognitive Behavioral Approaches to Psychotherapy*. London: Harper & Row.

Rachman, S. (1984). A reassessment of the 'primacy of affect'. *Cog. Ther. Res.* 8, 579–84.

Chapter 3
Autopoiesis and alternativism in psychotherapy: fluctuations and reconstructions

Vincent Kenny

Prefatory comments

For me, the perennial puzzle at the centre of the psychotherapeutic enterprise is that of personal change while retaining identity. 'Change' presupposes both something that changes and, while changing, something that manages to conserve invariance. This puzzle is classically illustrated by the ship of Theseus (Nozick, 1984). As he sails the seas he removed the planks of his ship, replacing them one at a time with a new plank. The old planks are thrown overboard. As the ship sails each part is gradually replaced until nothing of the original components remains. In what sense may we call this the 'same' ship? The story is now complicated, however, because we discover that an enterprising group of people were following Theseus on his sea voyage collecting all the planks that were thrown overboard. Gradually, they form these original planks into the exact configuration of their earlier existence until they have reconstructed the entire ship. When Theseus sails into his home port he is followed by the reconstructed ship. The question now is: which is the original? Which ship can be called the 'same' ship?

An answer to this puzzle, and to its psychotherapeutic counterpart, is to be found in the work of Humberto Maturana (1980a), a Chilean biologist, whose studies on vision have led him to develop a philosophical position extremely compatible with that of George Kelly. This chapter introduces his theory and draws implications for the practice of psychotherapy within PCP.

Introduction

Kelly and Maturana are both constructivists, but they differ in the type of constructivism they hold. Using von Glasersfeld's distinction of 'trivial versus radical' – where the trivial constructivist is one who, while endorsing the notion that we invent or construct our own reality at the same time believes in an 'objective, ontological reality' (Dell, 1985) – Kelly is a trivial constructivist, because he does really believe that there is an independently existing objective reality. Witness his reliance on external reality as the source of (in)validation of constructs. Kelly believes in the existence of two separate 'realities' (i.e. that objectively existing and that constructed by ourselves) which may ultimately converge. However, in discussing the philosophy of radical constructivism, Ernst von Glasersfeld introduces the idea that the best we can ever hope to aspire to in our knowledge of the real world is to discover what the world is not. It only reveals to us that certain aspects of our human endeavours are possible or viable. When we learn this, we are learning only about ourselves in the world, and not about the world we inhabit (von Glasersfeld, 1984). Maturana (1985) describes himself as being a '*radical* radical constructivist' in going beyond von Glasersfeld's descriptions, which on the one hand break with the notion of objective reality, and focus on the multiplicity of possible constructions of experience which may be validly made; on the other hand, Maturana goes further by developing his theory of structure determinism, which states that at the moment of perception there are no other possible constructions to be brought forth other than the construction actually made.

For Maturana the personal system is 'organizationally closed' (Varela, 1979) to the point where at the moment of experiencing we are constitutionally unable to distinguish between what we call a perception and a hallucination. We avoid the solipsist trap only through languaging-in a community of co-observers who, retrospectively, decide whether we hallucinated or not. This has obvious implications for working with so-called 'schizophrenics'.

Kelly also insisted on 'closing' the construct system in order to make sense of it and defined many of his theoretical constructs from 'inside' the person rather than from the point of view of an observer. The following quote illustrates Kelly's use of closure: 'he can never make choices outside the world of alternatives he has erected for himself' (1969, p. 88). The concept of organizational closure is central to Maturana's theory of Autopoiesis to which I now turn in order to briefly introduce it and some of its implications for PCT.

Autopoiesis: the word

In his book (with Varela) *Autopoiesis and Cognition*, Maturana describes how he invented this badly needed word following a conversation with a friend about Don Quixote's dilemma

> of whether to follow the path of arms (*praxis*, action) or the path of letters (*poiesis*, creation, production) . . . I understood for the first time the power of the word 'poiesis' and invented the word . . . *autopoiesis*. This was a word without a history, a word that could directly mean what takes place in the dynamics of the autonomy proper to living systems. (1980a, p. xvii)

Thus the word implies a recursive self-production (autos = self; poiesis = creation). With his new word, Maturana could 'bring forth' a new reality describing something novel about the organization of the living. However, the concept of Autopoiesis goes far beyond meaning simply self-production, as the following definition shows:

> A dynamic system that is defined as a composite unity is a network of productions of components that (a) through their interactions recursively regenerate the network of productions that produced them, and (b) realize this network as a unity in the space in which they exist by constituting and specifying its boundaries as surfaces of cleavage from the background through their preferential interactions within the network, is an autopoietic system. (Maturana, 1980b)

This definition is one that many people find hard to grasp. At the centre of it is the notion that there is a recursive network of productions which produces components (and relations) which in *turn* produce the network of productions that produced them, and so on. In such a recursive self-regeneration it is impossible to distinguish the product, production or producer (Varela, 1984). Furthermore, the components 'realize' or 'material-ize' the network of productions as a concrete unity (system) in space.

Let me illustrate this with the biological example of a single cell which may be seen as a factory literally producing itself, that is producing its components and their relations which in turn produce the network of processes which produce the components, and so on. It is impossible to distinguish the product from the producer. This is the 'organization of the living' which is called Autopoiesis. When Autopoiesis stops, the cell dies. While Autopoiesis is a very special type of organization applicable only to cells and cell aggregates, all systems whether biological or not can be characterized and identified in terms of their organization and structure. This distinction is precisely defined by Maturana as follows:

> *Organization*: The relations between components, whether static or dynamic, that make a composite unity a unity of a particular kind, are its organization. Or, in other words, the relations between components that must remain invariant in a composite unity for it not to change its class identity and become something else, constitute its organization.
> *Structure*: The actual components and the actual relations between them that at any instance realize a particular composite unity as a concrete static or dynamic entity in the space which its components define, constitute its structure. (1980b)

Organization only refers to *relations*. Structure refers *both* to concrete components *and* to the relations between them which *realize* or *material-ize* the organization in physical space. Hence, organization is a *subset* of structure. The organization must remain invariant for the system (unity) to survive. The structure may change endlessly while keeping the organization invariant. The system (e.g. us humans) is structure-determined (i.e. the organization can *only* be altered through the structure) since the organization is realized (materialized) only through the concrete structure.

Living systems are dynamic structure-determined entities which are continuously changing. A system lasts as long as its organization is conserved. Living consists in the conservation of identity. This is realized in structures which change all the time. Change is constitutive of living systems and change is completely dependent on structure. Thus we may understand Kelly's notions of Threat, Fear, Anxiety, and so on, as structural intimations that the conservation of the organizational invariance (= identity) is endangered. There are only two types of structural change possible – that which maintains the organization or that which destroys the organization. There is no continuum here. It is *always* discontinuous. An example of a structural change which maintains the organization would be to cut one inch off the four legs of a table. We *still* have a 'table' identity left but with a *different composition* (i.e. shorter legs). An example of destroying the organization is if I cut the table in two. Now we no longer have a 'table'.

Change/invariance

Returning to our central dilemma of change/invariance, how is it that we continue to consider ourselves the same person (identity) in spite of the profound structural (e.g. cellular recycling) changes over many years of growth and development? The answer is that as long as the changes do not cause a loss of organization, then you are 'the same', although now your invariant identity is realized through different components. From a psychological point of view, our identity remains the 'same' as long as our 'core constructs' or 'self-maintenance processes' are conserved throughout any structural variation.

Psychological difficulty arises either (1) when the person repeatedly uses some construct-system structure despite continuing invalidation of this structure (structural problems) or (2) when structural changes occur which are sufficient to destroy the current organization (organizational problems). Many of Kelly's professional constructs are to help identify, first, lack of 'fit' between structure and the world (structural coupling) and, second, actual loss of structure leading to loss of organization (e.g. personal identity).

Kelly identifies a central therapeutic version of the change/invariance dilemma in the following passage:

> Our position is that even the changes which a person attempts within himself must be construed by him. The new outlook which a person gains from experience is itself an event; and, being an event in his life, it needs to be construed by him if he is to make any sense out of it. Indeed, he cannot even attain the new outlook in the first place unless there is some comprehensive overview within which it can be construed. (1955 pp. 78–9)

Here again we have the awareness of the paradox that something must remain constant (i.e. the organization) while change occurs (i.e. structure). Kelly's theory attempts to spell out the limits to personal change (while retaining invariance), and in his Modulation Corollary he points out that 'for any one person there are limits in the extent to which he can go in either direction and still retrieve himself' (1969, p. 128).

Implications for PCT

In this section I would like to elaborate upon some implications of Maturana's work for PCT, first from a general perspective on psychotherapy and, second, examining Kelly's eight strategies for change.

The first implication from the Closure Thesis is that there can be no 'instructional interactions' between the therapist and client, or indeed between any two organisms of any kind. The concept of transferring information from one person to the other is now untenable.

This is not too alien a notion to followers of Kelly, since Kelly himself makes similar statements, for example: 'one does not learn certain things merely from the nature of the stimuli which play upon him; he learns only what his framework is designed to permit him to see in the stimuli' (1955, p. 79). We must therefore consider ourselves merely to be a source of perturbations in the other's medium. This means we must learn how to trigger transformations in the client, while remaining unable, of course, to determine such transformations. Whatever the outcome of our communications (or interactions), these results will reflect the organization and structure of the person's own system.

This brings us to the second point, 'listening to the listening'. If we wish our perturbations to have something made of them by the other person's system, then we must form a coherence (structurally couple) with the other in such a way that we come to know how the person listens. In the dynamics of the conversation we can listen (1) to the content and (2) listen to the listening of the conversation that is taking place, for example in a group, or family. This is why lecturing is so difficult because I have little clue as to what your systems may or may not be making of what I say.

Listening to the listening is obviously similar to Kelly's notion of subsuming the other's construct system. When we do this we know how to 'get into' the other's system (how to *use* it) through the *structural relations* that constitute the system. Thus I will better know how to trigger construct transformations, rather than being 'left outside' of the other's system.

The Closure Thesis states that 'every autonomous system is organizationally closed' (Varela, 1979). While a system (individual) may generate autonomous behaviour, it may also be seen by an observer to be 'controlled' by another system (society) and to play an allopoietic role in the composition of the larger system. To this extent, psychotherapy must always be anti-social and anarchistic since to raise any questions about the person in society may lead to interactions not confirmatory of the particular social system (Maturana, 1980a, p. xxvii).

Turning now to implications of the organization/structure distinction for therapy, I will summarize as follows.

The system can only do what it does at any given time (structure-determinism). In Kelly's terms, the construct system always moves in the direction with the greatest possibility for elaboration. 'A client can express himself only within the framework of his construct system' (1969, p. 83). Kelly's psychology of acceptance demonstrates how the notion of 'resistance' cannot be applied to clients as if they were being stubborn in not elaborating their system as the therapist wished: 'they bespoke more of the therapist's perplexity than of the client's rebellion'. To change the person's system we must get into what Maturana calls a 'co-ontogenic structural drift'.

Since all change is structure-determined then we can only approach the organization of the system through the components and relations of the system. What happens when you interact with a system depends *entirely* on its structure, (e.g. if I hit you on the head with a hammer, it is the structure of your skull that determines if you will die). What happens does *not* depend on the external perturbation. It is the structure which dictates what structural changes the system may undergo while maintaining invariance. The structure dictates what perturbation will constitute (a) changes in state or (b) destructive change.

The structure determines what will be accepted as an *interaction* and what will happen as a result, that is whether the interaction will result in self-maintenance or disintegration. It is this choice that the therapist must always keep in mind. Sometimes we are surprised and shocked when a client makes a 'destructive' conclusion about some data and kills himself as a result.

Conservation of invariance

Since, according to Maturana, 'living consists in the conservation of identity' then we should not be surprised at what appears to be 'resistance' in persons confronted with change. The organization/structure distinction makes this dilemma clear, as we have seen, since a (construct) system exists only as long as its organization remains invariant. Kelly's transitional constructs spell out the task of disintegrating one organization while inventing another.

Orthogonal approach

Given that (1) the system can only do what it does and (2) that all change is structure-determined and (3) that the system will attempt to conserve invariance, then what is a therapist to do? Where can you start? Should you begin at all? The answer is to begin by interacting with the person in an orthogonal fashion. In other words, to disintegrate the organization of a family, I must avoid becoming a member. Therefore I must interact through components (conversations, individual members, constructs) that do *not* constitute them as a family. We must discover what these are.

Recalling that we are multi-selves, only *certain* components of each individual are required to be constitutive of the system, and therefore there are many axes/components which are superfluous, that is dimensions *not* constitutive of the system. It is through these structural dimensions that the therapist must interact, thereby remaining orthogonal to the system. Whatever he does with the system structure must *not* confirm the organization. He must interact in a manner that the individual (component) will *listen* to him, and yet in such a way that (1) he does not confirm the organization and (2) that as a result of the interaction the person will undergo a structural change so that the person no longer serves to maintain the old system.

Kelly makes a similar recommendation in suggestions that we deal with peripheral or subsidiary components of the construct system.

Kelly's eight levels reconstrued

Kelly says that there are two ways to approach change of the system. We may either 'reroute' the person within existing channels, or we may create new channels. These correspond to the *Type I* and *Type II* levels of change that Watzlawick, Weakland and Fisch (1974) describe. In Maturana's terms Type I change (working within the existing system) is a 'change of state' while Type II change is destructive of the organization. Therefore we may look at Kelly's eight strategies (1969) and ask which of them are likely to be '*confirmatory versus destructive*' of the organization? In his own analysis it is Strategies 7 and 8 which may lead to radical reconstruction. Thus, in the first column of Table A3.1, under 'Organization', I indicate that the strategies most likely to disintegrate organization (and thereby create a new organization) are numbers 7 and 8. In contrast strategies 1 to 6 are likely to be confirmatory or conserving of the organization. In Maturana's terms all eight must be directed at the *structure* of the system, that is at the components and the relations among the components. (This is especially so since you cannot have direct access to organization. The therapist must move to change organization *through* changes in structure.)

The first three strategies use the components (but not relations), whereas strategies 4 to 8 use increasingly both components (constructs) and relations between constructs. Further, since triggering the 'observer role' (a degree of critical distance from oneself) in a client is implicit in Kelly's model of the person as a scientist, I have included a column for which strategies are most likely to induce the observer role. Apart from the first two (and perhaps strategy 6) most of the strategies would seem to imply an observer role for the client.

Table A3.1 Kelly's eight levels reconstrued

Level of change strategy	Org.	Structure		Induce 'observer' role
		C	R	
1 Slot rattle	■	√	■	■
2 Alternative construct	■	√	■	■
3 Pre-verbal constructs	■	√	■	√
4 System: internal consistency	■	√	√	√
5 System: reality contacting	■	√	√	√
6 Increase/decrease range	■	√	√	√
7 Alter meaning	√	√	√	√
8 New channels	√	√	√	√

Org. = organization C = component R = relations

Overall we see that major change – in terms of disintegration of current organization – is most likely to be triggered by strategies 7 and 8. However, it is possible that even these two strategies (the most creative and innovative) may succeed only in conserving the organization of the system, despite apparently significant achievement in creating new meaning and new axes. People avoid change because they fear 'psychological death', that is the loss of organizational invariance (identity). If strategies 7 and 8 fail to alter the superordinate core constructs which constitute the organizational invariance needing disintegrating, then we can only achieve adaptation within the existing channels (7 and 8 will then fall into the Type 1 category).

If we wish to invent further strategies of change – and Kelly mentioned that these eight were expandable – then this table provides some guidelines for innovation; that is, we must invent strategies that (1) may destroy or conserve organization, (2) must act through construct-system structure/components and/or relations among components, and (3) induce observer status in the client.

I would like to conclude by returning to Vico, an earlier constructivist, who in applying his Theory of *Verum* (the true) and *Factum* (what is made) to argue against the sceptics in 1710, made the following statement, which I think holds the essence of constructivism and which serves to bring forth the end of this chapter:

> Those truths are, indeed, human whose elements we fashion for ourselves, contain within ourselves and, by means of postulates, extend indefinitely: when we arrange these elements we make the truths which we come to know through this arranging; and because of all this, we grasp the genus or form by which we do the making.

References

Dell, P. (1985). Understanding Bateson and Maturana: toward a biological foundation for the social sciences. *Journal of Marital and Family Therapy* 11(1), 1–20.

Glasersfeld, E. von (1984). An introduction to radical constructivism. In P. Watzlawick (ed.), *The Invented Reality.* New York: Norton.

Kelly, G. (1955). *The Psychology of Personal Constructs*, Vols. I and II. New York: Norton.

Kelly, G. (1969). *Clinical Psychology and Personality: The Selected Papers of George Kelly.* Ed. B. Maher. New York: Wiley.

Maturana, H. (1980a). *Introduction to Autopoiesis and Cognition: The Realization of the Living.* London: D. Reidel.

Maturana, H. (1980b). Man and society. In F. Benseler and P. Hejl (eds.), *Autopoiesis, Communication and Society.* Frankfurt-am-Main: Campus Verlag.

Maturana, H. (1985). Personal communication.

Maturana, H. and Varela, F. (1980). *Autopoiesis and Cognition.* London: D. Reidel.

Nozick, R. (1984). *Philosophical Explanations.* Oxford: Clarendon Press.

Varela, F. J. (1979). *Principles of Biological Autonomy.* North Holland: Oxford.

Varela, F. J. (1984). The creative circle: sketches on the natural

history of circularity. In 'P. Watzlawick (ed.), *The Invented Reality*'. New York: Norton.
Vico, G. (1982). *Selected Writings* Ed. and trans. Leon Pompa. Cambridge: Cambridge University Press.
Watzlawick, P. Weakland J. and Fisch, R. (1974). *Change*. New York: Norton.

Chapter 4

Personal meaning and memory: Kelly and Bartlett

Peggy Dalton

Recently, I attempted to survey some of the literature on memory (Dalton, 1985). It was, on the whole, rather a depressing experience. It started well. I enjoyed reading what Aristotle had to say about *laying down traces*. He set out some conditions for such a process which would hold good today – the importance of the organisation of material to be remembered and the frequency of presentation or occurence, for example. He saw that memory traces could be associated, so that the recall of one experience would lead to the recall of another, largely through continguity in time and space. His point about the need for attention to similarities and differences between experiences for the formation of these associations caught my eye at once. But I was not to meet this idea again until I turned to Kelly.

From then on I found myself grappling with complex philosophical issues such as the mind versus body controversy, until I groped my way back to my theme, memory, where it seemed that Ebbinghaus (1885) set his seal on much of the work which was to come, with his reduction of the processes involved to the 'purity' of uncontaminated nonsense syllables, recalled in strict laboratory conditions. Only Bartlett (1932) was a lone voice insisting on the importance of other factors besides accuracy in remembering. Not until the work of people such as Tulving in the 1970s did I have a sense of remembering as the more unified experience of a whole person. Seamon (1980) gives a clear and comprehensive overview of what went on in the intervening years.

Bartlett on remembering

Bartlett is probably chiefly known for his use of the concept of *schemata* in relation to memory. He reluctantly adopted the term from the work of the neurologist Henry Head, although he felt that *active developing patterns* or *organised settings* would express his meaning better. Schemata may be seen as the structures which at once give meaning to the events perceived and are built up by the experience of that perception itself. Bartlett believed that the organism, the person, had hit upon a way of turning round upon its own schemata and making them the objects of its reactions, which makes it possible for the active organised settings to undergo change. Some schemata, he says, can be seen as completed models which are maintained by repetition, while others are still in process of change, are not dependent on the preservation of their chronological development for their use and thus we are free from over-determination by the immediately preceding event.

Bartlett found from his experiments that memory was far from being reduplicative or reproductive in nature and regarded literal recall not only as exceptional but 'extraordinarily unimportant'. Remembering, he states, is 'far more decisively an affair of construction'. Moreover, 'condensation, elaboration and invention are common features of ordinary remembering and these all very often involve the mingling of materials belonging originally to different schemata'. From the series of experiments on perceiving, Bartlett noted that people seldom took the situation detail by detail but rather tended to get a general impression of the whole, on the basis of which they constructed the probable detail. This was the case, whether the material was verbal narrative, pictures or faces. From his subjects' reflections on what characterised this general impression, he concluded that the major factor involved was 'attitude' – this, it seems, governed their construction of the situation as a whole. While acknowledging that attitude is a complex psychological state or process which is very hard to define, Bartlett sees it as largely a matter of feeling or affect. Justification of this attitude is the basis for a person's construction of a remembered event.

But this does not fully explain why some special features of recalled material are invariably dominant. Bartlett hypothesises that these features are related to the individual's 'appetite, instinct, interests and ideals'. Focusing on interests in the adult, he believes that they are very persistent and their materials collected from many sources.

> Consequently, striking features of a presented whole may, by the interest, be carried along in an individualised fashion and, in the form of sensorial images or of language, may directly influence reactions long after their original stimulus occurred. (Bartlett, 1932, p. 211)

From this argument Bartlett concludes that we may still talk of 'traces' in relation to memory, but these cannot be regarded as complete at one moment, stored up somewhere and then re-excited much later. They are, rather, 'interest-determined traces. They live with our interests and with them they change'.

Bartlett ends his theoretical discussion by attempting to answer the question of how our active organised settings, our schemata, are developed. He believes that Head is right in thinking that they follow the lines of demarcation of the special senses. But he points out that, in any given case these special senses are those of a single person, so that even if material which is touched, seen and also heard goes to different schemata, they are not isolated from one another. And if appetites, instincts or interests are the lines of organisation, they too are not isolated from one another. Their ranges of operation overlap continually. They are interconnected, organised together and display an order of predominance among themselves. This order of predominance forms *temperament* or *character*, and this is why, Bartlett maintains, memory is seen to have such a characteristically *personal* flavour.

Bartlett and Kelly

I am obviously not the first to find resemblances between some of these ideas and those of Kelly, published twenty years later (see Mancuso and Adams-Webber, 1983). Rereading Bartlett after some years of involvement with personal construct psychology was like listening to a familiar voice.

Although there are, of course, many differences between the theories of these two psychologists, not the least being the greater scope and complexity of Kelly's work, some links between them are striking. Central to Bartlett's approach to remembering, is his focus on a person's *effort after meaning*. His experiments on perceiving show his subjects trying to discriminate the material before them in the light of their previous experience and current preoccupations, just as Kelly sees people continually striving to make sense of their worlds. When asked to reproduce what they had perceived in this highly personal way, further modifications were found, governed not only by the strength of their interests but, quite clearly, by their *ways* of construing. When Bartlett describes the approach of his subjects to their tasks he differentiates between those who approach them with caution and concern for accuracy and others who are more confident, less organised, introducing more material from extraneous sources. The first he distinguishes as the 'vocalisers', the second the 'visualisers'. A construct theorist might view the former group as construing more tightly and the latter more loosely. Perhaps having greater access to visual imagery allows for a more dilated field in the second group.

Bartlett's schema is not the equivalent of a construct, nor his schemata the same as Kelly's networks of constructs. The bi-polar nature of constructs, so crucial to Kelly's theory, is missing from Bartlett's model. But the description of schemata as 'active developing patterns' and the idea that the person has the ability to turn round upon his own schemata and change them, carry with them some of the implications about the active nature of construing and reconstruction. Bartlett's reference to the processes of 'condensation, elaboration and invention' in remembering also have a familiar ring.

Where Bartlett speaks of the importance of 'attitude' in relation to how a person perceives and remembers events, stresses the 'justification of the attitude' as the governing factor, he is touching on something very like the notion of the influence of superordinate constructs and certainly implying the powerful effect of such processes at the pre-verbal level. The strength of 'interests', carrying with it the concept of high individualisation seems to relate to some extent at least to core-role construing. In his descriptions of 'temperament' or 'character' as represented by schemata which are organised, interconnected, with ranges of operation which overlap and have their own order of predominance, Bartlett comes very close to Kelly's delineation of the person in terms of a system of constructs.

As Bartlett is more interested in the constructive nature of remembering than in its accuracy, so Kelly is more concerned with what a person makes of things than with any objective reality. It is notable that, unlike experimenters before or since in the area of memory, Bartlett paid much attention to his subjects' personal experience and their reflections on their own processes of perceiving and remembering. For Bartlett, too, sociality seems to have been an important factor in his work with people, and his theory shows him subsuming their experience under his own system of professional constructs.

Kelly on remembering and forgetting

In *The Psychology of Personal Constructs* (1955) we would not expect to find a section headed 'Memory'. Since construing embraces every aspect of experience, segmentation under chapter headings, what Bannister and Fransella (1980) refer to as 'the intellectual carve-up' is totally inappropriate to Kelly's approach. He does, however, relate the phenomena of remembering and forgetting to his theory as a whole. He is interested, for example, in the nature of recollection within the context of a person's present construing of his situation. 'The recollection', he believes, 'is not the original "memory" but a cue which stands for the original memory or symbol of the context upon which the preverbal construct was originally formed'. The question for him is 'what the "remembered" event constructively stands for' (Kelly, 1955, p. 465).

In a section on *suspension* Kelly explores the phenomena of 'forgetting', 'disassociation' and 'repression' in terms of structure.

> In order for an experience to be remembered or perceived clearly it must be supported within a system of constructs. When one construct is resolved in favour of another one, some of the elements tend to drop out, especially those which do not fit so well into the new construct. Simultaneously, other elements which were once less available to the person are now more prominently displayed because the new structure provides a convenient peg to hang them on.

He goes on to discuss the relationship between a client's remembering events previously forgotten and signs of therapeutic movement. He sees 'suspension' of material as due to its incompatability with the overall system which a person is currently using and its restoration due to the development of new structures.

Kelly is also concerned with suspension due to implications. An event referred to by a client in the transcript of a tape which is the focus of a paper written in 1958, emerges as holding implications which he has forgotten, although the event itself is vividly remembered. The young man has recalled being pushed into a fish-pond by a friend as a child. The memory evokes intense emotion which he does not fully understand. Later exploration reveals that the intensity of the emotion is related to the client's confusion in the face of massive invalidation of his very limited construing of 'friendship' – limited because of his lack of experience in playing with other children.

A personal-construct view of remembering must clearly take account of both content and structure. It cannot be separated from other aspects of construing and will not make a great deal of sense without some knowledge of the person and his or her view of their worlds as a whole. An understanding of someone's typical ways of construing events (tightly, loosely or moving creatively between the two) will throw light on how the person might have perceived the original event. Learning what for him or her are superordinate constructions, which might relate to core structures, will help us to grasp the meaning of remembered material beyond the details of its contents.

Memory and the construing of self

Our sense of what we are and what we might become is derived from a number of sources. As children we are offered constructions of events by other people, by stories and the games we play, we make our own behavioural experiments and gradually form some kind of definition of ourselves as elements in the world around us. As Bannister and Mair (1968) point out, our view develops and changes over time and it is what we make of those early impressions as we go along that is of real importance.

It is often relevant for a person in therapy to review and perhaps reconstrue the past – his or her recollections of important figures or events may be altered as they are explored in a new light. Remembrance of the behaviour of a parent towards a child has been influenced by the need to make sense of the adult's present unhappiness, perhaps. A single episode, such as the one explored with his client by Kelly, can also be vividly but only partially remembered and turn out to have implications which may have played an important part in shaping a person's construing of self.

A man who had stuttered severely since his early childhood associated its onset with a highly unpleasant experience in hospital at the age of six. He remembered lying in bed before an operation, then waking up from an anaesthetic, attempting to call for his mother and failing to utter a sound. Only when he focused on his feelings of fear and helplessness before the operation and the terror of being alone when he awoke did he remember how he had felt abandoned by his mother, that she had left him in the hospital to die. He later discovered that he had been quite markedly 'disfluent' before this event. His memory of it as the cause, however, not only gave a basis to his theory about his problem but justified the sense he had carried with him for most of his life of being a victim of circumstances, helpless to help himself in any difficulty and only redeemable through outside intervention.

Vividly remembered episodes from childhood are not necessarily traumatic in nature, of course. Often we find we have filtered an experience out of its context and retained a glowing picture of a period or event in our lives which seems to have its strength partly through comparison and contrast with later periods or events. The contrast between the long hot summers and endless pleasure of early childhood is probably sharpened in memory if one's teens are fraught with the struggle to come to terms with one's changing body, difficult relationships, the pressure of examinations. As adults we can hopefully see ourselves as continuing both kinds of experience, with the capacity for play and enjoyment and the ability to go on learning from changing relationships and our response to pressure and challenge.

Levels of awareness and levels of memory

Throughout his book, Bartlett (1932) protests that although 'consciousness' is a meaningful concept to him, he cannot explain it. It has, he says, 'a definite function, other than the mere fact of being aware'. The organism's capacity 'to turn round upon its own schemata and construct them afresh' is 'where and why consciousness comes in; it is what gives consciousness its most prominent function'. But Bartlett can only wish he knew 'how it was done'.

Kelly, as always, found his own way of approaching this issue. He preferred to speak not of 'the unconscious' but in terms of *pre-verbal* construing, *suspension*, *submergence* and *levels of cognitive awareness* when he referred to constructions not immediately accessible to us. His theory seems to imply that, in some form, we 'store' all that we construe. Some of this material is experienced before we have words to put to it, some of it, though construed later, is never verbalised. We have seen how 'forgetting' is regarded by Kelly as 'suspension', either due to a construction's being incompatible with the rest of a person's system or simply because it is irrelevant at a particular time. He speaks of one pole of a construct being submerged, where it has either not been elaborated or is too threatening for a person to contemplate. Finally, he acknowledges that at any time constructs will lie at different levels of awareness.

The process referred to by Bartlett, of a person's turning round upon his or her own schemata, seems very like the movement of material from one level of awareness to another. When we reflect on some action or attempt to make some prediction about the outcome of our behaviour, we are drawing into awareness elements which are relevant to the matter in hand. We may be casting our minds back a moment or two or searching our longer-term memory for evidence which will help us to make whatever choices are before us. More often than not, a flash of remembrance seems to appear of itself without deliberate search. Sometimes the memory is at such a low level of awareness to begin with that it may be experienced as 'gut-reaction' – the fear which comes with the sound of a voice, a smell or the look on someone's face. Moments of joy will come to us without explanation and only later, if at all, be linked with an earlier happy experience.

There is clearly much more to be explored in relation to personal meaning and memory. A closer look at Kelly's basic theory should throw light on the ideas set in train by Bartlett and may perhaps yield some interesting reflections on the nature of construing processes. The effects on many aspects of a person's construction system with the experience of 'organic' memory loss will also be studied in a later paper.

References

Bannister, D. and Fransella, F. (1980). *Inquiring Man* 2nd edn. Penguin: Harmondsworth.

Bannister, D. and Mair, J. M. M. (1968). *The Evaluation of Personal Constructs*. Academic Press: New York.

Bartlett, F. C. (1932). *Remembering: A Study in Experimental and Social Psychology*. Cambridge University Press: Cambridge.

Dalton, P. (1985). Remembering as reconstruction. Project for the Diploma in Personal Construct Psychology (Therapy and Counselling). PCP Centre, London (unpublished).

Ebbinghaus, H. (1885). *Uber das Gedachtniss*. Dunker, H. Ruyer. Trans. C. E. Bussenius, *Memory*, Teachers College Press: New York, 1913.

Kelly, G. A. (1955). *The Psychology of Personal Constructs*, Vols. I and II. Norton: New York.

Kelly, G. A. (1958). Personal Construct Theory and the psychotherapeutic interview. In B. Maher (ed.), *Clinical Psychology and Personality*. Krieger: New York, 1979.

Mancuso, J. C. and Adams-Webber, J. (1983). *The Construing Person*. Praeger: New York.

Seamon, J. G. (1980). *Memory and Cognition*. Oxford University Press: New York, Oxford.

Tulving, E. (1972). Episodic and semantic memory. In M. Tulving and W. Donaldson (eds.), *Organisation of Memory*. Academic Press: New York.

Chapter 5

Kelly and Bateson: antithesis or synthesis?

Robert Foley

At first glance, the views of George Kelly and Gregory Bateson may seem difficult to reconcile. Kelly is portrayed as a personality theorist, primarily interested in 'cognitive structures' and how those structures (constructs) influence behaviour. In contrast, Gregory Bateson is viewed as a pioneer in the study of interpersonal phenomena. His search for 'pattern' and 'form' was in contrast to the traditional scientific preoccupation with 'substance' and 'quantity' and led him to conceive of the now classic double-bind hypothesis of mental disorder. If one surveys a sample of psychology textbooks, Bateson's is usually described as the father of systems-based therapy while Kelly is found drifting between the cognitive psychologists and the phenomenological psychotherapists.

My intention in this paper is to elaborate the similarities I see behind these apparently disparate views. My contention is that George Kelly in his personal construct psychology provides a theory and methodology which, if adopted, avoids many of those errors in thinking which Bateson described and elaborated in a more formal and academic manner.

Philosophy and psychology

Bateson and Kelly shared a deep personal interest in and familiarity with philosophical issues and also placed a priority on clarifying their own philosophical position for their readers. Kelly elaborated many times his basic 'constructivist' position, which he called 'alternative constructivism', and its implications emerge constantly within the psychology of personal constructs. Kelly's preference for constructivism liberated him from many of the constraints of the more traditional and established philosophical assumptions of science which he described as 'accumulative fragmentalism'. For Kelly accumulative fragmentalism is expressed in man's preference for *certainty* over *meaning*: 'We would rather know some things for sure even though they don't shed much light on what is going on'. It is no wonder that our identities often stand on trivial ground: 'If I can't be a man, at least I can be an expert'.

Now it would not be too bad if this were just a view held by a few scientists. The tragedy is however that it is a prevalent view among the majority of non-scientists too. We can see this view manifested when we ask people to state any proposition of truth. We find the tendency is to look backwards into past experiences for truth rather than as something we are looking for. Kelly expressed his position thus: 'What we think we know is anchored only in our own assumptions, not in the bed rock of truth itself, and that world we seek to understand remains always on the horizon of our thoughts' (Kelly, 1969). Thus, for Kelly alternative constructivism was an epistemological view of how we come to know anything.

In a similar manner, but expressed in a different language, Bateson was also highly critical of the prevailing epistemological view. He noticed that we tend to think in terms of abstract quantities – for example power, wealth, energy, and transitive actions (one thing acting upon another, e.g. 'If I work hard, I will become successful') – but these notions, according to Bateson, misrepresent the real world. We regard belief as the validating criteria for our views and hence 'we find what we want to find'. 'We create our world in that we look out at the universe through our own presuppositions, our own premises, our own expectations' (Bateson, 1976, p. xi). The similarity with Kelly is clear.

Bateson described the traditional epistemological process as occurring when we make splits in an effort to comprehend the world (e.g. mind/body: good/bad: nature/nurture). Then from those splits we draw boundaries and fool ourselves into believing that what we have just constructed actually exists. It is the old error of misplaced concreteness or reification as described by Whitehead.

Solidifying boundaries is comfortable as, among other things, it allows us to deny aspects of our experience – that is, we can disqualify what we do. For example, a mind/body split can be utilized to disqualify certain threatening experience. One often hears people say of a stomach ache or headache, 'Oh, it's only psychological', or of the experience of falling in love, 'Oh, it was pure physical attraction'. The most extreme examples of people using construed splits to disqualify aspects of their behaviour are found in what we call 'alcoholism' and 'anorexia nervosa', where individuals can completely disown an aspect of their existence.

More specifically, Bateson was critical of scientists, especially social and behavioural scientists who are preoccupied with studying quantities. For example, knowing the grooming habits of college undergraduates or the voting preferences of urban Jews does not give one any sense of the part they play in the larger system. It lends itself to an empty understanding of complex social phenomena. The alternative for Bateson is to look for the relations between interacting entities. Thus for Bateson any interpersonal behaviour, be it aggression, love, hate, dependency, competition, or whatever, is more fruitfully viewed as a phenomenon that can only be adequately understood as a pattern that connects individuals. His emphasis is upon the relationship that connects the parties together, rather than isolating one party and studying it intensively.

What both Bateson and Kelly sought was not a philosophical relativism; rather, they suggest that we become aware of our own biases ('constructs' for Kelly and 'patterns of punctuating events' for Bateson) and our own parochialness; that we take account of our contribution to any description or explanation we offer. As Brad Keeney says, 'A description tells more about the describer than the described'. They would have us always hold ourselves open to the possibility of altering the context within which we perceive and consequently interact with reality. Essentially, both were concerned with the dual problems of

1 coming to some adequate understanding of the bridge between self and others, self and the world
2 an understanding of the ontological development of systems of relationships.

My contention is that both Kelly and Bateson conceived this bridge between self and the world to be *formed of relationships*. Hence Bateson was principally concerned with relationships via 'communication patterns', while Kelly sought to elucidate the relationships between elements in the world and our personal constructs and the relationships between constructs themselves.

A few examples may illustrate their similar views. Brad Keeney commenting upon Bateson's views states, 'The fundamental act of epistemology is to draw a distinction – Distinguishing an "it" from what is "not it". . . . All that we can know rests upon the distinctions we draw' (Keeney, 1982, p. 156). Kelly never settled on any one definition of a construct, preferring to alternatively construe as his understanding developed. However, a construct, if it has to be reified (a construct is a process, not a thing), can be visualized as a reference axis upon which one may project events and elements in an effort to make some sense of what is going on: 'A construct is the basic contrast between two groups. When it is applied it serves to distinguish between elements and to group them. Thus the construct refers to the nature of the distinction one attempts to make between events' (Kelly, 1955, p. 13).

It is important to remember that the most important constructs (epistemological acts) are non-verbal and largely out of conscious awareness. They are channels of behaviour along which we consistently move. Our whole body is involved in drawing the distinction. Thus for Kelly constructs help us to locate events in relation to each other and to understand them and to anticipate them. Clearly, there is a large measure of similarity between 'an epistemological act' (punctuation of events) and 'imposing a construct'. Both are active processes coming from the person, not instincts or stimuli enforcing themselves upon a passive recipient. Both are intrinsically concerned with relations, not quantities. Both imply a relationship.

For Bateson the bridge between self and the world is similar to the bridge between a map and its territory. In the 1970s he became preoccupied with trying to understand the essence of what gets from the territory to the map:

> The answer to this question was obvious. News of difference is what gets across and nothing else. This very simple generalization resolves (at least for some time to come) the ancient problems of mind and matter. Mind always operates at one derivative (${}^{dx}/_{dt}$) away from the 'external' world. The primary data of experience are differences. From these data we construct

> our hypothetical (always hypothetical) ideas and impressions of the 'external' world. A report of difference is the most elementary idea – the invisible atom of thought. Those differences which are somehow not reported are not ideas. Bishop Berkeley would have been pleased. (Bateson, 1976, p. xiv)

For Bateson the mind dealing in news of difference will always be intangible, will always deal with intangibles and will always have certain limitations because it can never encounter the thing itself. It can only encounter *news of boundaries*, *news of contexts, news of difference.*

A few points about difference as emphasized by Bateson may clarify the point:

1 A difference is not material and cannot be localized; that is, if this apple is different from that egg, the difference does not lie in the apple or in the egg, or in the space between them. The difference is the 'relationship' between them as construed by the observer.

2 A difference is not quantity, it is dimensionless.

3 A difference or news of differences is information and must not be confused with energy, which is quantity with physical dimensions. The dimensionless quality of information becomes clear whenever that which does not happen triggers a response in an organism, for example the tax form you did not return, the silence you maintained in conversation.

4 Difference over time = change.

From the simple starting point that it is only news of difference that gets from the territory or map, many of the principles of systems theory may be derived.

The notion of recursiveness, for example, operates in two basic forms:

1 Self-correction or negative feedback. The main characteristic of self-corrective (quasi-purposive) systems is that the causal chains are always circular or more complex. Sub-systems are established which survive for a variable length of time.
2 The second type of recursiveness proposed by the biologist Maturana and mathematician Varela is a case in which some emergent property of the whole is fed back into the system.

Thus the notion of systems living-upon-themselves, of being self-determining or self-organizing (autopoiesis) becomes conceivable.

Bateson used the analogy of a smoke-ring as a basic illustration of the notion of a self-referential system. A smoke-ring is literally introverting, it is endlessly turning in upon itself: spinning on the axis of a cylinder and thus turning in upon its own inturned axis is what gives separate existence to the smoke-ring. It is after all made of nothing but air marked with a little smoke; it is of the same substance as its environment but it has duration and location and a certain degree of separation by virtue of its directional motion. In that sense a smoke-ring stands as a very primitive oversimplified paradigm for recursive systems that contain the beginnings of self-reference, or shall we say *selfhood.*

If we pause at this point and try to visualize a smoke-ring introverting upon itself; now think of the word 'information' and put it in its pure etymological sense of in-forming (forming from within) – we may just begin to get a sense of the process by which self-referential systems organize themselves and thus maintain their uniqueness and identity.

Bateson utilized notions from cybernetics and systems theory to aid his study of interpersonal behaviour. For example, concerning communication patterns he proposed the following views:

1 All behaviour occurring in an interpersonal frame may be regarded as a communication; that is, 'one cannot not communicate'.
2 All communication operates at different logical levels simultaneously; that is, they run along in parallel.
   (a) The 'report level' which is what we commonly associate with human communication; that is, a statement or gesture which follows what has gone before and contributes to the context of what happens next.
   (b) The command level, which operates at a different logical level: it refers to the implicit rules by which the communication is to be conducted. It refers to the relationship which is being tacitly negotiated between parties.
3 In any situation where at least two levels of interaction (report and command) are acting simultaneously, one exercising influence on the other, we then have the necessary and sufficient conditions for a recursive system to evolve.

A considerable amount of Bateson's work was an effort to investigate the context and conditions which are necessary for different forms of relationships to evolve and be maintained. The subject-matter has ranged from dolphins to alcoholism. Let me try to summarize the important issues and thrust of Bateson's position and then compare it to that of George Kelly. First, we must remember that there are two issues interwoven which can only be legitimately separated for descriptive purposes:

1 The bridge between self and the world (epistemology).
2 The evolution of living systems – human groups, families, and so on (ontology).

Luckily Bateson has paraphrased his position as follows:

> Conventional epistemology, which we call 'sanity', boggles at the realization that 'Properties' are only differences and exist only in a context, only in relationship. We abstract from relationship and from the experiences of interaction to create 'objects' and endow them with characteristics. We likewise boggle at the proposition that our own character is only real in relationship. We abstract from the experience of interaction and difference to create a 'self' which shall be 'real' or thingish, even without relationship.' (Bateson, 1976, p. xvi)

To accept this proposition requires an epistemological shift, which can be a threatening process (fear of loss of balance or support). In a similar manner major mental crisis (e.g. schizophrenia) can be viewed as a response to a 'threat of transition'.

To appreciate the position outlined by George Kelly in the psychology of personal constructs we should recall the context within which he worked. During the postwar period psychology in the United States was witnessing the *rise of Behaviourism*, which in the absence of effective biological treatments (no phenothiazines or anti-depressants) was being hailed as a major breakthrough in treatment of chronic mental disorder. Thus it was against a mounting wave of pragmatic-based psycho-technology that George Kelly put together his handbook of psychology. This was an altogether different context from that of Bateson, who was given every encouragement and facility to be creative within a multi-disciplinary team at Paolo Alto (1950s and 1960s). There was considerable pressure on Kelly to prove his case within an epistemology which demanded quantifiable measures and statistically significant differences. In the light of this context it is remarkable how Kelly managed to produce a theory which was 'scientifically' acceptable to hard technologists (no doubt wooed by the repertory grid technique), while at the same time managing not to compromise his philosophical and psychological differences. Unlike Bateson, who was encouraged to be as loose and speculative as he liked, Kelly was working within a constricting and hostile atmosphere. So in our search for similarities we will inevitably have to read between the lines somewhat.

Let us firstly remind ourselves of Kelly's notion of construing and see if we can see any hint of a relationship therein. Kelly reminds us that it would be best for us to envisage a construct as something devised by man for his own lively purposes: 'It must always be clear that the construct is a reference axis devised by man for establishing a personal orientation toward the various events he encounters' (Kelly, 1955).

Thus being a reference axis rather than a representation of something, a construct as described by Kelly is more clearly a psychological guideline against which objects may be referred rather than being either a limited collection of things or a common essence distilled from them. For Kelly what is most important in the life of a person is what *may yet occur* and the part he will choose to play in its realization. In personal construct psychology a construct is as much a personal undertaking (conscious or otherwise) as it is a disembodied scheme for putting nature in its place. This view suggests that human behaviour is to be understood in a context of relevance. Thus, for an adequate understanding of behaviour *one must be aware of what a person may have done but did not do.* The construct dimension which lends structure to the behavioural event does so by providing contrasting poles, and unless we take the trouble to explore both poles the directional trend of the behaviour cannot be plotted. What one does in life can be subjected to moral judgments only in context of what one might have done and did not. It is in such a manner that construct theory embraces both relevance (meaning in context) and responsibility.

From the above we should be able to detect Kelly's emphasis upon not only relationship (a construct is a reference axis devised by man for establishing a personal orientation towards various events) but also upon the paramount importance of meaning and context as essential to any adequate understanding of a person's actions.

We can now turn our attention to Kelly's view of human experience and see if we can detect any similarities with more recent systemic notions of recursiveness, and so on:

> If we are to have a psychology of human experience, we must anchor our basic concepts in that person's experience, not in the experience he causes others to have. Thus if we wish to use a concept of say hostility, we have to ask what is the experiential nature of hostility from the standpoint of the person who does it. Only by answering that question in some sensible way will we arrive at a concept which makes pure psychological sense, rather than sociological or moral sense. (Kelly, 1955, p. 122)

Here we see Kelly describing emotions from the standpoint of the person experiencing them rather than from the point of view of the speculative observer. Thus for Kelly an adequate psychological understanding of an individual and his actions demands a description of the whole person from the perspective of the person himself without necessarily any reference to the outside environment. In this sense Kelly refers to the autonomy of man by closing the boundaries and looking at it from the inside. This notion of closure is precisely what Varela (1979) points to in his distinction between operational and symbolic modes of description. Compare the above with Keeney's comments on the work of more contemporary systemic theorists:

> The contribution of Maturana and Varela to cybernetics was that they proposed a description of whole systems from the perspective of a whole system itself, without any reference to its outside environment. . . . To capture a system's autonomy requires, by definition, no reference to its outside. Instead the system must be described through reference to itself. Stated differently, the self-referentialness of a system becomes a way of pointing to the system's autonomy. (Keeney, 1982, p. 160)

Later he continues:

> In cybernetics of cybernetics, information is the In-Forming of forms, or as Bateson put it, the 'recursive transformation of

> difference.' When speaking of the autonomy of natural systems information becomes constructive, rather than representational or instructive. In this frame of reference in-forming is self-referentially defined. Here there is no outside information. (p. 162)

Kelly, working outside of the language and concepts of systems theory nevertheless grasped the recursive and self-referential nature of behaviour, within his concept of 'behaviour as a form of anticipation or as a question': 'The posture of Anticipation, which is the identifying psychological feature of life itself, silently forms questions and earnest questions erupt in actions'. Elsewhere he describes behaviour as man's independent variable in the experiment of creating his own existence. This view is in stark contrast to his contemporaries who tended to view behaviour as a dependent variable with environmental events as the independant variables.

For Kelly, behaviour is not the answer to the psychologist's question, it is the question – and just as all questions are anticipatory, behaviour is anticipatory. To ask a question is to invite a reply. Man's act of questioning changes himself:

> Within the realm of relevance his personal construct system defines for him, each man initiates what he says and does. Thus his words and his acts are not mere events consequent upon previous occurrence, but are expressions of what is relevantly affirmed and denied within his system. (Kelly, 1969)

The image that these notions evoke for me are very close to the systemic notion of 'coherence', that is where the system simply does what it does. It is constantly informing and unfolding itself. When we bear in mind that constructs are not cognitive entities but rather prescriptions for actions, often unconscious choices we make, I propose that Kelly's views are not only similar to those of Bateson but also share much in common with the work of Michael Polanyi and the later Wittgenstein.

With regards to clinical practice, the above views require the clinician to seriously reconsider or reconstrue much of what is currently accepted as professional practice. Thus symptoms, the stuff of clinical practice, may be reconstrued as an issue a person (or group of people) expresses through the act of being his present self, not a malignancy that fastens itself upon him. This reminds us of Kelly's view: 'What are expressed as symptoms are urgent questions behaviourally expressed, which have somehow lost the threads that lead either to answers or better questions' (Kelly, 1969). Concerning the *client–therapist relationship*, Keeney comments as follows:

> In the world of therapy we note that clients follow habits of punctuation that enable them to construct a particular world of experience. Knowing how clients construct their worlds becomes a task of epistemology. At the same time therapists follow systems of punctuation that prescribe how they describe. . . . A complete epistemology of therapy must therefore look at how both the client and therapist construct a therapeutic reality. (Keeney, 1982, p. 157)

The therapist joins his clients in the social construction of a therapeutic reality; he is therefore also *responsible* for the universe of experience that is created. When we accept that we are active epistemological agents we are therefore accepting that we are always participating in the construction of what happens. In our approach to therapy, we can no longer take comfort in the notion of the objective observer giving a value-free description of a situation. What we experience is the result of our personal participation and construction of a situation. We can no longer legitimately divorce ourselves from our subject-matter. As Keeney points out, 'The view of a participatory universe suggests that *ethics* rather than objectivity is the foundation of therapy' (Keeney, 1982, p. 166). In a somewhat similar vein, Kelly suggests that

> The significance of any successful clinical prediction we make or any therapeutic cure (intervention) we effect, is not disclosed by the degree of successes in reaching a goal but looms up only in the context of what might have happened. (Kelly, 1955)

Here Kelly is reiterating his view of therapy as a personal enterprise between people, not as technology done by one person to another, within the guise of objective science. Similarly, the whole issue of change becomes more complex when we accept that there are levels of change. One can go about changing the content of a client's constructions while missing the more fundamental level, that is '*his basic style of experimentation*'. A change in content alone is unfortunately only first-order change and may leave the fundamental *style of punctuation* unaffected.

In conclusion, following Kelly's counsel that we should continue to reconstrue PCT as our understanding develops, I have found it both profitable and illuminating to reconstrue PCT in the light of my study of Bateson and systemic theorists. While I accept that we generally see what we want to see, I feel that the exercise has broadened and deepened my appreciation of Kelly's PCT as a useful guiding model for practice.

References

Bateson, G. (1976). Foreword. In C. E. Slwzki and D. C. Ransom (eds.), *Double Bind: The Foundation of the Communicational Approach to the family.* New York: Grune & Stratton.

Bateson, G. (1972). *Steps to an Ecology of Mind.* New York: Ballantine.

Bateson, G. (1972). *Mind and Nature: A Necessary Unity.* New York: Dutton.

Keeney, B. P. (1982). What is an epistemology of family therapy? *Family Process* 21, 156–68.

Kelly, G. (1955). *The Psychology of Personal Constructs,* Vols. I and II. New York: Norton.

Kelly, G. (1969). *Clinical Psychology and Personality: The Selected papers of George Kelly.* Ed. B. Maher. Wiley: New York.

Varela, F. (1979). *The Principles of Biological Autonomy.* New York: Elsevier.

Chapter 6
Kelly and Popper: a constructivist view of knowledge

Francesco Mancini and Antonio Semerari

There is a myth about human knowledge contained within both common sense and scientists' philosophical notions. According to this inductivist myth something we may define as 'direct observation of phenomena' should exist; indeed, it must be the privileged source of any kind of knowledge. Modern epistemology, from Popper on, has largely discredited this myth; pointing out that a theory or an expectation, telling us 'what' we should observe, is always necessary if we are to take notice of something. Observation is possible only in the light of theory.

Nevertheless, the inductivist myth dies hard, even among constructivist psychologists. Perhaps this is because many scientists fear that giving up this myth would threaten the whole scientific framework. In fact, the notion, according to which theories do not depend upon facts, but, vice versa, facts depend upon theories, has often led to scepticism about the real possibility of attaining objective knowledge. Indeed, it easily leads to the belief that there are no 'rational' principles by which a standpoint on reality can be achieved; and only aesthetics and the principles of personal taste have any real existence (Feyerabend, 1975).

George Kelly has the merit of having constructed a psychological theory, which gives up the inductivist myth without leaving us sceptical about the possibilities of achieving human knowledge. Thus he represents for psychology what Popper represents for epistemology; that is, the attempt to reconcile constructivism to the possibility of knowing the 'real' world and of improving such knowledge, on a firm basis.

Kelly and Popper agree with each other on two crucial points:

1 Both of them consider observational evidence as the test, not the base, of our theoretical constructions. Observations always occur in the light of theories and expectancies, which show us what to look for.
2 They both think that knowledge is not simply a consequence of recurrent experience; on the contrary, it depends on the ability of the knowing system to recognize what is new and to build newer structures for better predicting events.

It is well known that Popper's starting point is the boundary-line between scientific and non-scientific knowledge, associated with the criticism of the inductive principle. Empirical science cannot be characterized by the inductive method, since it is logically impossible to obtain universal laws out of the addition of isolated factual observations. On the contrary, knowledge systems, commonly accepted as 'non-scientific', such as astrology, claim to be justified on factual grounds. Nevertheless, whilst it is true that isolated facts can tell us nothing about a general law, it is also true that they can disprove it (the rule saying that all swans are white receives no support from the direct observations of white swans, whereas the sight of a black swan can refute it). Scientific theories differ from all other kinds of knowledge because they must be so organized as to admit those events able to falsify them. So a theory built up to predict every possible event is essentially without (scientific) meaning. Vice versa, the more a theory 'forbids', the more informative it is.

In the theory of personal constructs, man-the-scientist's main purpose is to predict event. According to Kelly, anticipation is the outcome of the attempt to construct invariants, which impose an orderliness upon reality, so that its different elements may be assimilated and differentiated. Constructs are theoretical abstractions which have to cope with facts through prediction, since there would be no contact with reality at all without them.

Empirical experience gains learning value when it does not conform to theories and does not agree with expectations; it then becomes another datum to be fitted in a revised theoretical construction. A person's knowledge is not enriched by the amount of facts falling under his/her perception, but rather by the ability to discover what is new and to proceed to new constructions. There is no experience without this process.

The motion of knowledge

For the positivist scientist knowledge grows cumulatively with the increase of its observational content. Things are not so easy for the constructivist scientist. If theory has to precede observation, how can the empirical content of the latter increase? Does it make any sense to speak of progress and growth of knowledge. We have already apprehended that, in Kelly's opinion, man aims at making true predictions on a real universe, composed by real events. His/her system of constructs comes into touch with reality by validating and invalidating predictions. Obviously, no test can be considered a final test. No prediction can be validated once and for all, because new events might occur to refute it, or might prove themselves ambiguous. This calls for new constructions, for a development of the system and for a continuous evolution of man-the-scientist. The attempt to improve our representation of the future 'tantalizes' man; Kelly writes, 'the individual is not an object which is temporarily in a moving state, but he is a form of motion him/her self' (1955, p. 10). In our opinion, Kelly's (and Popper's) notion of the endless movement of knowledge joins the constructivist perspective to the idea of the progress of knowledge. From the positivist standpoint, progress consists in the increase of observational facts, each of which increases the degree of certitude of a theory. On the other hand, constructivism evaluates theories in accordance with their predictive efficiency. But if a theory could formulate precise predictions, it would have high logical (though not necessarily psychological) chances of invalidation – in Popper's sense – from the very large number of facts the construction 'forbids'. In other words, the more precise the predictions of a theory are, the easier it is to falsify it.

Therefore the relation between the empirical content and the degree of certainty and stability of a theory is turned upside down. The more empirical a theory is, the more it 'predicts immediate happenings, the more susceptible it becomes to changes or revisions' (Kelly, 1955, p. 13). But the very possibility of change and revision appears to the constructivist scientist as the best pledge that his constructions are coming into touch with (a part of) reality. The empirical content increases the vulnerability rather than the stability of a theory. However, when such a vulnerable theory overcomes every test, despite its poor starting chances, it proves to be a good approximation to reality.

A comparison among theories allows us to speak about progress whenever a non-invalidated theory takes the place of either an invalidated theory or of a non-invalidated one which has a smaller empirical content. Therefore, thanks to the comparison with Popper, and bearing in mind that from Kelly's point of view 'knowing reality' means continually trying to expand both the scope and the empirical content of our theory, we may conclude that his constructivism offers a realistic and optimistic position. The empirical content of our theories can be increased by an infinite series of approximations to reality, which are 'piecemeal tested for their predictive efficiency'. 'Essentially', Kelly writes (as Popper would), 'this means that any of our interpretations of the universe can gradually be scientifically evaluated if we persist and keep on learning from our own mistakes' (1955, p. 15).

Summary I

1 The giving up of the inductivist myth implies for constructivism the risk of solipsism and scepticism.
2 We attempt to reconcile constructivism with the possibility of knowing the *real* world and of *improving* such a knowledge.
3 Kelly and Popper agree that knowledge precedes experience.
4 Knowledge does *not* grow up from recurrent experience, *but* it is a process by which expectations are constructed and *invalidated* and new constructions are shaped.
5 A theory is better than another if:
   (a) it has a higher empirical content (wider and more precise predictions, and therefore more vulnerable to falsification)
   (b) it has not been falsified yet.
6 If there are better and worse theories, then we can speak of the progress of knowledge.

The problem of invalidation

The constructivist has to cope with two problems. The first concerns the principles according to which an event can invalidate a theory. The second concerns the extent to which a falsification invalidates a theory.

In other words we ask:

1 At what stage and according to which principles do we decide that our hypothesis is invalidated?
2 What part of our theory is called into question by a failed prediction, and to what extent?

Kelly answers the first question by saying that an invalidation is not caused by observational facts. It is 'subjectively constructed'. Later on, quoting Poch's research, Kelly asks himself the second question: 'when a person discovers that his/her prediction is wrong, what does he/she do about it?' (1955, p. 160) The conclusion is that

> validation can affect the construction system in its various levels. In their turn, these levels can be ordered into gradients, ranging from the less exposed down to the most exposed to risk, the latter being the construct upon which the original prediction was based. Therefore it is the most affected by validational tests.

The consequence of an invalidation depends on the kind of links and connections which join the different parts of a system together and on their strength. A loose structure allows several predictions owing to the weak relations among the constructs in the hierarchical scale (Bannister, 1960). Therefore the extent of an invalidation on the system may range between two extremes: the first includes extremely fragmentary structures, which virtually allow no invalidations; the other includes highly monolithic structures, so that to accept an invalidation would mean to break down the whole system. In other words, the outcome of an invalidation depends on the degree of integration of the system itself.

At this point, we may ask another question: what are the prerequisites for the 'subjective construction of an invalidation', or, in Popper's words, for the methodological decision of accepting a falsification? Both Kelly and Popper stress the comparative aspect of tests. 'In most cases, before falsifying a theory, we have another one in store; in fact, the falsifying experiment is usually a crucial one, which aims at deciding in favour of one or the other' (Popper, 1959, p. 77n). According to the theory of constructs, asking nature alternative questions is both a psychological and a logical necessity.

In our view, each construct represents a pair of rival hypotheses, each of which may be applied to a new element that the person tries to construct:

> each person designs his/her daily explorations of life around rival hypotheses, which are suggested to him/her by the contrasts in his construction-system. (Just as the experimental scientist designs his/her experiments around rival hypotheses.) On the other hand, any individual can try to refute only what his/her construct-system shows him/her as possible alternatives. (Just as the scientist cannot foresee possibilities that he/she has not somehow conceptualized in terms of hypotheses.) The construct-system sets the limits beyond which it is impossible to perceive. (Kelly, 1955, p. 129)

Summary II

The problem of invalidation:

1 *How is an event which invalidates a theory accepted?*
Subjective construction or methodological decision.
2 *To what extent is a theory called in question by a failed prediction?*
It depends on tightness and looseness of the system.
3 *What are the requisites for the subjective construction of an invalidation?*
Comparison between theories. Asking nature alternative questions is both a psychological and a logical necessity.

The problem of determinism

This passage from Kelly is undoubtedly very important since it demonstrates the consistency of Kelly's theory of knowledge; moreover, in this passage Kelly anticipates the problem of the

'Knowers' dependence upon his own conceptual framework, which is being discussed by all modern constructivist epistemologists from Lakatos (1973) to Feyerabend (1975). This trouble is usually identified with the notion that our possibilities of learning and working out hypotheses are limited by our theoretic structure as a whole or, in Kelly's words, by our superordinate point of view. Undoubtedly this notion provides the solution to a problem. If the constructivist scientist had no such principle, for defining a limited set of acceptable hypotheses, he should, logically, test all hypotheses. However, this notion also gives rise to another problem, because it might be suggested that the preliminary state of a knowing system contains all its future development. In such a case it would be hard to speak of growing experience and of new constructions 'whenever something unexpected happens' since the system would have to have foreseen every unexpected event to perceive it. Thus the theory of constructs would face difficult paradoxes. Man would be 'a kind of motion' but in a closed container. Now both Kelly and Popper accept the notion of dependence on conceptual framework but do not believe that it cannot be overstepped:

> I accept that we are always prisoners, caught in the net of our theories and expectancies . . . [but] we are prisoners only in the Pickwickian sense, as we can run away from our framework whenever we try. We would undoubtedly find ourselves in another framework, but it would be a better and roomier one; and we could once again run away from it at any moment. (Popper, 1963, p. 126)

To understand this belief, it is necessary to discuss the constructivist setting of the problem of determinism. In Kelly's opinion 'a theory defines or determines the events which are subordinated to it. It is not determined by the events themselves, but by the superordinating point of view of the theory' (Kelly, 1955, p. 19).

In structural terms this means that the relation between superordinate and subordinate constructs is deterministic, but not vice versa. We must remark that by the word 'deterministic' Kelly means only control and limit, so it does not carry the full prescriptive mechanistic sense. A superordinating construct 'forbids' incompatible subordinate constructions, but it does not prescribe which construction is to be adopted among the compatible ones.

In this sense, the superordinate structure limits the range of possible hypotheses. Therefore, the lack of the superordinating control generates a chaotic and infinite host of hypothetical constructions. This control can be more or less hard in compliance with the Fragmentation and Modulation corollaries.

The question having been so decided, it follows that the solution to the paradoxes of constructivism should be looked for in the answer to the question 'how is the superordinate structure modified?' We suggest a reference once again to Popper's standpoint to clarify this question. Popper dealt with this subject within a discussion about determinism that he ended in compliance with a Darwinian pattern of knowledge development. His reasoning is based upon the construction of living beings as invariant seekers and active problem-solvers, to whom the environment appears as a perpetual source of puzzling situations, to be coped with, by attempting randomly to achieve acceptable solutions. The final result depends on the selection of choices that the environment and the individual himself produce from these efforts. According to Popper, this process describes fully the growth of human knowledge: in solving a problem, we work out a number of theories that we select in conformity with criticism and under the guidance of experimentation. One aspect of Popper's pattern is of great importance: attempts at solution are randomly generated; that is, they are not deterministically (in the mechanistic sense) provided. In other words, it is not true that when the terms of the problem and the characteristics of the organism are known we can exactly foresee what solution will arise, because an undetermined element always occurs, and we might define it as the creative skill of the organism which grows along with the evolving complexity of the organism itself.

Randomly does not mean chaotically. Attempts at solution are generated inside a specific puzzling situation. The notion of chance stands for the occurrence of a novelty and of an opportunity for invention, which were not implicit in the starting conditions. The rational quality of the attempts is not ensured by building procedures but by the rational quality of the selective principles. Also, Kelly divides the creative cycle of new constructions into two stages. The construct-loosening stage essentially aims at allowing new structural combinations and new hypotheses to be built, to the detriment of the predictive accuracy of the system. During the other stage, structural links are tightened. Now, the range of applicability and the permeability of constructs are reduced, and hierarchic relations between the different parts are set up. This step aims at establishing a more exact predictive efficiency of the system, at the expense of creating new combinations.

In this case Popper's and Kelly's reasonings cannot be superimposed. However, they are so closely analogous that we can lawfully turn to Popper to clarify an important passage of Kelly's theory. According to both of them, man's characteristic is his/her active search for invariants. They both believe that the search occurs through the building-up of theories which are tested against reality. They both believe that theories are not determined by the facts they describe. If we agree with Popper when he asserts that a theory is basically due to the attempt at solving a problem, we might ask again the question 'How is a superordinate structure modified?' At first sight the answer is easy: by questioning the superordinate structure itself. But what does this mean? We said that, whatever happens to us, we can change our subordinate constructs only to the extent which is allowed by the superordinate constructs, whereas a change in the subordinate constructs does not necessarily imply a change in the superordinate ones.

The notion of chance, that we explicitly propose to introduce into the theory of personal constructs, shows that neither the moment when this may occur, nor the final outcome of the process, can be determined in advance. As happens in the theory of evolution, we cannot foresee when a mutation will occur in endangered species and if it will or will not be successful. The structure can undergo successive loosening, it can collapse or change towards new, better constructions. What we want to stress is the fact that at a specific moment the system is limited by the nature and ramifications of the superordinate constructs, but as time passes, its limits are to be found in its capacity for raising problems. The emergence of a problematic situation is a very undetermined event, and this becomes truer and truer as we rise in the hierarchical scale of constructs.

However much circumstances may affect the shaping of a problem, they cannot determine it in advance. Moreover, if it is true that determinism moves from upwards to downwards but not vice versa, it follows that the more superordinate a construct is, the more arbitrary is its change. Obviously, this applies to the formulation of the problem as well as the generation of attempts at a solution. As to this, Kelly returns Popper's favour. The theory of constructs includes a structural principle which aims to forsee the degree of arbitrariness in attempts at a solution. This is not present in Popper's approach. On the basis of what is known about superordinate structures, we can really say that the more concerned with the lower parts of a theory a problem is, the more determined and predictable the attempts at a solution are. On the contrary, the more concerned with the superordinate structure of the system a problem is, the greater the degree of freedom is and the more unpredictable the attempts at a solution are. This is the reason why we can conclude by saying that the superordinate system of constructs is the boundary-line of the prison of knowledge. A boundary-line we can pass at any time and in the direction that we ourselves choose.

Summary III

How can we recognize that something unexpected happens, since we must have foreseen the unexpected in order to perceive it?

The solution of this paradox is in the answer to the question 'How does a superordinate construct change?'

Popper's Darwinist pattern of knowledge development:
P1 S.A. E. E. P. . . .

Notice the *creative search* for new problems and capacity to *invent* solutions.
See also *creativity cycle* and the importance of *chance*.

References

Bannister, D. (1960). Conceptual structure in thought-disordered schizophrenics. *J. of Ment. Sc.* 106, 1230–43.

Feyerabend, P. K. (1975). *Against Method: Outline of an Anarchist Theory of Knowledge*. New Left Books. London.

Kelly, G. A. (1955). *The Psychology of Personal Construct*. Norton: New York.

Lakatos, I. (1973). *Philosophical Papers*. Ed. John Worrall and Gregory Currie. Cambridge University Press: Cambridge.
Popper, K. R. (1959). *The Logic of Scientific Discovery*. Hutchinson: London.
Popper, K. R. (1963). *Conjectures and Refutations*. Routledge & Kegan Paul: London.

Chapter 7
Kelly's eye: an alternative view of PCT

Mantz Yorke

The Fundamental Postulate and experience

In his Fundamental Postulate Kelly asserts the central importance of anticipation. The argument of this paper rests upon the view that his emphasis on anticipation, prediction and control led him (perhaps because of his antipathetic reaction to behaviourism – a nice irony) to give insufficient attention to reaction. Mancuso and Adams-Webber (1982) also avow an anticipatory perspective with regard to the Fundamental Postulate, but it should be noted that much of their discussion is, in practice, devoted to people's reactions to circumstances.[1] In contrast, this chapter concentrates explicitly on the reactive side of Kellian theory, and largely ignores (though it does not reject) the more fully explored proactive side.

I find a number of difficulties when I try to construe the Fundamental Postulate, but I can give here only a brief indication of my unease. It seems to me that the linear manner in which it is stated gives an inadequate representation of what emerges from the bulk of Kelly's writing. His elaboration makes clear that it is the ways in which a person *anticipates* events that determine behaviour, appropriate psychological channels being established in the light of anticipation. The linearity of the Postulate seems to conceal a circularity, for how can a person anticipate events without in some way having already established psychological channels towards them?

The circularity is not necessarily vicious, but the imprecision in Kelly's writing does not help the reader to avoid viciousness. Take, for example, 'processes'. In his discussion Kelly does not discriminate between various levels of process and, whilst he might have argued that all processes are interlinked via the construct system, to treat 'processes' in an undifferentiated way is unhelpful.[2]

I shall develop the point by taking, as broad examples of processes, cognition[3] and purposive behaviour. Figure A7.1, which is an adaptation of Kolb's (1971) experiential learning model tinted with Piagetian theory,[4] indicates that their relationship is cyclic rather than linear. Further, each cycle of experience includes progressively more content, whether it be concerned with the extension or definition of a construct system.[5]

Figure A7.1 exhumes the role of prior experience from its burial deep in the implications of the Fundamental Postulate and from its relatively insignificant position elsewhere in Kelly's writing.[6] People construe (interpret) events, whether these are adventitious

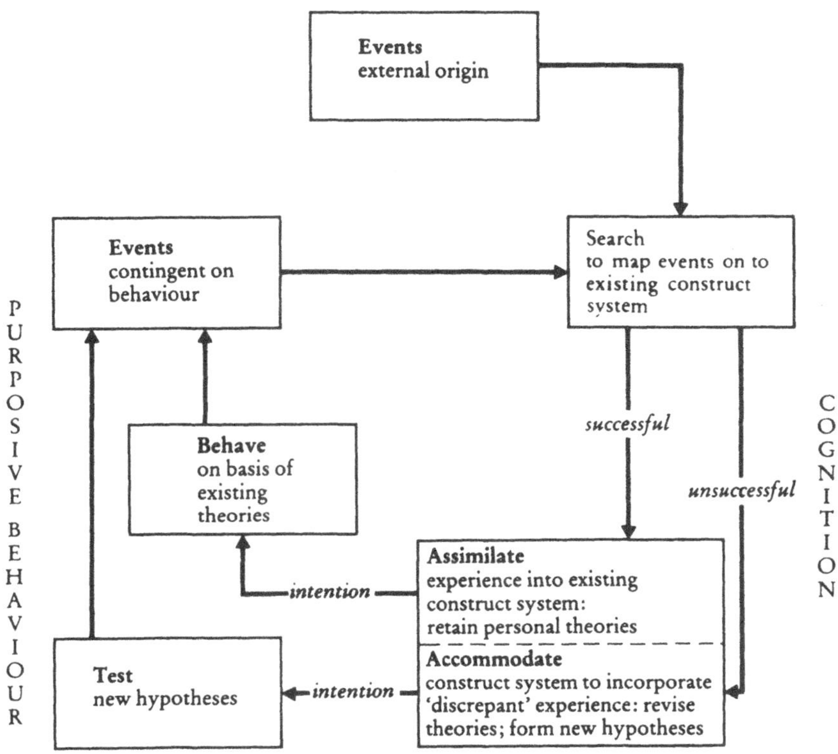

Figure A7.1 A schematic representation of the connection between cognition and purposive behaviour, illustrating the cyclic relationship between the construing of events and anticipation

or the outcomes of purposive behaviour,[7] and adapt their construct systems accordingly: the point here is that they must have undergone experiences in order to interpret them, and must also possess a construct system in order to have the capacity to interpret. Their anticipations – and, where relevant, their purposive behaviour – depend upon the interpretations they put upon their prior experiences. In Kellian language, I am arguing that a person's construction of events channelizes his or her anticipations.

Figure A7.1, though limited in respect of 'processes', is an attempt to define the Fundamental Postulate so as to incorporate the Experience Corollary, thereby giving the understanding and interpretation of experience a more central position in Kellian theory.

The interpretation of events

Consistent with the above argument, I take 'events'[8] (rather than 'anticipates') as the focal word in the Fundamental Postulate. Kelly (1955, p. 49; 1970) himself recognised the importance of events, although the significance of the word is not immediately obvious. To emphasise the construing of events is to move away from the scientific experimental paradigm and towards the understanding and interpretation of happenings whose antecedents are acknowledged as being imperfectly known and often uncontrolled.

Kelly (1955, pp. 940–1) describes how, as a psychotherapist, he explores why clients are as they are, in order that the derived understandings might provide a foundation for their subsequent experiments through behaviour. The process is exemplified where he kneads a self-characterisation sketch in his attempt to understand the client.[9] Further, Kelly admits to an eclectic subsumption of psychotherapeutic procedures within the framework of his theory, observing that the appropriate procedures vary from case to case and that 'a procedure which is used predominantly with one client may never be used in precisely the same way with another' (Kelly, 1955, p. 810); this is tantamount to construing each client as a unique event and is consistent with both the Individuality Corollary and Meehl's (1954) view of the clinician as reconstructive historian.

Kelly's wish to uncover the antecedent and current existential position of an individual requires him to act more in the manner of a historian than a scientist, though he only makes a direct link with the historian when he discusses the client's autobiography (Kelly 1955, p. 989). His approach to clients seems, therefore, to be subsumed rather uncomfortably under a theory which he sees as scientific. The implications of his philosophical account suggest that the pluralism inherent in constructive alternativism might find a more appropriate home under the banner of the interpretive and explanatory human sciences, and it is perhaps time to see what is offered by an alternative metaphor to 'Kelly the scientist': that is, 'Kelly the historian'.

Some implications of 'Kelly the historian'

Following Meehl, the researcher's task under this approach is to build, as accurately as possible, a representation of the relevant parts of the respondent's construct system. Figure A7.2 shows three main sources of evidence: the respondent's

1 behaviour in respect of an original event E
2 verbalised construing of E
3 behaviour whilst talking about E (i.e. a new event F).

As Kelly might well expect, the respondent's construct system may exhibit inconsistencies. As in a historical analysis, the interpreter must test part against part, and part against the progressively emerging total picture, using the rules of 'procedural evidence' (see Rychlak, 1968). This is necessarily a *post hoc* approach which accepts the imperfect knowledge of antecedents, and which is dependent upon the respondent's and interpreter's construct systems (with their abstracted knowledge of cognate events, their blinkers and their biases).

Rigorously conducted, interpretation is not a simple matter. It is a hermeneutic process which, following Ricoeur (1981), is divalent.

1 It accepts at face value what the respondent offers, and probes its deeper significance.
2 It puts 'under suspicion' what is offered.

One might, for example, find a teacher asserting a belief in children being active in the classroom even though this might result in noise which others might find unacceptable. Probed in the first

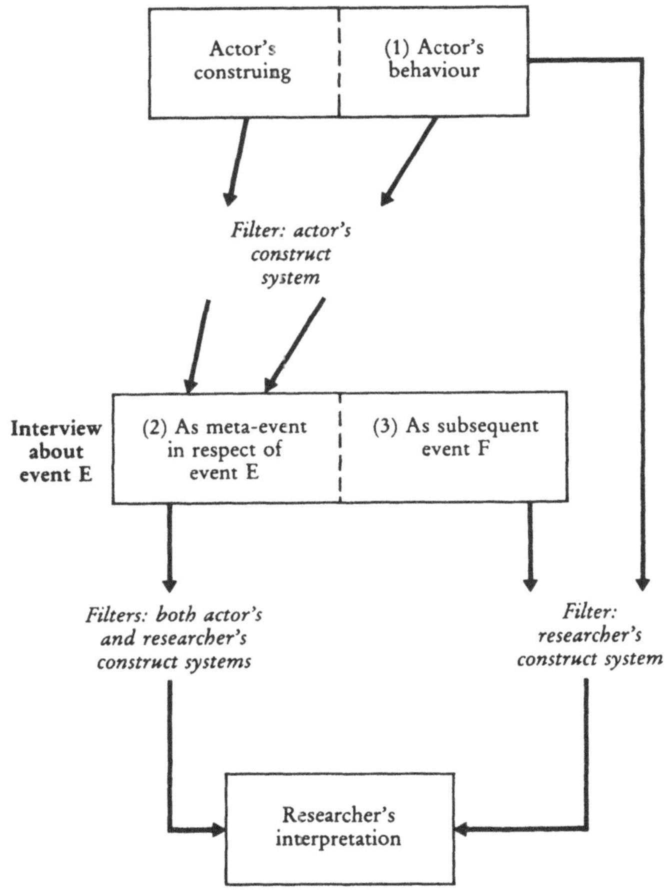

Figure A7.2 Routes via which a researcher might seek access to an actor's construct system

way, this might (rather easily) lead to the identification of an attitude which preferred liberalism to authoritarianism in education. On the other hand, the 'suspicious' approach might unearth feelings of inadequacy regarding class control. Even this simplistic example is sufficient to show that a hermeneutic human science, with its emphasis on meanings in context, goes beyond the relatively descriptive implications of Figure A7.2.

Construing the construct system of the respondent is clearly of central importance to a hermeneutic approach. Kelly (1955, p. 95) is aware of the naïve psychologism of construing things as the other does, and his notion of a social psychology based upon construing the other's outlook requires further exploration of how this might be achieved.

Husserl's (1962) distinction between the noetic and noematic properties of action suggests a useful way forward. The noetic refers to the psychophysiological qualities which characterise a mental act as being of a certain kind (such as a belief or an intention). In contrast, the noematic is concerned with the conceptual qualities of a mental act, and thereby subsumes the rationale for action. Neither the noetic nor the noematic can be re-enacted by an observer: all that the researcher can do is to gain some indication of their nature by construing the other's behaviour in the light of his or her own experience. The relationships involved are represented schematically in Figure A7.3.

In Figure A7.3 the respondent's actions and reportage are shown as providing clues to the noematic, which may allow inferences to be made about the noetic:[10] the noematic can be grasped (not re-enacted) without entailing a psychologistic re-creation of the noetic. Thus I can identify the motives behind the murder

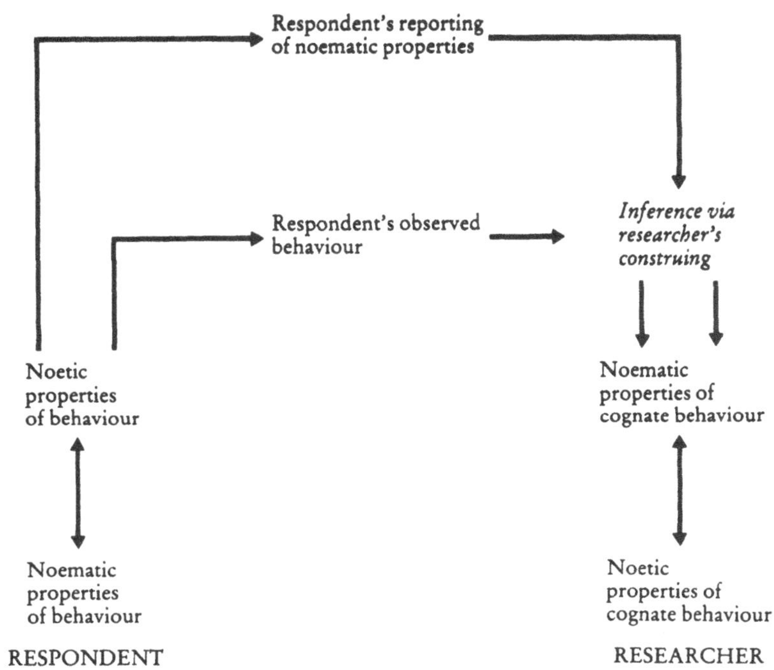

Figure A7.3 Construing the construct system of another via the 'noematic bridge'

committed by a jealous lover without re-creating the murderer's state of mind. But I can only do this because I exist within a culture in which motives for such actions are widely exposed and because I have experienced the emotion of jealousy. There would be no possibility of my interpreting the murder in terms of jealousy if I came from a culture in which jealousy did not exist.

Schutz (1967) offers three indirect ways in which the observer of an act might attempt to interpret an actor's motives:

1 To search the memory for similar actions of his or her own, and in effect project the relevant 'in order to' or 'because' motives on to the other (i.e. putting the other in the self's place).
2 Failing (1), to fall back on knowledge of the other's customary behaviour in order to deduce underlying motives.
3 Failing (1) and (2), to try to infer the motives by asking whether the act in question would further them, and then – while observing – to interpret the act in terms of its outcomes, assuming them to be intended.

Schutz bridges the gap between the phenomena being observed and the noematic, though his categories omit any reference to the normative aspects of the relationship between thought and action (the abstracted replications) in the researcher's construct system. One might also suppose that, where possible, rigorous interpretation would need to make use of all three of Schutz's methods.

However, Schutz does not consider the possibility of enquiring into the respondent's own construing of the observed event. In the next section I shall address this omission, though restrictions on space confine me to a few brief observations.

Some methodological implications

Accounts of the respondent's experience (here given primacy) can be mapped as partially completed networks of relationships between elements and constructs which can incorporate any of the four kinds of meaning-relationship identified by Kreitler and Kreitler (1976):

1 The attribution of qualities.
2 Comparison.
3 Exemplification and illustration.
4 Metaphor and symbolic representation.

The Kreitlers observe that the first two tend to occupy the realm of communal meanings, whereas the last two more closely reflect the personal and idiosyncratic aspects of experience.

It has to be pointed out that repertory and implications grids elicit only constrained accounts of experience[11] and are likely to allow little scope for the last two of the Kreitlers' categories of meaning-relationship to emerge – a paradox for methodologically individualistic techniques. Deficient as it is, grid methodology points to the need to be systematic in one's attempts to elicit evidence, and the succeeding paragraphs sketch – somewhat speculatively, from a base of personal experience, reflection on Kellian philosophy, and Eden, Jones and Sims's (1979) development of Hinkle's (1965) work on implications – an approach which can be applied to the elicitation of belief systems and the construing of specific events. It is implicit in Figure A7.1 that belief systems and the construing of specific events are inextricably connected. The researcher's interest, however, may emphasise one at the expense of the other: the argument of this chapter is that 'events' are of great significance in either case.

It is difficult, when placed on the spot, to articulate personal beliefs about an aspect of one's being (such as one's approach to child-rearing or criminal behaviour), or to produce some form of self-characterisation. Personal experience here suggests strongly that if one focuses upon relevant specific events, it is far easier to produce a set of constructs – and the process is far more rapid than grid administration typically permits. Belief systems can then be inferred – and may reflect personal 'theory in use' rather than 'espoused theory' (Argyris and Schon, 1974).

Alternatively, one might set out with the intention of eliciting constructions of a specific event (for instance, how a teacher construes an encounter with a class), since this might provide insights on which to base therapy, counselling or further professional training. One way into the respondent's construing is to inquire what was considered to be significant, and why, thereby eliciting a list of significant items within the event, together with a set of attached constructs.

A researcher with experience of cognate events is necessary in order to establish the 'noematic bridge' shown in Figure A7.3. Such a person, particularly if present at the event in question, is in a good position to suggest the significance of items hitherto unacknowledged as such, and to invite (but not press) the respondent to construe them.

At this point, only 'proto-networks' will have been produced, and these will require to be elaborated. Elaboration might be achieved by asking the respondent to indicate further connections between the elements and/or constructs, and to provide contrast poles where the constructs have been elicited in unipolar form. The opportunity exists to elicit new elements and constructs, and to encourage clarification through the use of illustration and metaphor. Further, one might 'ladder' constructs in order to gain a greater understanding of the framework within which the respondent is construing: this would be a different procedure from Hinkle's (1965), since the laddering would refer to specific circumstances rather than abstractions. The work of Eden, Jones and Sims (1979), focusing on managers' construing of specific problems, is indicative of what can be done.[12]

Probing the respondent moves beyond the elicitation of a freely produced account, and has considerable potential to assist a hermeneutic appraisal of evidence since it may render more visible both deeper significances and contradictions. There are, however, two intermediate steps: first, to map out the relational network (here some interpretation would inevitably occur) and, second, to present the respondent with the map (or perhaps, a more intelligible summary) in order to test its validity and allow for further exploration. Not that the respondent's view should necessarily be taken as the yardstick of validity, since he or she – like Hinkle's (1965) enuretic bride-to-be – may be uncomfortable with the emergent picture.

It is quite possible that more than one interpretation would be broadly consistent with the evidence. The researcher would then be required to assess, probably in qualitative terms, relative plausibilities and to justify the choice of the 'most valid' (see Hirsch, 1967) interpretation.

Qualitative analysis in the human sciences is less well developed than quantitative methods and lacks the crispness with which statistical tables can summarise findings. If one is interested in understanding how people construe their worlds, one cannot avoid using inference when tackling the problems of meaning and meaning-relationships, and the findings are likely to end up as an untidy and incomplete conglomeration. However, is not this to be preferred to the constrained tidiness of the output from grid analyses, and the massive assumptions necessarily made in the conversion of statistics into meanings?

Coda

Limitations on space have meant that this chapter has been somewhat sparsely argued. That stated, I believe that the argument I have sketched is sustained by a philosophical consistency that is not always apparent in research based upon construct theory (and particularly where studies have relied upon a rather positivistic grid-based approach). The methodological points which I have made are suggestive rather than prescriptive – and the best criterion against which this chapter should be judged is, perhaps, that favoured by Kelly in respect of theory: its fertility.

Notes

1 There is, throughout their discussion, a marked tension between anticipation and reaction. This can be seen, for example, when one tries to unpack their statement that anticipations are 'the schemata that are assembled to assimilate the incoming information' (Mancuso and Adams-Webber, 1982, p. 31).
2 The same criticism may be made regarding Kelly's ambiguous use of 'ways' and 'events'.
3 This paper gives its emphasis to what may be cognitively available to a researcher or clinician. Kelly would, of course, have been unhappy with the separation of the cognitive from the affective and conative.
4 Kolb's model emphasises accommodation at the expense of assimilation, though these would seem not to be mutually exclusive categories. Rosch's (1975, 1977) work on 'prototypes' and Schank and Abelson's (1977) script theory suggest that a pattern-matching operation might determine which of assimilation or accommodation would be predominant.
5 Figure 7.1 is, in the interests of brevity, an oversimplification. It is worth consulting Mancuso and Adams-Webber (1982) for a useful account of the complexities involved when construct systems undergo change.

6 I have in mind here Kelly's discussion of experience in Kelly (1955, pp. 72ff, 170ff).

7 Dewey (1916) makes the distinction between trying (activity) and undergoing (passivity) and draws attention to the 'end-in-view' as a hypothesis or plan-guiding activity. Schutz (1967) begins to differentiate 'processes' when he suggests that action is carried out in accordance with a plan that is more or less implicitly perceived, thereby implying a prior psychological channelling towards the projected event.

8 Like 'processes', 'events' is an undifferentiated construct which is not easily unpacked. The word can subsume, for instance, both the totality of a class lesson and the raising of an eyebrow.

9 See Kelly (1955, pp. 326ff).

10 The noetic and noematic are logically distinct (see Oakes's introduction to Simmel, 1980, p. 64 and p. 90, n. 23).

11 See Yorke (1983) for an extended discussion.

12 See Eden, Jones and Sims (1979); Ch. 7 gives three case studies in which implications are represented diagrammatically.

References

Argyris, C. and Schon, D. (1974). *Theory in Practice: Increasing Professional Effectiveness*. San Francisco: Jossey-Bass.

Dewey, J. (1916). *Democracy and Education*. New York: Macmillan.

Eden, C., Jones, S. and Sims, D. (1979). *Thinking in Organizations*. London: Macmillan.

Hinkle, D. N. (1965). The change of personal constructs from the viewpoint of a theory of construct implications. Unpublished PhD thesis, Ohio State University. Ann Arbor, Michigan; University Microfilms, 66–1790.

Hirsch, E. D. (1967). *Validity in Interpretation*. New Haven: Yale University Press.

Husserl, E. (1962). *Ideas: General Introduction to Pure Phenomenology*. Trans. W. R. Boyce Gibson. New York: Collier. First published in German (1913).

Kelly, G. A. (1955). *The Psychology of Personal Constructs*. New York: Norton.

Kelly, G. A. (1970). A brief introduction to Personal Construct

Theory. In D. Bannister (ed.), *Perspectives in Personal Construct Theory*. London: Academic Press, pp. 1–29.
Kolb, D. A. (1971). On management and the learning process. In D. A. Kolb, I. M. Rubin and J. M. McIntyre (eds.), *Organizational Psychology: A Book of Readings*. 2nd edn. Englewood Cliffs, NJ: Prentice-Hall, pp. 27–42.
Kreitler, H. and Kreitler, S. (1976). *Cognitive Orientation and Behavior*. New York: Springer.
Mancuso, J. C. and Adams-Webber, J. R. (1982). Anticipation as a constructive process: the Fundamental Postulate. In J. C. Mancuso and J. R. Adams-Webber (eds.), *The Construing Person*. New York: Praeger, pp. 8–32.
Meehl, P. E. (1954). *Clinical versus Statistical Prediction*. Minneapolis: University of Minnesota Press.
Ricoeur, P. (1981). *Hermeneutics and the Human Sciences*. Trans. J. B. Thompson. Cambridge: Cambridge University Press.
Rosch, E. (1975). Cognitive representations of semantic categories. *Journal of Experimental Psychology: General* 104, 192–233.
Rosch, E. (1977). Human categorization. In N. Warren (ed.), *Studies in Cross-Cultural Psychology*, Volume 1. London: Academic Press, pp. 1–49.
Rychlak, J. F. (1968). *A philosophy of Science for Personality Theory*. Boston: Houghton Mifflin.
Schank, R. C. and Abelson, R. P. (1977). *Scripts, Plans, Goals and Understanding: an Inquiry into Human Knowledge Structures*. Hillsdale, NJ: Lawrence Erlbaum Associates.
Schutz, A. (1967). *The Phenomenology of the Social World*. Trans. G. Walsh and F. Lehnert. Evanston, Ill.: Northwestern University Press. First published in German (1932).
Simmel, G. (1980). *Essays on Interpretation in Social Science*. Trans. and ed. G. Oakes. Manchester: Manchester University Press.
Yorke, D. M. (1983). The repertory grid: a critical appraisal. Unpublished PhD thesis, University of Nottingham.

Chapter 8

Constructing environments that enable self-organised learning: the *principles* of Intelligent Support

Laurie F. Thomas and E. Sheila Harri-Augstein

Introduction: early days

Since 1965, when the CSHL was formed as a post-graduate research institute at Brunel, one strand of our research has concentrated on the development of a conversational grid methodology for individuals, pairs and small groups to represent their personal experiences in ways which enable reflection, exchange and effective transformation of the quality of their learning. Another strand of research has investigated personal processes of learning; treating reading, listening, discussion, writing and creative thought as learning skills, has led us to a reflective methodology for learning-to-learn and to a theory of Learning Conversations.

At the Oxford, Utrecht and Brock PCP conferences we reported how we had developed the repertory grid as a content-free conversational tool to aid people to navigate the deeply personal processes of learning. They were enabled to construct a personal language to converse with themselves about learning, to enhance their capacity to learn from experience and to take better control of the direction, quality and content of their living (Thomas, 1978; Thomas 1980; Harri-Augstein, 1980; and Thomas and Harri-Augstein, 1983a). More recently a textbook-style compendium of this work has been published (Thomas and Harri-Augstein, 1985a).

FOCUS, SPACED FOCUS and TRIGRID provide psychic mirrors for the analysis and display of patterns of personal meaning for optimal use in conversational feedback. DEMON, PEGASUS and ICARUS offer progressively refined computer-aided conversations with oneself, thus introducing the computer as a powerful aid in our exploration of the mysteries of reflective conversation. PERCEIVE and EVALUATE take individual grids into perception. CHANGE grids uses successive grids to contract into directions of change. INTERACTIVE PAIRS and EXCHANGE & CONVERSE enable two people to compare and negotiate a deep-level understanding. SOCIOGRIDS illuminates the similarity of construing amongst a group or within a 'community of selves'. STRUCTURES OF MEANING, THESAURUS and CHART move beyond the grid into alternate forms for representing thoughts and feelings. Behavioural records, including the CSHL Reading Recorder, Writing Recorder and Listening Recorder, computer interface logs and a modified Bayles discourse-analysis procedure were invented and refined to produce a technology for Kelly's 'behaviour as an experiment'. Such behavioural records provide controlled and systematic aids for the reconstruction of the personal experience of events. The process of the conversation itself has been systematised and formulated into a science of Learning Conversations, to enable learners to self-organise their own behaviour and experience to initiate changes which they themselves value. Self-organised learners have the inner freedom and the skills to converse about and so develop their learning competence.

In the spirit of Kelly, who saw his own theory as a transmutable stepping stone to other positions, the central theme of this chapter explores the challenge of what Kelly's own position might have been thirty years on. We shall imagine our own Kelly clone working with us, interested in the things that interest us, and influenced by the demands made on us. We like to think that Kelly the practical, scientifically trained psychologist with his wartime experience of simulators, would have got over his central preoccupations with therapy and returned to industrial psychology and moved more fully into social and educational psychology. Undoubtedly, he would also have become involved in the wonderland of the microcomputer, information technology, inferential machines and the adventures of the fifth-generation game.

What happens in a grid conversation: mind touch?

Clients often remark upon how revealing and rewarding a grid conversation can be. But for them, after the event, the tangible evidence (i.e. the grid and its analysis) seems only a very partial and unsatisfactory record of what has taken place. Despite all the power of the grid in eliciting a client's thoughts and feelings, and despite all the care and precision of the FOCUSing and talkback procedures, much of what is most useful happens in the conversational process and is not recorded in what remains.

Representations of elements and constructs mediate a conversation which enables the client to achieve new awareness, to reflect and to initiate change.

We have tape-recorded many such conversations and have used these recordings to guide the client's reconstruction of the original experience. What emerges is that much of the inner psychological process provoked by the grid conversation remains unrevealed in the exchanges. Two related but separable conversations appear to go on in parallel. One is what is recorded as passing between the grid practitioner and the client, or the PEGASUS program and the client, and the other is clients' inner conversation with themselves. This inner process often illuminates the hidden power of the reflective-grid technology. It is the resource from which the client feeds the external conversation. Even when 'fully' reconstructed, one's understanding of this inner conversation remains incomplete, its language is largely non-verbal, and the second deeper contributor to it usually takes no part in the conscious reconstruction; but it is at this deeper level that some of the more significant effects occur: changes revealed later as new perceptions, insights, expectations and ways of behaving.

It is this secondary 'conversational effect' which explains how an inadequate two-way static representation of a psychological state (i.e. the repertory grid) has over thirty years grown to be the main tool of a professional aggregate that views man as an active, meaning constructing, event-anticipating animal – a view in which a person, as personal scientist, is building, using, testing and revising personal 'theories' that create and validate a personal reality.

If the grid mediates a certain type of inner conversation, if this conversation transmutes meanings and if the converser is constructing meaning the better to anticipate and thus manage the future, then we can begin to appreciate the power of the grid conversation in facilitating personal change. The grid with all its elicitation procedures, methods of analysis, forms of visual display and processes of talkback is a uniquely effective tool for enabling conversational change. Elements, constructs and the positioning of elements on constructs are not descriptions of psychological process: they are artifacts of Kelly's model of psychological process and hence of the form of the grid. The ultimate psychological entity is the *conversational encounter* (the C-indi). The grid and the construct system are merely a convenient and very powerful model for enabling practitioners to provoke and support creative inner conversations.

Meaning modelling and MA(R)^{4}S

At a PCP seminar convened by Peter Stringer two or three years ago, Don Bannister and Laurie Thomas were discussing 'anticipation'. Don (the novelist) saw it as a story-telling process (see Part H, 'The Arts'), where the internal logic of the story, up to and into the present, reveals probable futures. Laurie, with his science and engineering background, saw it differently. If we perceive the outside world by modelling it within us and checking the evidence to guide and validate this construction, then 'working models' of reality can be run more quickly than in real time, thus producing meanings ahead of the evidence for them. Modelling (or story-telling) seems to be a way of representing the creative process of meaning construction stimulated by replications of experience. Meaning is changed in such conversational encounters, but meaning is never fully knowable since part of the inner conversation always remains unrevealed. All we can do is represent our meanings (in appropriate forms) and by conversing with these representations the inner meaning is transmuted.

We have found it useful to represent this process as shown in Figure A8.1 (Thomas and Harri-Augstein, 1985b). MA(R)^{4}S stands for seven stages in the conversational cycle.

1 *M – monitor.* Observe yourself in action (process) and keep (remember or record) a sequential record (file, protocol) of what is happening.
2 *A – analyse.* Run the record (memory) of (1) through the model

(pattern of meanings) which drove the event (monitored in 1) to identify and pull out those features essential to an adequate reconstruction (thought, feeling and perception).

3 *R – record.* Make an external record (e.g. entry in the grid) which summarises sufficiently to later enable an adequate reconstruction of one's intentions.

4 *R – reconstruct.* Run the record through the model to re-recruit and revise the original experience, including (in particular) that which was *not* captured in the monitoring and that which slipped out of the analysis and record stages (i.e. the inner game). (Since MA(R)⁴S is essentially a hierarchically organised process, the most telling level of reconstruction may best be tapped minutes, hours or even days later.)

5 *R – reflect.* Having reconstructed the experience as veridically as possible, now *evaluate* it in terms of the original intention-

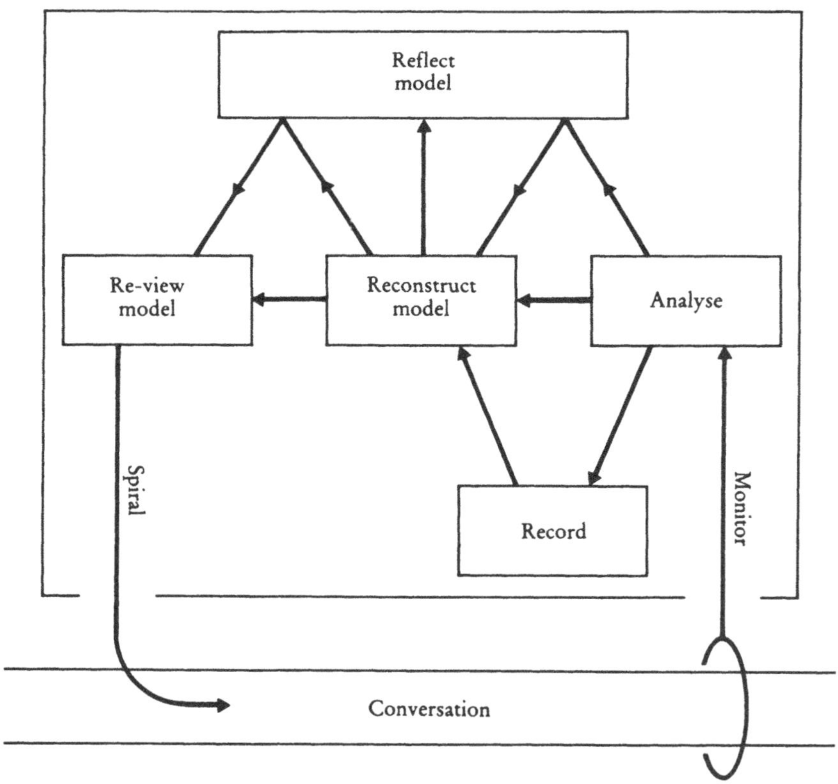

Figure A8.1 MA(R)^{4}S

ality of the event(s). Detect inadequacies, flaws, mismatch, poor timing, wrong emphasis, badly distributed effort, and so on.

6 *R – re-view.* Take the model apart, amend and reconstruct it so that it will more veridically embody the structure of the domain being modelled and thus, when run faster than real time, will better anticipate events.

7 *S – spiral.* Try another event and go through the cycle again (e.g. fixed role therapy, play another match, sit another exam, talk again in public).

Gödel and a conversationally evolving system

Whilst investigating what goes on in the grid conversation, our attention returned to Kelly's notion of 'reflexivity'. This remains for us one of the most revealing ideas about the nature of human beings. In 'Walden 2' the Skinner surrogate is left on top of a hill, outside, looking down, and in, upon the ideal society he has psychologically engineered. On the other hand, in *The Magic Mountain*, Hans Castorp is advised by Thomas Mann (1961) that a true creator stands between nature and spirit, subject and object, as 'lord of the counter positions'. The process of construction is all. Kelly's model of 'man the scientist' contains similar elements of awareness. It enables psychologists to rejoin the human race saying, 'I understand you, by understanding me understanding you, and vice versa'. In computer terminology the boot-strapping power of this idea is mind-boggling. If we substitute 'I construct and validate meanings about' for 'I understand', and if we continue with the idea that meaning is constructed conversationally, where does this idea take us? If we acknowledge that part of the inner conversation inevitably remains unrevealed, then we can never fully know our own knowing. Reflexivity has to be seen as open-ended. A theory that can explain its own existence should be capable of driving its own evolution. *PCP should not replicate itself; rather it must bootstrap itself into conversational science.*

Gödel (1962) has shown that we can never fully explain a system from within the system itself. We must always recruit in at least one more idea to complete the explanation. Thus we must either join Skinner on the outside looking in or we can join Kelly from within, *but* forever having to conversationally break open one's current system to achieve fuller understanding (Hofstadter, 1980).

For us as researchers, the interactive bootstrapping relationship between theory and method is central to what we do. Sometimes the idea system is ahead of the methods, and one looks around for (or is forced to invent) methods that allow one to operationalise one's ideas. Then suddenly one finds oneself with methods that produce all kinds of surprising results that do not seem related to the ideas that gave rise to them. Often this is because one develops all kinds of insights and skills in using the techniques. It is here that by turning the MA(R)^{4}S idea back on ourselves (see p. 118) we have been able to more truly represent the nature of our own action research models to ourselves.

Our action research projects require that we help a person, a couple, a group or an organisation become both more self-organised and more skilled, competent, creative or effective. It is in the nature of most learning requirements that the learner/client cannot know what it is that he or she wants to know until he or she knows it. This is the function of MA(R)^{4}S. It enables a directed search, for a successively more well-defined outcome, to be made from an ill-defined or even totally confused or apathetic starting point. We have found MA(R)^{4}S and a theory of 'support conversation' useful tools for conceiving how these 'don't know where we are going until we are there' but 'we will recognise it when we see it' issues can be tackled constructively.

If self-organised learning is (by definition) inner driven and not controlled by others, it follows that the responsibility for learning (both the processes and the products) remains with the learner. So what does the TC (teacher, trainer, tutor, therapist, counsellor, custodian, consultant and coach) practitioner contribute? He or she contributes constructive support. Thus our activities have revealed the need for a theory of Constructive Support Conversations. We not only need a theory of conversation, but we also need a theory of support systems. Let us take these one at a time.

Reflective conversation

Conversation involves a degree of creative encounter, either with another being, with an 'intelligent' machine or with oneself. The essence of conversation is that there is more than one autonomous node of control within it, and these nodes synchronise so that the passing of control back and forth between them achieves an encounter that neither can create separately. What is contributed by each is not predictable by the other. Indeed, what will be contributed is not predictable by the contributors themselves, since it is dependent upon what will be contributed by the other. Thus, without a totally preconceived notion of the form which the conversation will take, nor of the content, the conversants, within a conversational paradigm, enter upon a collaborative enterprise for which they can only have significant expectations.

Whilst practioner and client are both clearly separate nodes of control within a conversation, the nature of the control operated is different. Hence one can identify asymmetrical conversations. In the early stages of an encounter, the practitioner may control the process whilst the client controls the content. But an essential characteristic of the conversation is that is must allow for growth and for a negotiated agreement about who controls what and when. When the capacity for process and content control becomes shared, the conversation takes on a symmetrical form. The very essence of becoming a self-organised learner is the development of an ability to conduct symmetric conversations with oneself and to manage asymmetric and symmetric conversations with others.

We have identified five distinct levels of exchange. These operate in the two modes of conversation, both *content* and *process*. Figure A8.2 illustrates this. There are levels of content to be contributed and also levels of process by which the conversation may be guided.

The *constructional* and *creative* levels of content and process have a bootstrapping, positive-feedback effect on the conversation. It takes off. This ability to grow both the process and content, separately or together, is one crucial mechanism in producing an encounter. To be truly creative according to Maslow's criteria (Maslow, 1962), the conversation must transcend the evaluative system out of which it arose. Kelly's 'personal scientist' falls into the constructive conversation level. *The conversational scientist can engage in creative levels of encounter which can only be valued from a perspective which evolves out of the event itself.* It is both transcendent and self-referent.

The constructive and creative levels of conversation offer the minimum conditions of personal learning. It allows for the construction, reconstruction, negotiation and exchange of personally relevant and viable meaning, which typifies self-organised

PROCESS	CONTENT
Creative	Creative
Constructive	Constructive
Explanatory	Explanatory
Instructional	Informational
Ritualistic	Factual

Symmetrical ⟷ Asymmetric

Figure A8.2 Conversational theory

learning. In the absence of construction and creativity, lower levels of exchange in our conversational hierarchy will build up layers of impersonal representations, which alienate the person from themselves and exclude creative encounters with others.

The constructive level of content implies development within an existing evaluative framework; the creative level of content implies a symbolic change in content and values. The constructive level of process can have an experiential effect on the quantity of personal learning and leads in to learning-to-learn. The creative level of process can have an experiential effect on the quality of personal learning since each time it operates it is generating a change in the conversational paradigm. Within this paradigm, meaning is essentially a conversation between the constructor (that which attributes meaning) and the referent (that to which meaning is attributed). It is not a property of either but a relationship between them. It cannot be fully knowable and can therefore only be represented as a model of the conversation. The five different levels and two modes of conversation result in the representation of different levels of meaning, and these in turn affect the anticipatory mechanism which guides the nature of the conversation that can take place. The $MA(R)^4S$ configuration is an attempt to depict this.

Rote-Factual meaning leads to exactly identical cycles of anticipation. Instructional-Informational meaning leads to more variable anticipations, but these are nevertheless repetitive as a logical or categorical consequence of known positions in a static structure. Explanatory meaning leads to anticipations which are the consequence of causal chains, system characteristics or multi-causal networks. Constructive meaning introduces new components and structures from outside the system, and anticipations will involve new parameters and patterns of consequence. The conversational scientist and the self-organised learner have the capacity to converse and generate meanings at all levels and can so construct and create freedom to direct their own personal destinies.

The nature of self-organised learning

In looking at the process by which someone learns a task it is possible to identify three stages in moving from the unconscious doing of the task (i.e. the 'skilled' task-robot) to fully self-organised learning. (Thomas and Harri-Augstein, 1983b). Figure A8.3 illustrates these three stages.

1 In the first stage of learning the person does the task by dogged practice and repetition. With an implicit tactic of 'trial and error' they acquire some level of competence. Many years of such practice leads to the skilled technician, but he is totally content or task-bound.

2 In the second stage of learning the person stands back, observes and reflects upon the implications of their practice, thus raising the blind trial-and-error method into a more rational and coherent approach to the process of doing the task. But, at this stage in the development of learning, the task is still the total focus of attention. Awareness is concentrated on observing the process of doing the task and using the results of these obser-

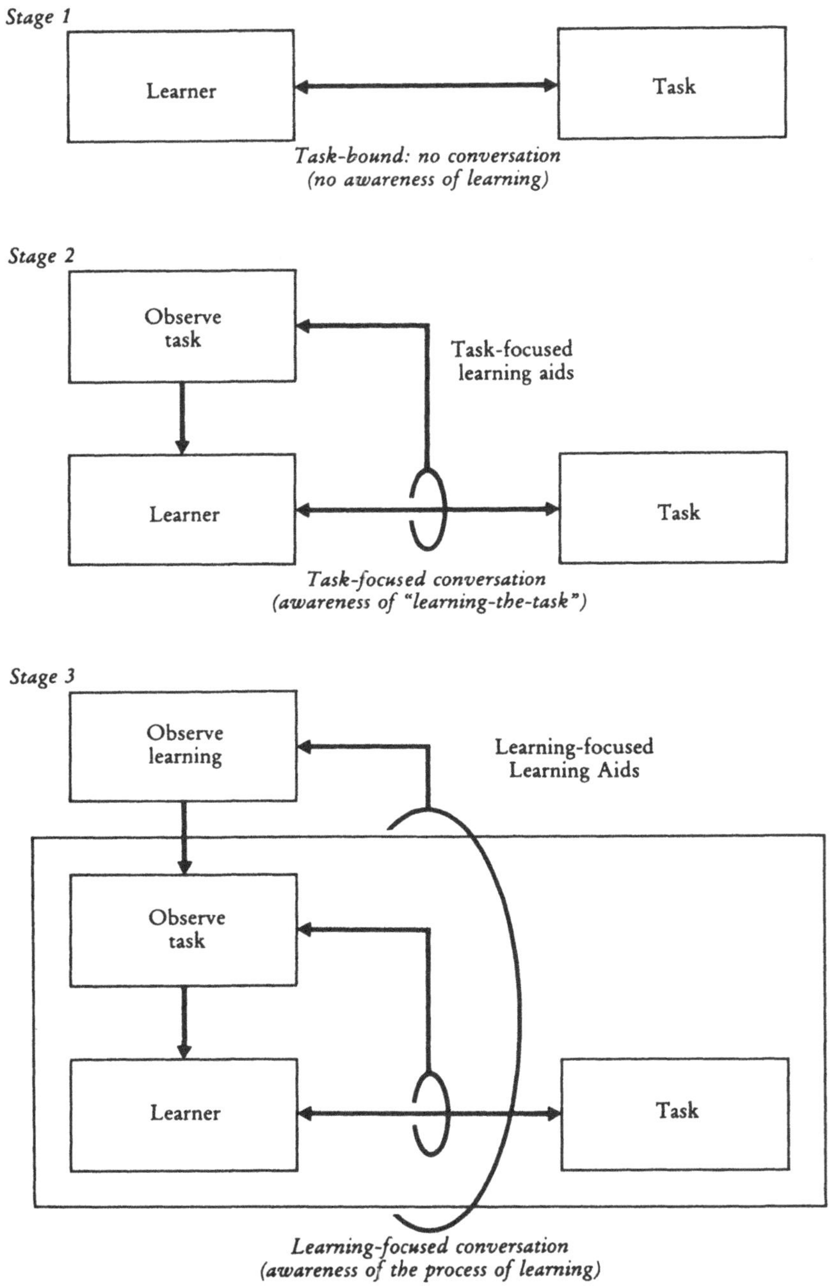

Figure A8.3 Three stages towards self-organised learning

vations to systematically experiment and improve one's performance.

3 At the third stage of learning, the focus of attention shifts. At certain intervals of acting out in stages 1 and 2, the person stands back one further step to take stock not only of how one is doing the task but also to reflect upon the process of learning itself. It is this second phase of awareness which is the crucial trigger to total self-organisation in learning.

Truly self-organised learners are conscious of experience and behaviour at the stage-3 level of awareness and thus understand their own learning processes. They are self-directing and able to function purposefully towards self-defined goals, and they are self-critical and construct their own evaluative criteria and assess achievements and progress in their own terms. They can interpret the behaviours and understandings of others, including experts within their own evaluative scheme, and make productive use of the comparisons with themselves. Above all, self-organised learners can sustain Learning Conversations with themselves and so continue to develop their competence.

Meta-theory of Intelligent Learning Support

'Intelligent' Learning Support

If we look upon the construction of meaning as a conversational process, then meaning becomes stuck if the conversation is frozen. We have already argued that in the absence of constructive and creative levels of conversation, meaning is impersonal and actions can become ritualistic and habituated. We cease to become aware of our thoughts, feelings and actions at an operational level, and these drop into non-consciousness and consequently are no longer under our control.

Most of us are almost totally unaware of how we attribute meaning to the events in our world. As learners we are unaware of how we learn to understand the displays of public knowledge offered in the educational setting (stage 1 of learning, see p. 101). Reading, listening, discussion, writing, thinking, feeling, judging, deciding and doing are long-established habits which have become so fixed that as learners we are prisoners of our own incompetence. We have found it useful to talk of such learners as having a set of personal learning robots. As a set of over-learned but not necessarily effective skills, learning itself has become robotish. Self-organised learning consists in an ability to observe oneself and reflect on processes of learning, and to search, analyse, formulate, review, judge and act on the basis of such encounters.

Becoming a self-organised learner depends upon overcoming an almost universal tendency towards the ultra-stabilisation of our thoughts, feelings and actions. It is partly a question of negotiating a personal balance between structure and freedom, between certainty and provisionality. In our experience, people need support to break free from existing habits and to distance themselves from their own processes in order to converse about alternative ways of modelling or representing meanings. The power of a reflective technology is such that learners can be supported to free themselves to explore alternative competencies. Let us identify the essential characteristics of a support system that enables learners to elevate themselves to become constructive and creative conversationalists.

Learning is itself a construction invented by mankind. Evidence about learning can only be evaluated and inferred from within a particular perspective. A self-organised learning perspective presumes that changes in both experience and behaviour are necessary and valid indications. The learner alone has direct access to the personal experience, but only an observer (human or machine) of learning can record the learner's behaviour with accuracy and precision. Hence the fundamental prerequisite of self-organised learning is that the emerging behaviourial and experiential evidence be conversationally exchanged. Once this is recognised, the functions of a reflective technology for supporting learning can be articulated.

Now we have the ingredients for explaining where we are 'thirty years on'.

1 Man is a meaning-constructing, meaning-driven animal.
2 Meaning is constructed conversationally.
3 Whilst conversation is the door through which Gödel (i.e. open-mindedness) may enter, it is possible for the MA(R)^{4}S process to cease to function, shutting this door, freezing the conversation and ultra-stabilising the meaning.
4 Ultra-stabilised meanings lead to robotishness.

5 A theory of support must offer insights into how the robot may be challenged, how the quality of the conversation may be improved and how the client may move towards self-organisation both in doing and learning.
6 A theory of support indicates how a system of related conversations can be structured into a Self-organised Learning Environment (both the learning and the environment are self-organising).
7 This SoL Environment is designed to become obsolescent. Support is gradually withdrawn as the learner becomes able to take over its function and to continue learning autonomously.

In essence, support consists in enabling a reflective conversational engagement with a given domain. This raises awareness of personal experience and behaviour as a coherent process. If the interface, person–domain interaction, is monitored, learners can be supported to converse with themselves and others about the processes of learning. $MA(R)^4S$, described earlier, indicates the modelling facility which helps to achieve this. Various forms of psychotherapy can be seen as different models of support. For example, Carl Rogers' view of the conversation is that it should operate as a reflector of the inner conversation. He therefore makes only reflective comments which challenge the inner conversational robot and break it open, back into awareness. Congruence, empathy and unconditional positive regard are the parameters of his model of therapeutic reflectors. The reflective repertory-grid technology, the beyond-the-grid techniques and the various forms of behavioural records referred to earlier provide resources for our $MA(R)^4S$ Learning Conversation support facilities.

Our model for an 'Intelligent' Learning Support System (ILS) has gradually emerged from attempts to reproduce, in a machine, some of the attributes found in the expert human Learning Conversationalist. This man/machine research effort has a utility beyond that of machine implementation of a natural support system. By analogy the results feed back to more precisely articulate how the human support system can manage learning in more natural habitats.

Let us imagine that the learner engages with the domain via an interface (the teaching–learning interface offered in the educational setting, or more artificially through interaction with a machine). This interface serves for the communication of guidance and support, either by a human Learning Manager/Conversationalist or a machine Support Generator. The system is able to make itself intelligible to the learner by virtue of its knowledge of the learners' behaviour and experience. This knowledge is acquired by direct monitoring of the behaviour domain, and conversational interogation of the learner through the interface. This results in the construction of behavioural and experiential 'models' of the learner. The system also includes 'referent models' with which the learner model can be compared. A referent model may represent an expert onself earlier or peer learners, but in any case are only offered to the learner as referents for the construction of their own understanding, and do not have an absolute or authoritative status (Fig. A3.4).

Within this system a (machine) Support Generator or a (human) Learning Manager guides the learner's interaction with the domain, recruiting appropriate modelling resources to support the learner. As part of the MA(R)⁴S it engages the learner in the three dialogues of the Learning Conversation, which reflectively raise awareness of process of learning, of the need for support through periods of disintegration of robotish skills, before systematic process reflection replaces these with new, more flexible skills, and

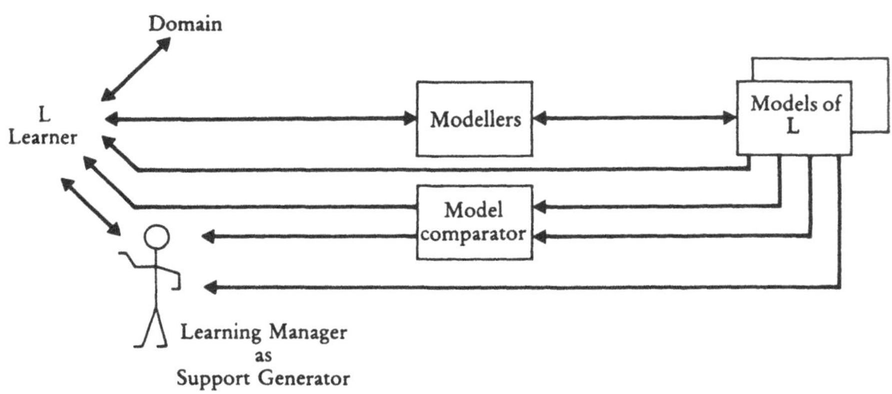

Figure A8.4 A simple version of an ILS (Intelligent Learning Support system)

of the need to build a personal system of referents for evaluating competence. It also guides the learner into the Tutorial Learning Contract, Learning-to-Learn or Life levels of the Learning Conversation as the dynamics of their conversational encounter require (Thomas and Harri-Augstein, 1979). Thus Learning Conversations are themselves monitored and supported within a wider context of self-organised learning.

The system of support reflects the conversational approach and is itself reflexive; that is, it contains within it the requirement that the Support Generator/Learning Manager gradually relinquishes control as learners become able to sustain symmetric conversations with themselves. The implementation of this shifting control between the manager of learning and the learner within the support system is one of the most challenging aspects of our current research efforts. Control depends on a capacity to monitor and regulate asymmetric content and process conversations described earlier and enabling these to evolve into symmetric forms which the learner is capable of internalising for themselves.

Self-organised Learning Environment: seven systems as a whole

Figure A8.5 offers a summary of our current view of how constructive support can be offered by a system of related Learning Conversation resources. The practical implications of this are elaborated in our paper in Part B, 'Education'.

References

Gödel, K. (1962). *On Formally Undecidable Propositions.* Basic Books: New York.

Harri-Augstein, E. S. (1980). *The Change Grid: A Conversational Method for Self-Development.* CSHL Monograph, Brunel University: London.

Hofstadter, D. R. (1980). *Gödel, Escher, Bach: An Eternal Golden Braid.* Penguin: London.

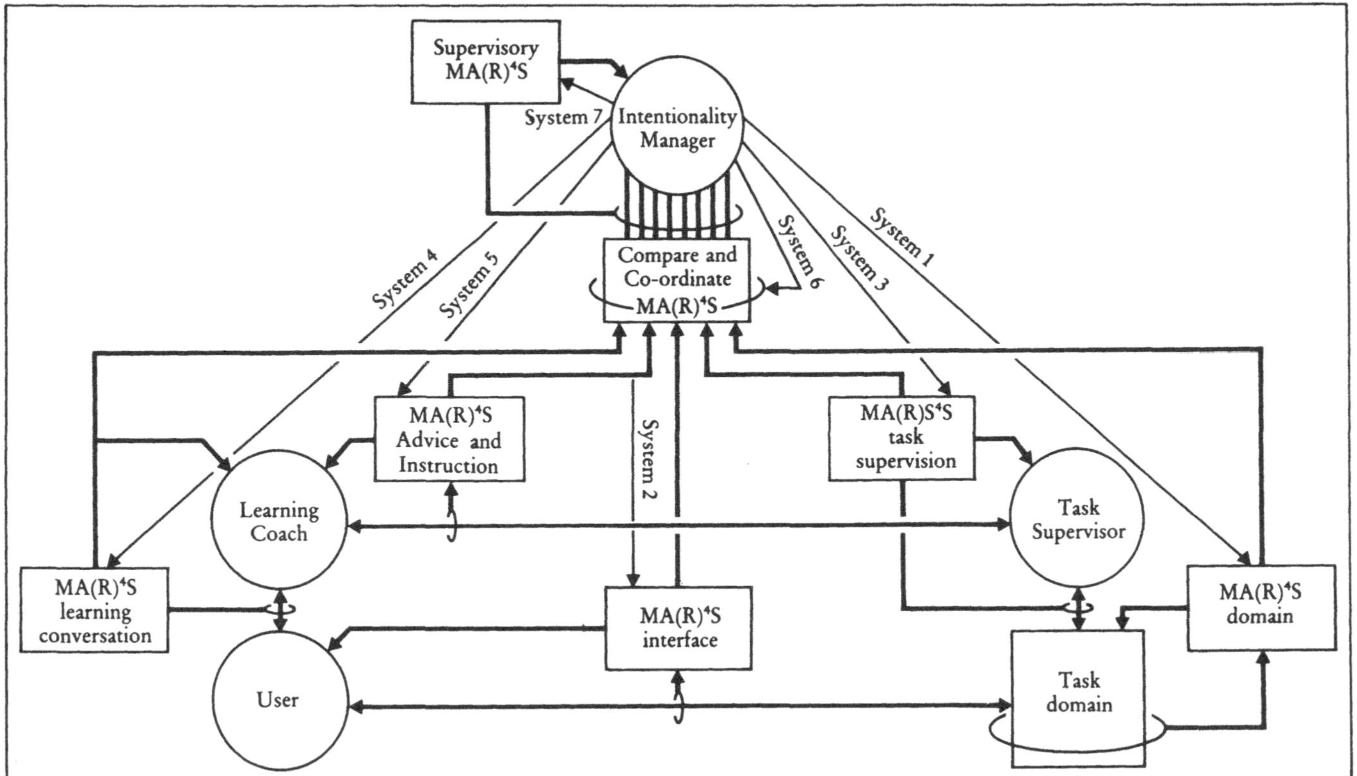

Figure A8.5 SoL (Self-organised Learning) environment: Seven Systems

Maslow, A. H. (1962). Notes on being: psychology. *Journal of Humanistic Psychology* 1, 47–71.

Mann, T. (1961). *The Magic Mountain*. Secker & Warburg: London.

Thomas, L. F. (1978). A personal construct approach to learning. In F. Fransella (ed.), *Personal Construct Psychology 1977*. Academic Press: London.

Thomas, L. F. (1980). *What Is More Practical than a Good Theory?* CSHL Monograph, Brunel University: London.

Thomas, L. F. and Harri-Augstein, E. S. (1979). Self-organised learning and the relativity of knowing: towards a conversational methodology. In D. Bannister and P. Stringer (eds.), *Constructs of Sociality and Individuality*. Academic Press: London.

Thomas, L. F. and Harri-Augstein, E. S. (1983a). The self-organised learner as personal scientist. In J. R. Adams-Webber and J. C. Mancuso (eds.), *Applications of Personal Construct Theory*. Academic Press: Toronto.

Thomas, L. F. and Harri-Augstein, E. S. (1983b). *Self-organised Learning and Computer Aided Learning System*. Final report of a three-year study sponsored by the Ministry of Defence. CSHL Monograph, Brunel University: London.

Thomas, L. F. and Harri-Augstein, E. S. (1985a): *Self-organised Learning: Foundations of a Conversational Science for Psychology*. Routledge & Kegan Paul: London.

Thomas, L. F. and Harri-Augstein, E. S. (1985b). *Implications of Self-organised Learning for an Intelligent Learning Support System*. Final report of a three-year study sponsored by the Ministry of Defence. CSHL Monograph, Brunel University: London.

B

Education

Chapter 1

Software for use in Self-organised Learning Environments: the *practice* of Intelligent Support

E. Sheila Harri-Augstein and Laurie F. Thomas

In our paper in Part A, 'Theory', we explained that self-organised learners have a capacity to consciously monitor their own learning processes and to use others as a resource for developing their competence. Furthermore, they can sustain Learning Conversations through life and so continue to develop the directions, quality and range of their experiences. Towards the end of our paper we outlined a Systems Seven SoL Environment for constructing 'Intelligent' Learning Support. Let us examine this in more detail and consider its implications for education and training.

The Systems Seven SoL Environment consists in five nodes of meaning construction and seven Learning Conversations. The related MA(R)^{4}S monitor and support the pattern of conversations. It can represent a 'community of selves' (Mair, 1977) where all the functions (see pp. 107–8) go on in one head. It can represent a whole organisation where the 'Learner' is many people and there are departments concerned with separating and running the various functions. The System can be controlled either by the human or machine 'tutor' or all functions are taken on by the 'learner' as insights and skills are acquired.

Thus it is necessary to clearly separate the functions in the SoL Environment from their location in particular human heads or software systems. Broadly speaking:

1 The *user* is the naïve client or Learner.

2 The *Learning Coach* is responsible for generating a Learning Conversation with the user.

3 The *Task Supervisor* organises the domain and is the expert on it.
4 The *Intentionality Manager* gives the system direction and purpose coordinating activities and the flow of conversation to negotiate, define and achieve its intentionality.
5 The *Domain* is what the user works on in doing his tasks.

Each MA(R)^{4}S monitors, controls and enriches one significant component in the pattern of Learning Conversations.

The learner is working at a domain. If the learner were an air-traffic-control trainee, the domain would be the air-traffic work-place in the control tower with its radar screens, information boards, intercoms, telephones, instruments, and so on. If the learner were an outpatient in psychotherapy the domain might be the home/family situation. The user could be a child in primary school, a manager on a man-management course or an Olympic pentathlon hopeful. The Systems Seven configuration is powerful in the insights it offers, and general in its areas of application.

As with the grid in Kelly's original system, the Systems Seven/SoL Environment offers a *content-independent procedure* through which to elicit and converse about what is going on. It offers a means of representing the conversational-support system.

Let us take an example. A student, in what was a teacher training college, is studying biology and education. The domain is the biology course. Only the student knows what she does and how she spends her time so the MA(R)^{4}S (interface) is in the student. The Task Supervisor is an uncoordinated mix of people including the course organiser, the biology-course organiser, the resource-centre tutor, and so on. The Learning Coach, in the guise of her tutor, conducts only a task-focused Learning Conversation. The tutor has little or no conversation with the Task Supervisor(s); in fact, the tutor sees himself as competent to offer advice and instruction but has no direct contact with the Domain. There would appear to be no Intentionality Manager. Without going further we can see that Systems Seven can be used to elicit and illuminate the condition of the user; it can be used as a reflective device to challenge the robots in the situation. In practice we have found that the representation feels right to the various people involved. It offers a content-independent facility with which to provoke some parts of the system into a Learning Conversation.

Let us take a more enlightened example. Our student is learning via reading. Take her education course. The Task Supervisor knows the literature and suggests certain books and articles. The student (as user) attempts to read the books and can make no headway. The Learning Coach begins to conduct a task-focused Learning Conversation in which the student's needs are explored and negotiated into purposes, strategies for achieving these purpose with the resources on offer are planned, the outcomes to be expected are identified, and criteria by which she can judge how well she has achieved her purpose are clarified.

She tries again but cannot carry out this Learning Contract

The Learning Conversation identifies a Learning-to-Learn problem. The Learning Coach switches into the learning-focused conversation. The Task Supervisor temporarily restricts the domain to one printed article and the MA(R)^{4}S (interface) is amplified with a Brunel Reading Recorder, which monitors and produces a record of exactly how the text is read. This can be done using mechanical hardware or Reading-to-Learn Software. The behavioural record is used to talk the student back through her specific process of reading to enable her to reconstruct the experience of attributing meaning to that text. She begins to get some insights into the ineffectiveness of her reading strategy and the inadequacy of her learning purpose.

She has not been instructed how she should read the text nor has she been offered a generalised freedom to learn. The MA(R)^{4}S (interface) has been temporarily amplified to challenge her reading robot and get her conversations with the books going again. The quality of the reading conversation is monitored by the MA(R)^{4}S (interface). The nature of the conversation is negotiated in the Learning Conversation. We could expand on the function of the Learning Coach at some length and have done so elsewhere (Harri-Augstein, Smith and Thomas, 1983); suffice to say in this context that the student's Reading-to-Learn skills increased rapidly but only after the MA(R)^{4}S (advice and instruction) process was severely challenged. The person apparently in the role of Task Supervisor did not at first understand the learning-focused activity; but with the MA(R)^{4}S (advice and instruction) amplified for monitoring and enhancing the quality of the Learning Coach–Task Supervisor conversation, he eventually produced a series of articles on reading which were suited to the Learning-to-Learn task in both process and content terms. It was in fact this choice of materials that raised the whole quality of the experience. As the person serving as Intentionality Manager began to appreciate what was going on in the Learning Conversations, at the reading interface, in the advice and instruction conversation and in the Task Supervisor's 'conversation' with the domain, she was able to modify and coordinate these conversations to much enhance the quality of the results and to change the intentionality, that is the emphasis and direction of what was going on.

In the air-traffic-control example we had spent two years advising on the design and implementation of a skills trainer for air-traffic controllers (Thomas and Harri-Augstein, 1983). This consisted of a computer-driven simulator of the radar screen and associated controls, coupled to a whole battery of computer-based task-learning aids. This trainer was the product of a feasibility project and was merely meant to serve as a vehicle to try out a variety of sophisticated techniques in the domain–Task Supervisor and domain–learner interface areas of Systems Seven. However, we had carried out a detailed task analysis in the real domain so that we could represent something worth simulating in the experimental skills trainer. When it was complete it was demonstrated to the 'natural habitat' course organisers who were very impressed (probably by the Hi-tech image) and immediately ordered a high-quality replicate of the experimental version for their own use. This was duly installed. Eighteen months later we were visiting the training site and were shown with some pride how they were getting on with the skills trainer. It was being used as a practice device by the trainees in their 'off duty' hours. There was no Task Supervisor and no Learning Coach. They were getting 70 per cent failures on their course. We tactfully suggested that perhaps better use could be made of the trainer. The instructor staff were very dubious but during their next twelve-week course offered us one day in the second week to brief the trainess about the learning facilities addressed by the trainer, and one day in the eleventh week to check on what had happened. The instructors said that they themselves were too tightly scheduled to be involved. We spent our first day explaining to the trainees what a Learning Conversation is, demonstrating it in depth with one of them acting as 'user', and getting them all to write Learning Contracts for their next session on the trainer. We also got them to refer to the manual, which explained the task-learning aids, and went through the contents page. We asked them each to keep a learning diary over the ten weeks.

When we returned we were very impressed by the fact that they had all kept diaries, even more impressed by the quality of what they had been doing as Users, as Task Supervisors and as Learning Coaches for each other. It emerged later that everybody on that course passed.

Finally, a different example demonstrates the universality of this approach. On a short (four week) course for supervisors the trainees were expected to work largely in syndicates. The Learning Coach and Task Supervisor functions were operating quite well, but the discussion process across the user–domain interface was hopeless. We identified the problem, used video-recording to amplify the $MA(R)^4S$ interface and used trainees working together in pairs to reconstruct from the recording exactly what each individual's personal experience had been. This was not chit-chat about the syndicate experience, it was a disciplined, carefully controlled sequential reconstruction of what had been going on in each inner conversation. The change was amazing: from frozen conversation the syndicates became lively, purposive and exceedingly productive. So much so that the trainers were much stressed by the creative demands being made of them by these unusually enthusiastic trainees. They had been classed as stupid.

These examples illustrate how, if one understands the minimum requirements of a Self-organised Learning Environment and have specific and powerful enough tools to challenge the robots that are strangling any particular component of it, amazing changes in productivity will almost automatically occur. But the systems must all be functioning together and coordinated by the Intentionality Manager.

Self-organised Learning Environment: Intentionality Management

Perhaps the name 'Intentionality Manager' itself needs some explanation. We have used this same system design to run a conversational evaluation and development project on a sophisticated software system, and to advise an organisation about the severe problems they were having in making a newly installed automated office work for them. In the examples already offered, we used the term *Learning Manager*; in the product evaluation study we used the *Conversational Researcher*; and in the automated office example we called it *Implementation Consultant*. Having finally recognised that the structure of each system was essentially the same, we tried to see what they had in common.

The top node in Systems Seven can represent models and compare them one with another. It can also monitor each conversation to ensure that the system functions effectively. However, we discovered that 'effectively' meant different things in each situation. In fact, it meant different things in the same situation at different times. It gradually dawned on us what was happening. It was that, depending upon how the conversations were managed, the system pursued and achieved different purposes. If it was mismanaged or unmanaged, as it often was in real 'natural habitat' situations, one could get purposes distributed around the system which were in conflict or were unrelated and unsynchronised. What the top node does when it functions properly is to conversationally negotiate the intention of the system and then guide, select, diagnose, direct and synchronise the various conversations to achieve the emerging intentionality. We could expand on this at length, but suffice to point out that different intentionalities require a different pattern of MA(R)^{4}S settings to drive the conversations. Hence the term 'Intentionality Manager'.

We have in a different context developed a simple taxonomy of learning–teaching relationships from the expert demonstration, through expert instruction, to the traditional tutorial situation in which there is conversation but it is ruled by the experts view of correct practice or established objective knowledge. Additionally, we have the two SoL modes of the task-focused (user-defined) Learning Conversation and the learning-focused (user-defined) Learning Conversation (Thomas and Harri-Augstein, 1983). These different modes of the teaching–learning activity call for different types and mixes of conversation in the SoL Environment.

The demo requires a Learning Conversation prior to the demonstration which allows the user to establish expectations and a receiving state in which he/she can use this valuable opportunity of observing the expert in action. Ideally, the MA(R)^{4}S (interface) should be set to record the demo so that it can be re-run and analysed in retrospect. It also requires some advice and instruction conversation so that the task expert can set the domain context in which the demo is to take place.

Similarly, each teaching–learning mode requires its own coordinated mix of conversations. If there is no Intentionality Management, what actually gets learned will be much degraded (as it usually is) and controlled by happenstance.

Another way of looking at Intentionality Management is to use what we have designated the five faces of teaching–learning (Figure B1.1). Each of these faces represents a unique configuration of the *Systems Seven* conversational network. The first three relate to the task-focused Learning Conversation and involve the Task Supervisor in setting up the domain and conversing with the Learning Coach so that the user can be enabled to set an appropriate Learning Contract. The remaining two relate to the learning-focused conversation and involve the Intentionality Manager guiding the Learning Coach into the level and form of Learning Conversation with the User. The Learning Coach also makes use of the $MA(R)^4S$ (interface) to reflect the process of learning back to the user.

In selecting to put the systems into any one of these configurations the Intentionality Manager needs some overall model of the structure and purpose of the processes he is configuring. He needs to monitor each conversation to collate and compare the emerging models (meanings) and to progressively define the direction the system is taking. This must be fed back for comment and reaction in each conversation. The consequences of the emerging intentionality must be used to set and control the pattern of conversations.

Self-organised Learning Environment: information technology

Much of the software on offer in education and training falls into the area of the task-focused conversation in Figure B1.1. Most of it also has a very restrictive and authoritarian Task Supervisor built in. Just occasionally the function of the Task Supervisor is made available so that the teacher/trainer or even the learner can configure the domain for different purposes. *Very little of the available software offers any of the functions of the Learning*

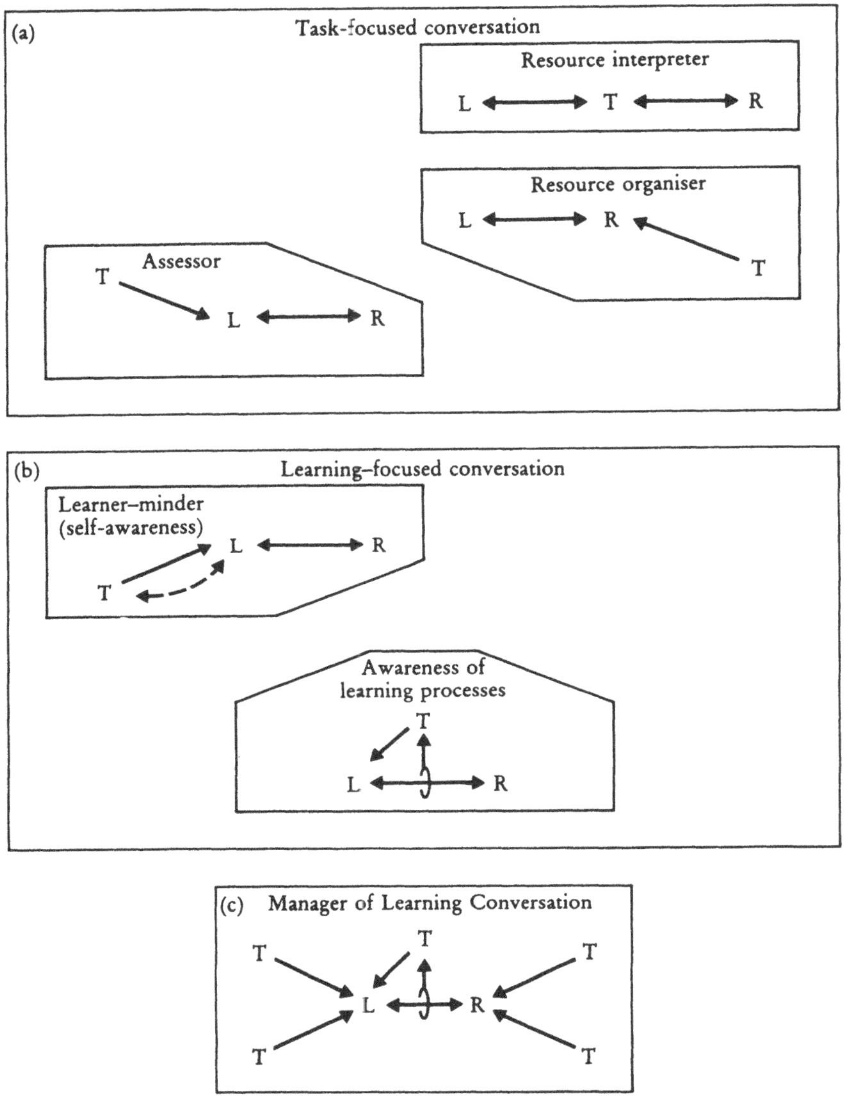

Figure B1.1 Roles within a full learning conversation

Coach. This seems to us to be a significant opportunity that is being missed.

In the CSHL Symposium our post-graduates and associates have referred, where relevant, to various forms and versions of the CSHL Reflective Learning Technology. Some of this is in the form of paper-and-pencil techniques which can be recruited into the SoL Environment to act as amplifiers of some component of one of the MA(R)^{4}S processes. Individual FOCUSed grids, STRUCTURES OF MEANING and CHART serve to represent meaning in different forms so that it may be reflected upon. Other techniques such as INTERACTIVE PAIRS and exchange and converse serve more directly as enhancers of the process of conversation. Many of these techniques are now available as CSHL software packages (Thomas and Harri-Augstein, 1985a). The microcomputer and the power of information technology can be recruited into the enhancements of various component conversations in the SoL Environment.

We are now concerned with building a software-driven SoL Environment around specific domains. We have so far made three attempts at this. The first is in a Ministry of Defence project, which is concerned with developing an Intelligent Learning Support System for Naval Command and Control (Thomas and Harri-Augstein, 1986). The second is an attempt to build our Reading-to-Learn techniques into software.

Reading-to-Learn

The Reading-to-Learn software has been designed as an aid for learners to work independently to further develop the effective use of reading as a learning skill and to use texts which they encounter in their normal studies as a more effective resource for self-organised study. The software replaces the Learning Coach and to some extent the Intentionality Manager and enables learners to develop their skills in the following ways:

1 *Purpose*. Identify a wide variety of needs and purposes in order to plan specified strategies. P
2 *Strategy*. Select from a wide variety of strategies in order to achieve specified purposes. S
3 *Outcome*. Assess the quality of reading outcomes within the context of specified purposes. O
4 *Review* systematically the whole process (Purpose–Strategy–Outcome) in personal terms. R

The software is divided into two major groups of programs. The Reading-to-Learn programs are located on the Pupils Reading Activities Disk (PRAD). The Organisation of Resources programs are located on the Teachers Resource Organisation Disk (TROD).

TROD allows teachers to examine text resources provided by CSHL on a Text Resource Engineering Disk (CSHL-TREND) and to prepare, copy, file and organise their own text resources on their own Teachers TREND Disk. PRAD enables pupils to become more aware of their own reading processes and to examine, reflect upon, review and develop their Reading-to-Learn skills. One central activity of the system uses MA(R)[4]S based on a behavioural record of reading the text. This enables the learner to model their Reading-to-Learn process and so to review and develop their skills. A Personal Record Organising Disk (PROD) allows them to keep a record of the results of their reading-to-learn activities, so that they can progressively review their progress. The CSHL-TREND disk offers twenty-seven texts for use with PRAD. These are grouped into eleven major categories which offer teachers and pupils a flexible and wide-ranging resource. Figure B1.2 outlines this ILS Reading-to-Learn software.

Our third endeavour is a domain-independent Learning-to-Learn software system.

Chat-to-learn

The system comprises a suite of programs which explain themselves to the learner, offers them choices of activity, and leads them through the elicitation procedures of model-building, that

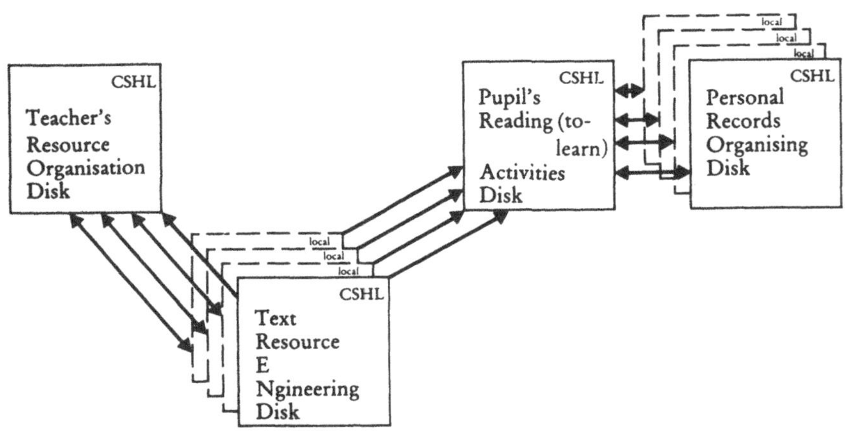

Figure B1.2 CSHL Reading-to-Learn software

is MA(R)^{4}S. The learner can choose to be addressed as a 'Novice', when they will receive full explanatory annotations to the procedures, or as an 'Expert', when the explanations are withheld. The learner is free to traverse the elicitation and associated procedures in almost any order they choose, although some routes are suggested as more sensible than others. The dialogue conducted via the VDU and the keyboard is augmented by hard-copy printouts of the learner's models which may be accompanied by non-evaluative comments which draw the learner's attention to omissions in the model or suggestions for the learner to reflect on. The software system cannot comment on the meaning of any of the contents of the learner models because it has, as yet, no 'intelligent' language-understanding mechanism. However, a human Learning Coach, where available, can take on this function.

There are essentially three activities available to the learner, corresponding to the three modellers; PSOR Learning Contracts, Intensive Conversation, and Reflect-and-Review. *The system provides no constraints on the contents of the learner's contracts.*

The PSOR modeller leads the learner through the elicitation of their contract, prompting them always to formulate their contract with the utmost care and to revise its contents, repeatedly if necessary. This emphasis reflects the importance attached to the process of contract-making as one which itself induces change in the learner. Together with the definition of the contract *topic*, its *purpose*, *strategy*, *outcome* and *review criteria*, the learner is asked to specify the *resources* they will need to draw upon to execute their contract. A more intense conversation involving an expansion of the contract follows, although here as elsewhere the learner can opt out of the suggested sequence. The learner is asked to specify both a superordinate context and a set of subordinate elements for each of the components of their contract (ie P, S, O, R) so that they are constructing a *three-level hierarchy*. Again, they have the opportunity to revise their contract. When they are at least provisionally satisfied, they can attempt to execute it. The suggested sequel is the contract Reflect-and-Review procedure, in which the learner reconstructs all the components of this contract and their resource list in the light of their experience. A comparison of before- and after-task versions of a contract is provided as a hard-copy printout (ORACLE) and the learner invited to reflect on the differences and plan future activities.

Each of the three modelling activities conducted in the current version of the system is self-contained and can operate in the absence of a human Learning Coach. However, the system does not include a Support Generator (see p. 106), which can steer the learner between activities, and this function has to be performed in person at present. Figure B1.3 outlines the current version. The three modellers can be supplemented by a pencil-and-paper

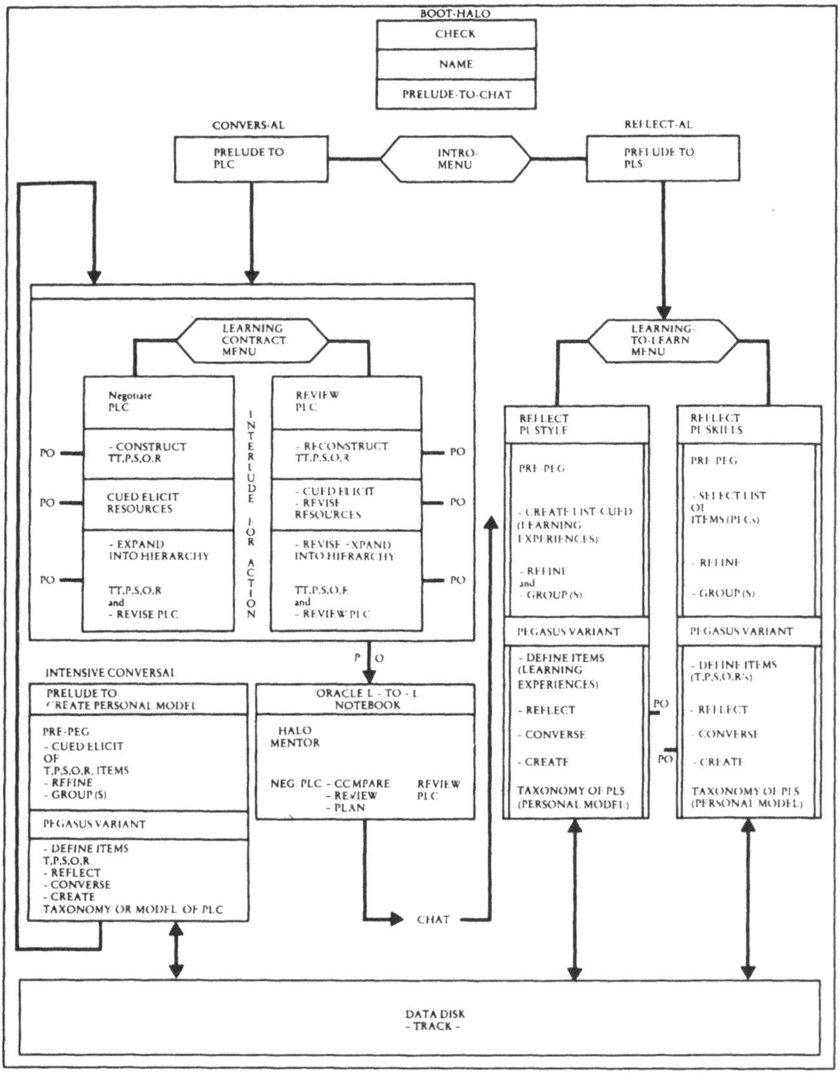

Figure B1.3 CSHL-ILS-SoL: chat to learn

version of the DEBRIEF, which is most effectively used after task execution and before contract review. The pencil-and-paper version of a procedure can be seen as an intermediate stage in the implementation of a procedure which initially exists only in the head of the skilled Learning Coach. This process of externalising and articulating the art of the Learning Coach is the first step towards a machine implementation and is served by a research strategy based on empirical study.

Starting from the assumption that in the early stages a human being is more likely to be able to offer a facility than a machine, we find that with experience we begin to be able to describe the models that drive us sufficiently clearly to write computer programs to do all or part of the job for us. In theory this saves time and effort in not having to repeatedly offer the same human services and enables us to offer a distant-learning software resource. In practice the computer programming can become all absorbing in itself, and until recently our programs could not (like us) learn from experience. However, the programs do serve a very useful purpose by implementing what we think is our model of an activity and then offering it at a distance, without us. The program illustrates how well or badly we understand what we, as researchers, are doing. It acts as a dynamic representation of our meaning upon which we can reflect. This is almost always salutary. Either we realise that we have only partially captured what we should have meant, or we realise that much of what we are doing could be done much more simply and economically. Either way, as conversational researchers we learn a lot. Thus the action-research approach to software development is incremental, and the results at each stage feed back to increase the range and sharpen the precision of our MA(R)^{4}S modelling facilities.

We have briefly outlined how we have embodied various aspects of Systems Seven/SoL Environment into software, and we also have a whole variety of software aids that can be recruited into the human Learning Conversation to sharpen this and improve its quality. We are now well into our first attempts to fully implement Systems Seven as a concurrently running 'learning shell' around certain specialist domains such as a ship-command simulator and a complex knowledge base. We are also introducing the SoL Environment as an aid to help us conduct Learning Conversations throughout one large organisation, namely the British Post Office.

Where do we go from here?

Let us speculate where the idea of SoL Environments might take us and our Kelly clone, or others and their Kelly clones, in the future. Our experience in using Systems Seven to enable self-directed change convinces us that the quality and effectiveness of learning in most educational and training situations could be many times greater than it is. In fact, we are convinced that a SoL Environment could quite transform current ideas about many different areas of endeavour. Self-organised learners go on learning in the absence of the TC (see p. 98) practitioners. In creating their own destinies they will extend the range of convenience of the constructs in our 'mind pool' (Harri-Augstein and Thomas, 1979). Bodily health is one other major area in which SoL Environments could make an impact. Yoga and the Alexander Technique demonstrate what can happen when we learn to reflect on our own body processes. Bio-monitoring techniques being used within a supportive Learning Conversation might transform the treatment of heart disease and respiratory problems. As medicine develops more non-intrusive diagnostic techniques, the range could expand.

We would like to think that George Kelly, thirty years on, would have appreciated the power of Systems Seven as a content-free environment for channelling and amplifying creative activities such as design, psychotherapy and even the philosophy of science itself. We know that Don Bannister, one year on, certainly would.

References

Mair, M. (1977). The community of self. In D. Bannister (ed.), *New Perspectives in Personal Construct Theory*. Academic Press: London and New York.

Harri-Augstein, E.S. and Thomas, L. F. (1979). Self-organised Learning and the relativity of knowing. In D. Bannister and P. Stringer (eds.), *Constructs of Sociality and Individuality*. Academic Press: London.

Harri-Augstein, E. S., Smith, M. and Thomas, L. F. (1983). *Reading-to-Learn*. Methuen: London.

Thomas, L. F. and Harri-Augstein, E. S. (1983). *Self-organised Learning and Computer Aided Learning Systems*. Final report of a three-year study sponsored by the Ministry of Defence. CSHL, Brunel University: London.

Thomas, L. F. and Harri-Augstein, E. S. (1985a). *Self-organised Learning: Foundations of a Conversational Science for Psychology*. Routledge & Kegan Paul: London.

Thomas, L. F. and Harri-Augstein, E. S. (1985b). *Implications of Self-organised Learning for an Intelligent Support System*. Final report of a three-year study sponsored by the Ministry of Defence. CSHL, Brunel University: London.

Chapter 2

Initiating the management of learning in a junior school

Graham Crosby and Laurie F. Thomas

Schooling and a conversational methodology

School is suggested as an example of a social, interventionist, learning environment which is institutionally organised. In it tasks are constructed to serve as change agents in one group of persons, frequently to satisfy criteria set by others. It has been said that a school, as an institution, is 'an immensely complex social reality quite as complex as "hospital" and more complex than "factory" or "holiday camp" ' (Harré, 1978, p. 111). This being so, its interventionist activities are complex and uniquely related to the needs of a particular society. They are not therefore directly related to the processes of 'natural' learning.

The term 'schooling' can be used to signify this non-naturalistic institutional organisation of activities designed to promote learning. In a five-year longitudinal study (Crosby, 1984) we have shown that this essentially social activity can be examined through a framework based on aspects of the personal construct psychology of George Kelly (Kelly, 1955).

An initial focus of this investigation was, as headmaster, to offer the eight teachers and the 230 children of an ordinary junior school (between four and eleven years of age) an opportunity to engage in the mutual and personal management of their own learning events. The method was to introduce the ideas of learning-to-learn through the use of suitably designed 'procedures'. These procedures were each a simple content-free method for enabling some part of the learning process. They are described elsewhere (Crosby, 1984). These serve as a means to encourage them into self-organising learning strategies. The procedures were used to establish conversational processes within an action-research paradigm. Part of the intention was to explore the extent to which children and teachers could experience learning as the 'personal construction and exchange of meaning' (Thomas and Harri-Augstein, 1976). Another part was to devise ways in which the procedures could enable the management of task events, within an institutional learning context, to be expressed as 'a catalyst of a systematic metabolism which is already at work' (Beer, 1975) in the participants.

Conversational interactions in school learning events

The teacher–learner interaction is a relationship which can be represented as a pair of intersecting axes. Initially each axis is an expression of the experience and understanding in either the teacher, or the learner. A conversational encounter between learner and teacher is intended to make both dimensions explicit to both participants. As the dimensions are caused to overlap in a learning conversation they become combined into a matrix of mutual understanding. This arises in reality, for example, as each becomes aware of the needs, purposes and criteria relative to a school task. The awareness is of self and of the other, at both task and personal levels of the matrix. Within a conversational methodology, support is provided by the teacher so that the learner is able to 'remain a spectator of his own process long enough to explain it in depth' (Harri-Augstein, 1976) whilst the matrix is developed. As such it can be defined as an essential element of the control processes which are operated within the changes occurring in the learner. The investigation suggests that its inclusion in the child is a complex process. If support is omitted from schooling at any level, then learners, whether adults or children, cannot effectively operate the quality and executive elements of their control process within task events at any stage.

Conversations in which such exchanges occur are usually asymmetric in favour of the teacher. They express the functions which enable the teacher to teach and the pupil to learn within an acceptable and supportive mutuality. When they are frequent and purposefully used the interactions make the underlying model of understanding explicit and articulate. In them each participant increasingly learns what to say to maintain their end of the conversation. They learn how to negotiate learning events from the perspective of their own pole of the teacher–learner dimension. Whilst doing this they develop an understanding of the other as an alternative construction of similar events. Thus Kelly's constructive alternativism can be expressed through the negotiations of ordinary classroom encounters about learning tasks.

A consequence arising from a mutual awareness of significant elements of the opposite pole is that it provides the possibility that each pole can adopt necessary elements of the other's needs, purposes and criteria for personal use. Thus, most importantly, the learner can learn to operate some of the dimensions which usually arise in the teacher. Initially this is at a task level of activity and language. It leads to, and is an essential part of the development of, the more abstract levels of process called 'learning how to learn the content of the curriculum'. The experience generated by these levels of specific-task activity when reflectively operated on, provides a basis for a multilevel process of personal management which can eventually be termed 'self-organisation'. In this the learner is able to personally and internally operate a significant part of the 'teacher role' in a conversation. However, in schooling, even though the development of parts of the roles of both teacher and learner occurs in the learner, it does not detach the teacher as a person from the learner. Neither does it enable the learner to become an autonomous or isolated person within the institution. The change for both is one of level of operation on the task elements.

As extended and complex levels of process are developed on teacher and learner axes in the mutual conversational matrix, available, personal, usable experience of operating on school tasks is enhanced. Both roles become more significant within the personal-change processes of the participants. Thus self-organised learners operate a learning process at multiple levels. Within the reflective processes which become established, past is more readily related to future in the reality of present actions. In this, each level, in every person, is embedded in cognitive structures of increasing commonality. Teachers and learners are differentiated by the degrees of complexity and points of focus which they can manage at any particular time.

To encourage this development of self-organised learning as a basis for the mutual and personal management of learning within this experiment, an appropriate system had to be created which permitted people in teacher and learner roles to complement each other. The traditional strategies of imposed competition and its resulting antagonism were undermined and replaced by mutually supportive procedures. Within the exercise of a conversational methodology, the divisive elements were redirected into positive activities. In many ways the developments which were played out at the project school could be summarised by the Complementality Corollary devised by Thomas (1979) as an extension to Kelly's original corollaries.

Initiating the experiment

At the start of the experiment there was an intention to use some of the ideas developed at the Centre for the Study of Human Learning at Brunel University as part of the philosophical and professional basis to the study. An initial inhibiting factor was the fact that many of the CSHL's key terms were not generally present in the teachers' language. At the project school, therefore, neither the terms nor the ideas they expressed were capable of immediate or simple transmission. A process of translation had to be evolved before transmission could occur.

For this reason the ideas were initially presented to teachers encapsulated in operational (i.e. procedural) forms. As technical aids to facilitation these were designed to enable particular typical tasks to be accomplished in the day-to-day transactions of classroom activities. Using them, teachers were able to create the necessary concrete experience of learning to learn from which they could construct their own context-specific descriptive language. As first-generation users of this, they were increasingly able to use it in their transactions with children.

In execution, the procedures had to serve two distinct but related sets of purposes. First, they had to be a means to satisfy the requirement for children to learn effectively as is demanded by the cultural criteria for all outcomes of schooling. Second, they were a means to develop, encourage and support learning to learn as part of a process of personal development in the participants. To make the task-related purposes served by the procedures articulate and understandable to the user population, a series of apparently simple models, related to well-founded scientific understanding were identified.

Identifying models in an institutionalised learning process

A number of apparently simple models contribute to a description of a theory of self-organised learning in an institutional context. For example, a model consisting of the elements 'pre-novice', 'novice' and 'expert' can describe the performances of children and adults in school as they construct new usable experience (Crosby, 1984). These elements can be related to the stages of the development, negotiation and exchange of usable experience within the framework of a control model. Briefly, the categories can be described in the following manner:

1 A pre-novice is identified as a learner with none of the experience needed to attempt a particular task. As such he or she is entirely within the control processes of the teacher as an external environmental change agent. At this stage the learner has simply to submit to being taught. Unfortunately, this represents the ultimate stage reached by many in institutionalised learning systems.

2 A novice, whilst still being practically incompetent on particular elements within a task, has sufficient experience to create a limited personal representation of it. He or she still requires extensive, externally supplied control. Such a person can begin to observe their activities at a task level. They cannot consciously execute adequate criteria of appropriate quality to multiple levels of outcomes, nor, in general, can they act diagnostically in their own actions or on their own outcomes. They do not have well-developed content or process languages to perform in these ways. It is a stage of learning how to learn an external subject-content offered by a teacher.

3 An expert in relation to a specific task can operate as a self-organised manager of personal learning. At this level of performance the person can observe themselves performing the task and operating as a learner. They can monitor outcomes and can apply criteria appropriately. From the outcomes of

their reflective and reflexive processes they can adequately predict their needs, purposes and criteria for inclusion in future tasks. The extent and integration of their tasks becomes increasingly generalised.

This third level of being 'expert' was not found to exist widely in young children or even in their teachers. Attention was therefore focused on identifying a category which bridged the categories of novice and expert and permitted the dynamic elements of precocious development to occur. This intermediate category was termed 'becoming more expert'. It eventually became more sensible and descriptively useful for identifying the strivings of both children and adults to achieve more competent performances in relation to tasks.

pre-novice \\ // novice → (more) expert

When related together in a model these categories permit the view that even though a person is 'more expert' in one task, the same person could be, at the same time, a 'pre-novice' in another. Thus the model shows a relativistic structure which is compatible with a broad curriculum of apparently unrelated tasks. It demonstrates the inappropriateness of many of the global categories of imposed values which are frequently appended to the participants in schooling as if they were descriptively factual. Everyone starts a new learning event as a pre-novice.

Having become novices in any particular activity, learners develop towards 'becoming more expert' by a process of looping from theory to practice and back. Their progress depended on how effectively this activity is matched to their existing experience at any moment. As George Kelly said of learners' new constructions, 'What is discovered (by a person) is a correspondence – a practical correspondence – between what our theoretical invention leads us to anticipate and what subsequently our instrumental invention leads us to observe'. Thus practice and theory linked by reflective/predictive processes, is another elementary model of institutionalised learning made explicit in this study.

Developing personal experience in schooling

A process with these intentions can be described through a new and apparently simple model which expresses the process of consciously developing personal experience in schooling. The model demonstrates and relates significant loci in the network of controls which a person appears to need to execute to have the necessary levels of conscious control in their task events. It is constructed of four interacting categories.

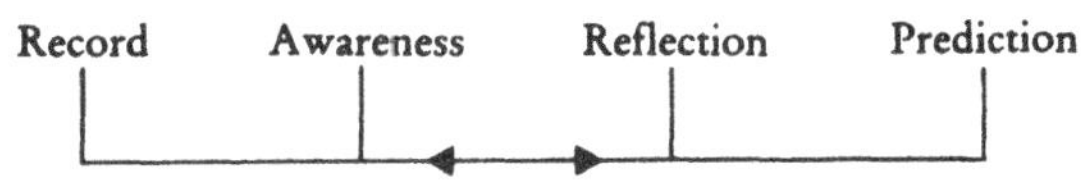

The RARP model describes a dynamic process in the learner–teacher relationship. It permits the proposition that data (from practice) and concepts (as theory) can be mutually constructed into new experience in an institutionally organised learning environment. In traditional schooling, with its mainly book-based academic studies (often presented without an adequately negotiated context) structured conversational interactions are frequently ignored. This actively inhibits the pre-novice to expert development of learners' personal reality in their experiences. A lack of support for task and learner interaction frequently allows the construction of simplistic, often emotionally based outcomes and can provide a pernicious recipe for the failure many now suffer.

The RARP model provides a general formula for converting well-practised and familiar techniques into personal learning to learn facilitators. It was part of the structure of every procedure at the project school. A learner-centred, self-organising process arose from a combination of the participant first being able to perform on tasks at an improved level of competence, and second, having both improved and systematic means to reflect on task and personal outcomes at multiple levels.

Conclusion

Insights into human learning which have arisen from the long-term application of elements such as those described above show that they have a potential for a wider application in a variety of social environments.

They appear generally applicable in a wide range of contexts which include some form of institutionally organised learning. For this to occur it would appear that:

1 Significant elements of a scientifically well-founded body of expert ideas has first to be partly translated into the users terms before it can become the theoretical basis for any specific social-learning system. This can be achieved initially, for example, by creating practical procedures which make them capable of non-expert use as a practical technology. People in teacher and learner roles can, by using such procedures, more competently develop appropriate usable experience.

2 The practical, context-bound procedures need to be constructed as complex technical devices with multiple levels of application. Each level in itself should be easy to use. As the members of the user population become more expert, they can then make use of the deeper levels of process supported and encouraged by the procedural structure as an intellectual scaffolding.

3 As a descriptive-predictive methodology this initially permits the expert basis of the procedures to be demonstrated and used and then to be reconstructed as new usable experience in the learner. A framework of models in which usable generalisations are described can be made in relation to a continuity between current and future developmentally related performances.

4 At every stage the models, as expressions of a range of control processes, can be offered to all participants for their own use. Ultimately the 'teacher model' can in this way be offered to each learner. Thus mutuality can be introduced into the asymmetric relations between teachers and learners so that each complements the other within task events related to a teacher–learner role construct.

5 Support which enables each participant to remain engaged in personal-change activities, at multiple levels, within a relativistic process in the institutional context of schooling, can be generated by the social outcomes of mutuality.

6 A conversational methodology is both viable and useful in insti-

tutionally organised learning. It induces self-organisation in learners. Through its constructive mutuality, an institutionalised learning process can become 'the negotiation and exchange of meaning'. As a result the participants (of whatever ages) can be shown to be able to productively engage in mutual and personal processes of managing their learning in relation to a prescribed curriculum.

7 An outcome from using a range of elements, which includes 'expert' ideas, models, procedures, theory and practice within a conversationally based action-research paradigm, can be a self-sustaining and systematic personal technology of self-organised learning which is better for all in school.

References

Beer, S. (1975). Management in cybernetic terms. In *Platform for Change*. Wiley: London.

Crosby, G. C. (1984). The management of learning: applying a conversational methodology in the development of a system of self-organised learning at the junior stage of schooling. Unpublished PhD thesis, CSHL, Brunel University, Uxbridge.

Harri-Augstein, E. S. (1976). *How to Become a Self-organised Learner: A Conversational Methodology for Learning to Learn in Action*. CSHL Monograph, Brunel University: Uxbridge.

Harré, R. (1978). Notes on the childhood conceptions of social order. *Educational Review* 30(a).

Kelly, G. A. (1955). *The Psychology of Personal Constructs*, Vol. I. Norton: New York.

Thomas, L. F. (1979). Construct, reflect and converse: the conversational reconstruction of social realities. In D. Bannister and P. Stringer (eds.), *Constructs of Sociality and Individuality*. Academic Press: London.

Thomas, L. F. and Harri-Augstein, E. S. (1976). *The Self-organised Learner and the Printed Word*. Final report, SSRC. CSHL Monograph, Brunel University: Uxbridge.

Thomas, L. F. and Harri-Augstein, E. S. (1985). *Self-organised Learning*. Routledge & Kegan Paul: London.

Chapter 3

A qualitative approach to the study of students' learning

Marie Luisa Figueroa and E. Sheila Harri-Augstein

Introduction

This paper offers an initial report of field work carried out by the main author to investigate how personal construct psychology and the Centre for the Study of Human Learning 'Self-organised Learning' approach might add new insights to the study of students' attitudes and their ability to learn. The emphasis throughout has been to develop systematic methods which reveal the personal nature of student learning whilst improving its quality. Two studies are briefly reported.

The first is a descriptive study of two groups of students in the National University of Mexico. A distance teaching system is compared with a more traditional face-to-face lecture and tutorial system (Castrejon Diez, (1982); Jimenes and Oehler, 1982; and Saljo, 1979b; 1980.

The second study carried out with students from Brunel University and Kingston Polytechnic (UK) uses the 'descriptive' techniques (i.e. questionnaire and interview) as the starting points for learning conversations designed to improve the students' capacity for learning.

The Mexican study

The distance teaching system (SUA) of the National University of Mexico has been operating since 1972. At present there are nine faculties that offer courses in co-ordination with SUA. The Modern Languages and Literature Department in the Faculty of Philosophy has achieved considerable success in the development of its courses at a distance. These course follow the same curriculum as the studies offered in the regular lecture courses in the faculty (FAC). However, students in SUA attend only a two-hour seminar every week and a full teaching day every six weeks.

As with other departments working with SUA, the Literature Department concentrates its efforts in the definition of the course objectives and the development of teaching material. In addition to this, the department gives special emphasis to the co-ordinated action of the tutors amongst themselves and their relationship with the students. Staff meetings have the double purpose of organising the tutors' activities and of discussing ways in which they can update and improve their role as tutors.

Although there seems to be a general acknowledgment of the differences between students in SUA and those in the regular courses in the faculty, there is no systematic attempt to describe such differences in terms of students' learning. The present study is an effort towards a qualitative profile of students' learning in both populations (Pask, 1976a; Morgan, Gibbs and Taylor, 1980).

The design

The general aim of this study is to describe differences in students' attitudes towards learning and how these relate to a sample of their learning activities. Such a description will result in a qualitative profile of the chosen student population which may complement quantitative information when decisions on changes to the curriculum are made.

Relevant points of departure for this project have been the studies that reveal the importance of qualitative aspects of students' learning and the value of understanding *how* students learn rather than how much they achieve (Marton and Saljo, 1976a; Thomas and Harri-Augstein, 1979a).

The two main questions with which this project is concerned are as follows:

- What relations exist between students' attitudes and personal views on learning and a sample of their learning activities?
- In what ways do students from one population (distance

learning) (SUA) differ from the other (face-to-face lecture courses) (FAC)?

The design of the project includes the use of three measuring techniques: a questionnaire, an interview and a reading activity. These techniques were applied in the order stated to obtain a profile of the population ranging from general to specific aspects of student learning.

The questionnaire

The questionnaire was based on the Lancaster Inventory of approaches to studying (Entwistle, Hanley and Hounsel, 1979). The number of questions was reduced but the main categories in the original version were maintained. The categories in this questionnaire are an attempt to integrate different studies in students' learning styles and approaches to learning, mainly those of Pask (1976a), Marton and Saljo (1976b), Biggs (1976) and Entwistle *et al.* (1979). The inventory was originally used as a means for investigating the relationship between study methods and academic achievement. However, research using these tools has not yet revealed much evidence of such a relationship (Biggs, 1979; Brumby, 1982; Marton and Saljo, 1976b).

The use of the questionnaire in this project should be interpreted as a way of systematically looking at students' learning attitudes in order to make these more accessible to analysis and not as a way of assigning fixed traits to individuals or groups.

The interview

The content of the interview was based mainly on the work of Marton (1979). The purpose of the interview is to find out to what extent learning can be a subject of analysis and reflection for some students and to what extent its meaning it taken for granted by others. The interview consists of eight questions. The first four questions are related to the students' perception of their educational environment (course, teaching staff, evaluation system, etc.). The last four concentrate on learning as it is experienced by students themselves and as it is perceived in others.

The reading activity

The reading record is an activity based on the work of the Centre for the Study of Human Learning (Thomas and Harri-Augstein, 1974, 1979b). The basic idea behind the technique is that reading for learning is a process of meaning attribution, construction and reconstruction of the contents of a text. The technique consists of a set of conventions and symbols that enable the reader to trace his own reading and obtain a record of the way he approaches the text. The record is considered a tool for raising awareness of the process of meaning attribution when interacting with a text.

The CSHL has developed more accurate methods for obtaining such records. The Reading Recorder and Computer Interactive Reading for Learning Programs are examples of these. However, for reasons of availability, a paper and pencil version of this technique was used in this project.

The main purpose in obtaining these records was to have a sample of students' learning. To achieve this, the activity was designed in such a way as to meet the following criteria:

- In terms of content, it should resemble as much as possible the type of texts that students read in their literature courses. A text by the writer J. L. Borges on Nathaniel Hawthorne was selected. This is a long literary essay, the level of difficulty of which was not too advanced for the students in the first years and not too simple for those in the third and fourth years. The text was selected with the help of some tutors and the choice was made on the basis of their agreement of the level of difficulty and relevance of the text.
- In terms of process, the activity should simulate what students do when learning from written materials.
- In terms of demands, it should make demands on the students at the level that is required in a university course. A set of questions was designed to obtain a record of students' comprehension of the text. Again, the tutors participated in the formulation of the questions and provided an agreed version of the answers to those questions.

The reading outcome taxonomy developed by CSHL is based on Bloom's (1956) and Barret's (1968) taxonomy of levels of comprehension and it has the purpose of making a more accurate appraisal of students' responses; one can not only obtain a register of whether the student response was right or wrong, but also know the quality of its rightness or probable reasons for its failure. Two students may both have correctly answered question three but one of them may have gone beyond the minimum requirements. In the same way a student may have attempted a complex evaluative judgment about the text, but failed to make the basic relationships in the context of the information of the text. This procedure, apart from allowing one to obtain an accurate way of recording students' information, may also provide a wider frame of reference within which to evaluate students' responses. It can also be a useful source of feedback for the students. The questions in this exercise were designed to demand a re-organisation level with the exception of two: no. 8, which demanded a level of appreciation, and no. 10, which required a literal level of understanding.

The sample

The sample consisted of two groups of twenty students each, one belonging to the distance system (SUA), and the other to the regular courses in the faculty (FAC). All students were attending the courses in the Modern Languages and Literature Department. Students participating in this project ranged from the second to fourth year and they participated on a voluntary basis. A brief written summary of the project was presented to both teaching staff and students. The teachers were rather sympathetic with the project and this helped to encourage student participation.

Data collection

The administration of the questionnaire was carried out in small groups of three and four students and occasionally with individuals. The time allowed to answer the questionnaire was thirty minutes, but the average time taken by students was twenty minutes.

The interviews were carried out individually with the exception of a group of three students who were interviewed at the same time, but nonetheless they each answered the questions individually. The interviews lasted from thirty to forty-five minutes, and students could expand as much as they wished on their answers. All of these sessions were taped with the exception of two, in which the students involved had rejected this idea so written notes were used instead. The schedules offered for these interviews were rather flexible and this helped to facilitate a more relaxed atmosphere, often at the student's home, in which to carry out these sessions.

For the reading activity, students were approached individually. They were given a familiarisation exercise which enabled them to know what to expect and what to do when the 'Reading to Learn' exercise was given. Some of the students found the 'Reading Record' technique rather disruptive of the way they normally read. They were encouraged to use the technique with other reading assignments before the exercise on Borges were given (Harri-Augstein, Smith and Thomas, 1983).

Analysis

1 Questionnaire

Personal construct psychology leads us to be rather wary of taking the responses to questionnaires as objective measures of attitudes. Firstly, the wording of any item will almost certainly be interpreted differently (i.e. have a different personal meaning attributed to it) by different respondents. Secondly, the personal meaning of each item is achieved relatively (i.e. in the context of all the other items in the questionnaire). The 'results' from the two groups were therefore analysed not absolutely in terms of specific responses to individual items, but relatively in terms of how the cluster linkages among items varied between the two groups.

2 Interview

The interview presented the problem of processing open-ended answers. The analysis of the information was approached as follows: students' answers to one question were grouped according to a similarity criterion, and a superordinate category name was assigned to each coded cluster attempting to reflect the commonality in all answers. For example, question no. 6, 'Why are some people better at learning?', elicited responses such as: 'it has to do with the family background, the school you attended', 'it is related to his economic position: if you belong to a large family, if you work, if you are badly nourished', 'if you do not have the means to go to a private institute to learn English'. All of these answers were grouped under the category 'causes in external, mainly socio-economical factors'. This way of organising the information allowed the results to be structured to a certain degree without losing the variety of responses that students gave.

3 Reading

The text was a ten-page essay, and was numbered every fifth line. A record was taken on the basis of the students' markings on the right-hand side of the text. The simple version of the technique used in this project does not allow an accurate record of the time structure of the reading.

Each student's reading was analysed using three criteria:

- the read record (i.e. pattern of reading)
- number of responses which correctly answer the question
- number of comprehension levels above or below that expected for each question.

The reference for marking the 'correctness' of students' answers was an agreed version given by two tutors and validated further by two external teachers of literature.

Results and conclusions

1 Questionnaire

Figure B3.1 shows simplified correlation matrices for the two groups. Correlations below 0.7 are omitted and the items are re-ordered to highlight the cluster linkages. Visual inspection reveals that:

1. Students on the distance learning courses have a more differentiated view than those on the traditional lecture course.
2. Distance students relate personal learning (items 27 and 25 plus associated items) to student independence and responsibility (items 28 and 26 plus associated items), whereas traditional lecture course students separate these.
3. Traditional lecture course students associate items 6, 5, 10, 9, 8, 20, 12, 18 and 19 together. The content of these items is revealing.

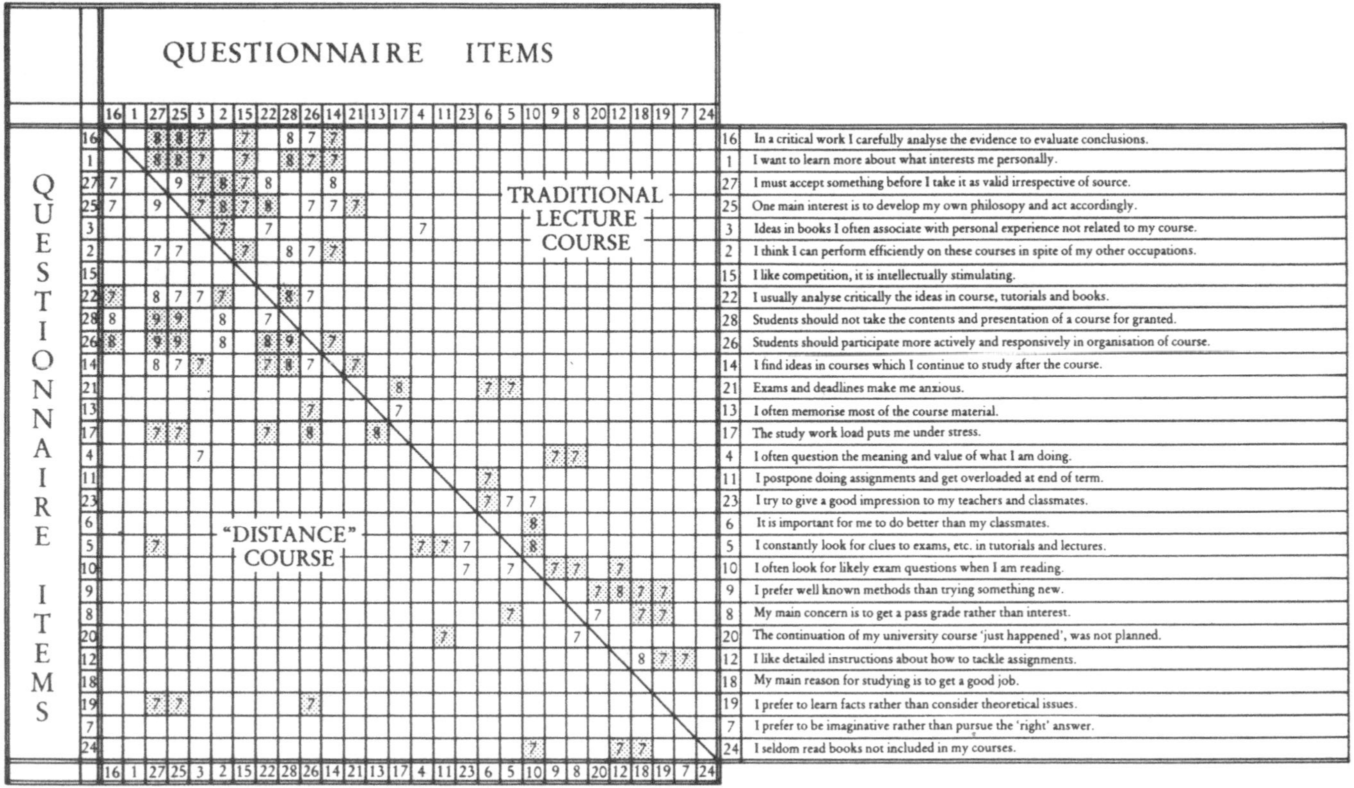

Key 1. Numbers (i.e. 7, 8 and 9 show high correlations (+10) between items.
2. Shading indicates where correlations are higher than in the other group.

Figure B3.1 A comparison of patterns of questionnaire responses for two groups of Mexican students

4 This method of comparing the patterns of meaning embedded in questionnaire responses warrants further development.

2 Interview

Coding of responses to the eight topics raised in the interview again shows marked differences between the groups. Figure B3.2 shows tables for each of the eight topics. The participants in distance learning group generally take a more positive attitude than those pursuing the traditional lecture courses.

Relationship with teachers	Distance	Traditional lecture course
It is positive, they are helpful and understanding.	9	—
It is a good relationship. Teachers are well qualified.	4	—
Good. But there are problems with the personalities of some tutors.	5	2
It is a good relationship.	2	7
It depends upon the type of teacher and type of student.	—	4
It is a very tense relationship.	—	7

The university teaching system	Distance	Traditional lecture course
It is a very good system.	8	—
It works. It is efficient and it is well organised.	5	—
It is a good system. It gives you freedom and demands responsibility.	3	—
It is good, but it has some weaknesses.	4	4
I do not think it is adequate.	—	4
The courses are well planned but the teachers are not very good.	—	6
There are problems with the organisation of the contents.	—	6

3 *Reading*

The distance learning students scored marginally higher than the traditional course students on the set questions. However, neither the levels of comprehension nor the patterns of reading differentiated the two groups. The most significant result was that students in both groups became very interested in *how* they read and in how their methods of reading related to the outcomes of their learning activities. Moreover, this interest was sustained well beyond the reported experiment.

Evaluation	Distance	Traditional lecture course
Fairly adequate, fails to give feedback to students.	4	—
I contrast my view of the quality of my work with that of the teachers.	3	—
It is adequate. Teachers know how to do it.	9	5
It is not very good. Lacks objective criteria.	4	4
It is inadequate.	—	3
Some aspects of it should be changed.	—	8

The importance of GRADES	Distance	Traditional lecture course
They are important. I set out good marks as my objective.	7	—
They are important. They reflect how much I have learned.	5	—
They are not important. Their value is often arbitrary.	8	5
They are not a good representation of the students knowledge.	—	4
They are important for future plans.	—	5
They relate to students progress.	—	6

Reasons why some people are better than others at learning	Distance	Traditional lecture course
It is related to motivation and to having a personal interest in what you are studying.	9	—
It depends on the background knowledge that the student brings to the course	4	—
It is related to creativity and perceptual sensitivity. It is partly innate and partly acquired.	3	—
The causes are to be found in external factors. Mainly socio-economic.	4	6
Defects stem from a lack of previous knowledge and training.	—	3
Defects stem from a lack of method, techniques and study skills.	—	5
The educational environments do not help students' learning	—	6

What does 'learning' mean	Distance	Trading lecture course
Learning is to modify certain behaviour	3	—
I know I have learned something when my views coincide with others'	3	—
Learning is something that relates to memory	3	—
Learning is an increase in knowledge.	3	3
Learning is considered to be a personally meaningful experience.	8	8
Learning is related to practical experience and application	—	9

Views about the quality and/or quantity of learning	Distance	Traditional lecture course
Quality and quantity go together. When you learn better you learn more, not vice versa.	5	—
The freedom in distance learning systems helps improve the quality.	3	—
Everybody should try to learn better. They should study more.	3	—
Quality in learning is identified with personal and meaningful experiences.	5	4
It is good to have both types.	2	2
Quantity refers to numbers and facts. Quality refers to how much you understand.	2	9
Quality in learning is related to the application of knowledge.	—	5

Style of learning	Distance	Traditional lecture course
It is personal, apparently disorganised, intuitive but coherent.	6	—
I have difficulties in learning.	4	—
I learn by association	5	4
I organise my work according to the task	5	6
It is a question of trial and error	—	5
I base my learning on what I get from classes and my teachers.	—	5

Figure B3.2 Tables of interview results

Conclusion

Distant students are more concerned with personal learning and value their tutors and the university system more highly, whereas the traditional students take a rather negative stance (Goldbergh, 1980). Discussion with the Mexican students after the descriptive study revealed that the questionnaire, the interview and the reading exercise had encouraged them to think about how they learned. The CSHL techniques for conducting learning conversations were seen to be very suitable for translating this largely fortuitous 'awareness-arising' activity into a more systematic process for enabling students to become more self-organised and effective in their own terms (Thomas and Harri-Augstein, 1985).

The learning conversations experiment

A systematic study was designed to investigate how the questionnaire, the interview and the reading activity could each be used as the first phase of an extended learning conversation with a student.

Pilot studies showed that the reading activity, although powerful, was too specific in the issues it raised to be directly comparable with the questionnaire and the interview. Another CSHL technique in which the student evolves a personal learning contract and evaluates the PSOR (Purpose, Strategy, Outcome, Review) structure of the consequent learning activity proved more amenable to our purposes.

Restrictions in available space prevent us from reporting this study in detail but the following paragraphs summarise how the study was carried out and the major results.

Design

The investigation was carried out initially with twenty Brunel students (final year degree students and postgraduates) and was then refined and repeated with twenty trainee teachers at Kingston Polytechnic.

Each group of twenty was divided into four sub-groups of five.

Every student participated in six individual one- to two-hour meetings.

Meeting 1
A repertory grid on the students' learning was elicited. Twelve elements were rated on twelve constructs.

Meeting 2
Each sub-group had different treatment.
Sub-group 1 (Questionnaire) completed the questionnaire and discussed the implications of the responses given.
Sub-group 2 (Interview) were taken through the learning interview which then opened out into a discussion of learning methods and problems.
Sub-group 3 (PSOR) were taken through the process of setting themselves a personal learning contract.
Sub-group 4 (Control) were encouraged to discuss their learning methods and problems in an unstructured format.

At the end of the second meeting all the participants were briefed on how to keep a 'learning diary'.

Meetings 3, 4 and 5
Each student, irrespective of sub-group, was encouraged to take part in a one-to-one conversation using the results of 'meeting 2' and the developing contents of their learning diary as the basis for the discussion.

Meeting 6
Another repertory grid on learning was elicited. It contained all the elements and all the constructs elicited for the grid completed in 'meeting 1' plus six extra elements and six extra constructs which *now* seemed appropriate to the students' view of their own learning.

Analysis

Comparison of the repertory grids elicited during meeting 1 and meeting 6 allowed each student to act as his or her own control.

Change was measured in three ways:

1 The overall change in ratings (on the elements and constructs which were common to each grid) was calculated to identify movement towards the students' own preferred poles.
2 An average correlation was calculated for all the new (meeting 6) elements with all the initial (meeting 1) elements. The lower this average correlation, the more 'personally original' were the new constructs. A similar measure was calculated for the new constructs.
3 All the construct poles of all the constructs were independently classified by three judges who then pooled their results and worked out a consensus classification system. The source of the construct pole descriptions were not revealed to the judges. Three more judges then independently assigned each pole description to the resultant hierarchical classification system. The distributions of poles from each sub-group were then identified and compared with those from other sub-groups.

Results

1 Change in ratings

The learning conversations resulted in movement by each sub-group towards the preferred poles of the individuals' constructs, i.e. improvement in their own terms.

The 'PSOR' sub-group moved significantly further than the 'questionnaire' and 'interview' sub-groups, who moved further than the 'control' sub-group.

2 Personal originality of new constructs

Again, the 'PSOR' sub-group's new constructs were more personally original than those from the 'questionnaire' and 'interview' sub-groups, which were more personally original than the control sub-groups. Similar results were obtained for the new elements.

3 Content of constructs

The content of new constructs as revealed by position in the hierarchical classification system could be directly related to the nature and quality of the learning conversation which had taken place.

Comparison of 'Brunel' and 'Kingston' groups

The results from the 'Kingston' group were more significant and clear-cut than those from the 'Brunel' group (although the Brunel results were also significant).

This was probably due to a mix of two influences. Firstly, the Kingston group were more homogeneous and therefore the changes were more easily identified. Secondly, the Kingston study followed the Brunel study and the researchers' skill in conducting learning conversations had considerably improved. This improvement was the topic of a separate 'reflective' investigation.

Implications of the two studies

Whilst the questionnaire and the interview were both useful as starting points for learning conversations which help students to increase their capacity for learning, the PSOR-learning contract proved a more systematic and powerful organiser of the conversational process. In Mexico both the distance teaching system and the traditional faculty system could benefit from the introduction of these awareness-raising techniques to improve the quality of students' learning and performance (Saljo, 1979a).

References

Barret, T. C. (1968). In T. Clymer (ed.), *What Is Reading: Innovation and Change in Reading Instruction. 67th Year Book of National Society for the Study of Education.* Chicago: University of Chicago Press.

Biggs, J. B. (1976). Dimensions of study behaviour: another look at ATI. *British Journal of Educational Psychology* 46, 68–80.

Biggs, J. B. (1979). Individual differences in study processes and the quality of learning outcomes. *Higher Education*, 381–94.

Bloom, B. (1956). Taxonomy of educational objectives. *Handbook I. Cognitive Domain.* New York: Longmans.

Brumby, M. N. (1982). Consistent differences in cognitive styles shown for qualitative biological problem-solving. *British Journal of Educational Psychology* 52, 244–52.

Castrejon Diez, J. (1982). *El Concepto de Universidad.* Mexico: Ediciones Oceano Mexico.

Entwistle, N., Hanley M. and Hounsel, D. (1979). Identifying distinctive approaches to studying. *Higher Education* 8, 365–80.

Fransso, A. (1977). On qualitative differences in learning IV: effects of intrinsic motivation and extrinsic test anxiety on process and outcome. *British Journal of Educational Psychology* 47, 244–57.

Goldbergh, J. C. (1980). Counselling the adult learner: a selective review of the literature. *Adult Education* 30(2), 67–81.

Harri-Augstein, E. S. (1971). Reading strategies and learning outcomes. PhD thesis, CSHL, Brunel University, London.

Harri-Augstein, S., Smith, M. and Thomas, L. (1983). *Reading to Learn.* London: Methuen.

Jimenez, B. and Oehler, A. (1982). *El Sistema de Universidad Abierta.* Coordinacion del Sistema de Universidad Abierta UNAM, Mexico.

Marton, F. (1979). Skill as an aspect of knowledge. *Journal of Higher Education* 50(5), 602–14.

Marton, F. and Saljo, R. (1976a). On qualitative differences in learning: outcome and process. *British Journal of Educational Psychology* 46, 4611.

Marton, F. and Saljo, R. (1976b). On qualitative differences in learning: outcome as a function of the learner's conception of the task. *British Journal of Educational Psychology* 46, 115–27.

Morgan, A., Gibbs, G. and Taylor, E. (1980). Students' approaches to Studying the Social Science and Technology foundation courses: preliminary studies. *Open University IET: Study Methods Group*, Report 4. Milton Keynes: Open University Press.

Pask, G. (1976a). Styles and strategies of learning. *British Journal of Educational Psychology* 46, 128–48.

Pask, G. (1975b). Conversational techniques in the study and practice of education. *British Journal of Educational Psychology* 46, 12–25.

Thomas, L. and Harri-Augstein, S. (1979a). Learning Conversations: a person-centred approach to self-organised learning.

CSHL *British Journal of Guidance and Counselling* 7(1), 80–91.
Thomas, L. F. and Harri-Augstein, S. (1974). Reading to Learn. In J. Merritt (ed.), *New Horizons in Reading*. Newark, US: International Reading Association.
Thomas, L. F. and Harri-Augstein, S. (1979b). *A Reading to Learn package* London: CSHL, Brunel University.
Thomas, L. F. and Harri-Augstein, E. S. (1985). *Self-Organised Learning*. London: Routledge & Kegan Paul.
Saljo, R. (1979a). Learning about learning. *Higher Education* 8.
Saljo, R. (1979b). Informe sobre los Sistemas Abiertos en la Educacion Superior en Mexico. *SEP*, Mexico.
Saljo, R. (1980). Universidad Abierta en *Revista Mexicana de Ciencias Politicas y Sociales*. UNAM, Mexico.

Chapter 4

Report on learning-to-learn techniques based on PCP

Rosamond Nutting

Introduction

Learning problems

The Australian Commonwealth School's Commission Report (1980) drew attention to major problems confronting the school system, particularly those concerned with the high degree of ineffective learning that was reported from all states.

It is well recognised that a large percentage of these lower-level achievers move from secondary school into the technical and further education (TAFE) system as a last attempt to gain useful knowledge before they enter the working world. They see TAFE as being the only place where they have the chance to succeed in their education.

Many Queensland technical college (TAFE) students experience problems with their learning. Some of these students can be helped by traditional remedial programmes. However, there are many for whom such help appears to be of limited value. For some, psychological barriers are the main hindrance to learning, for others the problem is an inability to fit in with traditional learning systems.

If any study is to be made of the cause and treatment of ineffective learning, it is first necessary to define clearly the parameters involved when the words 'effective/ineffective learner' are used.

The term '*effective* learner' could be applied to a person who possesses the following characteristics:

1 Able to apply new behaviours in new situations and to generate new solutions to new problems (Johnson, 1972).
2 Able to act independently of others, to think for themselves, and to widen their thought processes (Thomas and Harri-Augstein, 1985).
3 Able to see what is really happening to them in the learning environment without a blocking or narrowing of perceptual ability (Kelly, 1955).
4 Possessing appropriate attitudes and values towards learning (Kelly, 1955).
5 Able to perceive themselves as effective learners (Purkey, 1970).

'*Ineffective* learner' is an overall term which could be used to describe an individual who possesses the following characteristics:

1 Unable to adapt to new situations (Ashley, Laitman and Faddes, 1979).
2 Dependent and compliant learning behaviours. (Harri-Augstein and Thomas, 1983).
3 Unable to see what is really happening to them in the learning environment, thus blocking and narrowing their perceptual abilities (Kelly, 1955).
4 Possessing inappropriate attitudes and values towards learning (Kelly, 1955).
5 Perceiving themselves as ineffective learners (Purkey, 1970).

The problems of ineffective learners appear to be made worse by the demands made upon them by the changes occurring in our society; changes which are causing considerable stress, alienation and dependence. Two major needs can be identified relating to the problems of ineffective learners when they have to face up to changes in their living and working environment; the need for flexibility and the ability to change, and the need to develop independent learning skills.

Too many schools appear to encourage dependent learning, when what students should be achieving is self-organised learning (Thomas and Harri-Augstein, 1985). Schools appear to be teaching students how to passively submit to learning rather than being encouraged to 'learn how to learn'. The dependency model is not appropriate in a society trying to cope with rapid change because this model encourages compliance rather than independent problem-solving behaviour. Compliancy reduces the individual's ability to cope creatively with, and to capitalise upon, change (Toffler, 1970; Elule, 1964).

More than ever, today the modern education system should be aiming to teach individuals how to become independent, self-reliant learners; to learn how to learn; to change the negative views they have of themselves as learners (Harri-Augstein and Thomas, 1985). But one of the basic problems with present-day education is that the skills it teaches are the ones needed to cope with life's problems as they were in the past (Nutting, 1985).

Every student needs the ability and confidence to cope successfully with life as it will be in the future. Yet students who reject traditional syllabuses taught in traditional ways in a traditional education system are labelled as failures. The result for many can be a loss of self-confidence, a lowered self-image and an increase in negative attitudes about the self, the opposite of what the education system should have created in them.

Since these issues are critical variables in any study of effective and ineffective learners, it is important at this stage to outline some of the essential concepts involved.

The self as a major factor in learning

The study of the 'self' has a long history and is currently receiving considerable attention. Many theories have been espoused, and definitions abound in psychological and educational literature regarding 'self-concept', 'self-esteem' and 'self-efficacy'.

Calhoun and Morse (1977) have advanced three definitions that assist in clarifying what people refer to when they use the term 'self':

1 *Self* is defined as the sum total of all one can call hers/his.
2 *Self-concept* is the substantive description that one employs to identify his/her nature.
3 *Self-esteem* is the degree of one's satisfaction with her/his self concept.

Students with positive self-esteem are more able to achieve learning success.

> The self-esteem and self-confidence of learners is critical to their learning success. Students whose self-esteem and self-confidence are low appear to set goals for themselves far lower than they are capable of achieving, and even fail in the achievement of the goals they do set, more often than those students whose self-

esteem is high. They tend to regard themselves as failures also in their personal lives. (Thomas and Harri-Augstein, 1981)

Self-esteem is a specific state of mind. It varies according to the degree of negative or positive attitudes towards one's self-concept. Coopersmith's (1967) studies suggested a high positive correlation between (1) low self-esteem and high stress and anxiety, and (2) high self-esteem and low stress and anxiety. He suggested further that people with high self-esteem were less likely to be troubled by self-doubts about their abilities to achieve. Those with high self-esteem are more motivated towards the achievement of realistic personal goals.

The achievement of a positive self-concept is vital to the academic success of an individual (Purkey, 1970). He defines the characteristics of the self-concept of learners and theorised that the development of the self-concept is an experience vital to the academic success of the individual. Like Kelly, he theorised that the self-concept was a map of what people believed about their 'self'.

Two factors appear to be critical to the ways in which low achievers perceive themselves as learners. It appears that the negative development of the self-concepts in underachievers is likely to have been influenced at some stage by (1) a teacher's criticism of their learning ability and/or (2) the grades as subjectively assigned to them by their teachers. Students with long histories of failure could be expected to be suffering from low self-concept, low motivation towards personal achievement. They could also experience a high degree of stress and anxiety, particularly in competitive situations.

A solution to the problems

A learning approach which is compatible with the concept of independent self-organised learning has been developed using Kelly's (1955) theory of personal constructs. This theory offers useful techniques upon which teachers can develop a deeper understanding of their students' learning characteristics. Once these have been identified it is possible for teachers and students to cooperate in the creation of self-organised learning environments that make full use of these characteristics instead of forcing students to fit their traditional teaching styles.

It is important, therefore, that people are able to understand and analyse their own constructs. Kelly saw people being able to do this. He described the process by which every individual could become what he called 'their own personal scientist', using their own individual interpretation of their constructs in a way that had the most personal meaning for them. They could then develop what Kelly called a *mental map* of their own world (as they saw it).

Because learning behaviour is controlled by individuals' mental maps, Kelly believes that the analysis of a person's mental maps is a technique which can help both learner and teacher to understand more about the process of learning. That is if their maps are inadequate, their learning behaviour will be inadequate; if their maps are complex, their learning behaviour will be complex.

Eliciting a map: the repertory grid technique

Kelly placed special importance on individuals being allowed to analyse their own constructs. To enable people to do this, he developed the repertory grid technique so the individual could identify his/her personal constructs as a unique and special set of meanings different from those used by any other individual. Having recognised one's own 'mental map' of the world and the ways in which it affects one's views of that world, it becomes much easier for the individual to see how his/her behaviour is governed by this map. It also makes it easier to see why others place different meanings on supposedly 'standard' words and symbols used in interpersonal communication.

The teacher/researcher's role is to mirror these processes to the learner, to allow learners the freedom to explore their views of themselves as learners and to come to conclusions about themselves as learners and their own learning. Learners gain heightened awareness and insight that allows them to explore their learning skills at a deeper level and eventually move at their own pace towards self-organisation, independence in learning and learning competency.

Thomas and Harri-Augstein's (1979) studies show that the conversational methodology offers procedures for enhancing awareness and the development of insight which makes it easier for students to take conscious control of their own learning processes. Harri-Augstein (1976) states that it is the internalisation brought about by the learning conversation that produces self-organised learners. When this happens she suggests that students are also able to create more positive opinions of themselves. Thomas (1982) states that the teacher's role should be in helping students to become more aware of how they learn and so become more positive in the way they perceive themselves as learners. His research involves techniques to help learners to identify the personal myths they may hold about themselves as learners, and thus help them develop a better self-concept. His aim was to monitor the students' learning environment and the people within that environment. Through this insight, he was able to achieve greater learning effectiveness in individuals.

Developing positive attitudes to personal change

This concept of change in learning behaviours has also been researched by Randall (1982), who states that when people experience change, they are forced to learn. He adds that once people become better learners, they are better able to cope positively and effectively with change.

The need for support during change

Learners need the support of a counsellor while they are undergoing change following a grid elicitation. Keen (1977) studied changes in construing between the test–retest method of grid elicitation and the test–conversation–retest method. He found the test–retest reliability on elicited grids to be not significant, suggesting no change in construing. But when conversations took place, he noticed a significant reliability between the two grids, suggesting that a significant change in construing had taken place. This he said had been due to the psychological support during the conversations which took place between the two elicitations.

Statement of aims

The initial aim of the study was the analysis/review of current personal construct theory as a means of developing learning techniques previously unused in Australian TAFE colleges. Personal construct theory offers some unique and relatively novel ways of dealing with three interrelated barriers to effective learning.

The second aim of the study was to evaluate the effectiveness of a range of currently available techniques based on Kelly's personal construct theory, and to assess their value for use with Australian TAFE students.

The third aim was to identify possible methods or interventions based on Kelly's Personal Grid and the Brunel Learning Conversations that could be used in TAFE to identify the cause of negative thinking by ineffective learners and so assist in restructuring their attitudes to learning.

An additional aim of this study was to develop ways of gaining a broader understanding of the behaviour of Australian TAFE students as learners. This information is necessary as a guide to the development of appropriate TAFE courses, particularly for under-achievers.

Methodology

Subjects

Pre-vocational students (106) from three sections of the Bald Hills college of TAFE took part in the study. These students were chosen at random from the Catering and Hospitality section, the Business Studies section and the Trades section of the college. A pilot study involving six pre-vocational students was run and modifications were made to the research design.

Procedure

Students selected (randomly) for the study attended meetings called by the researcher to explain the study briefly and to give them the opportunity not to take part if they wished. Students were randomly assigned to four experimental groups, A, B, C and D.

Group A received learning conversations.
Group B received a placebo treatment.

Group C did not receive a treatment or a placebo treatment. Subjects assigned to these three groups were given a repertory grid elicitation at time 1 and again at time 2.
Group D did not receive a treatment nor a placebo treatment. They were given a repertory-grid elicitation at time 2 but not at time 1.

Repertory-grid elicitation (time 1)
Students in group A (treatment), B (placebo group), and Group C, (*not* D), were given the reportory grid to complete. They were given the grid in small groups if attainable, or individually if college timetables would not permit a group to be used. The elements, modified following a pilot study, were used to elicit the constructs from eighty students in groups A, B and C, at time 1.

The modified elements for the grid were as follows:

1 Me – the learner I am now.
2 Me – the ideal kind of learner I'd like to become.
3 Mother – or the person who took the role of mother to me when I was growing up.
4 Father – or the person who took the role of father to me when I was growing up.
5 Brother/sister closest to me in age.
6 Best friend.
7 Two successful learners I know.
8 Two unsuccessful learners I know.
9 The two best teachers I have ever had (were able to teach me well).
10 The two worst teachers I have ever had (were not able to teach me well).
11 The most successful person I know.
12 The least successful person I know.

Seventeen constructs were elicited from students, the eighteenth construct was supplied by the researcher. This was the bi-polar construct successful–unsuccessful.
The grid elicitation took place during late March and early April, at least six weeks after the commencement of college courses.

Test battery (time 1)
All students in the study were exposed to a test battery. This included the following:
1 ACER Study Skills Inventory and Rosenberg Self-esteem Scale.
2 Tasmanian Mathematics Test.
3 ACER Cooperative Reading Test.
Teachers were given a learning-effectiveness instrument to complete, one for each student taking part in the study. This measure was developed by the researcher for use in this study. An earlier reliability test confirmed its suitability in the measurement of learning effectiveness.

Grid analysis (time 1)
Grids for students in group A were analysed using the computer program FOCUS.

Learning conversations (treatment) and placebo conversations
Only those students assigned to group A were exposed to learning conversations. They attended two or three individual sessions with the researcher. They also attended a group learning-conversation in groups of three to five students.

Group B students received placebo conversations. These conversations were also both individual (with the researcher) and group.

Grid elicitation (time 2)
Students in group A (treatment), group B (placebo), group C and Group D, completed a second repertory grid at the end of August/beginning of September, five to six months after the first grid had been used and after all learning conversations, both treatment and placebo, had been completed.

The elements for the grid at time 2 were the same as those chosen for the time 1 grid elicitation. Constructs were elicited and rated following the same procedure as at time 1.

Test battery (time 2)

All students taking part in the study were again exposed to the test battery before they completed the second grid. The tests were the same as for time 1.

Teachers were again asked to complete the perceived learning-effectiveness questionnaire (teacher questionnaire), one for each student.

Analysis of data

For each test in the test battery, the data analysis consisted of a multivariate analysis of variance. Grids were analysed using programs FOCUS and SOCIOGRIDS.

Results

Perception of self as learner

Grid scores were tested for indications of significant differences in the way individuals saw themselves (The learner I am now/ the learner I would like to be) as indicated by student responses on the repertory grid.

Group A showed considerable improvement in the way they perceived themselves as learners. In the case of group C there was a negative significance where the mean at time 1 was lower than the mean at time 2 (Table B4.1).

Table B4.1 Grid means (Difference between 'Learner I am now' and 'Learner I'd like to be')

Group	N	Means – Grid Differences Time 1	Time 2
A	(26)	18.6923	11.8846
B	(20)	14.45	16.15
C	(17)	13.3529	20.9412
D		(no test at time 1)	

Individual group means on 'Learner I am' and 'Learner I'd like to be' at time 1 and at time 2 were calculated (Table B4.2).

Table B4.2 Group means: 'Learner I am' and 'Learner I'd like to be' at time 1 and at time 2

Group	N	Learner I am Time 1	Time 2	Learner I'd like to be Time 1	Time 2
A	26	45.5	29.5	24.346	22.19
B	20	38.85	39.85	24.45	24.8
C	17	38.68	39.5	25.125	22.06
D	15	–	46.15	–	22.846
Left	25	42.09	–	25.27	–

Table B4.2 shows a difference in the perceptions students had of themselves as learners at time 1, although the ideal kind of learners they would like to become was relatively the same. At time 2, however, group A has shown an improvement in individuals' perceptions of themselves as learners. Groups B and C, however, appear to show a deterioration in individuals' self-perceptions.

It is interesting to note that between times 1 and 2, students in all groups had increased their expectations of themselves as learners from 'Learner I'd like to be' at time 1 (mean 24.79) to 'Learner I'd like to be' at time 2 (mean 22.97).

Further testing involved a 2 × 2 Analysis of Variance (ANOVA). Significant differences were found for the group/time interaction $F(2, 60) = 15.268$, $p < 0.001$.

In order to determine where the differences within the group/time interaction occurred, a *post hoc* test, using the Newman–Keuls test revealed a significant difference (0.001) between:

Group A at time 1 and group A at time 2
Group A at time 2 and group C at time 2
Group C at time 1 and Group C at time 2

Self-esteem

The self-esteem test mean of group A showed a highly positive trend in improvement between times 1 and 2. The mean of groups B, C and D remained relatively constant between times 1 and 2.

However, ANOVA Analysis of Self-esteem test data revealed no significant results in the main effects, and no significant interaction effect.

Maths test data

The means of groups A, B, C and D, on Maths test data revealed a surprising stability of scores over time. No major improvements were found in any groups between time 1 and time 2. The ANOVA Analysis of the Maths test data revealed no significant results.

Study Skills

Groups B, C and D means for Study Skills showed a negative trend at time 2, compared with those of time 1. Group A, however, did not show a negative trend and remained relatively stable between times 1 and 2.

The group/time interaction for Study Skills data did not approach acceptable levels of significance. However, the ANOVA analysis on the data indicated an overall main effects difference between time 1 and time 2, $F(1, 74) = 7.560$ $p < 0.007$. This indicated a significant drop in test scores between times 1 and 2 in Study Skills data. The means showed that the drop did not occur in the treatment group (A).

1 Group A showed a positive trend for improvement between times 1 and 2.
2 Groups B, C and D, however, showed negative trends at time 2.

Reading test

Reading test means show that all groups improved between times 1 and 2. However group A showed a greater change than the other groups. The reading test ANOVA results revealed a main effects (time 1 and time 2) significance, $F(1, 74) = 47.437$ $p < 0.001$, and a significant interaction-effect between time and group, $F(3, 74) = 6.469$ $p < 0.001$. A Newman–Keuls analysis showed that:

1 Group A, Time 2 results were significantly different at 0.01 to group A, time 1 results.
2 Group A, time 2 results were significantly different at 0.01 to group B, C and D, time 2 results.

Learning Effectiveness

The mean for group A showed a large difference between times 1 and 2. There was a trend, however, for groups B, C and D to show deterioration means at time 2 less than those at time 1 (Table B4.3).

Table B4.3 Learning Effectiveness means table

Groups	N	Means – Learning Effectiveness Time 1	Time 2
A	(26)	68.6923	80.5
B	(20)	77.40	75.1
C	(17)	77.4706	73.7059
D	(15)	68.4667	67.667
Total N	(78)		

The Learning Effectiveness ANOVA test data showed a main effects (time 1 and time 2) significance, $F(1, 74) = 5.054$ $p < 0.05$, and a significant time/group interaction, $F(3, 74) = 10.693$ $p < 0.001$.

The Newman–Keuls test determined that:
1 Group A at time 2 showed a significant difference at 0.01 from group A at time 1.
2 A significant difference (0.01) between groups A and D at Time 2.

Although the mean for group A showed a large difference between times 1 and 2, the test showed no significant difference between group A at time 2 and groups B and C at time 2.

Attrition rates

Although 106 students were in the initial selection, only seventy-eight remained in the study by the end of the year. Twenty-seven students had decided to terminate their studies at the college.

Table B4.4 itemises student numbers at the beginning and end of the study in the pre-vocational courses from which students were selected.

Table B4.4 Student attrition rates

	Groups					
	A	B	C	D		
Trade Based	11	11	11	11	Started	(44)
	9	7	9	8	Finished	(33)
Cater. & Hosp.	9	7	5	7	Started	(28)
	9	6	4	4	Finished	(23)
Business Studs.	9	9	8	8	Started	(34)
	8	7	4	3	Finished	(22)
Totals	29	27	25	27	Started	(106)
	26	20	17	15	Finished	(79)

Strategies for change

During the learning conversations with students, and particularly during the laddering stage, specific personal problems (e.g. stress, guilt, learned helplessness) were identified by students. Strategies for change (e.g. relaxation techniques, assertion training, conflict management) were incorporated into the methodology to help the individual to overcome these individual learning blockages. These interventions were not planned when the initial conversation methodology was drawn up but were considered appropriate at the time to increase overall learning effectiveness.

Discussion

The results derived from the test battery analysis and grid data provide a demonstration that improvement in learning can be acquired by students who undergo the learning-to-learn approach as modified for this study from the Brunel model.

Learners within the treatment group changed their construing in three ways. They changed the ways in which they perceived themselves as learners to become more positive; they extended their range of significant meanings; and they changed their pattern of significant meanings. This, in Kelly's view, is learning. This is the kind of learning that Harri-Augstein and Thomas (1983) described as 'heightened awareness', which enables individuals to explore skills and move towards competency, creativity and responsibility for their own learning.

The learning approach developed in this study appears to be successful in changing students' self-image in a positive direction in spite of the influences that caused a negative trend in the self-perceptions of those students who did not take part in the learning programme.

Many Queensland technical students underachieve. They hold negative views of themselves as learners when they begin their courses, and from this study it appears that these views become even more negative during their time at the college. These negative perceptions of 'self' have been reinforced throughout their lives by their teachers and their parents and peers. Expectations of failure have lessened their ability to succeed academically; poor self-images have resulted from their failures; and a vicious circle has been built up during primary and secondary school. Expectations of failure appear to be the major factor which restricts students' learning effectiveness from the very beginning of their courses. When they come to college, many students expect that they will fail, particularly in the more academic and theoretical subjects which require them to be proficient in the skills at which they were failures in secondary school. When they fail to achieve in these subjects at college, they become more discouraged ('they can't even pass a subject'). Failure to achieve in a subject appears to be the factor which is critical to their self-images.

Following the grid exercise, and during learning conversations students were able to question their own ideas of reality, revise ideas, discuss them, test them, develop them and also change their learning behaviours. The methods, techniques and the specific-change strategies that were used in conjunction with the learning conversations, helped to hasten the process of change in more positive directions. As students' perceptions of themselves changed, so too did their learning behaviours.

Increased motivation as learners

According to teacher perceptions of learners, the students in group A who experienced the learning-to-learn programme were seen by them to have changed their learning behaviours. These students showed a strongly positive change towards learning effectiveness based on the constructs teachers hold of what learning effectiveness means to them. Those students assigned to groups B, C and D showed negative trends towards ineffective learning habits as these were perceived by their teachers.

Students assigned to the treatment group (group A) reported few changes in their study habits on the Study Skills inventory; however, students in the other groups showed a negative trend in test-score results. The treatment appeared to keep students' motivation in group A at a relatively even level throughout the duration of their course, whereas in other groups this motivation for study appeared to decrease.

During the learning conversations those students in group A changed their learning behaviours and appeared to become more positive in their attitudes towards college teachers, their college courses and in their own achievements. Several students who were not involved in this group identified changes in their friends who had taken part in the study and requested that the researcher help them to learn also. Even some teachers sought an opportunity to share what they perceived as a highly positive activity.

The treatment group also increased their reading efficiency significantly. This was not a surprising result considering that most students in the treatment group reported that they had increased the time spent studying and reading during their spare time and their study time. They reported doing this without being told to by teachers or parents. They had increased their motivation to obtain knowledge. They were learning how to learn independently of others. They were beginning to take responsibility for their own learning.

Other effects

Another interesting effect was the fact that the treatment group lost fewer of its members than groups B, C and D during the year. One of the three students in group A who did leave, decided soon after her first learning conversation to return to high school and finish grade 12 (HSC). More students from each of the non-treatment groups left after gaining full-time employment. A proportion of those assigned to groups other than the treatment group reported that they found their course too difficult for them to cope with, but none of the students who left from group A gave this as a reason.

Warnings on the use of the repertory grid

Whenever long-term beliefs about any concept are questioned, individuals experience anxiety, and the concepts they have regarding learning are no exception. An individual does feel threatened by any perceived change which is about to take place. Denial is sometimes experienced by those undertaking the grid exercise, followed by later acceptance and finally a change in behaviour. In the words of one student, the repertory grid exercise 'lays it on the line'. Students are confronted by their own judgments of themselves as learners. They become sharply aware of the degree to which they alone are in control of their learning. They recognise that if they fail, it is their responsibility. Improvements in learning are suggested by themselves during learning conversations, and the grid exercise points directly to areas where improvements can take place on their own terms.

Group conversations

The conversations that took place in groups questioned some individuals' ideas (constructs) regarding learning. By introducing one individual to the constructs of another, a change in construing can occur in that individual. This study would seem to imply that this does occur. The individual, prior to the exchange, may not have considered a particular construct as being related to her/his learning. However, when the construct was discussed during the group session the changed construct would be subsumed into the individual's construct system and thus would be an added benefit to the individual's learning effectiveness.

During group learning-conversations, this issue was of major importance, and the discussions that took place regarding it took up a major proportion of the time allotted to the conversation.

Need for teacher awareness

Teachers should become aware that students judge them according to the student's own constructs. If this awareness could be achieved, teachers would be able to improve their understanding of learners and, through this understanding, to improve communications with students. It would also be hoped to produce more caring, friendly, democratic attitudes in teachers. Coupled with more independent, self-sufficient learners, the overall efficiency of both teaching and learning could be increased.

Personal-change strategies

During the learning conversations with students, and particularly during the laddering stage, specific personal problems (e.g. stress, guilt, learned helplessness) were identified by students. It was clear that in almost every case these problems were causing blockages in the learning process for that particular student.

Strategies for change (e.g. relaxation techniques, assertion training, conflict management) were incorporated into the methodology to help the individual to overcome these individual learning blockages. These interventions were not planned when the initial conversation methodology was planned but were considered appropriate at the time to increase overall learning effectiveness.

Major problems were:

1 Low self-esteem and self-efficacy, and a conviction that personal change is impossible (learned helplessness).
2 Stress in the student's personal life (anxiety, threat and pressure).
3 Lack of a goal, demotivation, disorganised life, a sense of hopelessness for the world in the future.
4 Withdrawn, compliant, dependent learning behaviours in students.

Many of the above problems stemmed from a fear of teachers, particularly those who used aggressive, authoritarian, highly directive techniques. These not only created emotional stress (i.e. fear, guilt, etc.) but also reduced the students' abilities to learn independently.

References

Ashley, Laitman and Faddes (1979). *Adaptability: perspectives on tomorrow's careers.* A Symposium, National Center for Research in Vocational Education, Ohio State University, Ohio.

Australian Commonwealth Schools Commission Report for 1980: Response to Government Guidelines, ACS Commission: Canberra, November 1980.

Bandura, A. (1977). *Social Learning Theory*. Prentice-Hall: New York.

Bandura, A. and Adams. (1977). Analysis of self-efficacy theory of behavioural change. *Cognitive Theory and Research* 1, 287–310.

Bannister, D. and Mair, E. (1968). *The Evaluation of Personal Constructs*. Academic Press: London.

Calhoun, G. and Morse, W. (1977). Self-concept and self-esteem: another perspective. *Psychology in the Schools* 14(3), 318–22.

Coopersmith, S. (1967). *The Antecedents of Self-esteem*. Freeman: New York.

Elule, J. (1964). *The Technological Society*. Vintage Books: New York (translation from the 1954 original).

Harri-Augstein, E. and Thomas, L. (1983). *Learning Conversations: Reflective Techniques for Learning to Learn*. Centre for the Study of Human Learning, Brunel University: London.

Johnson, W. (1972). *Living with Change: The Semantics of Coping*. Harper & Row: New York.

Keen, T. R. (1977). TARGET – Teaching Appraisal by Repertory Grid Techniques. A paper presented at the Second International Congress on Personal Construct Theory, Christchurch College, Oxford.

Kelly, G. (1955). *The Psychology of Personal Constructs*, Vol. I. Norton: New York.

Nutting, R. E. (1985). *Skills for Positive Living: A Guide to Personal Growth*. Pitman: Melbourne.

Peters, R.S. (1973). *Youth Self-Concept and Behaviour*. Charles E. Merrill: New York.

Purkey, W. (1970). *Self-concept and School Achievement*. Prentice-Hall: Englewood Cliffs, NJ.

Randall, G. (1982). Conducting learning conversations with an organisation. British Conference on Personal Construct

Psychology Papers, Brunel University: London, September 1982.

Rosenberg, M. (1965). *Society and the Adolescent Self-Image.* Princeton University Press: Princeton, NJ.

Shaw, M. (1980). *On Becoming a Personal Scientist.* Academic Press: London.

Stewart, V. and Stewart, A. (1981). *Business Applications of Repertory Grid* McGraw-Hill: Maidenhead, Berks.

Thomas, L. (1982). *Education and the Negotiation of Meaning.* Centre for the Study of Human Learning, Brunel University: London.

Thomas, L. and Harri-Augstein, S. (1981). The dynamics of learning conversations. In T. Boydell (ed.). *Handbook of Management Self-Development.* Gower: Farnborough.

Thomas, L. and Harri-Augstein, S. (1985). *Self-organised Learning.* Routledge & Kegan Paul: London.

Toffler, A. (1970). *Future Shock.* Pan Books: London.

Chapter 5
Turning-on teachers' own constructs

C. T. Patrick Diamond

A theory and clinical method

After Kelly (1955) construed people generatively as inquirers, and pre-emptively as nothing but bundles of constructs (i.e. as the intersect of many personal construct axes), he devised the repertory grid as one of the possible systematic methodologies for eliciting and then comparing and contrasting their differing psychological space structures. In order to place themselves in a position to play a role in helping teachers, teacher-educators need to understand how the teachers build their own matrices of approval. Since the repertory grid provides a mathematical basis for expressing and measuring the perceptual relationships between the role elements or figures which are characteristically interwoven in any person's meaning space, Kelly sought a simple way of factoring such space. However, while it is one thing to articulate teachers' personal construct systems in this way, it is quite another for teacher-educators then to subsume them within their own systems in ways that enable them to deal effectively with their teacher-students. In Kelly's words:

> Can we, as rank outsiders, crawl into this subject's skin and peep out at the world through his eyes? Perhaps not. But it should be possible to derive data from this protocol which can be meaningfully perceived within our own personal construct systems. (1955, p. 277)

The present paper seeks to offer some advice about the interpretation of rated versions of pedagogical grids by making some basic and practical points about how to help teachers become more aware of their tacit understandings and how to explore what they involve. This requires that teacher-educators enter into teachers' perspectives together with them. Other accounts relevant to this collegial role are provided by Thomas (1979) and by Pope and Keen (1981).

Exploration of teachers' constructs

The FOCUS technique

If, as the Organisation Corollary suggests, teachers' systems of constructs are not just chaotic jumbles but rather related, hierarchical and integrated complexes, these networks of pathways may be regarded as being more or less similar and their equivalence or functional overlap (and also that of elements) can be determined. While primarily psychological in nature, this degree of similarity was expressed by Kelly in a coefficient of similarity that resembled the old Simple Matching Coefficient (Rathod, 1981, p. 119).

Several other relational measures have since been introduced for discovering the principles of inclusiveness which underlie groupings. While the Pearson Product Moment Correlation Coefficient is most familiar and widely used, the City Block metric is a mathematically more sophisticated distance measure of similarity with respect to the construct of matching. This metric provides a cumulative distance score. For constructs the coefficient is an association or similarity measure and it ranges from maximum or perfectly reversed similarity, through complete dissimilarity, to maximum or perfect similarity. For elements the coefficient is a distance measure which ranges from maximum distance or dissimilarity, to minimum distance or perfect similarity. The matching scores are used in the FOCUS algorithm (Thomas, 1976) to generate matrices of dis/similarities between constructs and elements respectively, which are then used to form clusters.

The FOCUS technique also provides criteria for reversing a construct if it is better matched in its reversed than in its actual form. Kelly (1955, p. 283) used a process of reflection or reversal in analysing grids, and this operation is important since the assignment of left-hand or emergent and right-hand or implicit poles to a construct is clearly artificial. Unless some additional rationale is operating, these poles may be reversed providing the assignment of the elements to the poles is also reversed.

An advantage of the presentation is that the sorting only 're-presents' the original grid organised by the 'neighbourness' of constructs and elements. The main patterns are identified and there is nothing mystical in the way that the parts of the grid are rearranged. The analysis process can be easily understood by both the generator and the user of the grid without there being any credibility gap. The teachers project meaning onto the results and confirm this directly in terms of the original grids.

The SOCIOGRIDS technique

This technique was developed by Thomas *et al.* (1976) to map one grid onto another so that either grids elicited from the same teacher (or group) over a period of time can be compared and contrasted or the constructions among a group of teachers can be explored. Independently of the words used to label constructs, the PAIRS algorithm computes the measure of similarity or overlap between each two grids. This matrix of similarity measures, serves as the basis for generating a sociometric type of display, called SOCIONETS, showing who construes what most like whom. Every occasion where two constructs from different grids are adjacent is considered and then the occasion is weighted with the level of match in which it occurred. All the constructs from all the grids are then listed to produce a continuum ranging from those which are most shared by the group to those which are least common. A MODE grid is extracted from the most common constructs.

While there may be reservations about the legitimacy of grouping such diverse perceptions into a common view, Kelly (1955, p. 318) hoped for some methodology that would prevent grids becoming bogged down in the particularistic approach. If the elements are comparable from protocol to protocol, it is possible to extract a group stereotype or factorialised figure such as, for example, of self, the teacher I am and pupils. As the Commonality

Corollary assumes, there may be areas of shared or continuing meaning between and within individuals.

A workshop interpretation

Although Kelly has discussed the characteristics which make for greater flexibility in construct systems, more attention might be paid to specific ways in which the development of systems could be effectively helped or hindered. Carefully guided talkback through the patterns of meaning hidden in the display of the original raw grids can help teachers to interpret the data in significant and personally relevant terms.

A workshop in several steps was designed as an adaptation of procedures devised at the Brunel Centre for the Study of Human Learning to take teachers and others back through their individual and shared grids. Grids were completed by seventeen beginning teachers during a year-long course of teacher preparation (Diamond, 1985a) and by fifteen experienced teachers before and after individually designed interventions in the form of Kelly's (1955) Fixed Role Treatment (Diamond, 1985b). As a conversational heuristic, the FOCUSed grids proved a useful, speculative tool which reflected back to the teachers their changing views of themselves and teaching as seen through their own eyes.

Each grid and each sequence of two or three grids were discussed. The shared list of elements consisted of sixteen figures for the beginning teachers and of fifteen for the experienced teachers. Twelve constructs were elicited from each teacher on each occasion using the same figures – that is, self, past self, ideal self, teacher I am, teacher I would like to be, teacher I fear to be, mother, father, siblings, spouse/steady, friends, pupils, principal/deputy subject master, supervising teacher/inspector and university tutor (if applicable). The effects of enacting the alternative scenarios were thus able to be monitored. The workshop helped focus and discipline the teacher educator's awareness by attending first to the exploration and then to the elaboration of teachers' constructs.

Exploration of teachers' constructs

Though the elicitation process itself may trigger off reflexive mechanisms, careful talkback can further enhance the teachers' awareness of their own construing – that is, if good questions are asked rather than pat answers being found. Salmon (1978, p. 36) has described such questions as those which 'avoid confusion and transcend the obvious or the trivial'. A renewal in teaching may begin by the construing of self and the teacher I am with a view to producing something new rather than preoccupying itself with discrediting prior constructions. Teaching is then regarded

> as open to an infinite variety of alternative constructions – some of them better than others, to be sure – and with most of the best ones yet to be concocted. In such a system the function of an answer is not to make further questioning unnecessary but to hold things together until a round of better questions has been thought up. (Kelly, 1969a, p. 116)

Easterby-Smith (1980, p. 11) warns, however, that the potential for quantification can lead to an over-emphasis on the numbers in the grid, and these can exert something of a mesmeric effect upon the teacher-educator. Indeed, Neimeyer (1982, p. 183) has shown that over 95 per cent of published empirical studies in personal construct theory employ some variant of the grid. Serious studies of the evolution or flow of conceptual structures are rare. It would be deeply ironic if 'one-off' interpretations of FOCUSed constructs and elements were to displace intelligence as the notorious example of reification in psychology.

If they use the grid, teacher-educators may need to be reminded that a construct or a cluster of constructs is a psychological process of a live teacher. It is not

> an intangible essence that floats from the owner to the interpreter of the grid on the wings of an uttered word. While [teacher-educators] can fill the air with words that symbolise their own notions, they must avoid confusing the [teachers] by helping them to develop new constructs out of the materials they are able to furnish. (Kelly, 1955, p. 1088)

The words passing between them need to be valued in terms of what they mean to the teachers and not because of the alleged natural correctness of the teacher-educators' interpretations. All the interpretations that are understood by teachers are perceived in terms of their own construct systems. The teachers can be asked to conceptualise in some new or generalised form what they have been talking about only if it is stressed that not only is a construct personal but also it is a process that goes on inside a person invariably to express anticipation. When this point is forgotten, the clusters are reduced to static, geographic concentrations of ideas. However, if pupils have been construed as stupid and yet calculating, and teachers as wise and cruel, that is something to guide action in tomorrow's classroom.

By extrapolating from Erikson's (1959, p. 86) insights on subjectivity, teachers' association of constructs and elements may be considered as one of the best entry points into the meaning of teaching as teachers are currently negotiating it. There is a synthesising function which can be assumed to associate, cluster or condense, mostly without conscious knowledge, such items into strong images and affects. Teacher-educators can rely on the teachers' capacity to produce such sequences of themes, thoughts and affects which seek their own concordance and provide their own cross-references, as for example in grids. This synthesising trend permits teacher-educators to observe with 'free-floating attention' and to expect a confluence of the teachers' search for clarification and their own endeavour to recognise meaning and relevance. Kelly advises that the need at this time is to 'stop wondering what the words literally mean. Try to recall, instead, what they sound like. Disregard content for the moment; attend to theme' (1969b, p. 229).

Care needs to be taken that the teachers still play a major part in interpreting the grid and that the printout does not form a barrier to understanding and action. FOCUSing adds nothing new to a grid but only makes it easier to identify the latent patterns. By summarising and condensing the data, interpretation is made easier.

The FOCUSed grid provides an economical, spatial representation of how teachers classify teaching, and these perceptions can be extended by asking them further questions around the grid. As the teachers seek to enter their own (and group) construing, some personally significant perceptual, cognitive and affective organisations or schemata may be challenged as new constructions of familiar figures emerge and the teachers find themselves thinking, feeling and perceiving differently (Thomas, 1979, p. 59). Construing is to be construed as essentially a temporal activity.

Elaboration of teachers' constructs

Kelly's most distinctive theme is his concern not only with the exploration of systems of personal understandings but also with their elaboration. If there is no test of their validity, there is a little point in the most detailed and careful inquiry into teachers' psychological theories. The mere identification of their ways of knowing does not guarantee their validity. Once explicated, their meanings require further experimentation and validation. A focus on and an evaluation of the teachers' central assumptions requires that the teacher-educators act as tentative 'process consultants' (Schein, 1969).

Individual sessions with members of the two groups of teachers outlined above, and especially with the experienced group, were based on their individual FOCUSed grids, the MODE grids and SOCIONETS, the construct and the element trees, the self-delineations of centrally important elements and the distance scores for these selected elements. As closing or widening gaps between elements were hit upon, it often had the effect of 'a crystal seed in a supersaturated solution: a rush of other insights and explanations quickly formed around it' (Tiberius, 1980, p. 6). The seed acted as a kernel of truth in the limited hermeneutic sense of truth as an interpretive view of things rather than as a 'once and for all time', settled view of the actual state of affairs.

As puzzling elements seemed to fall into place, the teachers showed surprise followed by recognition. There ensued a natural process of building, shaping and clarifying which yielded information sufficiently detailed to be useful in helping the teachers to construe their ongoing or slowing processes of development. It was possible to grasp the details of a particular issue and then to design a course of action (such as enactment of an alternative teaching scenario) to effect possible improvement or resolution. The ratings assigned on each of the constructs to key elements such as the teacher I am, the teacher I would like to be, and pupils helped to regulate the design of such Fixed Role Treatments (Diamond, 1985b).

The process of dialogue or of a 'learning conversation' (Thomas, 1978) was enhanced by the experience of mutual stimulation, which generated a more narrowly specific and deeper appreciation of their own teaching circumstances. The initial analytical or exploratory stage was thus followed by a productive or synthetic phase of elaboration so that the set of personally significant issues suggested by the grids was followed by the design of a behavioural experiment. While a large number of potentially useful resources and recommendations might have been offered, the teacher-educator made specific suggestions in the form of questions to help launch the teachers further into their own voyages of self-discovery. Often, by acting not as a detached expert but rather as a facilitator, mediator, co-problem-solver and advocate, it was found that successful recommendations were developed cooperatively.

The matrices of element-matching scores, described by Easterby-Smith (1980, p. 21) as 'standard scores for the grid', proved to be a particularly rich source of prompting questions and, when embodied as Fixed Role Treatments, helped the teachers' ideas evolve over time. The distance between the teacher I am and self was initially construed for beginning teachers as an index of role identification; the distance between the teacher I am and the teacher I would like to be, as a measure of self-esteem or of realisation of positive teaching ideals; the distance between the teacher I am and the teacher I fear to be, as a sign of escaping from a negative pedagogic self-image; and the distance between the teacher I am and pupils, as a measure of empathy for or of alienation from them. However, it is essential to establish the behavioural significances and the interpretations of the teachers themselves of such shifts and to keep clear the rationale for their construction. For example, increasing distance between self and the teacher I am, might not automatically indicate a lack of dedication to teaching as a career but rather a conscious decision to have a personal life quite independent of teaching.

Conclusion

The goal of a more clinically based method of inquiry is to help teachers understand and either remedy problems or confirm solutions in classroom teaching and learning. Such a method is distinguished from more narrowly scientific modes by the intensive study of individual teachers; by the use of repeated grid measures in conjunction with collaboratively designed interventions; and by role changes consonant with more collegial relations among the participants.

The FOCUS and SOCIOGRIDS techniques produce results about distances, connections and relationships as expressed through Kelly's basic notions of similarity and matching. A workshop approach can help teacher-educators to talk teachers back through their FOCUSed grids so that together they can learn to experience teaching as a current enterprise and not as an accomplished fact. While the teacher-educator uses the grids as the basis of the conversation, the teachers increasingly take responsibility for the content and meaning of the exchange.

Exploring and elaborating teachers' construct systems confirms that teaching is about making sense of things and that the sense that is achieved is not some generalised, abstract or disembodied knowledge; it is understanding framed within personal contexts, constraints, opportunities and time scales (Salmon, 1978, p. 43). Finally, the central feature of it all, despite the generalisations of the MODE grids, is the absence of any one final version of teaching. Indeed, teaching teachers may usefully be construed as helping them to 'turn on' the navigation lights of their own construct systems. A clinically based methodology helps demonstrate that nothing is as theoretical as good teaching practice.

References

Diamond, C. T. P. (1985a). Becoming a teacher: an altering eye. In D. Bannister (ed.), *Issues and Approaches in Personal Construct Theory*. London: Academic Press.

Diamond, C. T. P. (1985b). Fixed role treatment: enacting alternative scenarios. *Australian Journal of Education* 29, 161–73.

Easterby-Smith, M. (1980). The design, analysis and interpretation

of repertory grids. *International Journal of Man–Machine Studies* 13, 3–24.
Erikson, E. H. (1959). The nature of clinical evidence. In D. Lerner (ed.), *Evidence and Inference*. Glencoe, Ill.: Free Press.
Kelly, G. A. (1955). *The Psychology of Personal Constructs*. New York: Norton.
Kelly, G. A. (1969a). The strategy of psychological research. In B. Maher (ed.), *Clinical Psychology and Personality*. New York: Kreiger.
Kelly, G. A. (1969b). The language of hypothesis: Man's chief psychological instrument. In B. Maher (ed.), *Clinical Psychology and Personality*. New York: Kreiger.
Neimeyer, R. A. (1982). The development of personal construct theory: a sociohistorical analysis. Unpublished PhD thesis, University of Nebraska, Lincoln, Nebraska.
Pope, M. L. and Keen, T. R. (eds.) (1981). *Personal Construct Psychology and Education*. London: Academic Press.
Rathod, P. (1981). Methods for the analysis of repertory grid data. In H. C. J. Bonarius, R. Holland and S. Rosenberg (eds.), *Personal Construct Psychology: Recent Advances in Theory and Practice*. New York: St Martin's Press.
Salmon, P. (1978). Doing Psychological research. In F. Fransella (ed.), *Personal Construct Psychology 1977*. London: Academic Press.
Schein, E. H. (1969). *Process Consultation: Its Role in Organization Development*. Reading, Mass.: Addison-Wesley.
Thomas, L. F. (1976). *Focusing: Exhibiting Meaning in a Grid*. Centre for the Study of Human Learning, Brunel University: London.
Thomas, L. F. (1978). Learning and meaning. In F. Fransella (ed.), *Personal Construct Psychology 1977*. London: Academic Press.
Thomas, L. F. (1979). Construct, reflect and converse: the conversational reconstruction of social realities. In P. Stringer and D. Bannister (eds.), *Constructs of Sociality and Individuality*. London: Academic Press.
Thomas, L. F., McKnight, C. and Shaw, M. L. G. (1976). *Grids and Group Structure*. Centre for the Study of Human Learning, Brunel University: London.
Tiberius, R. (1980). Consulting to improve university teaching. *Options* 7 (Fall), 4–6.

Chapter 6

Personal and impersonal constructs of student teachers

Sylvia Chard

Learning is a process so fundamental to human life that there have been countless attempts to describe it and improve it. Kelly's theory of personal constructs offers a perspective on psychological functioning which enables teachers to provide learners with the means to monitor and organise their own learning. In higher education teachers continue to be important to the self-organised learner but, hopefully, more in the role of guide and interpreter in an unfamiliar domain than as presenter of a prespecified body of knowledge. The problem is not that such a body of knowledge cannot be agreed among a given social or professional group, however difficult that may be. It is rather that the individual person's access to that knowledge depends on the facility with which she can acquire new constructs which map easily on to her own existing construing of relevant personal experience.

The research I am reporting in this paper was carried out to monitor the developing constructs that teacher education students applied to children early in their course and to see how these changed over an extended experience of working with children in the classroom (Hucklesby Chard, 1985). The findings have led me to new insights into the role of the teacher-educator who wants to help students to acquire professional understandings that are well grounded in self-aware personal experience.

Personal and impersonal constructs

Personal constructs are imbued with personal meaning. They also reflect the negotiation for public meaning by the individual with the social groups of which she is a member. Some constructs are more idiosyncratic, some more publicly agreed. A family group may have unique constructs but a professional group is constrained by the demands of its work to be explicit about the shared and public nature of its constructs. Upon initiation into a professional training or education many familiar constructs continue to be used, but some new constructs are learned. These may be of a technical nature. They involve the learning of a new and specialised language used by the professional group. At first their use by the novice is restricted, they are in a sense 'impersonal constructs'. They have more in common with supplied than with elicited constructs and as such tend to be less meaningful (Cochran, 1977).

Early in this study of teacher training, students were expected to use school-specific constructs (e.g. those concerned with children's intelligence, achievement, work habits and motivation) even though they would have as yet little experience of their use. Such constructs are important in the professional teacher's personal-construct system. They will eventually become part of each student's personal-construct system. At the beginning of the teacher education programme, however, it was assumed that they would be rather inflexibly applied, learned from the class teacher and college supervisor. They would be impersonal, part of the student's 'espoused theory' rather than part of her 'theory-in-use' (Argyris and Schon, 1976). It seemed likely that the more personal constructs would be applied more meaningfully to children in the unfamiliar setting of the classroom. The study reported here offers support for the view that *impersonal* and less familiar constructs are applied less flexibly by first-year students and are less open to modification than *personal* and more familiar ones. Discussion of the findings raises questions about alternative methods of introducing new constructs in the context of professional training.

Report of the study

This study was concerned with what was being learned about children by the students in the school experience arranged for them in their first year. Evidence was sought for a relationship between the students' construing of children and related strengths and weaknesses in their work with children in school.

Context

The personal constructs applied by students to children were investigated at the beginning and end of a six-month period. During this time each student worked with children in an infant school classroom as part of the first-year requirement of the teacher education course, a BEd in an English college of higher education. The first-year school experience began with two whole-day visits to the classroom in October followed by two full weeks there in November. The student continued close contact with the same class through weekly whole-day visits until May. At the beginning of the summer term she spent three whole weeks in the classroom working with the same children.

Elements and constructs

Repertory grids were elicited dyadically in individual, conversational interviews from a sample of forty-three students after the first two weeks of full-time contact with the children in November. These were compared with grids completed in the summer at the end of the school experience to provide measures of change. Follow-up interviews with a subsample of thirteen students with varying data profiles provided supporting evidence for the information obtained from analysis of the grids.

It is important in any study of personal construing that a given set of constructs applies appropriately to a given set of elements. The elements in this study were the *children* with whom the student worked in school. Here the set of 'children in your class' represented a set of elements which could be construed within a common set of parameters. In Kelly's (1955) terms, it fell within the 'range of convenience' of a set of personal constructs. The domain or topic of children was considered of particular relevance to students because work with children was a central part of their teacher education programme and also a major professional concern (Lacey, 1977). It was a domain about which students would have some previous experience, and some preconceptions when they had chosen the professional preparation of teacher education. Both layman and professional alike can be articulate about children. The domain was also considered to be of sufficiently limited scope for detailed study.

Two aspects of the students' construing of children were of primary concern: first, the *content* of their constructs; second, the *integration* of constructs. These were examined in relation to the *students' teaching performance* and progress throughout the year in their work in school as judged by the college supervisors.

Construct content

The content of the constructs used by the students was analysed and two major categories of construct were identified. The first group were those normally used only by teachers within the classroom context (impersonal). These were concerned with the intelligence, achievement, work habits and motivation of the children. These constructs are associated with the professional role of the teacher; for example, 'intelligent/slow', 'reads well/poor reader', 'well-developed language/restricted language'. The second group were those more generally applied by people to children or other adults in any context outside classrooms (personal). Examples of more generally applied constructs are 'happy/sad', 'cooperative/uncooperative', and 'easy-going/is easily upset'. Students were expected to use a combination of classroom specific and more generally applicable constructs, a combination of impersonal and personal constructs.

Integration

The second aspect of students' construing concerned the integration of the constructs. The term *integration* here refers to how the constructs covaried in the way they were applied to the elements. Integration varies according to how similarly or differently individual constructs within a system are applied to members of a set of elements. Kelly used the terms 'tight' and 'loose' construing to refer to what is here termed integration within the construct system. In this study an integration score was calculated from the relationship between the set of ratings on every pair of constructs in a grid, expressed as a Spearman Rho.

The sum of the Spearman Rhos is the integration score (called the Intensity score by Fransella and Bannister, 1977, p. 60). Related concepts elsewhere in the PCP literature are 'cognitive complexity' (Bieri, 1955), 'functionally independent construction' (Landfield, 1971) and 'interconnectedness' (Hayden, 1982).

There is an optimum level of integration for most effective construing in the middle range between high and low integration (Adams-Webber, 1979). Integration is therefore in this context, a neutral term. Highly integrated construct systems provide less discriminatory capability than systems that are moderately low in integration; where there is high integration, thinking tends to be stereotyped. Where integration is too low, there is little pattern or relationship seen among the constructs and construing tends to be fragmented.

Integration has been shown generally to be lower concerning an unfamiliar domain and to increase with familiarity (Benjafield, Jordan and Pomeroy, 1976; Bodden and James, 1976; Crockett, 1982). In this study it was expected that the students' construct systems would show greater integration among constructs at the time of the second rating of children on the constructs at the end of the school experience.

Students' teaching performance

The study was primarily concerned with the way construct content and construct integration related to the students' teaching performance in the schools. A measure of performance was obtained by means of ratings given by college supervisors for the purpose of the research. It incorporated judgments on the students' teaching performance and on the progress they had made throughout the year in their work in school. The college supervisors of the school experience were deemed the persons best fitted to make these judgments as they have within the BEd programme a major role in guiding students' thinking and assessing their work in school.

Findings

Construct content

A measure of change in students' ratings of children between the first and second repertory grid interviews was calculated from a comparison of the grid data. It was found as expected that the ratings on constructs that are more generally applied to children, personal constructs, changed significantly more than the ratings on school-specific constructs, impersonal constructs, over the time of the school experience, Wilcoxon's $T(43) = 166$, $p < 0.005$. At the beginning of a teacher education course, when students have little experience of children in classrooms from a teacher's point of view, it seems important for them to bring their currently operating personal constructs into the classroom context in order to make sense of what is happening there. New and impersonal constructs of the school-specific type may certainly be adopted but will probably be less useful at first than the familiar, personal and more generally applicable constructs in discriminating among the children.

Also as expected, those students showing more change in construing were judged to be more successful in their teaching. A significant correlation was found between degree of change and supervisors' ratings: Spearman's $r(43) = 0.331$, $T = 2.25$, $p < 0.025$. An illustration from one of the follow-up interviews gives an example of a change of view on a personal construct. The student at first saw mainly advantages for the teacher in children's assertiveness and leadership qualities at the beginning of the school experience:

> I thought it was better for children to be more outgoing and assertive at first, as they were the children who got noticed, but now I don't think it is such an advantage. Ruth was very outgoing and always pushed herself forward, but then I found she needed a lot of encouragement to do any work on her own, she just wanted attention all the time, so she'd just stop work and come up so that you'd tell her to carry on. Several of them were like that.

The findings that students' ratings change more on constructs that are more generally applicable and that change in rating is positively related to teaching performance have possible implications for the working of the supervisor–student relationship. While students appear to be quite ready to adopt school-specific constructs which they have little experience in applying, they are likely to use such constructs more rigidly, and appear to learn less in ways reflected by changed construct application. The more generally applicable constructs have been used in meaningful ways over a long period of time and applied to other people the student knows besides children. These constructs refer to personality differences such as 'easy-going/easily upset', 'talkative/quiet'. Students should be encouraged to talk about children in these terms first, rather than to use the more school-specific constructs early on.

The supervisor ratings of students' teaching performance show that supervisors value evidence that the student-teacher is thinking independently and personally about children and not just repeating statements made by the teacher. Such independent thinking takes place within the construct system the student already uses, her 'theory-in-use'. This is further evidence that the students concerned do not 'short-cut the gradual shaping of thought by experience' that is recognised by some teacher-educators as being so necessary a part of teacher development (Floden and Feiman, 1981). There is a justifiable scepticism about the value of teaching students to talk as though they were experienced teachers without the weight of experience to substantiate their views.

Integration

The findings of this study indicate that most students' construct systems have increased in integration by the end of the school experience compared to the beginning. A test of the difference between first and second integration scores showed this increase to be significant: Wilcoxon's $T(43) = 291$, $p < 0.025$. The increase in integration is thought to indicate the emerging perception of patterns of relationships among constructs as these apply to children. Supervisors gave significantly higher ratings to students showing an increase in integration score than to those showing a decrease, Mann-Whitney test: $U(27, 12) = 70$, $p. < 0.005$.

Students whose construing was tight at the beginning of the

school experience, either showed little change in their construing or decreased in integration. High integration at the beginning of the school experience may indicate a lack of flexibility and openness in the face of unfamiliar challenges with children in the classroom. Where integration decreased, it could be inferred that the student had preconceptions which had to be unlearned because they were disconfirmed by the experience of children in the classroom. Interview material supported this inference.

Discussion

For a few students, learning through the school experience appears to involve some significant restructuring of the construct system, changing from high to lower integration, becoming less ready to stereotype children, more flexible and independent. The anxiety associated with high integration in the construct system was evident among some of those students with high integration scores. They seemed to talk more about their problems in the follow-up interviews. Highly integrated construing has been found elsewhere to be related to anxiety (Fransella and Bannister, 1977). The students' anxiety was reflected in recurrent problem themes. These were rooted in misconceptions about children which could be detected by means of the repertory grids and their analysis. Grid elicitation enables a student to make explicit problematic aspects of her thinking which might otherwise be difficult for a supervisor to discover. Thomas and Harri-Augstein have suggested a range of related awareness-raising procedures which enable the learner to examine his own learning processes (Thomas and Harri-Augstein, 1985). Students can be encouraged in a variety of ways to talk about their difficulties and try out alternative constructions of them.

Supervisors may learn to recognise the very different problems of students who, on the basis of little experience, see few relations among constructs (low integration) and those, on the other hand, who see many relations (high integration), make many unvalidated assumptions, and so tend to think stereotypically. These two types of student appear to correspond in socialisation and learning style to Lacey's (1977) and Grimmett's (1984) 'internalisers' and 'compliers.' The internalisers are likely to be independent and flexible in their thinking, preferring to use supervisors and class teachers to help them solve problems which they themselves identify. The compliers, on the other hand, are described as being more dependent on the authority figures and anxious to do what is expected of them. Thus it might be best to encourage some students to ask their own questions and to try out their own ideas. Other students may be more anxious about trusting their own judgment and may best be helped to learn by means of relatively detailed instructions and guidance while at the same time being encouraged to be reflective about the outcomes of their teaching activity.

The personal construct psychology methods, however, are of greatest value as teaching/learning devices when supported by informal interview data. Here is an example of the kind of individual learning insight which is not uncommon and is fundamental to the formation of a professional identity:

> At the beginning I thought he just wasn't very clever, was very slow, but now I sort of look at other things, like he doesn't listen or he's sort of naughty. Perhaps that's why he doesn't pick things up. He's very disruptive and easily led by others. . . . Well, I think now that if that was just the way he was you'd just have to try and put up with it and hope he'd pick some things up some day, whereas if it's sort of influenced by other things, you can do something about it. Perhaps try to give him things that are going to interest him, or put him in a different group or something, so that you can help him a bit.

In talking about individual children in relation to this kind of insight a student can appear to make far-reaching and important discoveries about her own approach to the responsibility of teaching.

Conclusion

As a student progresses through an extended period of professional education she is socialised into the terminology, technology, network of rules and principles, and code of ethics which constitute the expertise of that profession. It would appear from a personal construct psychology perspective on learning that the transmission model of teaching and learning on which many courses are based is insufficient. The understanding of a concept such as 'intelligence' or 'motivation' is not only a matter of knowing when to use the word. It involves reading the concept into a set of relevant personal constructs, diffusing its application in a variety of contexts, negotiating its meaning with fellow novices and tutors and with peers over a period of years. The recent innovations in methods of teaching in higher education promoting peer-group learning supported by an appropriate range of interactive computer software will facilitate the 'construction of personally satisfying, significant and viable meanings' (Harri-Augstein, 1978). The college tutor will be free to become more responsive to students as guide and interpreter according to the very different needs of the individual learners on the course.

There is much scope for further research in the areas outlined in this paper. The stability of the tendency to approach unfamiliar situations with a highly integrated construct system could be studied together with possible ways of helping students and teachers to become more flexible and independent learners throughout their professional development. It would be interesting to see the extent to which recurrent themes in students' construct content might change over the years they spend in initial teacher education and also in the first few years of teaching. A set of core constructs for the profession of teachers of young children and some account of how these become personally meaningful would be a useful addition to resources in the field of teacher education.

Note

This paper is based in part on a doctoral thesis submitted to the Department of Elementary and Early Childhood Education at the University of Illinois at Urbana-Champaign. I would like to thank Lilian G. Katz, Theodore Manolakes and James D. Raths for their advice in this research.

References

Adams-Webber, J. (1979). *Personal Construct Psychology: Concepts and Applications*. New York: Wiley.
Argyris, C. and Schon, D. A. (1976). *Theory in Practice: Increasing Professional Effectiveness*. San Francisco: Jossey-Bass.
Bannister, D. (1960). Conceptual structure in thought-disordered schizophrenics. *Journal of Mental Science* 106, 1230–49.
Bieri, J. (1955). Cognitive complexity–simplicity and predictive behaviour. *Journal of Abnormal and Social Psychology* 51, 263–8.
Benjafield, J., Jordan, D. and Pomeroy, E. (1976). Encounter groups: return to the fundamental. *Psychotherapy: Theory, Research and Practice* 13, 387–9.
Bodden, J. and James, L. E. (1976). Influence of occupational information giving on cognitive complexity. *Journal of Counseling Psychology* 23, 280–2.
Cochran, L. (1977). Differences between supplied and elicited considerations in career evaluation. *Social and Behavioural Perspectives* 4, 241–8.
Crockett, W. H. (1982). The organization of construct systems: the organization corollary. In J. C. Mancuso and J. R. Adams-Webber (eds.), *The Construing Person*. New York: Praeger.
Floden, E. R. and Feiman, S. (1981). Should teachers be taught to be rational? *Journal of Education for Teaching* 7, 274–83.
Fransella, F. and Bannister, D. (1977). *A Manual for Repertory Grid Technique*. London: Academic Press.
Grimmett, P. P. (1984). The supervision conference: an investigation of supervisory effectiveness through analysis of participants' conceptual functioning. In P. P. Grimmett (ed.), *Research in Teacher Education: Current Problems and Future Prospects*. The Monograph Series, University of British Columbia.
Harri-Augstein, S. (1978). Reflecting on structures of meaning: a process of learning-to-learn. In F. Fransella (ed.), *Personal Construct Psychology 1977*. London: Academic Press.
Hayden, B. C. (1082). Experience – a case for possible change: the modulation corollary. In J. C. Mancuso and J. R. Adams-Webber (eds.), *The Construing Person*. New York: Praeger.
Hucklesby Chard, S. C. (1985). A study of teacher education

students' personal constructs about children. Unpublished PhD thesis, University of Illinois, Urbana, Ill.

Kelly, G. A. (1955). *The Psychology of Personal Constructs*, Vols. I and II. New York: Norton.

Lacey, C. (1977). *The Socialisation of Teachers.* London: Methuen.

Landfield, A. W. (1971). *Personal Construct Systems in Psychotherapy*. Chicago: Rand McNally.

Thomas, L. F. and Harri-Augstein, S. (1985). *Self-organised Learning*. London: Routledge & Kegan Paul.

C

Children

Chapter 1
PCP and children

Rosemarie Hayhow, Richard Lansdown, Jenny Maddick and Tom Ravenette

Introduction
Richard Lansdown

During the Boston Congress in 1983, several people noted that there appeared to be little work done in the area of PCP and children. Accordingly, a small group of interested people met in the Centre for Personal Construct Psychology, London, to discuss work we were all doing. It became clear that none of us felt it appropriate to regard children as essentially different from adults in terms of their psychological processes. Equally, we were concerned with the practical application of PCP in our everyday professional lives. The three pieces that follow were developed in order to illustrate three aspects of our work and children's development within a context.

Tom Ravenette sets the scene with a discussion of theory and practice. As an educational psychologist he has had many years' experience of relating one to the other. Rosemarie Hayhow is a speech therapist who uses PCP to illuminate much of her work. Arguing that one cannot understand children if they are viewed in isolation, she gives an account of how PCP can help one understand young mothers, thus illustrating the opening theme set by Dr Ravenette.

Jenny Maddick, also an educational psychologist, tackled one facet of a presently topical subject: the integration or segregation of handicapped children within the education system. Discussions on this have been long on emotion and short on data; Mrs Maddick shows how valuable a PCP approach can be in coming to some conclusions on arguments for and against integration.

PCP and practitioners who work with children
Tom Ravenette

Introduction: theory as a tool for the practitioner

It is frequently forgotten that personal construct theory originated in practice. Although in its early development practice and theory went together, once the theory was launched and became an entity in its own right, the practical origins tended to be overlooked.

The potential practitioner wants to use theory, but since his familiarisation with the theory has frequently been in the hands of non-practitioners, he may well have verbal knowledge of its propositions and be well armed with research and theoretical questions about the theory itself. He has not become aware, however, that for the practitioner theory is a tool to be used, not to be debated academically. His questions, therefore, need to centre on the value of the theory as a tool, and the ways in which the tool can be used in face-to-face situations.

In the practical context within which a practitioner develops his skills, any theory about people demands to be looked at from four different angles: What is the theory's stance about the fundamental nature of persons? What is its stance about change and the promotion of change? What are the propositional contents of the theory? Where does the theory stand in relation to other theories? These four questions provide a basis for studying and understanding any personality theory. It is recursive since it applies to all personality theories, it applies to the specificty of personal construct theory itself, and since each individual is also his own personality theory in action, it applies to the individual as well.

These questions provide perspectives for the practitioner within which his tools take on practical value.

Personal construct theory viewed within a practitioner's perspectives

The theory has two epistemological roots and these are specifically important to the practitioner. On the one hand, 'construction alternativism', the notion that there is always a different way of seeing, and therefore acting, provides both an aim and a hope for his interventions. On the other hand, the principle of 'difference' and its complement 'sameness' as the essential basis for all discrimination points theoretically to the 'construct' and practically to strategies of interviewing: 'We do not know the meaning of an assertion until we know what it also implies, what it denies and the context within which it is useful'. In elaborating these epistemological roots two caveats need to be made. The first is against equating a person's psychological processes with the theory; the other is against misunderstandings inherent in Kelly's use of the three cognate expressions 'construe', 'construction' and 'construct'. This particular difficulty arises from the fact that language may carry either everyday meanings as in ordinary discourse, or precise meaning as in theoretical discourse. Whereas Kelly uses everyday meanings for 'construe' and 'construction' by contrast he loads 'construct' with a very heavy theoretical content. A failure to recognise this essential difference can lead the practitioner into unnecessary difficulties.

It is instructive to apply the four questions posed above to the formal content of the theory as expressed in its Fundamental Postulate and corollaries. This can be done by a simple reordering from Kelly's own presentation. Specifically:

- *Its stance vis-à-vis the individual.*
  Fundamental Postulate, Construct and Individuality corollaries.
- *Its stance vis-à-vis growth and change.*
  Choice, Experience and Modulation corollaries.
- *The individual's own theoretical system.*
  Organisation, Dichotomy, Range and Fragmentation corollaries.
- *The individual in relation to others.*
  Commonality and Sociality corollaries.

From theory to practice

Children do not refer themselves to a psychologist. Referrals of children, therefore, always arise out of the referrer's construction of a child, the events in which the child is involved, and implicitly the referrer's construction of himself. It follows that the practitioner needs to direct his investigations not only to the child but also to the ways in which the referrer makes sense of the situation (which includes the teacher himself) at the centre of the referral. He will also have in mind the need to promote change in the referrer's constructions.

It has become apparent in practice that teachers' referrals usually reflect their own failure of understanding or of action, their sense of what is properly their job as teachers or their inability to build safeguards for a child's future. In fact the referral is a function of their constructions of themselves and their circumstances.

In the light of this argument, a number of questions appear to lie behind the construct practitioner's enquiries.

1 What are the events which are the occasion for the referral? Who is complained about? Who complains?
2 What are the constructions within which the complaint takes on meaning for the referrer, and what are the constructions of the child about his circumstances whereby he is complained about? For each description, what is also implied and what is denied?
3 What are the ways in which changes in the protagonist's constructions may be promoted? Is there new information for old constructions or new constructions for old events? Is change to be encompassed through reflection or imagination, or through experimental enquiry or directed role change? Is the main work to be done with the child or the referrer, or both?

Attributes which might usefully be developed by a personal construct practitioner

Since language acts both as a revealer and an obscurer of an individual's ways of making sense, the practitioner needs to develop an attitude of *sceptical credulity* to what the client says. Further, if he is to attempt some reconstruction in his client's system, he needs the *detached awareness* of a detective but at the same time *empathy, compassion and concern* to match his clients distress and dilemmas. At the level of action the art of the story-teller and the skill of the stage director are valuable adjuncts when the practitioner seeks to promote change.

These attributes and skills may not obviously be aspects of 'man the scientist', but they each contribute vitally to the hidden view of science. The practitioner, therefore, does not need to see himself as an outsider in the scientific enterprise, but rather as a balancing contributor.

PCP and parenthood: some observations of a participant in a mothers' study group

Rosemarie Hayhow

Six women met weekly for nine weeks to discuss areas of difficulty that they were experiencing with their children. The author aimed to explore the value of Kelly's model when considering the day-to-day problems that arise when caring for young children. The group generated an enormous amount of material and only a small portion can be considered here.

Although initially there was an emphasis upon our children, as the group evolved we became more concerned with understanding ourselves and the commonalities within our experiences as mothers. Among the issues that were important for this group there were two that are interrelated and interesting to consider from the viewpoint of Kelly's theory. They are (1) the fear of loss of self and (2) the weariness that can get in the way of being a satisfyingly good mother.

The Fragmentation Corollary considers inferentially incompatible construct sub-systems. Mair (1977) illustrates this by proposing a 'community of selves', where disagreement on the running of some aspects of the community can be tolerated provided there is consistency at a superordinate level. Full-time motherhood removes the context in which some of the pre-mothering selves were meaningful, and consequently these members of the community appear lost. In addition, long-lost selves may reappear when living with a child. Not only might the mother rediscover earlier, pre-verbal selves but also the much less sophisticated ways of construing associated with these. She might be in the perplexing situation of losing some of the selves that she knows and loves and regaining some of the selves that she had forgotten she ever had. The women who continued some work outside the home also had the fullest social lives. It seemed that maintaining some pre-mothering selves made it easier to keep others, and this could be a more important factor than time, money, and so on.

The experience of fragmentation could occur when different

selves are competing. For example, 'childlike me' may construe through the senses and be able to construe the needs of a young baby or delight in playing with mud and water with a three-year-old. 'Childlike me' may become angry at never being able to finish anything and respond to the frustration of incomplete experimentation with foot stamping and shouting. 'Good mother me' is then likely to feel guilty. A battle may ensue as the mother struggles with the anarchy within her community; alternatively, she may grieve for the lost selves, feeling that she will never be the same again. More hopefully, she will find ways of integrating, accepting and keeping alive her important selves.

An unsettled 'community of selves' and the experience of fragmentation with its inevitable accompanying guilt is bound to have an effect. Attempting to subsume a couple of little construct systems is hard work. If you add to these the lack of short-term validation and the effects of sustaining the sometimes large amounts of aggression that need to be directed towards the mother, then there is ample explanation for the exhaustion that overcomes most mothers at some points in these early years.

In a different context, the Individuality Corollary is also relevant. The importance of personal meanings was evident in several different ways. Discussion usually generated a variety of constructions of events, and this encouraged an experimental approach. The results of experimentation were also construed differently by the group members. This was often extremely helpful, but there were times when shared verbal labels initially masked the extent to which personal meanings were at odds.

Discussions of the meanings of different types of work that motherhood involves were also interesting. One mother was able to sweep a floor full of toys to the sides of the room where they would rest like drifting snow while her children created more chaos in the newly cleared spaces. For another, the state of her house symbolised the state of herself. As her family grew in number and demands, so she needed to keep the house increasingly tidy and organised. Contrary to appearances, she felt more capable and confident when her house became more untidy.

There were other times when our early experiences became a focus. A discussion on aggression quickly lead into fear and the unresolved fears that we all experience. For all of us, having children had increased our fearfulness, partly due to fear for our children's lives and safety, partly our need to remain healthy enough to bring up our children and also partly a result of re-experiencing some of our childhood fears. The ease with which the women could, at times, get in touch with their own early fears could determine their ability to help their children reconstrue a frightening experience. The value of story-telling and poetry in offering both alternative constructions and ways of coping was discussed. So too were the differences between the ways that boys and girls experience and act out fear and aggression.

It was extremely difficult to assess how successful I was in achieving the original aims of this experiment. The mothers all found the meetings helpful but could not identify which parts were most useful nor anything in particular that had changed. Some 'problems' were reconstrued from the child's point of view and were no longer problematic. Some women felt more confident knowing that others had the same types of problems. Most mothers increased the range and number of approaches that they had towards different problems. Taking the child's point of view encouraged a respect for our children and their experiences and maybe we were all, for a while at least, rather more tolerant.

I did not set out to teach the women personal construct psychology but tried to maintain a Kellian perspective in my contributions. This was often difficult since although Kelly's ideas make a lot of sense on a theoretical level, they do not always lead easily to solutions to problems. This seems especially true when as a parent you are involved in the experiment or several experiments that your child or children are conducting. It can be extremely difficult to stand back and subsume. For me the experience of participating in the group was extremely useful, interesting and enjoyable, and hopefully in time further groups will evolve.

Children's construing and physical disability
Jenny Maddick

This study arose out of a wish to investigate the self-construing of young people with a physical disability in both special and mainstream school situations to see whether segregation or integration tends to facilitate a more positive self-image. It may be that to construe oneself as valued and having something to offer society one needs an opportunity to mix; alternatively, it could be argued that if society's view of the disabled is a very negative one, to spend one's education to some extent insulated and without having one's constructs invalidated could lead to a more positive self-image in the longer term.

Beail (1978) looked at how adults with a physical disability construed themselves in terms of self-image, ideal self, future self, self without a disability and public attitude to the physically handicapped. He concluded that society had a strong effect on the self-image of the physically handicapped since self, future self, public self-image and public attitude to the physically handicapped were highly correlated. However, he did not look at how non-physically handicapped adults construe themselves or the handicapped so that some of his conclusions, including differences between physically disabled men and women's construing, may need to be reconsidered in the light of this.

The study described looks at the self-construing of young people both with and without a disability. The first stage involved young physically disabled thirteen- to fourteen-year olds in a national residential special school for the physically handicapped and compared their self-construing with that of a similar number of young people of the same age in a comprehensive school. As well as extending the study at a future date to include physically disabled young people integrated into mainstream schools, it is also intended to examine construing at different ages as differences at ten years and sixteen years, for example, would have significance for ages at which integration might be easier to achieve.

The two groups of physically disabled young people in the study were those with very severe physical disability affecting mobility (twenty-one boys and nineteen girls, the majority of whom were in a wheelchair, the remainder only able to walk with extreme difficulty and supporting aids) and thus to society obviously disabled, and a numerically smaller haemophiliac group (n = 5), who clearly have a severe disability which can limit their activities considerably at times but, except during a 'bleed' generally show no outward visible sign of their disability. The experimental groups were matched with similar numbers of boys (n = 20) and girls (n = 19) in mainstream schools with no disability. All pupils were of verbal reasoning ability appropriate to a mainstream, as opposed to slower learning, curriculum.

Three tasks were carried out by the subjects of the study:

1 Using bi-polar constructs previously elicited from groups of physically handicapped and non-handicapped young people together with added constructs relating to attractiveness, independence and aggression, they rated themselves on an eight-point scale with twelve constructs and eight elements, which were as follows: (i) self now, (ii) as adults see me, (iii) as peers see me, (iv) ideal self, (v) future self, (vi) parents' view of future self, (vii) self without a disability and (viii) how the public see the disabled. Non-disabled subjects rated themselves as self in a wheelchair instead of self without a disability.

To try to offset the need to use imposed constructs, subjects were all asked to rank constructs in order of relevance to themselves, but this proved unreliable and subjects found it difficult, often rating in terms of preference rather than relevance. A teacher's rating of pupils was not obtained because of industrial action.

2 A picture sorting task (after Davey's 1983 study looking at preferences of young people in friendships) was used to obtain a measure of dominant constructs and see whether colour, sex or handicap was likely to be a dominant feature for possible discrimination. Subjects were asked to sort pictures containing equal numbers of black and white children, wheelchair-bound and able-bodied boys and girls into two equal piles. One pile was removed and the task repeated, the procedure carried out once more to include the final 'forced choice' of criteria for sorting. The forced-choice situation proved of interest as a number of young people, especially in the group with physical disability, were very reluctant to sort on grounds of colour and, indeed, some initially tried to balance all the characteristics in the first sorting until asked to sort by the specific feature they first noticed.

Many subjects, except those with severe co-ordination problems, were able to do the first task in a group administration. The picture sorting was done individually, which also allowed time for comments on relation to the third task.

3 This task asked pupils to indicate whether or not they felt pupils with a physical disability should be in mainstream school, special school, or, if this depended on certain factors, to indicate what these should be.

The preliminary analyses so far completed suggest the following results:

1 Similarities in self-rating by physically disabled and other young people are more striking than differences, which has implications in considering Beail's findings. A particularly interesting difference, however, was that girls *without* physical disability appeared to have the poorest self-image in terms of intelligence, popularity, attractiveness and other constructs. Boys, both with and without disability, rated themselves as more independent. However, caution is needed in interpreting this result as young people with a disability tend to use the term 'independence' differently in a physically handicapped school where independence is so strongly encouraged. All groups perceived the public as viewing the disabled in very negative terms, but the able-bodied tended to be less negative in terms of intelligence but more inclined to expect depression and dependence. All groups expressed most dissatisfaction with attractiveness (based on looking at differences between self and ideal self). Intelligence and sense of humour were not expected to be factors that change in the future, in general.
2 On the picture-sorting task girls, especially without disability, seem less aware of handicap than boys. Handicap, however, was consistently sorted out first and colour last in all groups.
3 Boys without physical disability were more inclined to think a special school appropriate than other groups, but this was a very small number and the overwhelming majority of all subjects felt that pupils with a physical disability should have a chance to attend mainstream school. Provisos mentioned by non-disabled pupils usually related to risk of teasing as well as more obvious access factors. Only pupils with a disability, in a few cases, mentioned appropriateness of curriculum and possible learning difficulty.

Some of the results relating to the haemophilia group show differences from both the other groups, but the small number involved in this particular group means that further investigation is needed before conclusions can be drawn.

References

Beail, N. (1978). The dimension of self of physically handicapped people: a repertory grid study. Presented to the BPS Social

Psychology Section Annual Conference Nottingham, September 1978.

Davey, A. (1983). *Learning to Be Prejudiced: Growing Up in Multi-ethnic Britain*. London: Edward Arnold.

Kelly, G. A. (1955). *The Psychology of Personal Constructs*. New York: Norton.

Mair, J. M. M. (1977). The community of self. In D. Bannister (ed.), *New Perspectives in Personal Construct Psychology*. London: Academic Press.

Chapter 2

Representing the parent-role construing systems of expert parents

Michael F. Mascolo and James C. Mancuso

Cognitive psychologists working in the area of *problem-solving* have made considerable advances in exploring the knowledge systems of experts in various domains (Larkin, McDermott, Simon and Simon, 1980). The following discourse contains a constructivist analysis, using personal construct theory (Kelly, 1955) as a basic model, of the ways in which the concept of *expert problem-solving* can be used to explore the processes involved in successful parenting. The discussion then turns to a delineation of the ways in which one might use grid technology to test some hypotheses pertaining to the knowledge systems of persons categorized as *expert parents*.

Problem-solving and the functioning of the cognitive system

Substantial progress has been made in exploring the processes by which persons solve problems. A problem-solver must reduce the *discrepancy* between some *representation* of a problem, referred to as the *present state*, and a *goal state* (Newell and Simon, 1972), which produces the feedback input patterns that are compared to the representation. To reduce the discrepancy, it is assumed that the problem-solver must assemble a problem-solving strategy by consulting knowledge, organized in memory, pertaining to the input which defines the situation as a problem.

Kelly's (1955) Fundamental Postulate states, 'a person's

processes are psychologically channelized by the ways in which he anticipates events' (p. 42). Mancuso and Adams-Webber (1982) have proposed that a person's *anticipations* 'are nothing more than the schemata that are assembled to incorporate, integrate, or assimilate incoming information' (p. 14). Thus, to the extent that sensory input presents a discrepancy with one's schemata (representations), which are assembled by consulting knowledge represented in memory pertaining to the knowledge domain at hand, the person as cognitive system becomes physiologically mobilized to reduce the input–representation discrepancy (Mancuso and Hunter, 1983). In this sense, one might think of the resolution of input–representation discrepancies, which are implicated in every psychological act, as basic acts of problem-solving.

The expert problem-solver

Efforts to explore the knowledge systems of expert problem-solvers in various domains have been based on the assumption that experts can engage in more efficient problem-solving than do less expert persons. Chase and Simon (1973) reported evidence consistent with the proposition that the ability to organize chess information into larger and greater numbers of 'chunks' of information facilitates a master chess player's reconstruction (recall) of non-random configurations of chess pieces, relative to the recall skill of less experienced players. Chi, Feltovich and Glaser (1981) found that physics experts categorized physics problems on the basis of the problem's underlying 'deep structure,' that is according to underlying physics principles; novices categorized problems on the basis of their surface structures, that is on the basis of similarity of the literal features of the problems. By analyzing the order in which computer language reserve-words were recalled by expert and novice computer programmers, McKeithen, Reitman, Reuter and Hirtle (1981) found that experts produced recall organizations that were more similar to each other than did intermediate- or novice-level programmers.

One can take these data as indicative that experts share a rich, hierarchically organized, domain-specific knowledge organization which they call upon to solve problems in their area of expertise.

One might suggest that the expert's early categorization of a problem's 'deep structure' automatically (Schneider and Shiffrin, 1977) activates hierarchies of specific procedures that may be applied for problem solution.

The parent as problem-solver

One can readily conceptualize the process of parenting as problem-solving in the domain of parent–child relations. It is assumed that the person adopting the parent role has constructed, over his or her lifetime, a *parent-role construing system*, which specifies the knowledge base which guides the parent's construing of his or her child's response to novelty, arousal reactions, and rule transgressions. To the extent that inputs associated with a child's behavior provide discrepancies from standards (representations) specified by the parent's parent-role construing system, the parent becomes mobilized to reduce the discrepancy (Mancuso and Lehrer, 1985). In so doing, the parent will call upon subordinately embedded structures within his or her parent-role construing system to formulate a *reprimand* strategy to reduce the input–representation discrepancy. Thus one can define 'reprimand' – a major component of the parent's problem-solving activity – as any attempt of person A, upon his having observed person B transgress from person A's construction of an event, to persuade person B to accept person A's construction of the event (Mancuso, 1979; Mancuso and Handin, 1985). The parent's reprimand activities strongly influence the building of the systems of constructions which the child will use as he or she defines his or her roles in relationships with other persons, including persons who attempt to provide growth-inducing stimulation and reprimand.

The metaphor of parent as problem-solver prompts the exploration of the parent-role construing system which a parent might use as he or she construes parenting activity, including attempts to formulate discrepancy-resolving reprimands. More specifically, an investigator might attempt to represent and to quantify the knowledge systems of those parents who might be described as *expert parents.*

Differentiating expert from inexpert parents

Mancuso and his colleagues (Mancuso, 1979; Mancuso and Handin, 1980, 1985; Mancuso and Lehrer, 1986) have explicated a constructivist theory of reprimand. Mancuso (1979) has suggested that one may usefully categorize reprimanding activity along the dimension *relevant–tangential. Relevant* reprimands address the transgressor's constructions of the event and prompt an elaboration of his or her system relative to the transgressive act. By elaboration, we refer to an increase in the differentiation of constructs about the event in a normative direction, and simultaneously, the integration of these constructs with other standards which guide the child's construings. In contrast, *tangential* reprimands induce little elaboration of conceptions about the rule-related event.

To illustrate the proposed dichotomy, consider the following reprimand scenario. Three-year-old Sarah, playing with her two-year-old sister Alice exclaims, 'Alice, you're a jerk!' The mother, Mrs Scalzo, looks up from her reading, orients toward Sarah and admonishes, 'Sarah, we don't use that kind of language in this house! Mind your manners!' Sarah's facial expression conveys a question. Mrs Scalzo continues, 'Imagine how you would feel if Alice said that to you!'

Consider Mrs Scalzo's first strategy, 'we don't. . . .' If one considers the mismatch between Sarah's and her mother's conceptions, one might say that this reprimand was not particularly elaborative for Sarah. However, the mother's second strategy – 'How would you feel if . . .' – prompts Sarah to take the perspective of another and thereby calls upon the basis of the standard, that is of the rule, set by Mrs Scalzo's construings.

From these propositions, it is suggested that a parent's focus on the transgressor's construction system (Kelly's, 1955, Sociality Corollary) represents a major feature distinguishing the construings of the expert parent from those of the inexpert parent. We suggest that the expert parent's focus on the child's construings parallels the expert problem-solver's consideration of the deep structure of problems in his area of expertise. Additionally, the parent's construction of the transgressive act according to its 'deep structure' – the child's construction system – prompts the formation of *relevant* reprimands. Thus, just as the expert problem-solver's deep-structured categorization of problems would cue hierarchies of problem-solving procedures, we suggest that the expert parent's focus on the child's construings cues hierarchies of relevant reprimand procedures. We suggest that the inexpert parent's failure to consider the construings guiding her child's transgressions increases the likelihood that she will 'bootstrap' tangential reprimands by considering only the surface features of the child's transgression (the transgressive act itself).

Accessing the expert parent's construct system: the development of a Parent Role Repertory Analysis technique[1]

Building from the assumptive base described above, Mancuso and Handin (1980, 1983) adapted Kelly's (1955) Role Repertory Grid to access and to represent the organizational properties of parent-role repertories.

To complete the Parent Role Repertory Analysis (ParRep), the participant provides data to fill a 16 × 14 matrix. A statement of parenting practice *belief* stands as the label of each of the sixteen rows of the matrix. Each of the fourteen columns in the matrix is labelled by a description of a parent *role*. The roles and belief statements were constructed to provide stimulus items which might reflect the extent to which a participant's constructions of parenting include constructions about the ways in which the parent might or might not address a child's construction of events. (See the Appendix and the end of this chapter for a sample listing of role and belief descriptions.)

For each of the role descriptions, which are computer-presented serially in a random order, the participant is instructed to try to develop a definite impression of the parent described. Each respondent then judges the extent to which the person filling the role description would agree with each of the sixteen parenting belief statements, which appear serially in a random order with each of the fourteen parent roles. The respondent registers his judgment by pressing the 1, 2, or 3 key to indicate that the displayed role-parent 'Wouldn't believe it at all,' 'Might believe it,' or 'Would believe it completely,' respectively. When a respondent has completed his or her 224 judgments, the resulting 16 × 14 matrix may be subjected to a variety of multidimensional analyses, including (1) a principle components analysis and varimax rotation of components, (2) a cluster analysis (Rosenberg, 1977; Rosenberg and Jones, 1972), and (3) a prototype analysis (Gara and Rosenberg, 1979). As readily available sources provide explications of the ways in which factor analytic (Slater, 1977) and cluster analytic (Shaw, 1980) techniques may be used in the ParRep Analysis, the following section will describe briefly the linkage between PCT and the indices extracted from the prototype analysis.

The prototype analysis

One can readily conceptualize one's construing of parent roles in terms of the process of categorization. In so doing, one can bring PCT into line with a large body of research surrounding the concept of *prototypicality* (Rosch, 1978). A *prototype* refers to the clearest case of category membership. (For example, a *robin* is judged consistently as more prototypical of the category *bird* than is *chicken*.) Rosch and Mervis (1975) have found that prototypical exemplars are judged to share attributes with many other members of the category in question, while sharing attributes with fewer instances of contrasting categories.

To link these concepts to the analysis of the ParRep, one might take the parent roles as events which are to be construed, that is events that are to be categorized. One might take the belief statements as the attributes which may be assigned to each role. One may then ask, 'Which parent roles emerge as prototypical exemplars of various categories of parents?'

The basic output of the prototype analysis is the implication phi (Francis, 1961). The implication phi (adapted from Gara and Rosenberg, 1979) indicates the extent to which an event, in this case a parent role, has been assigned features shared with many other elements of the subset to which it belongs. The parent role which produces a high implicative phi has been assigned a larger percentage of a category's features than other exemplars of the subset, and that role is designated as a prototype.

The EASY parent (see Appendix), for example, could emerge as a prototype in a particular respondent's grid. In that case, the respondent has indicated that the EASY parent holds a larger percentage of the beliefs held by other parents in the cluster in which the EASY parent is located. In short, the EASY parent can be taken as 'more prototypic' of the role class than is any other member of the cluster of roles to which it belongs. (See McDonald and Mancuso, in press, for a more complete description of the ParRep Analysis in conjunction with a case study of a parent-in-training.)

Some validating results of the ParRep Analysis

Several small studies have supported the use of the ParRep Analysis to represent parent-role construing systems. These studies assess relationships between the ParRep structural indices and important parenting practices in reprimanding a transgressor. Although these studies do not specifically involve the use of expert or inexpert parents as participants, the results clearly indicate the utility of the ParRep Analysis for representing the structure of parents' systems. One might even assume that the results of the studies reported below follow from a successful differentiation of participants who had acquired 'more expert' parent role construing systems from those who had acquired 'less expert' systems.

Kanner (1985) asked twenty middle-adolescent-age respondents to complete the ParRep grid. Kanner's participants also responded to Eimer's (1981) interview for analyzing a person's perspective on the functions and purposes of reprimand. Eimer's stage analysis follows from the view that persons in our culture progress through a series of levels during which they call upon different constructions of the purposes and functions of reprimand. In the last stages of this progression, Level II-A, a person can believe that a reprimand will have no effect on forestalling future transgressions unless that reprimand effects change in the transgressor's construction of the situation in which the transgression occurred. Half of Kanner's participants were classed as level II-A status, whereas the remaining participants were classed as Level I-A or I-B.

A prototype analysis showed that independent prototypical roles emerged more clearly from the ParRep grids of the adolescents who used 'more sophisticated' constructions of reprimand (Level II) than from the grids of the 'less sophisticated' participants (Level I). While at least two prototypes emerged from the grids of Level-II respondents, the ParRep grids of Level-I respondents yielded but one prototype (X^2 (1) = 10.76).

Labreque (1985) asked college students who had completed the

ParRep Analysis to discuss in writing a reprimand which would be directed toward a boy who had held up the family's departure for a picnic. Labreque rated the participant's discussions using a rating scale developed by Heerdt (1983). The reprimand rating scale provides an index of the extent to which a participant had formulated a reprimand aimed at the transgressor's guiding construction system. A positive correlation emerged between the number of independent-role prototypes extracted from the ParRep Analysis and the reprimand ratings ($r = 0.31$, $p < 0.001$). These data indicated that a ParRep structural measure which indicates that a participant uses a more sophisticated parent-role construing system can predict the extent to which he or she would endorse a relevant reprimand strategy.

Application of the ParRep Analysis to expert parenting

In extending these findings directly to the domain of expert parenting, we plan simply to compare the findings of ParRep Analysis of parents who have been identified as physically abusing their children and parents known not to abuse their children. We expect that the findings of such a study would converge more directly with the findings of investigations of the systems of experts in other domains.

Specifically, one would expect, following the work of Chase and Simon (1973) that expert parents (the nonabusers) would call upon a richer, more highly integrated knowledge base than would less expert parents (the abusing parents). The structural indices of the ParRep, particularly the prototype analysis, would provide a means for testing this hypothesis. One would expect, among other results, that one could extract a greater number of independent prototypes from the ParRep grids of expert parents than from those of inexpert parents. The greater number of prototypes would allow for an economy of processing in the parenting domain for the expert parents, relative to the inexpert parents, and a greater reliance on relevant rather than tangential reprimands.

One would expect that the expert parent's parent-role construing system would be organized around highly principled, 'deep structure' representations pertaining to parenting roles, rather than around surface features of the parenting roles (as in

Chi, Feltovich and Glaser, 1981). It has been suggested that, in the reprimand context, the parent's framing of a reprimand by considering the construings of the transgressor is indicative of a 'deep structured' understanding of the reprimand process. From this proposition, the expert parent's ParRep grid should provide evidence of differentiation between those parents' role descriptions who are perceived to endorse relevant reprimands from those who are perceived to endorse tangential reprimands. One might expect that role prototypes might emerge from the grids of expert parents which are assigned belief statements indicative of the endorsement of relevant reprimand practices.

Finally, one would expect, following McKeithen, Reitman, Reuter, and Hirtle (1981) that the group of expert parents would share a more similar knowledge structure pertaining to parenting activities than would a group of less expert parents. Shaw (1980) has developed a suite of computer programs which allow facile on-hand analysis of repertory-grid data. Shaw's SOCIOGRIDS and MINUS programs allows an investigator to compare the structural similarity of sets of completed repertory grids. Thus, one could use Shaw's algorithm to compute an index of the extent of intergroup similarity of construing. One could then compare the structural similarity of the expert's ParRep data with that of the inexpert data. A finding of higher intergroup similarity of expert parents over inexpert parents would support the hypothesis that expert parents share a common knowledge structure, while less expert parents construe parent roles in a more idiosyncratic fashion.

Conclusions

In conclusion we must acknowledge a point implicit in much of the discussion. If we set out to assess expert parent-role construing systems, we must believe that we have some idea of the problems which could be solved by that system. That is, we are setting out to assess the system of an expert in the domain of psychological development. As psychologists we should immediately see that we have entered a paradox. We are setting out to assess the expertise of a system pertaining to a domain in which we, as professionals, would want to regard ourselves as experts. Yet, as experts, we continue to equivocate about the parameters which account for effective problem solution in that domain. Could we find ten psychologists who would agree that a particular solution to a child-rearing problem can be regarded as one which came out of an expert system? We know that every proposed solution would be the product of a favored theory. How can we expect to demonstrate the presence of the expert system we are trying to demonstrate?

We speak for ourselves in response to the last question. As indicated, we take the position that a person whose child-rearing practices derive from a constructivist perspective will guide the kinds of psychological development which we would regard as positive. Further, our efforts would proceed from the assumption that a system which allows flexible construction of parent roles will stand as more expert than one that is limited in this respect. Thus we will continue to develop ways to index the structures of persons' role-construing systems.

Appendix

Selected parent-roles descriptions

9 Ruth Kramer is a mother who knows the best thing to do when children get upset. (CALMWELL)

11 Barbara Moore has a child who can't stand being in new situations. Barbara just hasn't helped her child to put up with anything new – new food, new places, new people. Barbara's child really fusses whenever the family tries something different or new. (CH-NOVEL)

13 Joe Hooker is the kind of parent who doesn't always try hard to get his children to do what they are told to do. He's kind of easy on them. (EASY)

14 John Powers is a man who is known to be very fair with his children. John's friends, and all the other kids always say, 'John Powers is fair in whatever he asks his children to do.' (FAIR)

Selected child-rearing belief statements

2 The child who has done something really bad deserves a really hard punishment, and the child who has done something that is not so bad deserves an easier punishment. (PUNFITCR)
4 Whenever a child has done something that a parent doesn't like, talking to the child works better than punishing the child. (TALK-PUN)
11 Punish a child whenever he does not do what he is told to do. (DOWATOLD)
15 When it's time to put a child to bed, do things in the same order each night – like, a bath first, then a snack, then a story – the same order each night. (ROUTINE)

Note

1 A thorough discussion of the ParRep Analysis can be found in Mancuso (in press). Microcomputer versions of the ParRep Analysis are available from James C. Mancuso, Department of Psychology, State University of New York at Albany, 1400 Washington Avenue, Albany, New York.

References

Chase, W. G. and Simon, H. A. (1973). Perception in chess. *Cognitive Psychology* 4, 55–81.

Chi, M. T. H., Feltovich, P. J. and Glaser, R. (1981). Categorization and representation of physics problems by experts and novices. *Cognitive Science* 5, 121–52.

Eimer, B. N. (1981). Children's conceptions of the purposes, outcomes, and styles of reprimand. Unpublished PhD thesis. State University of New York at Albany, Albany, New York.

Francis, R. G. (1961). *The Rhetoric of Science: A Methodological Discussion of the Two by Two Table*. Minneapolis: University of Minnesota Press.

Gara, M. A. and Rosenberg, S. (1979). The identification of persons as supersets and subsets in free response personality

descriptions. *Journal of Personality and Social Psychology* 37, 2167–70.
Heerdt, W. A. (1983). The implicative structure of self-role constructs and the formulation of reprimand that is relevant to the transgressor's construing of the transgressive event. Unpublished doctoral dissertation. State University of New York at Albany, Albany, New York.
Kanner, B. (1985). Adolescent's conceptions of parental reprimand, parenting roles, and child rearing techniques. Unpublished Master's Thesis. State University of New York at Albany, Albany, New York.
Kelly, G. A. (1955). *The Psychology of Personal Constructs.* New York: Norton.
Labreque, M. C. (1985). An examination of various measures of differentiated integration in construction systems. Unpublished paper. State University of New York at Albany, New York.
Larkin, J., McDermott, J., Simon, D., and Simon, H. (1980). Expert and novice performance in solving physics problems. *Science* 208, 1335–42.
McDonald, D. E. and Mancuso, J. C. (in press). A constructivist approach to parent training. In R. A. Neimeyer and G. J. Neimeyer, (eds.), *Casebook in Personal Construct Theory.* New York: Springer Press.
McKeithen, K. B., Reitman, J. S., Reuter, H. H. and Hirtle, S. C. (1981). Knowledge organization and skill differences in computer programmers. *Cognitive Psychology* 13, 307–25.
Mancuso, J. C. (1979). Reprimand: the construing of the rule violator's construct system. In P. Stringer and D. Bannister (eds.), *Constructs of Sociality and Individuality.* New York: Academic Press.
Mancuso, J. C. (in press). Analyzing cognitive structures: an application to parent systems. In J. C. Mancuso and M. L. G. Shaw (eds.), *Cognition and Personal Structure: Computer Access and Analysis.* New York: Praeger Press.
Mancuso, J. C. and Adams-Webber, J. (1982). Anticipation as a constructive process: the fundamental postulate. In J. C. Mancuso and J. Adams-Webber (eds.), *The Construing Person.* New York: Praeger.
Mancuso, J. C. and Handin, K. H. (1980). Training parents to construe the child's construings. In A. W. Landfield and L. M. Leitner (eds.), *Personal Construct Psychology.* New York: Wiley.

Mancuso, J. C. and Handin, K. H. (1983). Prompting parents toward constructivist caregiving practices. In I. E. Sigel and L. M. Laoss (eds.), *Changing Parents*. New York: Plenum Press.

Mancuso, J. C. and Handin, K. H. (1985). Reprimand: Acting on one's implicit theory of behavior change. In I. Sigel (ed.), *Parental Belief Systems*. Hillsdale, NJ: Lawrence Erlbaum Associates.

Mancuso, J. C. and Hunter, K. V. (1983). Anticipation, motivation, or emotion: the fundamental postulate after twenty-five years. In J. R. Adams-Webber and J. C. Mancuso (eds.), *Applications of Personal Construct Theory*. Toronto: Academic Press.

Mancuso, J. C. and Lehrer, R. (1985). Cognitive processes during reactions to rule violation. In R. Ashmore and D. Brodzinsky (eds.). *Thinking about Parenting*. Hillsdale, NJ: Lawrence Erlbaum Associates.

Newell, A. and Simon, H. A. (1972). *Human Problem Solving*. Englewoods Cliffs, NJ: Prentice-Hall.

Rosch, E. (1978). Principles of categorization. In E. Rosch and B. B. Lloyd (eds.), *Cognition and Categorization*. Hillsdale, NJ: Lawrence Erlbaum Associates.

Rosch, E. H. and Mervis, C. B. (1975). Family resemblances: studies in the internal structure of categories. *Cognitive Psychology* 7, 573–605.

Rosenberg, S. (1977). New approaches to analysis of personal constructs in person perception. In A. W. Landfield (ed.), *Nebraska Symposium on Motivation: Personal Construct Psychology*. Lincoln: University of Nebraska Press.

Rosenberg, S. and Jones, R. (1972). A method for investigating and representing a person's implicit theory of personality. *Journal of Personality* 22, 272–86.

Schneider, W. and Shiffrin, R. M. (1977). Controlled and automatic human information processing: I. Detection, search, and attention. *Psychological Review* 84, 1–66.

Shaw, M. L. G. (1980). *On Becoming a Personal Scientist: Interactive Computer Elicitation of Personal Models of the World*. New York: Academic Press.

Slater, P. (ed.) (1977). *The Measurement of Intrapersonal Space by Grid Techniques*. New York: Wiley.

Chapter 3
Self-characterisation: dimensions of meaning

Sharon R. Jackson

Kelly encourages us to ask the troubled person what is wrong, for they may just tell you. In the same spirit, self-characterisation is an invitation to identify ourselves in personally relevant ways.

Kelly suggests that we request a self-characterisation in the following way:

> I want you to write a character sketch of *Harry Brown*, just as if he were the principal character in a play. Write it as it might be written by a friend who knew him very intimately and very sympathetically, perhaps better than anyone ever really could know him. Be sure to write it in the third person. For example start out by saying '*Harry Brown* is . . .' (Kelly 1955)

Kelly uses the term 'character sketch' to emphasise structure rather than detail. The 'third person' calls for a perspective in the character sketch. The wording 'as if' invites the person to do the sketch from an external point of view and again encourages perspective. Being 'intimately' and 'sympathetically' known implies that something more than superficial appearances be covered and that the person consider their self acceptable, avoiding a catalogue of faults, dwelling on 'what is' rather than 'what ought' or 'is not'. Then to avoid it being written as some other actual person would write it, we add, 'perhaps better than anyone ever really could know him or her'.

In presenting this request to children and adolescents Jackson and Bannister have used this rewording:

> Tell me what sort of boy or girl *Sally Jones* is. If you like I will be your secretary and write down what you say. Tell me about yourself as if you were being described by an imaginary friend who knows you and likes you and above all understands you very well. This person would be able to say what your character is and everything about you. Perhaps you could begin with *Sally* is . . . and say something important about yourself. Try to fill this page.

Volunteering to be secretary and wording the characterisation in such a way reduces threat and so enables young persons to describe themselves in personally meaningful ways. The aim is to see 'how persons structure their immediate world and how they see themselves in relation to these structures and the strategies they've developed to handle their world' (Bannister and Fransella, 1971). In analysing the self-characterisation Kelly points us to the credulous approach and says, 'Remember the customer is always right' (Kelly, 1955). This instruction is the first learnt by many junior sales clerks, who quickly realise that it makes for good business. It makes just as good sense to adopt this approach as we seek to understand persons in their own terms in order to play a role in a social process. People working mainly with children often fear they will not gain a 'true' picture of the child from their characterisation. Kelly points out in accordance with constructive alternativism that our present perceptions should be open to question and reconsideration. Obvious events appear different if we construe them differently. If we can understand a child or adult in their own terms, a fear of 'lies' will not be an issue.

An eleven-year-old girl, Tracy, came to paediatric attention because of the 'fits' she was having at school. The school nurse was confused about these as the symptoms were all there but in the wrong order. The paediatrician referred Tracy for psychological investigation and discharged her from hospital. A short while after getting to know Tracy she took a 'fit' in my office. This was construed and dealt with as her attempt to gain readmission to hospital and so avoid the difficulties of both home and school. As part of the work with Tracy she was taken round her new school to familiarise her with the surroundings and routine. As we passed an artwork case she claimed to have made a very professional piece of pottery. Rather than confront the deception it seemed important to see her statement as a longing for creativity just as her 'fits' were a meaningful comment on her experience of school and home. Kelly's ideas were useful; he says we should not be taken in by lies but should strive to make sense both of what persons are trying to say about themselves now as well as what they are striving to become. As with self-characterisation our invitation is for persons to identify themselves in ways relevant to them, and it is these ways which should also be relevant to us.

The Modulation Corollary suggests that we look at the type of constructs used in the characterisation when we come to analyse it for therapeutic use. Kelly stresses to us that we restate the argument in our own terms and that we use professional constructions to view the issues before us. We can scan the character sketch for pre-emptive, propositional and permeable constructs and can apply the constructs of transition (hostility, threat, aggression and so forth) as well as tightness, looseness, range of convenience, the creativity cycle and many more. The Range Corollary suggests we look for what is missing in the characterisation. We can also look at the developmental context to note if the concerns are in line with the context and age of the person. It is also important to check if the person is aware of the interactive cyclic process through which we all gain a usable picture of ourselves and through which we can elaborate our notions of others, as we give and gain varying validation in respect to behavioural experiments.

Three self-characterisations follow, all from twelve-year-old boys, one each from the groups of problem, 'rebel' or 'unorthodox', and normal children. The first is by Gary, who had seen a psychiatrist, was a problem to his teacher, his peers and himself.

Gary

Gary is bad in school. He gets bossed easily. When he is asked a question he can't find the answer in his head. It is rubbish being Gary, life's not worth living.

He is always getting picked on at school by the teachers. He forgot to get his report signed – always forgets about it.

Mum and Dad would call him an idiot cause he doesn't get on at school. He's only got one or two friends.

Gary likes his brother's friend's CB. He likes going on to the farm. He goes up there in October, helps with the tractor and helps out with other stuff. His friend got that CB pinched and he couldn't do now't about it cos they were illegal then, but he's getting a new one, an FM.

He would say that Gary is spoiled. Gary liked watching TV, the only thing he can do.

The second characterisation is by Tom, designated 'rebel' or 'unorthodox'. He had been in trouble, been on probation and was a problem to his teacher. He was not, however, a problem to his peers or to himself. He could predict what other children would say about him and could understand how he was seen by others. He was popular and felt he could understand himself.

Tom

Tom is bad at times. He likes jumping over people's hedges. He likes lighting other people's bonfires. He plays football for the school and for the Rangers and he is bad tempered at the teachers. He likes taking motor bikes to pieces with his brother and riding them. He tells his Mum off if she gets him mad.

Parents say he is bad, fighting all the time, throwing stones and running off. He gets on all right with the man across the street 'cos he learns him about motor bikes and cars. He likes picking locks on people's huts. He broke into a school and got caught in the past and was on probation for a few months. His mates would say he is always fighting them. He likes playing tig. He flies pigeons with his Dad. He likes swinging in the toilets and kicking a football about in the sinks. He usually chases next-door's cat and puts it in a cage with the dog to see who wins. He goes rabbiting. Teachers would say he was bad tempered and always chewing gum. If they tell him to take it out, he argues.

Craig was not a problem to himself, his teacher or his peers.

Craig

Craig likes sports a lot. He is very active. He finds he can learn sports quite easily and new things quite easily like woodwork and crafts. He is quite competitive in sports. Quite a few of his friends are and they think he is as well. He thinks he is quite mentally mature in his head because he understands life and why people do things. Because he is an only-child, he prefers to be with friends and other people, but he can amuse himself when he is alone; for example, going to the cinema.

He would like to be something unusual when he grows up like an astronaut, not an office job, as it would be boring, but whatever job he does, it has to be active as when he's not active he is quite bored. He is keen on comics, for example, Marvel as it gives a bit of people's problems and makes him able to understand people.

One of his qualities is he knows when some others are lying, or what they are going to do. He is interested in people whether they are intelligent or different from him, not that he is super-intelligent himself.

Eight scores were derived from the theory, to score the characterisations for research purposes. The scores for each child with totals are given in Table C3.1. The score allotted to each child is the mean of two judges. Gary, who showed problems all round, scored the lowest with 35; Tom, the 'rebel', scored 45; Craig, who did not have problems, had the highest 'good psychologist' score with 55. These scores are in line with the overall results of the research (Jackson and Bannister, 1985).

Table C3.1 Self characterisation scores

	Gary	Tom	Craig
1 Self-esteem	2	7	10
2 Non-psychological statements	7	9	0
3 Psychological statements	14	18	20
4 Personal history and future	0	1	3
5 Conflict	5	4	0
6 Insight	3	0	1
7 Views of others	2	5	1
8 Psychological cause and effect	2	1	20
Totals	35	45	55
Grid scores			
Problem to teacher	Yes	Yes	No
Problem to peers	Yes	No	No
Problem to self	Yes	No	No
Social agreement	Average	Low	Average
Agreement (own and others view of self)	Poor	Average	Good
Hard to understand (self)	Yes	No	No
Hard to understand (others)	Yes	No	No
Articulation	Poor	Average	Good

1 The Sociality Corollary suggests that we examine the extent to which the views of others are taken into account and dealt with. From this we derive the first score.

Views of others: a count of the number of times the child refers to the view taken of him or her by other people. For example: Gary – 'Mum and Dad would call him an idiot 'cos he doesn't get on at school'; Tom – 'Parents say he is bad, fighting all the time'; Craig – 'they think he is [competitive] as well.'

2 The Experience Corollary suggests we look for the implications of the person's *history* in their characterisation and how far they are construing the past and noting changes in their construction over time.

Personal history and future: a count of the number of times the child refers to his or her past or possible future in psychological terms. For example: Tom – 'He broke into a school in the past and got caught and was on probation'; Craig – 'He would like to be something unusual when he grows up, not an office job, it would be boring but whatever he does, it has to be active.' Score 3 for three separate ideas of what his future should hold. Non-psychological past/future ideas are not counted (e.g. 'I used to live in Barnsley').

3 The Construction Corollary suggests we look at the characterisation for replicated 'themes', that is constructs stated or implied which seem to thread their ways through the characterisation. Kelly says, 'Behaviour is the living interplay of persons with each other and their world which continually recreate new variations in these replicated themes of our experience' (Kelly, 1955).

Psychological cause and effect: a count of the number of times a child makes an assertion of a cause-and-effect kind in psychological terms. Explicit psychological cause-and-effect statements were scored 3, implicit statements scored 1. For example: 'Tom is bad at times. He likes jumping over people's hedges' (implicit, score 1); 'Craig likes sports a lot. He finds he can learn sports quite easily' (implicit, score 1); 'He [Craig] thinks he is quite mentally mature in his head because he understands life and why people do things' (explicit, score 3). A score of 1 is given for children's implicit statements as children's constructions are not always accessible to them, if events have not been construed, yet the connection is clear and they tend to link the ideas together.

4 The Dichotomy Corollary directly suggests that we simply list

the number of constructs given in the characterisation and make some kind of guess as to the unstated contrast poles.

Non-psychological statements score: a count of the number of non-psychological statements. These are often purely behavioural statements, activities or physical descriptions. For example: Tom – 'He plays football for the school'; Gary – 'His friend got that CB pinched'.

5 The Organisation Corollary suggests we look for the level of abstraction at which the self-characterisation is written and try and sort out our superordinate/subordinate constructions.

Psychological statements score: a count of the number of psychological statements of any kind made by the child. Note that if the child listed a series of likes or dislikes in the same sentence which were all on the same topic (school subjects, sport, food, and so forth) the total list was given as a score of one. For example: 'Tom is bad at times'; 'Gary likes watching TV'; Craig – 'He is interested in people whether they are intelligent or different from him'. An example of a list which was scored one, would be, 'he likes running, jumping, climbing and rope swinging in PE'.

6 The Fragmentation Corollary suggests we look for contradictions and inconsistencies in the characterisation and consider ways in which they are resolved, or how they are dealt with by more superordinate constructions, if they are dealt with at all.

Contradictions score: a count of the number of pairs of themes or general assertions which were contradictory in some way. Marked contradiction between two assertions was scored 3, a mild degree of contradiction between two assertions was scored 1. For example: Tom – 'His mates would say he is always fighting them', 'He likes playing tig' (score 1); 'Gary likes watching TV – the only thing he can do' and 'He helps with the tractor and other stuff' (score 3).

7 The Choice Corollary suggests we look for barriers and possibilities inside the characterisation. In other words, what kinds of choices can the person make, and in general are they concerned with extension and definition of life or vice versa.

Insight score: a count of the number of statements reflecting the child's awareness of his or her own shortcomings and resulting problems. For example: 'It is rubbish being Gary, life's not worth living' and 'He's only got one or two friends'; Craig – 'When he's not active, he is quite bored.'

8 Individuality and Commonality corollaries come into play when

we compare one self-characterisation with another rather than simply analysing one single self-characterisation. The process of attaching a self-esteem score implies comparison with others, so we look at what is actually said about the self.

Self-esteem: awareness of claims of competence were given up to five points and another five points for claims of moral virtue, depending on intensity and frequency of statements.

Jackson (1980) and Jackson and Bannister (1985) have argued that construing of self and others is integral and develops in harness. The children in their studies scoring well on the 'elaboration of self' measures derived from self-characterisation, grid and other predictive tests, are called 'good psychologists'. It is from this work that the self-characterisation scores and grid measures were tested out and examined. There is a small but significant group of children who are labelled 'problematic' by their teacher and their peers but who nevertheless, score well on 'good psychologist' measures and are able to predict and construe other children. They can be thought of as 'rebel' or 'unorthodox' children who are confusing but not confused.

There was a significant positive relationship between various self-characterisation measures: taking account of the views of others relates positively to high insight and both go with a high number of psychological cause-and-effect statements. Many of the self-characterisation and grid scores also relate positively; for example, taking account of the views of others goes with high salience of self constructs from grid scores. Those scoring high on personal history and future as well as psychological statements show a higher social agreement on a social dictionary compiled as a table of the average construct relationship scores for constructs on the grid. Those with high insight scores of self-characterisation have more complex structure on the grid, have less residual constructs and the ideal self construct is more salient. Self-esteem relates to popularity and children high in these scores show more social agreement (i.e. they use their constructs in the same way as others), they understand how they are seen (i.e. have higher predictive ability) and they can be predicted by others. They also agree with the views of others, and their past self has low salience and they want to change.

Self-characterisation contributes to our understanding of another's way of making sense of themselves and others. Its use as a clinical tool has been recounted. It radically enhances the picture we gain of a person through the use of the repertory grid, and its dimensions can be tightly defined for research purposes. Like the grid, it embodies the spirit, as well as the letter, of personal construct theory.

References

Bannister, D. and Fransella, F. (1971). Inquiring man: the theory of personal constructs. Penguin: Harmondsworth.

Jackson, S. R. (1980). The development of self-construing in children. Unpublished DACP dissertation, University of Stirling, Scotland.

Jackson, S. R. and Bannister, D. (1985). Growing into self. In D. Bannister (ed.), *Issues and Approaches in Personal Construct Theory.* Academic Press: London.

Kelly, G. A. (1955). *The Psychology of Personal Constructs*, Vols. I and II. Norton: New York.

Chapter 4

A child of four could tell you: a study of identity in the nursery school using situations grids

Anne Edwards

Personal construct psychology and child development

The current focus on the social construction of identity (Yardley and Honess, 1987) has educational implications, as the object of inquiry becomes the system and not the child. Such emphasis may divert the psychologist in teacher education from the pedagogical concern of learning processes.

Personal construct psychology hence has a role to play in refocusing attention on the child. Interpretations of an extension of personal construct theory to the developing child have much in common with the social-interactionist view of child development elaborated by Newson (1974), Schaffer (1977), Trevarthen (1977, 1978) and to some extent by Shotter (1984). Salmon (1970) described Kelly's child as changing as a result of his own efforts to 'grasp the nature of the world' and engaged in a process to 'find out what possibilities life may hold for him'. O'Reilly (1977) advises that we construe children as 'Scientists holding theories about their world which provide ways of acting towards events'.

Salmon's description particularly captures the tension between the individual and social found in Shotter's (1984) image of childhood as the niche 'which a society constructs for the development of its newborns into autonomous members'. Shotter's debt to Mead and social interactionism is clear. However, his allegiance to social constructionism is evident when he elaborates the notion of niche in terms of the 'political distribution of opportunities for development' and explains action in the context of 'localised affordances'. It is at this point that the individual may be seen to disappear under the strength of social determinism.

However, personal construct psychology would exclude such a shift. Mair (1977) suggests 'Kelly invites us . . . to consider self as a personal construction', which is a means by which a person can order his action in the world. This places considerable responsibility on the individual. Holland (1970) makes the point that Kelly, 'the reluctant existentialist', attracts the criticism 'commonly directed at the existentialists – that they put too much responsibility on the individual person'. However, Radley (1978) restates the essential reflexivity in personal construct psychology when he writes, 'when we are engaged in any task, when we commit ourselves in any way, we make changes in the world through our actions, which in turn make changes in us' (p. 125).

This reflexivity with local affordances is inherent in the fundamental postulate of personal construct psychology that a person's psychological processes are channelled by the ways in which events are successively construed. In this way credence is given to the meanings the child imposes.

The ontogeny of the process of mutual imposition of meaning can be explored with equal ease within personal construct psychology and within a social-interactionist, intersubjective, framework. Newson (1974) used the term 'intersubjectivity' to describe a shared understanding of what both partners in an event see as significant in that event. Trevarthen (1977) describes how this develops in terms of a shifting power relationship between mother and infant. Trevarthen's starting point shows commonality with the anticipatory thematics of personal construct theory. Talking of the neonate, he states, 'Any immature organism will show organs in a strange anticipatory state of adaptation, with intrinsic organisation in excess of essential function of that time' (p. 229). For Trevarthen the infant is endowed with 'potentialities for psychological action'.

In the neonatal period, according to Newson (1977), the mother engages in 'as if' behaviour, acting towards the infant 'as if' he or she has intentions, with the result that initially the mother controls the meanings placed on events. Pawlby (1977) supports this observation: 'almost from the time of birth there seems to be a marked tendency for mothers to reflect back . . . certain gestures which occur spontaneously'. Hence, there is maternal control of meanings and appropriate behaviour in the early stages.

However, the relationship experiences a relatively rapid shift during the first few months of life as mother and infant mesh their behaviour and as increasingly the infant's own intentionality enters the joint negotiation of meanings. In personal construct psychology terms the child comes to understand his or her world through 'an infinite number of successive approximations'. A healthy relationship between infant and caregiver easily accommodates such shifts as they are considered part of the 'people making process', a move towards differentiation and the end of symbiosis.

Kelly (1955) uses people making terminology in his discussion of the Commonality Corollary and culture. Cultural similarity between two people is to Kelly a similarity in what 'they perceive is expected of them'. It is this anticipatory nature of personal construct psychology which lends itself so easily to an integration into a social-interactionist understanding of child development, as the potentialities described by Trevarthen are selectively elicited by adults, and adult responses selectively sought by the infant. Additionally, personal construct psychology's commitment to the individual allows exploration of the role of responsible agentic selfhood in the negotiations of identity construction between individual and situation.

Having observed the ease of integration of personal construct psychology and one of the major child development paradigms, one is struck by the dearth of child development data in the personal construct psychology literature. A certain reluctance persists in working below the period of middle childhood because of children's problems with the adult-style methodology, specifically the cognitive and linguistic demands made. There has been a range of studies with children of primary-school age and mentally retarded adolescents (Wooster, 1970; Allison, 1972; Salmon, 1976; Honess, 1978). As a result there is now a common body of knowledge on which to draw when working with children over the age of six years.

Nevertheless, although the use of grids with children no longer presents the completely unknown territory it did when Ravenette began his pioneering work (1964), at the lowest end of the age range with nursery and young infant-school children, unexplored ground still exists. Allison (1972) included seven children in the four-to-seven age range in his study of the development of personal construct systems in children. But the mean ages were 6.5 for the girls and 5.6 for the boys, and the number of four-year-olds was not given. Neither does he describe the specific methods he used at each age. Hence, although the age range of grid experience has been lowered over the last twenty years, any attempt at systematic use of grids with nursery-school age children has little shared experience from which to draw support.

In addition to a narrow concern with adapting an adult methodology for use with children, another weakness has been noted. Salmon (1976) suggested that the full potential of grid methodology with young children was not being exploited as she notes that studies by Brierley (1967), Little (1967) and Allison (1972) were concerned with the categories of constructs used by children at different ages. This tradition was continued by Bannister and Agnew (1976) and has much in common with Applebee's 1975 study.

The Study

In an examination of the construction of personal identity in four-year old children, repertory-grid methodology provided a way of accessing the children's own constructions of their world. Consistent with a social-interactionist perspective on pedagogy was a concern with the tension between the children's personal agency and the expectations held by the school. This necessarily involved an exploration of the child's view of the classroom discourse using grids to explore the children's use of constructs.

Caution in an untried area necessitated extensive pilot work. First, 'self' and 'other' descriptors were collected from local pre-school children. This provided a pool of constructs for use in the final study to supplement those elicited from the study children themselves. There were a series of attempts at grid procedure using pictures as elements. The children coped better with simple line drawings of individuals or single objects than they did with more complex pictures or those comprising several items or action scenarios. Interestingly, they were able to deal with familiar situations as elements without visual signifiers. Simple ranking procedures were soon superseded by a rating response as, consistent with Piagetian theory, the four-year-olds resorted to random guessing as they were unable to focus simultaneously on more than one item. After initial trials of a dichotomous 'yes' and 'no' rating scale, it was decided to include 'sometimes' as a third alternative.

Three grid forms were given trials with local pre-school children before being incorporated into the final study. The first was a simple role grid with four characters, the child and three others as elements. These were represented by simple line drawings chosen by the child from a selection of twenty role cards. The constructs had one elicited pole with an implied negative (e.g. 'cries – does not cry') and were a mixture of supplied constructs common to all the grids, e.g. 'naughty – not naughty', constructs elicited in conversation with each individual child and constructs supplied where necessary from the 'pool' gathered from local children. The grid was used in the final study to ensure that the children understood the procedure.

The second grid was a traditional-situations grid in which the eight situations were those commonly found in the classroom (Table C4.1). This form allowed the exploration of identity constructed within the social-interactionist understanding of self in situation.

Table C4.1 School-situations grid

Grid 2: child NM

	Happy	Fights	Naughty	Another hits me	Laughs	Good at
Sand	2	1	2	1	1	2
Puzzles	2	2	1	1	1	2
Painting	2	2	2	1	2	2
Dressing-up	1	1	2	1	1	1
With my teacher	1	2	1	1	1	1
With lots of children	1	2	1	1	1	1
With a new grown-up	1	2	1	1	2	1
On the bikes	1	2	1	1	2	1

1 = Yes
2 = No

An additional construct, 'good at – not good at', was supplied in this and the third grid. The third grid examined the children's understanding of themselves in the more global situations of school, home and playing out (Table C4.2).

Table C4.2 Global-situations grid

Grid 3: child MC

	Happy	Silly	Naughty	(Others) Pinch me	Good	Cry
School	1	2	2	1	1	2
Home	1	2	2	2	1	2
Playing out	1	1	2	1	1	2

1 = Yes
2 = No

The two situations grids were administered as a game with each child individually. The children gave their 'yes', 'no', 'sometimes', responses to the questions (e.g. 'Is Louise naughty with other children?') by posting a card on which I had sketched a picture of themselves into the opening of a post-box labelled 'yes', 'no' or '?'.

Twenty-eight four-year-olds from two nursery schools were selected for the final study. One school was in an area of extreme socio-economic deprivation with consequent problems of linguistic deprivation among the children. The other was situated in a more enabling environment, but was not without its own difficulties.

Before attempting to elicit constructs in conversation from the target children, I visited each school frequently for six weeks to take group singing and story sessions and to generally become accepted by the children.

The grids were administered over a period of two days. Measures from the grids included a discrimination score on the second (the school situations) grid which indicated their ability to discriminate between classroom situations in their use of constructs (Edwards, 1984). Results indicated that each child used the constructs meaningfully even if he or she could not discriminate between elements; for example, if they were 'good at' dressing-up, they were happy and not cry during that activity. Figure C4.1 shows the linkage analysis using matching scores from the school-situations grids of both a high and a low discriminator.

A more detailed examination of the children's use of the supplied constructs 'good at' and 'naughty' gives insight into the children's perspective on the discourse.

The use of the construct 'good at' accesses children's perceived areas of competence and difficulty within the nursery school. In Figure C4.2 the problem areas indicated by a 'not good at' response are given. There are eight instances of perceived incompetence in cognitive or skills areas and ten instances of difficulty in social interaction with adults and peers. It is only in the area

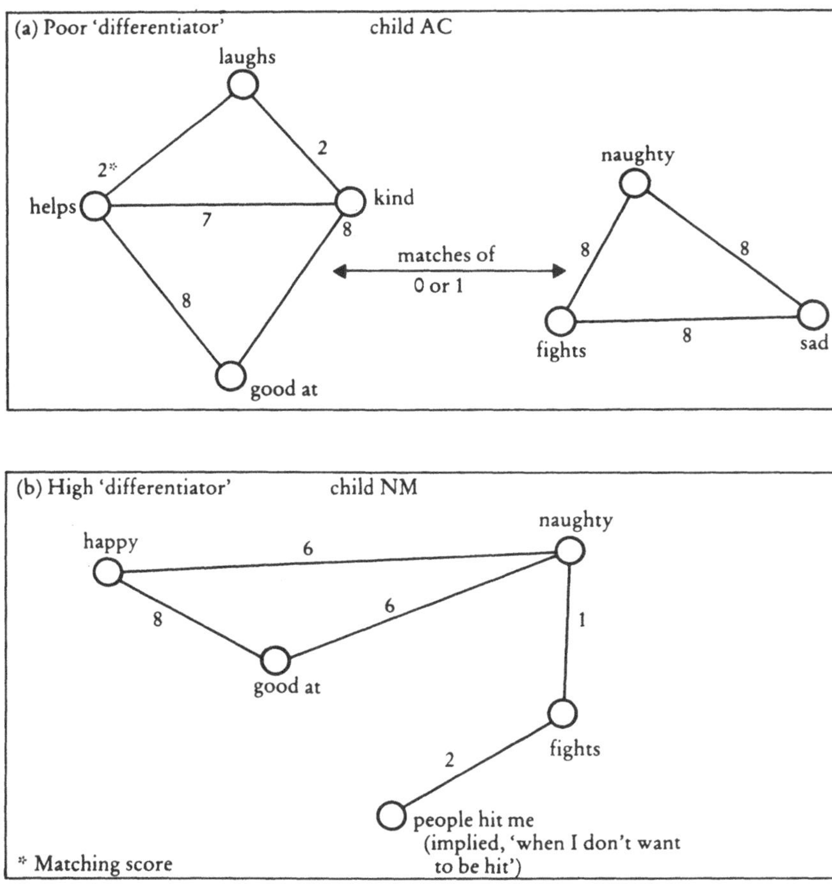

Figure C4.1 Examples of construct clusters using matching scores

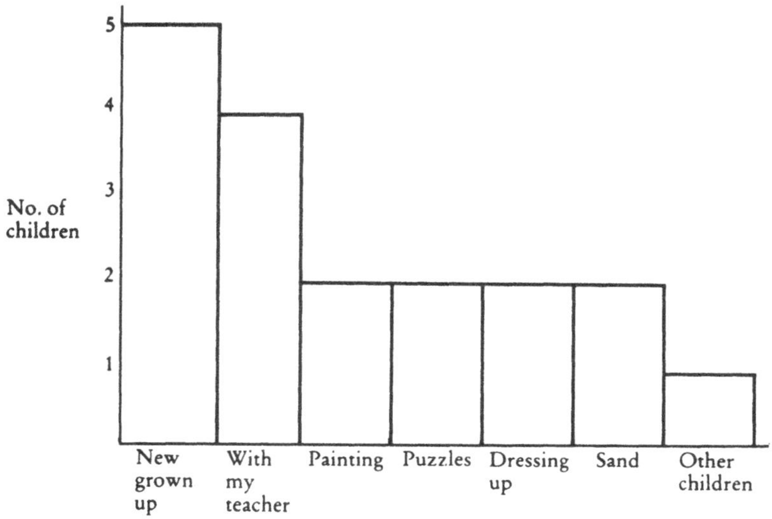

Figure C4.2 Children's own perceived problem areas as shown by responses on 'good at' construct in grid 2

of 'on the bikes' that no perceptions of incompetence appear to occur. However, of particular relevance to the earlier discussion of intersubjectivity and mirroring is that it is interaction with adults which presents the greatest problems to these four-year-olds.

The children's use of 'naughty' in both grids (Table C4.3) suggests that the children do not see themselves as naughty in school but do at home. This is despite quite definite teacher rating to the contrary.

Table C4.3 Children's constructions of themselves as naughty at home and school shown by responses to the supplied construct in grid 3

Construct	At home	At school
Naughty	13	2
Good	15	26

Two boys, David and Nathan, one from each school, said that they were naughty in school on the third (global situations) grid (see Table C4.2). Both stated that they were naughty with their teacher on the school-situations grids (the only children to do so), and 'good at' being with her. These boys also had the highest discrimination scores in their schools, indicating relatively high self-awareness, and most importantly were observed to have particularly close relationships with their teachers.

Although there is no suggestion of direct causality, an examination of these points within the framework of what Taylor (1977) describes as responsible agency may open up the nursery-school discourse to a form of analysis which reveals the patterns of power within it. Observing that in our modern notion of self, responsibility has a strong sense, Taylor notes that 'We think of an agent not only as partly responsible for what he does, for the degree to which he acts in line with his evaluations, but also as responsible in some way for those evaluations' (p. 118). Identity is therefore defined by certain evaluations which are inseparable from ourselves as agents. Without these we would cease to be ourselves, as we would lose the possibility of being a self who evaluates. In construct theory terms we would be unable to make our own interpretation of events.

This view of selfhood has implications for the analysis of the reception-class discourse revealed by Willes (1981). Noting that children learned very rapidly to perform in accord with teacher expectations, Willes argues that far from being a process of effective socialisation beneficial to learning, the discourse secures a dominant position for the teacher and a consequent passive role for the learner. Willes's observation of the process of this early socialisation offers quite novel insights into the construction of a school identity. She explains, 'once the children had settled, the teachers acted "as if" children knew how to behave and respond as pupils'. If teachers did not get an expected and acceptable response, they would interpret a look, a gesture or silence as if it were at least an attempted response, and evaluate it. Hence, we note that teachers hold expectations of responses, impose meanings on gesture and evaluate that meaning. To recall Taylor's model of agency, it appears that in the nursery-school study just described, most of the children were fed inauthentic (not naughty) evaluations of behaviour, designed to keep them powerless vis-à-vis the teacher custodian. Consequently, an inauthentic identity was created in response to these invalid external evaluations. This new identity is dependent on these situation-specific evaluations and, therefore, the teacher. An authentically agentic self, actively and responsibly engaged with the social world in the joint construction of identity, is hence denied to many children within a very short time of entering school as it is blocked by a dependency relationship which is axiomatic to the teacher's custodial role.

To the construct theorist the children are engaged in social roles vis-à-vis the teacher as they search among the implicit rules to effectively construe the other's outlook. However, this social process is not reciprocal, as teachers choose to impose their constructions on the other's.

This relationship is far removed from the shifting balance of power of mother–infant intersubjectivity documented by Trevarthen (1977) and Schaffer (1977) as the school goal is not differentiation but dependency. The inherent paradox is exposed when the outcomes are examined in personal construct theory terms. Kelly (1955) refers to the differentiated self as something that can be used, a datum: 'When the person begins to use himself as a datum informing constructs, exciting things begin to happen. He finds that the constructs he forms operate as rigorous controls on his behaviour' (p. 131). Here Kelly is enthusiastically advocating a responsible agency of the Taylor model in which behaviour is controlled in a process of personal mutual adaptation of individual and niche, the differentiated individual is able to react authentically to the real demands of the situation and becomes responsibly engaged in upholding those theories of selfhood developed in interaction with the social environment. In such a model the teacher's role as custodian becomes redundant.

The major issue here is as much the vulnerability of teachers, as the powerlessness of children. Their weakness originates in the custodial demands made by society and the lack of a commonly accepted pedagogy informing practice with which society's demands may be countered. Similarly, from the sociological perspective, Willes sees both teachers and children locked in sterile learning situations 'from which escape is difficult'. They are in a discourse that perpetuates itself.

The potential of personal construct psychology

Personal construct psychology, with its individual focus, may provide an escape route. Parsons, Graham and Honess (1983) have shown that repertory-grid methodology provides a useful way of working with teachers to deconstruct their expectations of learners. Salmon (1976) has suggested that the method be used to explore the exchange of meanings within education between teacher and pupil. The present study indicates that the methodology may be used with effectiveness to access even young children's perspectives on the discourse. A particular value of personal construct psychology hence lies in its power as a tool in the deconstruction process as a preliminary stage in the construction of a commonly accepted pedagogy. Axiomatic to this process is Kelly's constructive alternativism, by which we assume 'that all of our present interpretations of the Universe are subject to revision or replacement' (Kelly, 1955).

The central concern of this paper is the construction of an inauthentic school identity as the result of what may be described as inaccurate reflection of children's agentic actions. This occurs as the teacher does not merely select desired behaviour for approval and reflection, but returns invalid interpretations of the child's actions to enthrall the child and to perpetuate her power in the only way available to her.

Hence, it is suggested that the alternative constructions may be informed by a theory which redresses the balance of power within the learning situation and restores to the child the right to be an active inquirer in a relationship with others. That such a theory is totally compatible with personal construct psychology has already been argued. That its institution may depend on the processes available within personal construct psychology methodology is now being proposed.

References

Allison, R. (1972). The development of personal construct systems: a preliminary study. Unpublished manuscript. Memorial University, Newfoundland, Canada.

Applebee, A. (1975). Developmental changes in consensus in construing within a specified domain. *British Journal of Psychology* 66, 473–80.

Bannister, D. and Agnew, J. (1976). The child's construing of self. In A. W. Landfield (ed.), *Nebraska Symposium on Motivation*. Lincoln: University of Nebraska Press.

Brierley, D. W. (1967). The use of personality constructs by children of three different ages. Unpublished PhD thesis. University of London.
Edwards, A. (1984). The emergence of self in the pre-school child. Unpublished PhD thesis. Faculty of Education, University College, Cardiff.
Holland, R. (1970). George Kelly: constructive innocent and reluctant existentialist. In D. Bannister (ed.), *Perspectives in Personal Construct Theory*. London: Academic Press.
Honess, T. (1978). A comparison of the implications and repertory grid techniques. *British Journal of Psychology* 69, 305–14.
Kelly, G. (1955). *A Theory of Personality*. New York: Norton.
Little, B. R. (1967). Age and sex differences in the use of psychological, role and physicalistic constructs. Unpublished manuscript, University of Oxford.
Mair, M. M. (1977). The community of self. In D. Bannister (ed.), *New Perspectives in Personal Construct Theory*. London: Academic Press.
Newson, J. (1974). Towards a theory of infant understanding. *Bulletin of the British Psychological Society* 27, 251–7.
Newson, J. (1977). An intersubjective approach to the systematic description of mother–infant interaction. In H. R. Schaffer (ed.), *Studies in Mother-Infant Interaction*. London: Academic Press.
O'Reilly, J. (1977). The interplay between mothers and their children: a construct theory viewpoint. In D. Bannister (ed.), *New Perspectives in Personal Construct Theory*. London: Academic Press.
Parsons, J., Graham, N. and Honess, T. (1983). A teacher's implicit model of how children learn. *British Educational Research Journal* 9, 91–101.
Pawlby, S. (1977). Imitative interaction. In H. R. Schaffer (ed.), *Studies in Mother-Infant Interaction*. London: Academic Press.
Radley, A. (1977). Living on the horizon. In D. Bannister (ed.), *New Perspectives in Personal Construct Theory*. London: Academic Press.
Radley, A. (1978). The opposing self. In F. Fransella (ed.), *Personal Construct Psychology 1977*. London: Academic Press.
Ravenette, A. T. (1964). Some attempts at developing the use of repertory grid techniques in a child guidance clinic. In N. Warren (ed.), *The Theory and Methodology of George Kelly*.

A Report on the Proceedings of a Symposium on Construct Theory and Repertory Grid Methodology held at Brunel University.
Salmon, P. (1970). A psychology of personal growth. In D. Bannister (ed.), *Perspectives in Personal Construct Theory*. London: Academic Press.
Salmon, P. (1976). Grid measures with child subjects. In P. Slater (ed.), *Explorations in Interpersonal Space*, vol. I. London: Wiley.
Schaffer, H. R. (1977). *Mothering*. London: Fontana.
Shotter, J. (1984). *Social Accountability and Selfhood*. Oxford: Blackwell.
Taylor, C. (1977). What is human agency? In T. Mischel (ed.), *The Self: Psychological and Philosophical Issues*. Oxford: Blackwell.
Trevarthen, C. (1977). Descriptive analyses of infant communication Behaviour. In H. R. Schaffer (ed.), *Studies in Mother–Infant Interaction*. London: Academic Press.
Trevarthen, C. (1978). Instincts for human understanding and for cultural co-operation: their development in infancy. In M. Von Cranach *et al.* (eds.), *Human Ethology*. Cambridge: Cambridge University Press.
Willes, M. (1981). Children becoming pupils: a study of discourse in nursery and reception classes. In C. Adelman (ed.), *Uttering Muttering*. London: Grant McIntyre.
Wooster, A. D. (1970). Formation of stable and discrete concepts of personality by normal and mentally retarded boys. *British Journal of Mental Subnormality* 15, 24–8.
Yardley, K. and Honess, T. (eds.) (1987). *Self and Identity: Psycho-Social Perspectives*. London: Wiley.

Chapter 5

Choice and meaning in childhood illness

Auriol Drew

It may seem curious that I should wish to share such an intense and personal experience as the care of my chronically sick daughter, Louisa. But my studying of personal construct psychology at the same time profoundly affected my behaviour in this experience. Tying all together is the underlying theme of love, in particular mother love.

Louisa was born on the 3 January 1981 by emergency caesarian section after a trial of induced labour. Despite the severe pain and shock of the delivery, I experienced a surge of emotion, a mixture of love for another person and affirmation of self, the intensity of which surprised me. It was also the superordinate construct that guided all my subsequent choices and actions.

Louisa's weight at birth was on the tenth centile and her height on the fiftieth. My mildly expressed concern was easily dismissed by reassurance from medical staff as a consequence of her being born two weeks late, her messy stools, the consequence of my drinking too much orange juice. But the disparity between height and weight was not resolved despite my overabundant milk supply and demand feeding – often full feeds every one or two hours. Why did this greedy baby with constant food supply not gain more weight? The answer was that she was probably intended to be lightly built. During this time I grew to know the torture of sleep deprivation, wrestled with the weight of my inescapable responsibility and did not know how to cope with my poor postnatal self-image exacerbated by frequent drenching in excess milk.

In the first six months the bewilderment and fatigue gradually eased and, no matter how close I was to chucking the baby out of the window when feeding yet again in the small hours of the morning, the emotional 'high' (the continued validation of my core construct of 'self as mother') was seldom below the surface for long. But now my concerns gradually increased again. Why was a child so verbally and manually advanced, so clearly interested in everything, not more active physically? I was as keen as the health visitor to extort evidence that nothing was wrong with Louisa. My concern was that her weight started to fall below the tenth centile with the introduction of solids. The health visitor focused on the delay in gross motor development and she put the onus for this on me. Louisa was not crawling because I did not put her down on the floor enough; she was not walking because I did not provide enough motivation; her increasingly demanding and fretful behaviour was Louisa winding me round her little finger. For a while I took on board these suggestions; it was preferable to blame myself than to believe there was anything wrong with Louisa.

When she was nine months old I began to express serious concern. But all the various baby clinic doctors favoured merely recording Louisa's weight and seeing if she gained in a month's time. Her weight was now falling well below the tenth centile. I failed to recognise Kellian hostility in the people involved and repeatedly allowed their reassurance to quieten my anxiety. My anxiety was so great that I can only describe it as 'psychological tinnitus' – Louisa's name thrashed round my head whenever my thoughts were unfocused.

At last, after asking the doctor whether she did not think Louisa looked like one of the starving Biafran children, I was given a *routine* referral to see the paediatrician. I tried to get my general practitioner to bring the interview with the consultant forward but was told that malabsorption problems were rare and that I had been reading too much. By this time Louisa had given up the unequal struggle to eat enough and became very ill. I tried to contact the paediatrician directly without success and went back to the GP. Only then, when it was clear that I had tried to bypass him, I in tears and with my husband in tow, did I get an appointment to see the consultant the next day.

Louisa was eighteen months old on this first admission to hospital. She objected strongly to being examined despite the fact that the doctors and nurses did their utmost to be gentle and to win her cooperation. She appeared to have a pre-verbal construction along the lines that 'having my body examined by strangers is not acceptable and could lead to something nasty'. This was validated by the several sweat tests and a jejunal biopsy. She now cried whenever strangers approached her in a purposeful manner. She never lost a certain wariness and reticence in new company.

I thought that Louisa probably had coeliac disease until the nursing staff accidentally revealed that the other possible diagnosis was cystic fibrosis (CF). Immediately I knew that was what it was. All I knew of this disease was that it led to early death. I knew that Louisa was already dying and one of the doctors confirmed this and the diagnosis a week later. Only then were we given information and only then was any treatment offered.

The prognosis was better than I had thought. Many people with CF were now living into adulthood and Louisa's main advantage was in having clear lungs and having been diagnosed young. I now had grounds to cease grieving Louisa's dying and to hope for, or even expect, Louisa's health to improve, providing we followed the recommended treatment.

Returning home, diagnosis in hand, I received apologies from all those who had failed to recognise Louisa's illness. How frustrated I was that even in their very apology it was clear that no one had understood! They all apologised for not knowing what was wrong. I had never expected that they should be able to put a name to it. All I had asked was that if a child deviates from the norm and the mother expresses concern, she should be taken seriously.

I had tried to establish that I expected straight answers to straight questions, no matter how painful the answers. The pain was my responsibility. It took me a long time to realise that straight answers did not necessarily also convey the amount and depth of information I required. I therefore started to read everything I could lay my hands on. Very briefly, cystic fibrosis is a recessively inherited degenerative disease, which varies considerably between individuals in the severity of its clinical manifestation. All secretions from the exocrine glands are too concentrated; for example, the sweat is too salty and the thick pancreatic secretions block the ducts resulting in the malabsorption of food. The sticky mucus in the lungs leads to a susceptibility to life-threatening chest infrections. CF is still the major inherited cause of death in childhood. But something in the region of 75 per cent now survive until adulthood.

I think it probably takes six months to settle into any new job, and it took me about that to understand fully what it was I needed to grieve over. It was when Louisa was about two years old, and still improving, with her weight easing closer to the tenth centile, that I found little to rejoice over in her reprieve and plumbed the depths of grief and depression, even to the most basic choice: should I live or should I kill myself? My superordinate core construct of 'self as mother' governed this choice. To have killed myself would have entailed not mothering my child, therefore to commit suicide and remain 'mother' I would also have to murder my child. Quite apart from the practical difficulties of achieving this effectively and painlessly, it was apparent how much this dual killing would hurt others I loved. How could I avoid burdening them with such pain and guilt? By murdering them too? Even while still toying with the idea of my own suicide, the tragic farce of what its implications would also make me do, brought the simultaneous knowledge that I would choose life not death.

Another of my superordinate constructs is that I try 'to do things thoroughly'. So, in choosing life, I would utterly live just as surely as death would of necessity be so final. As I climbed out of these depths, I deliberately used the idea of spreading one's dependencies. It was the gradual and increasing dependence on many more people that enabled me to get through later, even more taxing, events.

Choices in management had to be made early on. Should we even embark on the treatment at all? Should I continue to work or not? Should we protect Louisa from contact with infectious children? How should we maintain discipline? It was quite plain that we should treat. Louisa's lungs were comparatively clear; her primary problem of malabsorption was readily responding to enzymes; using treatments more aggressively was proving very effective in other cases; and finally, anticipated advances in research justified at least moderate hope for better prospects.

I am glad I acted on advice to continue working, despite the extra stress entailed. First, I continued to share the care of Louisa with a nanny and maintained relationships with colleagues, thereby facilitating spreading my dependencies. Second, my community of selves could continue to include 'me as speech therapist', carrying with it the opportunity to elaborate a core self construct, the implications of which were enjoyable and without the pain entailed in my other core roles as 'mother' and 'physiotherapist'. Third, it was necessary to focus attention on something other than Louisa, to acknowledge the continuity of other people's lives and my involvement with them, which involvement provided respite and refreshment.

I am also grateful for the emphasis placed by hospital staff on the need to maintain normality in social life and discipline, despite the risks and costs involved. Normal social life meant continuing with playgroups and so on. These enriched Louisa's life and provided her with many friends, and provided me with frequent meetings with people who tolerated me even when I felt I was weighing down the atmosphere like a thunder cloud, and who supported me on my way up out of despair. The risk was heavy. When Louisa caught a cold she was severely affected – requiring several physiotherapy sessions during the night for example. People wondered if I wanted to keep appointments when their children had colds, and I found that I alone had to bear the responsibility for deciding on each occasion whether this was an acceptable risk. Would this be the cold that would kill her? Gradually I realised that it would be the cumulative effect of infection that would be fatal, and not one particular cold. I decided that if a child with a cold would have been sent to playgroup and was not actually sneezing, then I would take the risk. You might be surprised to learn that even this is a controversial way in which to manage CF, and that I shocked a visiting paediatrician who came to lecture our local CF group by the extent to which I involved Louisa in pre-school activities. He thought that it was vital to protect pre-school children with CF from infection and that anyway children do not really need the company of other children until school age!

And what about discipline? I carried on as before, but perhaps already handled this differently from many. Louisa was not a physically explorative baby and never needed the frequent physical restraint that so many children need and which so easily leads to smacking. I had always intended to avoid smacking if possible, preferring to use explanation, reasoning and reward. This was, at least in my view, very effective and I believe contributed to Louisa's elaborate and precocious ability to make inferences and to deduce the implications and consequences of events. I should emphasise that I always had in mind the need for a strong framework of limits to, and expectations of, certain behaviours. My hypothesis that this would be the best way to achieve and maintain discipline, was tested to its limits in relation to Louisa's physiotherapy. You will have to make your own judgment as to whether you would interpret the evidence as validating or invalidating!

Louisa's chest became noticeably worse when she was about three years old, and she began to lose rather than gain weight. The next six months continued to be emotionally gruelling. It was perhaps at this time that I learnt how hard it is to grieve for the unquantifiable, the incomplete, the all-pervading nature of chronic and degenerative illness. I had difficulty obtaining treatment I considered necessary. I knew that the outlook was now much worse. Underneath those rosy cheeks and lively manner, her health was deteriorating faster, but I was unable to convey the reasons for my certainty to those involved in her care. How can you convey a pre-verbal 'knowing' to a level which is not only verbal but also couched in someone else's language? How can you convey it urgently and assertively enough to break through the ever-present barrier of hostility with which people fend off the unacceptable? Ultimately one has to know what to ask for, and in our case I eventually learnt of and asked for a transfer to a regional centre for CF. Louisa was immediately admitted to hospital and given enormous quantities of antibiotics.

During this admission I became more aware of the issues surrounding treatment choices. What means are acceptable to reach the desired end? The end is contaminated by the means. Louisa's medication became the first element under my scrutiny. She had become very adept at taking enzyme tablets rather than the powder available for those not yet able to swallow tablets. It was therefore decided she should have her antibiotics in capsule form and she managed the first dose easily. However, I was not present when the night staff gave the evening and early morning doses in liquid form. This error was prompted by yet another example of pre-emptive construing 'children aged three and a half cannot swallow tablets'. The following morning Louisa was in tears; she had been given 'drinking medicine' and she knew this was wrong. Had it ended there, little harm would have been done. But she now refused all tablets, including the enzymes, for the duration of the twelve days in hospital. My choice was between waiting for Louisa to choose to start taking tablets again, losing essential nutrition all the while, or to force the tablets down her.

I decided against force. Louisa was sent home with a face-saving choice of powder, granules or tablets. At the very first meal she chose granules and never took tablets again.

Louisa's physiotherapy was a prominent feature of this hospital visit, especially so for me in that Louisa objected energetically to the physiotherapists doing it, and in the end it seemed less emotionally exhausting for me to continue to do the therapy rather than hold her down for them. Physiotherapy for CF patients consists of the person lying head down on a wedge-shaped piece of foam, so that gravity aids the drainage of excessive mucus which so predisposes the chest to infection. All sides of the chest are vigorously percussed to loosen the mucus, and older patients then learn to cough deliberately to complete the clearing of the chest. This process must be done for about ten minutes four times a day or, better, for about half an hour twice a day – this would be the absolute minimum. Extra sessions are needed when the person has a cold. One could trade a certain amount of physiotherapy for physical exercise instead, but it is the regular and thorough clearing of the chest which is the key to the enhanced health and life expectancy of people with CF. Therefore throughout the two and a half years she had physiotherapy, Louisa was never allowed to escape the minimum amount – discipline was absolute.

Physiotherapy was started when Louisa was eighteen months old. At first she was reasonably cooperative, although she preferred to play. She appeared to have two relevant pre-verbal constructions, 'playing – not playing' and 'not having therapy – having therapy'. The task was always to persuade Louisa to an alternative construction of physiotherapy, a construction which would enable her to see therapy as desirable, or at least not something to avoid. Alternative constructions were offered, such as 'there are things you can play with on the wedge', 'there are stories, music or conversation you can listen to on the wedge', and so on. Playing was not possible at the level of complexity Louisa desired, and the chest percussing often made it difficult for her to hear the conversation and stories easily. But for two and a half years, listening to music did make physiotherapy more or less acceptable. When this began to fail, a star chart for 'good' behaviour was tried. But it did not really work.

Now, for the first time, I was confronted with outright refusal of cooperation in a procedure that was essential to life. The choice appeared to be either not to do the therapy or to force it upon her. It was not as if I had not used force to some extent before, but it was the necessity to use ever greater strength and on every therapy session that proved so difficult for me. Could I be both 'loving mother' and 'good therapist'? It seemed impossible, but I had to try.

The physiotherapist and I had agreed that if that was the only way to obtain obedience then that was what I would have to do. It is a dangerous road to go down. When smacking for discipline in a state of such frustration, anxiety and fatigue, with the life of one's child at stake if one fails to obtain obedience – the proximity to a situation where one is battering the child to make it live becomes very alarming. Frightened and ashamed at my narrow escapes from the ranks of battering parents, I retreated to review the situation. I decided to continue therapy but to make use of a more elaborate star chart using specific behaviours. Each behaviour was assessed at every therapy session and if good enough was rewarded with a drawing of Louisa's choice on her chart; when a certain number of drawings had been acquired this merited a small surprise present. This system was effective for about three months. I now decided to make the rewards more immediate – a tickle, a 'horse-bite', a back massage or just a cuddle. At first a tickle was her favourite, but as laughing produced coughing, which was ever more uncomfortable, she increasingly disliked it. This revised method achieved a further month's grace.

A week or so before Christmas Louisa was worse and had a high temperature. Should she spend Christmas at home or in hospital? The implicative dilemma seemed to involve a choice between health *or* happiness, as I thought Louisa would judge it. I decided Louisa should spend Christmas at home. Over Christmas Louisa's deteriorating health and vociferous rejection of therapy coincided to raise again the issue of whether the end justified the means.

The pre-verbal construct evidenced by Louisa running away from therapy as a toddler, had been elaborated, modified and raised to ever higher levels of awareness as physiotherapy continued to dominate daily life. Now it had become a constellatory set of highly explicit verbal constructs: 'I don't want therapy', 'get your hands off me', 'don't you do that to me'. To continue would require one person to hold her down and another to do the therapy. Some people take the route. But for me there were too many questions with harsh answers. What meaning would

Louisa have given such force? Would she feel loved? I thought not. Would her health be sufficiently maintained to make it worthwhile? I thought not. The choice was between my now incompatible roles of 'mother' and 'physiotherapist' both highly correlated with love or longevity. If I consider that the meaning she gives to my actions is a lack of love, then this is the reality of our dyad. If she is seen by me as finding love in my actions towards her, then that is the reality for us. In my intimate, perceptive and elaborated knowledge of my child I am entitled to be an important judge of the meaning of the interaction between us.

You have probably realised that we stopped doing physiotherapy. Louisa recovered from the bad period over Christmas and there ensued about three months of comparative normality and health. I was mother not therapist, Louisa was child not patient, and so we could enjoy each other. Louisa was well enough to attend a full term at nursery, totally integrated within the community and able to maintain relationships with her friends.

By Easter Louisa was dying, but she was loved and felt loved and gave love. I knew she was dying when I took her to hospital in great distress. But no, they said, she is not dying; she is hungry, thirsty and possibly also has the blocked bowel to which CF people are prone. It turned out that she was dehydrated and therefore should have a saline drip. Their message was: 'You have an ambivalent attitude towards your daughter continuing to live; you not only expect her to die soon, but you also want her to die and unconsciously you convey this to her because of the intense and close relationship you have with her. Your daughter is merely trying to please you by not drinking. You have not tried hard enough to persuade her to drink.' Because of my belief that she was dying I rejected the idea of a long-term naso-gastric tube. So she had a long-line drip and began to eat more, but there was little change in her drinking.

They now suggested I take a week's holiday. In view of this and under intense pressure, I agreed to a naso-gastric tube. Putting in a naso-gastric tube is daily bread to hospital staff, but it made Louisa cough blood for the first time and it broke my heart.

I went away on holiday and Louisa started to eat and drink. On my return the tube was taken out and Louisa returned home.

The hypothesis that somehow I was the cause of Louisa not drinking appeared validated and my continued insistence that they were being hostile in refusing to allow a physical explanation for the start of the problem was evidence that I myself was being hostile. I refused at any level to allow even the plausibility of the various so-called psychological hypotheses. The cost to me of testing this hypothesis was the possibility of total invalidation of my core construct of 'self as mother'. How could I have been a good mother if, however unwittingly, I caused the near-death by dehydration of my own daughter? As I saw it, no matter how low the level of awareness of my activity, I would hold myself responsible and therefore guilty. I did not at first recognise my own hostility, and would not have done so without the clinical supervision I was having in the course of my studying personal construct psychology. During discussions with my supervisor (Gavin Dunnett) I came to understand why it was that I had felt the closest I had ever been to total personal disintegration. The only solution was to test the hypothesis.

It seemed to me that if it is a psychological problem, then we should deal with it on that basis and involve a professional psychologist. This changed the hypothesis straight away. It was now acknowledged that Louisa seemed to have something wrong with her 'thirst mechanism' and all that was required was that I merely have 'the expectation' that Louisa would drink. I insisted that a psychologist be involved, particularly as it looked as if I was still required to bully Louisa not merely to expect it. The involvement of a clinical psychologist obtained a reprieve for Louisa. She was able to spend two weeks at home without me or anyone else bullying her to drink. Her drinking was better than when she had first gone to hospital dehydrated, but it remained fragile and I knew another crisis was very near. When it came it was another trip in the early hours of the morning. This time there were no arguments about whether or not she was dying. She had heart failure.

During the final week Louisa's continued ability to play, albeit vicariously, and show interest in her surroundings, was always seen as evidence that her death was some way off despite her increasing weakness. The nurses involved in Louisa's last twenty-four hours showed an intuitive and deep empathy and care despite the fact that at a verbal level of awareness they did not think her death was so close.

In conclusion, I have a number of points to make. First, it seems to me that a person's engagement in life should be taken as evidence that dying is well managed, not that their dying is not happening. Second, we should look at what the child's behaviour is telling us. Remembering the difficulty I, an adult, had in being heard, I am confident that many children suffer from being unheard. Effective listening entails listening for the meanings the child gives to its experiences. It makes us think about the choices the child would make, given the power to do so. It leads us to consider the implicative dilemmas *for the child* in the choices we make on their behalf. As a result we might find better ways of helping children to construe their experience in alternative ways.

Third, both parents and professionals need to be more aware that *any* course of action is a *choice* of action. In particular, standard medical practice in any situation is a choice. In terms of Kelly's CPC cycle, just because one particular dimension is routinely pre-empted, does not mean that it is also innately right for all time and for all people. Greater awareness that any treatment choice is the final stage in a CPC cycle gives one greater freedom for fresh circumspection. Difficulties arise when people trying to agree on a treatment choice differ in the extent and depth of their circumspection, as happened with me. Following routine practice condenses the circumspection phase with the risk that one will make inappropriate decisions.

Fourth, there should be an awareness of the need for reflexivity. Pre-emptive construing and hostility in professional staff can have very serious consequences which threaten the life and mental health of the very people supposedly being helped. Reflexivity is needed in facing the issues arising in the face of death. These issues hurt us more when we consider them in terms of children dying, so there is a strong temptation to avoid thinking about them.

I feel now as I felt at the start, that if we see the child's best interests as paramount, then the only superordinate construct possible is that of love. For me, a child's feeling of pleasure in living, of goodness in being here is more important than 'mere preservation'. The care of children with CF ultimately forces one to choose between preservation and the child's sense of pleasure and goodness in being alive. If the latter is chosen, one has to develop a further elaboration of the construct 'love'. When children are dying or likely to die, do we love them enough to let them go?

D

Clinical

Chapter 1

Construction of psychological disorders as invalidation of self-knowledge

G. G. Gardner, F. Mancini and A. Semerari

In this paper we intend to discuss a particular psychopathological model that we have observed in a number of our neurotic patients. Our observations basically emerged from the following questions. How does the patient interpret his/her own disturbance? What conclusions does he draw and what predictions does he make about himself and his life when he interprets and takes into consideration his own symptoms?

Therefore, it is of greater importance to see how (i.e. from what point of view) the patient considers the problem a real problem rather than to establish which existential problems and which set of constructs in transition the problem in question corresponds to. It is worth noting that most of the patients did not seem to attribute reassuring, neutral or pacifying meanings to their own disturbances. Almost all of them said they were very worried, anxious and dejected about their own symptomatology. However, these simple, common and frequent facts cannot be overlooked simply by saying that a person feels dejected and anxious when he spends hours a day washing his hands or never goes out alone. Rather from a constructivist point of view, these facts should be interpreted bearing in mind how the person constructs them; if the construction is accompanied by threat or guilt, it would very likely mean that we were up against a transitional state of the patient's central constructs.

In our research on how patients, mostly neurotic ones, interpreted the symptom, we have observed the following:

1 The disturbance was related to how he applied his vision of self, i.e. the interpretation of the disturbance came about not only

on the basis of his knowledge in medicine or psychology, for example, but also through the constructs which channelize the maintenance of the subject's identity, i.e. his central constructs.

2 At least some of the central constructs of the patients were invalidated by the disturbance. Therefore, the disturbance was incongruous with the vision of self, not because the construction of self was not applicable, but because the construction had been invalidated.

3 The symptom was interpreted from the central constructions which the disturbance was attributed to and the symptom invalidated these constructions even further.

We intend to discuss the following thesis: the disturbance comes from the invalidation of some central constructs, but the disturbance in turn can cause a further invalidation of the constructs themselves: this vicious circle coexists with structures that are poorly articulated and this poor articulation makes it more difficult to change.

Using a clinical case, we will develop our thesis by attempting to answer the following questions:

1 What role does this vicious circle play in the genesis and maintenance of suffering?

2 To what point can this model be generalized? What are the phenomenological characteristics which make us suspect the presence of a vicious circle and which can be explained by it?

3 Can the knowledge of this mechanism supply useful information for selecting the therapeutic aim?

Clinical case

To better demonstrate our thesis we will present a clinical case and the relative procedure for reconstructing the personal meanings system.

The patient was a forty-year-old housewife who had been married for eighteen years and had three children. For fifteen years she had been suffering from an obsessive symptomatology essentially consisting in extremely complex, invasive and extenuating rituals which she carried out when she thought she had directly or indirectly caused harm to someone else. For example, if by chance she slightly cut her finger, she bandaged her hand very meticulously, disinfected everything she happened to touch dozens of times and avoided direct contact between her bandaged finger and objects; the reason for this was that her husband had caught hepatitis several years before and since she had heard about healthy carriers of the disease, she was afraid of transmitting the virus through drops of blood from her finger. This entire ritual, as in many other analogous ones, was to assure her that God would not accuse her of hurting others. She believed that God's severity was both obstinate and unpredictable. Her symptomatology wavered; periods of rather tolerable discomfort which lasted from ten to forty-five days were followed by longer periods of extremely intense suffering. She usually got worse abruptly, like a downpour coming over her, while her improvements were slow and gradual.

Schematically, the basis of her symptomatology was her fear of harming someone else's health and thus her ritual was an attempt to be absolutely sure that her fears did not materialize. Often intense emotional reactions of anxiety and depression accompanied her rituals.

Therefore, we asked ourselves the following questions:

1 Why was the patient afraid of causing harm to someone else?
2 Why did she try to exorcize her fears with rituals?
3 Which personal meanings did she attribute to the disturbance?
4 Why did she get worse so abruptly; that is, what events were likely to bring on the symptomatology and why did the symptomatology get progressively worse and worse?

To answer the first question, we followed a laddering type of procedure which, as we have already mentioned, demonstrated that if she did harm to someone, God would be displeased with her and would condemn her for eternity when she dies. She took precautions in order to eliminate any possible risk and she did not even consider the dimensions or the likelihood of the risk itself; her precautions were an attempt at being an extremely scrupulous and careful person.

To study this aspect, which is closely connected to self knowledge, we used a rating grid. We elicited fifteen constructs using triads of various people that the subject knew, but we were careful to present the element 'how I am' in each set of three.

The elicited constructs were grouped in two clusters: one around the construct 'scrupulous – couldn't-care-less attitude' and the other 'diplomatic – self-confident'. Starting from these two constructs, we tried to go back to the superordinate structures using the laddering procedure.

The patient had a great deal of difficulty responding when we asked why she preferred to be 'scrupulous' rather that assuming an 'I-couldn't-care-less attitude', and she spontaneously resorted to images and memories from the past. We found this difficulty particularly interesting because her answer indicated that she had a low level of awareness regarding the constructs because these constructs practically represented the boundaries of her cognitive abilities.

However, the patient responded that ever since she was small she had always attached great importance to being scrupulous because she wanted to excel at school so that people would say she was clever, which meant avoiding her father's displeasure. At this point, since the father and the husband were considered to be similar on the grid, we asked whether it was important for her to avoid her husband's displeasure. When she answered that it was, we asked her why. She responded that if she avoided displeasing her husband, it meant that the marriage was 'successful', and if she did not, it meant 'separation'.

It was not possible to go any further here because she could not even imagine how her life might be if she were separated, and therefore she could not even express from what point of view a 'successful marriage' was preferable. The breaking of this bond probably went beyond the patient's ability of looking ahead: her own meanings sank into the unknown.

The laddering procedure, starting from the 'diplomatic – self-confident' construct again led to the 'avoid displeasing the husband – displeasing' construct. At this point it is obvious how the fear of harming others and the rituals shared a common origin: avoid displeasing an authority figure who is severe or adverse (God, father, husband). In particular, displeasing her husband was negative because it was a strong threat in the Kellian sense. However, all of this did not explain certain facts: the symptomatology, after all, could be seen as an attempt (by being scrupulous) to solve a problem (displeasing a particular meaningful figure). Her attempt at being scrupulous often failed, which is evident if we take into account that she intended to reach a total scrupulosity – that is, the absolute certainty and not just a likelihood of not harming anyone.

Then why was the patient so dramatically distressed when she attempted to put these ritual solutions into practice instead of feeling distressed when these attempts failed? This is what happened, particularly when she worsened, and it explains a great deal of her dramatic suffering in those moments. It was precisely when she got worse that there was a parallel increase of rituals and suffering which occurred when she realized that she was performing them; in addition, the more she washed her hands, the more she despaired about doing it, and the more she despaired, the more she washed her hands.

How did the patient interpret her own disturbance, what did it mean to her? To answer this question, we used the laddering procedure once again and we asked the patient from what point of view and for what reasons she thought it was better not to perform these rituals instead of continuing the symptomatology.

Once again she answered that her husband showed signs of being very displeased every time he caught her performing one of her rituals. Therefore, substantially in order to save herself from the threat inherent in her prediction of breaking the bond, she tried to avoid her husband's displeasure by trying to be diplomatic; when this failed she tried to be very conscientious and scrupulous. However, this brought out the problem of her husband's displeasure one again. This vicious circle explained why the worsening of her condition was so dramatic. In fact, the typical sequence went like this: when the woman interpreted an event as a sign of the displeasure of some particularly meaningful person, her obsessive symptomatology was accentuated and this brought forth the possibility more and more that she would annoy her husband.

Afterwards, the patient realized, step by step and with great effort, that the relationship was not about to fall apart, so she was able to calm herself down. However, over the years her construction of self and her relationships had dwindled down to the point where her whole life revolved around the problem of how to avoid displeasing people that were important to her, by being scrupulous or diplomatic.

The relationship between the vicious circle and the genesis and maintenance of the disturbance

We believe that an invalidation arising from the construction of one's own disturbance is not always necessary to the genesis of suffering; on the other hand, we can intuit that vicious circles are a kind of amplification of the suffering which reach borderline cases where the main, most frequent and important invalidation derives from how a person constructs his own suffering.

Similar things can happen to patients whose problems revolve around the fear of losing control. It is worth giving a brief example on this subject. A twenty-three-year-old young man presented crises with very intense anxiety and moments of acute depression. It all began at the end of the summer when he returned from a vacation that he had spent with friends, and for the first time he was in Rome alone, without his parents or closest friends. During that period he realized that sooner or later his parents would die and he would no longer have their protection. This prediction provoked his first crisis of anxiety. These anxious symptoms worried him even more because he interpreted them as signs of his intrinsic weakness of character; in turn, this idea made him imagine that he could lose his self-control, go crazy or encounter terrible difficulties when he no longer had his parents' protection and control. In this case, the vicious circle revolved around the idea of being weak, without self-control and in need of external protection and control.

A few months after this symptomatology had begun, he started therapy and he was so taken up with his vicious circle that he admitted being very worried, and if we asked him why, he answered that the fact that he worried, worried him. The main threat was feeling threatened. The vicious circle was not necessarily related to external events.

In our opinion the vicious-circle mechanism can explain another rather frequent phenomenon – that is, feeling dramatically and suddenly worse not because of external events which invalidate the personal construct system. For example, for depressed patients the beginning of a depressive episode and a rapid worsening of the symptomatology can be explained by the fact that actually seeing themselves depressed triggers off catastrophic predictions which go hand in hand with emotions that confirm the catastrophic predictions. As a depressed patient once said, 'My feeling listless and dejected is proof of my inefficiency'.

For this patient many of the depressive episodes began with feeling very tired for rather trivial reasons, and this was accompanied by a gradual change from 'efficiency to inefficiency', and the the vicious circle went into action; within a few days, she actually was in a dramatic situation.

The role of this mechanism is more meaningful as far as the maintenance and not the genesis of suffering is concerned

In previous papers (Mancini, Chiari and Gardner, 1980; Mancini, Sassaroli and Semerari, 1981), we have discussed the importance not only of asking why people feel bad but also why they continue to feel bad, why change does not come about. If it is true that many patients, particularly neurotic patients, suffer from existential problems which are basically similar to those of many other people, why do they have such great difficulty in solving or overcoming them? If it is true that everyone can have an invalidation of central constructs, for example mourning, why do certain people stay in the same state of transition for years and years? On the other hand, these are psychological disorders: 'any construction which is used repeatedly in spite of consistent invalidation' (Kelly, 1955, p. 831). In this definition Kelly makes it clear that the system's lack of revision is more important than its invalidation or than a state of transition. A revision process or overcoming the state of transition are particularly difficult and unliked if there are not any alternative constructions. It is quite difficult to question one's own point of view if it is the only way one has to channelize one's own experiences. Likewise it is evident that if there are few alternative constructions, it is more likely that a vicious circle sets in.

If one does not have alternatives to the constructions in transition, the symptom will be interpreted by the same constructs. A vicious circle means poorly articulated structure with few alternative viewpoints. The presence of a vicious circle can make us think that the structure is not articulated, that is up to the point of making changes difficult.

Can the constant reverberation of invalidation due to the vicious circle make the structure even more poorly articulated? In our opinion not only does a lack of alternative viewpoints help vicious circles set in but also they can make the structure even more poor in alternative constructions.

If we take the example of the obsessive patient into account, we can draw attention to the fact that the rituals took the form of an invalidation of the pole 'avoid displeasing my husband' and simultaneously a validation of the opposite pole, 'displease'; the former was preferable because it kept the marriage together, which in turn was preferable because of its forecasting ability (it was the pillar of the patient's existence), the latter was not desirable because it implied a separation which was not preferable given the impoverishment of her ability to foresee (the patient said, 'I can't begin to imagine how life would be with a broken family due to a separation').

It should be pointed out that the symptom arose from the threat of separation, and separation was suggested once again by the symptom. Above all, it should be stressed that the application of the construct 'avoid displeasing – displease' or the problem of displeasing the husband were continually confirmed and reproposed by the symptomatology. The symptom was a threat, but it also confirmed that it was possible to apply a part of the system. Bearing in mind the particular role of the symptom, we will now attempt to analyze how the vicious circle contributes to the loss of alternative constructions.

From the Choice Corollary we note that human beings tend to choose and develop the part of the system that they consider more promising for the expansion of their ability to predict. Since the symptom repeatedly confirms that a part of the system can be applied, it becomes the patient's way of trying to increase his own power of forecasting, to the detriment of other alternatives.

The Choice Corollary tells us that the development of the system comes about as an attempt to increase the power of predicting, that is that people choose and therefore articulate those points of view that are more promising as far as forecasting is concerned.

On the one hand, in the vicious circle, the symptom elicits a construct; that is, the person continually faces a situation (the symptom) where it is useful for him to apply the construct. On the other hand, the symptom is an invalidation of one of the poles of the construct itself, the preferred one since it implies greater forecasting abilities. Precisely in this way the symptom is a new problem and the invalidated construct is problematic. So a subsystem is selected which is useful because it can be applied profitably to reality; however, at the same time it takes on the form of a threat. For the Choice Corollary the person has no motive for eliminating a subsystem that has given him the explanation for many events and that he is able to apply so frequently to reality; as a matter of fact, for these very reasons the subsystem will be chosen and further articulated, to the detriment of other subsystems, even if its application to reality creates a continuous threat and therefore suffering.

In the case of the woman patient, the symptom continually represented the problem of displeasing her husband, and her attention and interest were continually concentrated on this problem.

Thanks to the vicious circle between the problem of the husband's displeasure and her rituals, the patient became more and more specialized as time went on in preventing and handling her husband's eventual bad moods by using diplomatic and scrupulous behavior; but she had more and more overlooked problems which were useful for maintaining the marriage: progressively, she had stopped considering other aspects of her husband and their relationship, such as her interest in her husband or the affection he felt toward her, his involvement in bringing up their children, his possible worries about his job, her health or her obsessive rituals.

As far as the relationship between the vicious circle and the maintenance of suffering is concerned, the following conclusions seem possible:

1 A vicious circle starts more easily in poorly articulated structures, that is with few alternative viewpoints, making change more difficult.
2 The vicious circle contributes to the selection of a limited number of viewpoints with an implicit loss of alternatives.

How the model can be applied

Can the model suggested be applied to all patients or only to certain ones? And, what characteristics do these patients have?

In our opinion the model is applicable to subjects who, while considering the symptom (or the problem in question) as 'issuing from his person' (Wright, 1970), cannot give explanations for it nor modify it and it is dramatically undesirable for them. The more a person cites a problem that he acknowledges as his own but that he cannot explain satisfactorily even though he has made numerous attempts, that he cannot solve alone and he experiences it very dramatically, the more suited the model is as an explanation of his suffering.

Everyone experiences states of transition, even in central constructs during life, for example mourning. However, not everyone considers his own states of transition or their manifestations as something unexplainable, unalterable or highly undesirable.

In our opinion the basis of existential problems in neurotic disturbances are similar to the basis of many people's suffering. The sufferings of many neurotic patients have still other characteristics: to the patient it seems unexplainable and difficult to modify and he or she sees it in turn as a source of further suffering.

These three characteristics can be explained on the basis of the mechanism described above. The fact that the experience of transition or its manifestations in turn constitute an invalidation of the same constructs that are already in transition, is precisely the starting point of our discussion; therefore, it is unnecessary to re-examine the question. Rather, let's consider the fact that the problem cannot be explained; that is, in what sense do we think the symptom is unexplainable for the person? To find an answer, let's turn the question around: in what sense and under what conditions can we say that the symptom is explainable?

In our opinion a disturbance can be explained when the context of the existential problems where it goes into effect, is taken into account. It is necessary to have a viewpoint that makes it possible to simultaneously consider both the symptom and the personal meaning system where the disturbance fits in.

All of this is valid for the psychotherapist and for the patient, with a further consideration for the latter: the explanation must be integrated in the patient's system of central constructs. It must not be an academic explanation.

We have already established that a vicious-circle mechanism is accompanied by poorly articulated structures, that is with few constructions which act as alternatives to the invalidation that creates the symptom: a situation that does not satisfy the conditions because it activates an explanation of the symptom. In fact, there is no viewpoint that allows us to consider simultaneously the symptom and the framework of personal meanings where it is put into effect. Instead, the inevitably partial attempts to explain will be understood on the basis of these viewpoints, which should be included in the explanation.

If the explicandum is the symptom and the explicans is the personal meaning system, there must be a viewpoint from which we can complete the explanation. This will not be possible if the explicans coincides with the viewpoint from which an explanation is attempted, and that is what happens in a poorly articulated structure.

A widely accepted opinion in psychological common sense is that the roots of the symptomatology are unconscious because the patient has precise reasons for ignoring them. Such positions are no longer valid or in any case are superfluous if we bear in mind the mechanism mentioned above, and in particular the poorly articulated structure which accompanies it. In our opinion it is not necessary to think of a particular, specific, advantageous tendency to repress. Instead, the difficulty that many patients have in tracing the symptom back to their own personal meaning system comes from the fact that their attempts to understand are fulfilled on the basis of invalidated constructs, while an explanation should take into consideration precisely these invalidated constructs. However, the explanations a patient tries to give, even if they are unsatisfactory, are not useless and irrelevant rationalizations; a careful analysis can help us to focus in on the field of constructs in transition.

As far as the impossibility of changing is concerned, it should be pointed out that almost all patients report that attempts to modify usually fail, and as Watzlawick, Weakland and Fish (1974) asserts, are paradoxical. In a poorly articulated structure not only the attempts to explain but also the attempts to solve will paradoxically reproduce the logic of the invalidated constructions.

The lack of alternative viewpoints can account for the impossibility of modifying the symptomatology just as it can account for the impossibility of explaining it. It is a common opinion in psychology that the symptomatology is maintained in the course of time because it presents great advantages. We do not think it is necessary to postulate the advantages of a symptomatology to

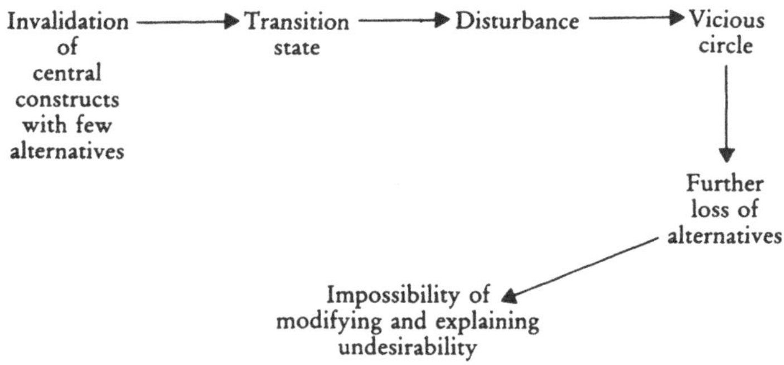

explain why it is maintained. On the other hand, this opinion contrasts with the recognition of patients' considerable suffering. Neither is it necessary to apply the idea of the symptom as the solution of a conflict between advantages and disadvantages. Instead, the absence of change can be explained by the lack of alternative construction: the attempts to solve fail because they re-present the logic of the problems which they try to solve, and they will go on failing until alternatives are constructed. Since patients' states of transition concern central constructs (i.e. the pillars of their existence), and since there are few alternatives available from the start, it is easy to understand that coming up with an *ex novo* alternative is not an easy or simple operation.

Psychotherapeutic aspects

In psychotherapy there is the important problem of defining the exactly right breadth of the intervention. We consider Bannister's (1984) question crucial: 'At what level of abstraction do we need to define the patient's problem?'

> One of the most worrisome things about psychotherapeutic literature is how arbitrarily problems are established at one level of abstraction or another as if it did not make much difference in the evaluation of results how the problems are presented in a broad or narrow sense. (Bannister, 1984, p. 255)

The vicious circle offers useful suggestions for solving this problem. In fact, it allows us to define the aims of the intervention avoiding both the constructs that are too superordinate as well as the too particularized and limited ones, choosing constructs of intermediate abstraction: those where the vicious circle closes (or the more abstract ones).

In the case of the obsessive patient in our example, the best intervention was to try to enlarge the alternative modalities used for avoiding displeasing her husband which are, however, useful for maintaining the marriage. Basically, we could think of two other aims: one consistent with the revision of the more abstract constructs – for example, broadening the patient's ability to predict a hypothetical separation – and the other made up of more subordinated constructs – for example, making the person find different ways, other than being diplomatic or scrupulous, which are useful in avoiding displeasing the husband. The first aims would certainly be sufficient: in fact, the threat inherent to the poor ability of predicting on behalf of the 'separation' pole, would crumble; however, there would be remarkable difficulty because an extremely superordinate and central construct, which is one of the cornerstones of the patient's vision of self and of life, would be questioned. We made this attempt, but simply asking the woman to think about the possibility of a separation or to put her sentimental bond with her husband in second place provoked an intense feeling of threat and notable resistance. The second aim would have been less threatening but partial and substantially irrelevant. In fact, for all the alternatives to being scrupulous that we could have found, it is difficult to imagine that they would always have been effective in avoiding the husband's displeasure. Therefore, sooner or later she would have gone back to being scrupulous again, the vicious circle would have been re-presented and then the invalidation would begin to reverberate.

We chose the following therapeutic strategy: first of all, we gave up discussing the importance, the centrality and the uniqueness of the construct 'maintain the marriage – separation', which we accepted as the frame of reference. Within these limits, we tried to explore other aspects of a marital relationship together with the patient so that the woman began, step by step, to discover that her husband was not just a divinity that she had to continually calm down but also that he was a person who ought to be involved in bringing up their children, someone who was at times weak and needed help, someone who was interested in her and considered their relationship fundamental and that he would have a lot of trouble leaving her even if he was unhappy.

To explain the positive outcome of the invention, it is necessary to discuss the therapeutic relationship, Our patient's vicious circle did not include the therapist, as happens in many cases. The therapeutic relationship was outside of the paradox. Evidently, other constructs were present that the patient could use to channelize her relationship with the psychiatrist, even if they were not as central as those in the vicious circle. After an opening period of general distrust, the woman established that the therapist was an admirable person because he was honest, interested and, above all, he respected the fact that she was religious even though he was an atheist. Having established these points, the therapeutic relationship was a good base for the revision of constructs without risking further paradoxes; for example, the problem of having to avoid the psychiatrist's displeasure never arose.

References

Bannister, D. (1984). Il cambiamento psicoterapeutico dal punto di vista della Teoria dei Costrutti Personali. G. Chiari and M. L. Nuzzo (eds.), *Crescita e Cambiamento della conoscenza individuale*. Franco Angeli: Milano.

Kelly, G. A. (1955). *Personal Construct Psychology*. Norton: New York.

Mancini, F., Sassaroli, S. and Semerari, A. (1980). Problem solving e organizzazione cognitiva in psicoterapia. *Arch. di Psicologia, Neurologia e Psichiatria* 41(2), pp. 194–215.

Mancini, F., Chiari, G. and Gardner, G. (1981). Un modello della psicoterapia come problem solving. In V. F. Guidano and M. A. Reda (eds.), *Cognitivismo e psicoterapia* Franco Angeli: Milano.

Watzlawick, P., Weakland, J. H. and Fish, R. (1974). *Change*. Astrolabio: Roma.

Wright, K. J. (1970). Exploring the uniquess of common complaints. *British Journal of Medical Psychology* 43, 227–32.

Chapter 2

PCT interpretation of sexual involvement with children

Li Chin-Keung

Introduction

Adult–child sexual contact is a sensitive research topic because it is a highly emotive social issue. A glance at the tabloid headlines on sexual offences involving children is sufficient to make us aware of this. Some people are keen to eliminate all possibilities of sexual contact between adults and children, and their viewpoints have found support in a Private Member's Bill introduced to Parliament in June 1984.[1] Under great pressure from the police and the court, paedophile organisations in Britain have virtually ceased to exist.[2]

In recent years, writings on paedophilia, incest and related topics have rapidly increased. This body of literature consists of demographic-statistical studies, treatment reports, evaluation of rehabilitative programmes and the elaboration of some aetiological theories.[3] Although different professionals and academic researchers have different views on the subject, most of them have conceptualised the phenomenon in terms of some psychopathological model. The study of the personal construction of adults who have had, or who desire to have, sexual contact with children, is very rare, despite the importance of such a task, and it is my wish to contribute a little to the closing of this gap in the literature.[4]

Means and ends of research

I started from the premise that the human person is an agent who acts rather than an organism which emits pieces of behaviour. In so far as the 'person' is restored to the rightful status of the 'subject' (in the sense of the 'I'), psychology must develop in the hermeneutical rather than the mechanistic direction if it is to become a meaningful enterprise about the human person.[5] Following this premise, my first task is to ask my informants to explicate their desire and activities in the language that *they* use in daily life. To me, Kelly's basic ideas are compatible with such a task. The starting point of Kelly's work is that a person acts according to how he or she interprets events.[6] A person construes reality as he or she is interpreting events and carrying out his or her actions in the direction that these interpretations lead. This is not a neat and linear process – one's actions always have feedback effects on how one construes further events, and the cycle of reality-testing-cum-reality-construction moves forward like a helix. This 'constructive cycle' constitutes the very essence of one's psychological life.

The objective of my research, in the context of a constructivist-hermeneutical framework, is a quest for 'meanings', not 'causes'. I am not pursuing the 'aetiologies' of paedophilic behaviour, rather I am trying to see how my informants construe their actions and how they make sense of their sexual experiences. Although a person's construing is not always on the verbal level, it cannot be denied that 'talk' is the most important source from which we can derive an explication of the sense we have of ourselves as persons who act with a distinct intentionality. As Rom Harré has argued, 'the fundamental human reality is a conversation',[7] and it is most appropriate that I should focus on my informants' talk. In so doing, I am using what Kelly called 'the credulous approach' – an attitude that treats the narrative of each of the informants as the most important source of information about him, and at the same time respects him as capable of explicating his actions.

The empirical work on which this paper is based consists of a series of individual interviews with twenty-five adult males contacted through various channels.[8] Basically, I asked each informant to provide his own account of his sexual involvement with, or desire for, children. Wherever possible, each informant was interviewed two or three times, or even more, so that feedback and 'account negotiation' could be carried out. The analysis presented in the following sections is based on the verbatim records of these interviews.

Informants' constructions

Five of the informants, who are exclusively attracted to boys, can see no particular precipitating events, experiences or factors which might be responsible for the development of their paedophilic desire. They feel that this desire is part of the constitution of their very self – the *leitmotif* of their accounts is 'This is me' or 'Just the way I am'.

While not all of them are definite about the inborn nature of their sexuality, some have indeed described it as 'inherent', 'inbred' or 'innate'. It is not a matter of choice (why would one *choose* an orientation that could bring endless troubles?), but a natural unfolding of their constitution:

> To be honest, you know, I think it's always been in me. I don't think it's sort of one stage, that happened that converts me over to that . . . I felt it was innate – it's not something that happened in my life that changed me totally. (Tom)[9]

Although these informants feel that their desire for boys is normal as far as they are concerned, yet they sometimes cannot help experiencing an anxious ambivalence:

> I do not consider it to be a perfectly normal situation because if it was, it would have to be more socially acceptable. Obviously, from my point of view, it would be very nice if the world accepts me as I was. Life would be so much easier. (Ben)

Added to this anxiety of self-doubt is the actual punishment (legal or otherwise) that society has imposed on these informants, and they feel that they are suffering for what they *naturally* are. One informant has remarked painfully that 'everyday is hell' to him because of the ostracism that he has to endure as a consequence of his sexuality.

In contrast, there are four informants who not only have shown no anxiety towards sexual activities with children but have actually construed sexual involvement with children as a perfectly normal part of human sexuality, not just for themselves but for *everybody*. These four men are not exclusively attracted to children; they simply do not feel it necessary to exclude children from adult sexual activities. They believe that the free expression of human sexuality could release much suppressed human potential. Not only is adult–child sexual contact harmless (provided no coercion is involved), it can actually be beneficial because it is 'practical sex education in the true sense of the word', which would help children avoid many future difficulties as they mature into full adult sexuality:

> If everybody could have an experience at an early age, some kind of experience, people would not have nearly, nearly as many problems, as what they do have. And I think that's why sex with children, with me, I think it's an extension of that – learning them what I've learned. But it got to be done in a nice, pleasant way, you can't force anybody. (Jack)

Another informant remarked that sexual contact with children is what every adult male would like to have:

> I do not think that sex is wrong, can ever be, irrespective of age, provided that no cruelty is inflicted. Frankly, I think most males would go with girls below sixteen were it not that the law is against it and it can mean trouble. (Kevin)

To these informants, the free expression of sex is natural; it is only because society has been so repressive that people are held back from spontaneous sexual interaction with children, who are by nature interested in sex even though they are young. There is no need to find an explanation for sexual attraction between an adult and a child, just as there is no need to find any explanation for similar attraction between two adults.

It is interesting to note that these four informants do not belong to any paedophile organisation. Moreover, they come from quite diverse backgrounds: two are successful businessmen, one is a retired journalist and the other is an unemployed lorry driver; one of them is a supporter of the Conservative Party, another is a professed Marxist, while a third is an amateur painter and the other a volunteer speech therapist. All of them have been married for a long time and feel satisfied with their adult sex life. Despite their obvious differences, the commonality in their construction regarding adult–child sexual relationship is very striking.

I have grouped another six informants into a third category. They have identified habitual childhood sexual activities with other children as playing a significant role in the development of their current sexuality: 'My intimate sexual connections with boys of my own age, from a very early age, were the beginnings of my Peter Pan outlook' (Paul). One of the six, while giving an autobiographical narrative, actually related, one episode after another, his sexual encounter with children from his childhood days up to the present, as if these experiences formed the core of his life. Indeed, he ended his account with the quip, 'So that's more or less the line of my life' (Adrian). These six informants, each in his own way, have construed a continuity between their childhood and adult sexuality, a continuity that seems likely to extend into their future.

The remaining ten informants of this study have construed their sexual involvement with children as a consequence of difficulties in adult relationships. They can be further categorised into two different groups, one in which marital problems are implicated, while in the other group (of five unmarried men) difficulties in approaching women have played a significant role. One common theme, however, is that informants in both groups tend to describe themselves as shy, unassertive and incompetent in social interaction.

According to the group of unmarried informants, they often experience a sense of sexual inadequacy and rejection with respect to grown-up females, and they find children much more approachable:

> Certainly I only commit these sorts of offences when I have met a woman who I'd like to get to know better sexually, but being unable to approach her, I then go away, I go round areas where I think that girls are likely to congregate – I'd look for girls. (Vincent)

In the case of the married informants, rather than a general sense of sexual inadequacy, it is a deterioration in emotional intimacy or in sexual harmony between the spouses, or both, which is construed as the crucial factor contributing to the emergence of the informants' sexual desire for children:

> It seems that when I'm able to have sex with my wife, whichever wife – the first or the second – everything was fine, I didn't want to touch any children. But, as soon as for one reason or

> another I can't have sex, I seem to start on the young children. (Matthew)

Thus in the accounts of these two groups of informants a link between some difficulty in adult heterosexual relationship and the development of a desire for, or involvement with, children has been explicitly articulated. While for some, a sexual encounter with a child is only a substitute activity when the opportunity for adult sex is lacking, for others it has actually become a much more enjoyable, and hence preferable, form of sexual fulfilment.

Significant features of constructions

I have in the previous section presented my informants' construction of the development of their sexual involvement with children. In this section some of the more significant features of their construction will be highlighted with the help of some of Kelly's concepts, in the hope that a better understanding of these men's experiences will be obtained.

'It doesn't happen unless the child needs it'

Nearly all of my informants have explicitly stated that their sexual relationships with children are of a consensual nature. They have construed a reciprocity in their relationships, free from any coercion:

> There cannot be any sense of doing against the child's will. That would negate it for me completely. (Ben)

> There is the saying: it takes two to tango. There must, obviously, be attraction for a young girl to 'go' with a male to talk or make love. (Kevin)

> Actually, the younger one asked me to put a finger on her vagina and then press, she said put your finger here, and now push, and I pushed, 'now push, push harder', so I pushed harder. (Daniel)

Because of this perception of reciprocity, some of the informants feel very angry about society's condemnatory attitude towards adult–child sexual relationships.[10] They feel that there is a clear commonality in the ways they and their child partners construe their sexual activities; they feel that a mutuality exists in their relationships. Yet there is also an absolute lack of commonality between their construction and that of society. Some of the informants, after getting into trouble with the criminal justice system because of their sexual contact with children, are trying to reconstrue their life in accordance with the norm of adult heterosexuality, but most others tend to affirm their own views even though they might have to be more discreet about their activities or to stop them altogether for a period of time.

In this connection the question of an ethical response to adult–child sexual contact must be raised. I want to suggest that Kelly's Sociality and Commonality corollaries might serve as a starting point for tackling this question, although they only constitute a necessary but *not* sufficient basis for such a task: 'To the extent that one person construes the construction process of another, he may play a role in a social process involving the other person'.[11] This is how Kelly construed the realm of 'the social'. As human existence is social in nature, a paedophilic-inclined adult must first be required to construe how a child would construe their possible sexual contact. The second requirement, then, must be the presence of commonality between their respective construction. It is only when commonality in construction exists that it could be reasonably assumed that the relationship is consensual.[12] Given the necessity of consensuality, it would be easy to formulate an ethical stand with respect to those adult–child sexual relationships where consensuality is absent.[13] The difficulty arises, however, in cases where consensuality exists. *Whether* children do give genuine consent to sexual involvement with adults cannot be settled *a priori* with reference to any psychological theory. It can only be tackled through empirical investigation.[14]

In this study, many of the informants have described how their child partners actively participated in the sexual activities. Can this be accepted as evidence of consensuality? We may argue that these informants might have *misconstrued* the actions of the children; yet on what basis can we put forward this argument? One solution is to check whether the child has actually said 'Yes' willingly to a request for sex. However, one informant has this to say:

> They have to be consenting – I use the word carefully, because, even at 13 or 14, a boy cannot verbalise this consent. It's something one has to sense. Because, you went to a boy of 13 and said, do you want to have sex with me, it would be a very rare occasion where the kid said 'Yes', because he would feel wrong to say 'Yes', even if, even if he wanted to. So it has to, it comes out of an instinctive understanding of the child's, the child's feelings – it has to be mutual. (Ben)

We can reject this on the ground that the informant is an interested party and so his perception would be biased. The difficulty is, *all* participants in any social encounter, including clinical or research interviews, must be reckoned as 'interested parties' – so why is a clinician's judgment taken as less biased than this informant's 'instinctive understanding'?[15]

One can suggest that children are *by nature* incapable of giving true consent to such sexual contact; indeed, this is the solution adopted by the law, which decrees that under a certain arbitrary age, a person is unable to act consensually in sexual matters.[16] In Kelly's terms such a solution can be described as pre-emptive, or even hostile, construing. As the general tenor of Kelly's work does not favour this type of dogmatic construing style, would it be wise for a personal construct psychologist to follow uncritically the law's 'pigeon-holing'?[17]

In Kelly's formulation the possibility of sociality lies in the effort a person makes in making sense of how other people make sense of reality. To develop an ethics for practical actions, one must try to makes sense of how other people view the world, since one's actions inevitably impinge on the reality constructed by these people. Beyond this, however, Kelly's ideas have not provided direct help as to how to handle situations where the other person does not construe my construing process (the lack of sociality on his or her part) or where the other person does not accept my construction (the lack of commonality). Of course, it may still be intellectually satisfying to say that I have nevertheless come to an *understanding* of the relationship, or the lack of it, between myself and this other person. Yet in practice the requirement to *act* in relation to the other person raises real ethical issues beyond the level of understanding. The way in which I, as a psychologist, construct a psychological report on a paedophile for the consumption of the court often does not have any logical link with the paedophile's own construing – the logic is apparent only within my particular construction of his acts, a construction (respected as 'clinical judgment') informed, perhaps routinely, by ideas and ideologies outside the realm of psychology. In this context the whole practice of psychological assessment and treatment must be called into question, and the role of the personal construct psychologist in relation to these controversies urgently discussed.

'Normality is subjective'

It is interesting to note that 'constructive alternativism', the cornerstone of Kelly's work, has found clear expression in the ways in which some of my informants make sense of, and cope with, their experience.

Given the strong social disapproval and legal sanction against adult–child sexual contact, most of my informants feel under great pressure either to suppress their inclinations completely or to carry out their activities with the utmost furtiveness. Yet many of them are adamant in affirming the legitimacy of their sexuality: 'Why should I be deprived of my sex life? Every human being has got a sex drive, if you can't get one, you're going after the other' (Adrian). In Kelly's terms, such construing can be described as 'aggressive' (an active elaboration of one's construct system), or even hostile (forcing events into Procrustean categories despite invalidation). It is a means of defence for these informants, with which they ward off the threat (in Kelly's sense) of the loss of their core identity.

A more sophisticated construction, employed by several of the informants, makes use of the argument of relativism: 'What is normal today may be abnormal tomorrow, what is abnormal today may be normal tomorrow' (Richard). In other words, they have discerned the changing nature of the notion of 'normality' and argue that society's attitude towards adult–child sexual relationships is only a function of the dominant *Zeitgeist*, not a universal truth. These social sanctions are time-bound artefacts – indeed, to call paedophilia a perversion or a disorder is a matter of *labelling* – socially produced, not necessarily reflecting the nature of the case:

> There is the historical aspect; in the middle ages children were not children in the sense we speak of these days. Probably it [paedophilia] went on regularly within and without families. . . . I assume that hundreds of years ago sex with younger females was just not noticed. . . . Before alcoholism was recognised, people who got themselves into a state were called lazy, good-for-nothing scoundrels, etc., etc. Get the point? (Kevin)

Can we, as personal construct psychologists, accept such 'constructive alternatives'?

'*Children are warm and generous*'

Over half of my informants have mentioned specific characteristics of children that are particularly appealing to them. Paedophilic relationships are thus often *in themselves* much more satisfying than sex with adults. These relationships are the informants' *first* choice rather than a substitute when they cannot get adult sex.

Children are portrayed as gentle, truthful, broad-minded, affectionate, perceptive and with an 'inquiring mind', whereas adults are narrow-minded, selfish and lacking any depth of feeling. Children possess 'spirit' and 'innocence', adults are just preoccupied with material gains. Children are warm and generous, and it is easy to communicate with them – one does not have to prove anything in their presence, one can simply be oneself. In addition, some informants have stressed the physical attractiveness of children. This ranges from a fascination with the *variation* in boys' penises to an adoration of young girls' budlike genitalia.[18]

These informants have sharply distinguished children from adults with the two superordinate constructs of *physical beauty* and *attractive personality*. They have construed children according to the construct pole of these two dichotomies and placed adults on the contrast pole. It is obvious where their preference lies. It would be interesting to study how these constructs of beauty and charm have been developed by these men, and whether their disappointment with adults is merely a matter of idiosyncrasies or indeed a reflection of general human experiences. From their accounts it is clear that they are holding society responsible for the suppression of these positive childhood qualities.[19]

'I'd never grown up, I'd always been a child'

Because of this stark contrast between childhood and adulthood, several of the informants have actually expressed the feeling of not wanting to grow up themselves:

> I am very much a Peter Pan, the boy who never grew up. My deep love for boys for so many years is so very much a part of me psychologically that growing up would be impossible. (Paul)

> I suppose, you can say that I'm slightly immature, haven't lost my childhood. Childhood is a very, very short, sort of time in your life, goes too quickly, and it's very sweet, you know, it's all innocent. (Keith)

Conclusion

They do not want to grow up, but this is clearly impossible.

> Looking into a mirror,
> Do I like what I see?
> This image of a child
> Staring at me.
>
> I know what he's thinking,
> But don't know why;
> Because this image in the mirror,
> Needs to cry.
>
> Are they tears of loneliness,
> Running down his face?
> Oh unloved image,
> Out of place.

Are you really a child,
Or really a man?
Are you truly the image
Of what I am?

This poem is written by Nick, one of the informants of this study. To him, the adult world is cruel, but love is possible with children; to him, paedophilia is a matter of relationships, not sex: 'I have to look for things worth living for . . . sex isn't the main thing, the main thing is being wanted, I suppose.'

Space does not permit me to elaborate further the richness of these informants' personal construction of their sexuality, but sufficient has been said to illustrate how intimate relationships with children have provided some of them with a *raison d'être* to anchor their human existence.

Notes and references

1 Paedophilia (Protection of Children) Bill, Hansard, 27 June 1984. This Bill was introduced by Geoffrey Dickens, MP for Littleborough and Saddleworth, and it aimed at banning all organisations that could be even remotely associated with anything to do with adult–child sexual contact. The Bill failed to get a second reading due to the lack of parliamentary time.

2 In the July 1984 issue of *Paedophile Information Exchange (PIE) Bulletin*, the PIE executive made an announcement to close down their organisation 'because of various difficulties'.

3 A review analysis of this literature has been carried out as part of my PhD dissertation, which is under preparation.

4 Of course, the study of the personal construction of the *children* involved in such sexual activities is equally essential to a better understanding of the phenomenon, but as I have failed to obtain permission from any public agency to meet and talk to such children who are under its care, I have to confine my research to the adults involved.

5 This position is ably articulated in the work of John Shotter; for example, Shotter, J. (1975), *Images of Man in Psychological Research*, London: Methuen; or Gauld, A. and Shotter, J. (1977), *Human Action and its Psychological Investigation*, London: Routledge & Kegan Paul.

6 This is how I understand Kelly's Fundamental Postulate. His work

is spelled out fully in Kelly, G. A. (1955), *The Psychology of Personal Constructs*, New York: Norton; and (1969), *Clinical Psychology and Personality: The Selected Papers of George Kelly*, ed. Brendan Maher, New York: Wiley.

7 Harré, R. (1983). *Personal Being*. Oxford: Blackwell, p. 20.

8 A summary of the characteristics of my informants is as follows:

Age distribution	*No. of informants*
20–9	3
30–9	5
40–9	4
50–9	11
60–9	1
70+	1
	25
Gender preference	
boys	11
girls	11
both boys and girls	3
	25
Occupation	
professionals	5
business and commerce	5
technicians	3
manual work	2
unemployed	6
retired	4
	25
Criminal record	
arrested for sexual offence against under-age persons	15
no such record of arrest	10
	25

9 All names of informants are fictitious for obvious reasons.

10 Rape and sexual murder of children do occur in our society, and my informants have expressed abhorrence over such incidents. Yet, as the occurrence of rape among adults does not logically negate adult sexuality, so the occurrence of similar violence against children does not logically exclude the possibility of consensual adult–child sexual relationships.

11 Kelly, *The Psychology of Personal Constructs*, p. 95.

12 While most of us would agree that consensuality is a necessary prerequisite, it should be noted that PCT cannot be invoked to support the argument that only consensual relationships are *morally* acceptable. PCT cannot, within its own logic, make any pronouncement on what is universally/objectively good (or bad). It may be able to say something on why people choose as they do (Choice Corollary), but not on the moral goodness (or badness) of these choices.

13 In such cases, presumably, the role of the personal construct psychologist would be to help the adult involved reconstrue his position with respect to children according to the requirement of sociality and commonality.

14 Of course, any 'empirical' investigation is always informed by, albeit implicit, *theories*, and the goal of obtaining absolutely 'objective' information on children's consent (or its absence) is impossible to achieve. The other problem is whether children would always tell researchers (or other professionals) how they truly feel. These are questions beyond the scope of the present paper.

15 Here the issue of the hegemonic *power* of professionals in modern society is relevant, and the work of Michel Foucault, especially his concept of power/knowledge (*pouvoir/savoir*) would be most useful to the discussion.

16 In Britain the age of consent is quite high: sixteen for heterosexual activities, and twenty-one for male homosexual activities.

17 I am not proposing that we should disregard the law but that it may not be possible to justify particular laws in PCT terms. The law, and morality for that matter, lies outside the range of convenience of personal construct theory.

18 One of the informants talked about boys' penises in this way: 'I'm attracted, I want to see boys' penises. Now, they say, everybody says, all boys are the same – now they are *not* the same. Some've been circumcised, some have little ones, some have big ones, some have long ones, fat ones, thin ones, I want to see them' (Adrian). Regarding young girls' genitalia, they are described as hairless, fresh, round, smooth, firm, dry and with a natural tightness, whereas those of grown-up women are said to be flabby, wet, smelly, ugly and repulsive.

19 Two quotations can illustrate this point: 'Children are immeasurably perceptive, but by the time they have grown up, society has dealt them a deadly blow, and their perception has fled for all time' (George); 'They are warm and generous and it is only when they get older and they learn the ways of the world and ask what's in it for me or what is it worth. When that happens they lose all their charm and enchantment' (Jack).

3

Understanding the disoriented senior as a personal scientist

Elizabeth Ann Hill

Foreword

This study assumes that aging with dignity and enjoying a quality of life should be an option available to all seniors. From the viewpoint of the consultant, the author of this study, the goal of helping one towards aging with dignity, is described in this manner: helping in areas where people need help in order to maximize each person's freedom of choice or change.

The stance taken by this author is that in order to help in this manner it is necessary to understand how seniors construe their particular situations. Through a specific senior's perspective, the author attempts to construe the world the way he does. This approach uses Kelly's 'man-the-scientist' as a basis for understanding how a senior, Dr Rager, gives meaning to his world of reality.

The dialogue that is generated between the consultant and the senior creates what has been referred to in an earlier paper (Rix, 1983) as a 'reflective epistemological conversation'; that is, not only does the consultant attempt to become aware of the senior's constructs but the senior as a result of the interaction reflects upon his own 'level of cognitive awareness', as Kelly used the term (1955, pp. 475–6). In this paper it is argued that continual, reflective, and intensive conversation (five hours a day for over two months) which constantly includes personally important matters, becomes a significant factor in positive observable change in behaviour.

Introduction

Stephen Leacock wrote that 'Old age is the "Front Line" of life, moving into no-man's-land. No-man's-land is covered with mist. Beyond is it eternity.' This study assumes that this misty no-man's-land, that is aging, should be accompanied with dignity and an enjoyment of a quality of life readily available to all seniors. The thesis I wish to put forward in this paper is that the quality of a senior's life, either an improvement or deterioration, is dependent upon many factors, one of which stresses the importance of how one construes reality. How one chooses to construe becomes a very important determinant of one's psychological and physical well-being. For the senior as a scientist, what is vital to good health are the choices a senior makes for the ways in which he/she anticipates events. I see this as an extension to the Fundamental Postulate, which states the 'a person's processes are psychologically channelized by the ways in which he anticipates events,' an extension in theory or perhaps at least an application in practice. This application suggests that a person's health is enhanced by the process of construing and, in particular, in this case, becomes less disoriented/confused, or gets better, feels better with the re-creation (recreation) of old constructs and, perhaps, the creation of new ones.

Tautological nature of the process of anticipating events: loop theory

As a senior construes or thinks about an event, a situation, an idea, or notion, he does it through a self-selected filtering process. The result of this process is anticipation. This anticipation affects the person in the way or ways one collectively combines his/her thinking, feeling, and acting. The integration of the various degrees of intensity of how one thinks, feels, and acts towards the construed event is likely to result in one of four responses: first, a state of *positive* response, such as feeling good, feeling a sense of happiness; second, a state of *negative* response, for example feeling terrible, sick, sad, or depressed; third, a state of *neutrality*; or, fourthly, a *vacillation* between or among any of these three states. The resulting choice of state is itself an experience. It is this experience which provides validation or invalidation for the choice of response selected. How one responds to the validation of one's behaviour or invalidation of one's behaviour will be directly related to how one begins to think or rethink about the same topic. Of course, the choice to begin a new or different thought of construction may be made. Hence, the process of anticipating events referred to as 'loop theory' (Fig. D3.1) begins again.

The observation in working with seniors, and specifically with Dr Rager, leads to a single observation in Figure D3.1, and that is that the greater the degree of validation of positive response, the greater the likelihood of continuity of motivation, stimulation, interest desire, will, and hope.

My interest in the study of construct uniqueness of disoriented seniors, and specifically in the case of Dr Rager, is concerned with the notion of dormant constructs and with the fact that these existing constructs in a state of rest or torpidity must be activated. If this occurs (see asterisk Fig. D3.1), one's constructs seems to flourish – not that new and different ones are constructed, although that is possible, but existing ones are examined from different perspectives. In other words, the person, in this case a senior, does an excellent job at being a scientist. Kelly could very well have been writing about Dr Rager when he states that 'A

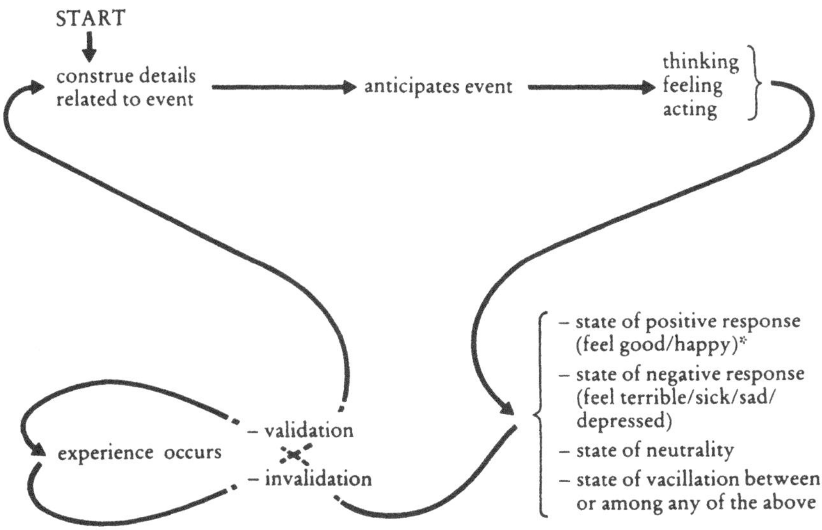

Figure D3.1 Tautological nature of the process of anticipating events: loop theory

good scientist tries to bring his constructs up for test as soon as possible,' and that 'testing of constructs . . . characterizes any alert person' (1955, p. 13).

About the agency

The agency that works with disoriented seniors asked me to help them with some of their clients, one of whom was a Dr Rager. The agency, called Friends of the Family, is a service for seniors providing the kind of temporary day-to-day help that family members or close friends would provide if they were available. It is called Respite Care Service for the Confused Elderly, a service with bonded staff specially trained in practical daily services and other skills needed to work with someone who is confused or disoriented due to the aging process. The mandate of Friends of the Family is to help the older person maintain his/her dignity and to supplement this independence when age or infirmity make it increasingly difficult.

About Dr Rager

The file for Dr Edward Rager (real name) indicated he had a distinguished career as attorney at law and had been admitted to practice in the United States Supreme Court, where, in New York City, he practiced for over forty years. He had been described by associates as a crusader for justice, a champion of human rights and duties, a dedicated public servant, lecturer, philosopher and author. There was also evidence to indicate he had endured several sufferings in life; for example, he was embezzled, defrauded and deprived of his properties, possessions and life savings. As a result, it would appear that he left the United States and now lives as it were 'in exile' on the tenth floor of an apartment building in a comfortable uptown residential area in Toronto, Canada. It is readily obvious through his conversation, behaviour and writings that justice, sincerity, and honesty are still his prime values, his core constructs.

The process of the reawakening of personal constructs: confusion reduction

My role on first being assigned to Dr Rager was one of counsellor. I was informed that he was a very 'difficult man', and that he needed to have his mind stimulated. Medically, he was well. He was an elderly person (eighty-six years old) who revelled in being well known for presenting pithy and controversial views expressed both verbally and in writing.

As counsellor to Dr Rager, I viewed myself as 'helper' with the goal that could be stated like this: to help in areas where help is needed in order to maximize his freedom of choice/change. Ultimately, he required protection and care, a type of help that would allow him to remain in his own home and to age with dignity.

Without planning it this way, it turned out that the process of reawakening personal constructs assumed three stages: clarification, formulation, and intervention. My early visits could be referred to as the *clarification stage*, where I was getting to know Dr Rager, who he was, and how he construed reality, his values, his constructs, or as my niece would say, 'getting to know where he was at.' About the third week of five-hour daily visits, our activities took on what I would call the *formulation stage*. At this point I started to plan how we would spend our time based on the discoveries I had made about him. A highlight of every day was the hour-long classical music concert from 2.00 p.m. until 3.00 p.m. every afternoon and always followed with a cup of tea. Other events that often occurred spontaneously were reading and writing of poetry, reading the doctor's array of articles he had written or ones that were written about him (e.g. his colourful speeches as counsellor of the Republican Party in the *New York Times*), reading the poetry of Edgar Allen Poe, James Joyce's *Ulysses*, *The Philosophy of Wisdom*, the Bible, or *The Rat Race* – the book he authored in 1954.

Towards the end of the first month I became aware that I was creating, purposely, what might be called an *intervention stage*. I was particularly interested in offering opportunities for a selection of choice in his behaviours and at the same time reducing confusion periods which occurred on occasion. This is how it happened. By fortunate coincidence an external intervention source presented itself. Josepha, his sister, whom he had not seen for several years, was to arrive on April 4. By now the process of transference had been occurring regularly and so we had a plan that would 'wean' Dr Rager from his dependence upon me so that he could assume the independence of free choice of actions and attitudes that would make him ready to host his sister's arrival. The intervention stage in this case also would become the culmination of the process for, as it happens, April 4 was also the date my assignment was to terminate; we had double motivations. Josepha, as a symbol, was the motivation for altering many of our client's behaviours. Reconstruction or reconstruing flourished most when together we decided upon the several choices of things to be done to get ready for Josepha's visit. As it turned out, Josepha never did come. Her telegram saying so left him for a short while in deep despair. But her use as the intervention agent served its purpose admirably: our client recovered quickly and went on to look for new stimulations. The doctor's ability to bounce back from sad events no doubt is directly related to being able to retain many of the changes that had been made.

Although April 4 was my last official day with Dr Rager, I have remained a close friend to both Dr and Mrs Rager; we chat on the phone and visit periodically. His recovery from disorientation appears complete.

Observable change over time

Specific areas within Dr Rager's present style of life were showing alterations. These were not so much new styles or new constructs as they were a revitalization of what had previously been a style of his person. It was as though the established and very stable constructs or modes of thinking which may have been dormant, now were restored. Several examples of these changes can be seen in Figure D3.2. In the first column of this figure are eleven actions and attitudes which, over a period of two months of reciprocal conversation, became the eleven actions and attitudes of the second column.

• From an emphasis about self	→	to a sincere interest in others.
• From feeling ill	→	to feeling well more often than ill (only ill again through over-exertion or having eaten the wrong food).
• Speaking in assertive sentences	→	to asking questions and getting another's opinion; he often said, 'What do you think?'
• From sitting idly	→	to returning to past activities in which he was so creative and productive (writing in particular).
• From a serious, sombre attitude	→	to a happy 'life really is worthwhile' attitude punctuated with outbursts of laughter. On commenting to him, 'You have quite a sense of humour' his thought-provoking response was, 'Yes, but it needs to be nurtured.'
• From a spectator stance in listening to music	→	to a type of participatory stance. On March 12 he sang along with and clapped after each movement of Bach's Brandenburg Concertos. On March 14 he sang two familiar songs.
• From continual conversation	→	to conversation as well as writing of narrative and poetry; he dictated and I wrote, until March 14 when he requested the pen and he wrote poetry while supper cooled on the table.
• From waiting until I arrived to get up and dress	→	to being fully attired in a style he had been accustomed to as a professional lawyer.
• From leaving the bed for me to make	→	to helping (without being asked) to make it.
• From no participation in domestic activities	→	to making himself tea and clearing the dishes off the coffee table. His exclamation to me that that was the first time (April 1) that he had ever made tea, was literally true.
• From smoking many cigarettes	→	to smoking one or two or none per day.

Figure D3.2 Observable change over time

The importance of the reciprocal conversation: the dialectic

A discussion of the importance of the reciprocal conversation will help to explain why changes resulted. At the July 1983 Congress on Personal Construct Psychology, I presented a model towards a reflective epistemology of educational practice, a model that assumed that both the teacher and the student were 'scientists' and through an effective conversation they discover the potential that the conversation can have for the relationship. Teacher and student can be substituted in this paper for counsellor and Dr Rager.

It would be close to accurate to say that Dr Rager and I spent five hours a day for two months dialoguing. At first our conversation was halted, often difficult and sometimes impossible. As we spent more time together our conversation became more natural and spontaneous. A degree of interpersonal trust, liking and respect was being established. It appeared to me that when his constructs, his values were perceived by him to be picked up by me, at this point in time things started to happen. Stated otherwise, changes occurred when he felt secure and comfortable. A major noticeable change was in the style of conversation. Interrogative sentences became commonplace; he started to ask questions, questions for information, questions for clarification, questions for receiving another's opinion. Kelly might have viewed Rager as 'A good scientist, bringing his constructs up for testing' (1955, p. 13). Up to this time he had spoken almost always in assertive sentences. Dr Rager's conversation became more complex, more in-depth, more personal. Our conversation became more cryptic (but understood), more creative, more poetic, more sensitive both mentally and spiritually. We often spoke in imagery, we laughed together, we cried together and especially enjoyed our conversation within the context of the sun glistening on the glass on top of his study table and other treasures in his front room where we spent most of our time together.

Communication was functioning and it appeared to be functioning well (for a formulation of principles resulting in functional communication, see Monaghan, 1983). As a scientist Dr Rager was construing my constructs at the same time that I, as a scientist, was construing his. The end result was that I helped him but he in turn helped me in so many ways. This is the synergism that can result in a dialectic that is affective by being reciprocal and conversational (developed in Rix, 1983). It is similar to the pervading spirit that Brown refers to when talking about administration as 'the science, the art and the magic' (1984, p. 200). Perhaps Dr Rager was putting to practice the suggestions he himself wrote regarding a lawyer's image:

> That a lawyer should try his utmost to be fully conversant . . . should be beyond doubt. That he should have an excellent command of the language as a means of expressing his thoughts with clarity and as a forensic tool of his art of advocacy is hardly debatable. . . . Those who attain skill in these talents may become artisans or artists and be celebrated for their dialectics which is quite rewarding (1964, p. 19).

Afterword

The findings of this paper are not concerned with extending life but rather to reduce disorientation and confusion periods thus extending the quality of a senior's life; one tends to lead a happier life. One concern that arises from this study is related to the issue of the time involved in procuring the results. Further examination of how the results of the study could be accomplished in less time would be valuable. It would also be useful to discover under what conditions the revitalized constructs are retained over time or slip back into dormancy once again. A further concern is the necessity for training and development of professional personnel who work with seniors as well as opportunities for relatives, friends or associates to become skilled in their interactions with seniors, disoriented or not, so as to improve the seniors' right to enjoy a quality of life.

References

Brown, A. F. (1984). How to change what teachers think about teachers: affirmative action in promotion decisions. In R. Halkes and J. K. Olson (eds.), *Teacher Thinking: A New*

Perspective on Persisting Problems in Education. Lisse, Holland: Swets & Zeitlinger.

Kelly, G. A. (1955). *The Psychology of Personal Constructs*, Vol. I. New York: Norton.

Monaghan, R. R. (1983). The communication process: principles on negotiation of meaning. Paper presented at the Fifth International Congress on PCP, Pine Manor College, Chestnut Hill, Boston, Massachusetts, July.

Rager, E. (1964). Legal education: toward what image? *Case and Comment: The Lawyer's Magazine* 69(5), 16–22.

Rix (Hill), E. A. (1983). Towards a reflective epistemology of educational practice. Paper presented at the Fifth International Congress on PCP, Pine Manor College, Chestnut Hill, Boston, Massachusetts, July.

Chapter 4
Personal identity in disturbed marital relationships

Greg Neimeyer and Alison Gold Hall

At the interface of social and clinical psychology lies a growing interest in disordered relationships. Central to this interest is the need to determine those interpersonal processes which distinguish disordered from more healthy and satisfying relationships. A recent literature has begun the empirical assessment of psychological processes underlying these disturbed but intimate relationships (Doster, 1985; Duck and Gilmour, 1981; Finchman and O'Leary, 1983; Neimeyer, 1984). This paper extends these efforts by applying to marital relationships a developing account of relationship disorder based on Kelly's (1955) personal construct theory (G. Neimeyer, 1985; G. Neimeyer and Hudson, 1985; R. Neimeyer and G. Neimeyer, 1985). According to this account, marriage provides partners with a relationship which simultaneously supports and extends their social constructions and their personal identities (G. Neimeyer and Hudson, 1985; Wright, 1984). One way of understanding the nature of this support is through self-identity theory (Breakwell, 1983; Schlenker, 1984).

Identity theory views relationship satisfaction as a function of the person's ability to enact his or her 'desired identity image' within the relationship. In other words, partners are more satisfied with their relationship to the extent that it supports and confirms their important images of themselves. In this way intimate partners provide one another with *self-affirmation* value by 'characteristically behaving in ways that facilitate the expression and recognition of one's more important and highly valued self attributes' (Wright, 1984, p. 120). Kelly (1955) referred to these important self-images as 'core role constructs,' by which he meant those dimensions that operate to define the individual's personal identity. These constructions operate as forms of social hypotheses that require social validation (Duck and Sants, 1983), and intimate relationships can serve as one important means to this end.

One implication of this reasoning is that more satisfying marriages should be characterized by higher levels of personal validation (G. Neimeyer and Hudson, 1985). The effect of validation is to secure the system of understandings by tightening the relationship among its constructs (Bannister, 1963). Psychologically, validation assures the individual of the utility of existing constructions and contributes to his or her efforts to better understand and anticipate social experience.

By contrast, disturbed marriages provide much higher levels of *invalidation* (G. Neimeyer and Hudson, 1985; R. Neimeyer and G. Neimeyer, 1985) Because construct systems are forged within interpersonal contexts, the repeated invalidation which characterizes distressed marriages should impact the way in which interpersonal relationships are anticipated. For example, a woman's expectation that loving relationships are characterized by kindness is invalidated by her husband's insensitive or abusive behavior. This invalidation loosens the relationship among constructs in the system (Bannister, 1963), thereby reducing the predictive power of her construct system. In this case she may become less likely to expect kindness in an intimate relationship. The net effect of repeated invalidation is to reduce the predictive value of the construct system until the person experiences 'chaos in the whole area of his [or her] anticipations of other people' (Kelly, 1955, p. 501).

Despite the negative consequences of distressed or abusive relationships, most women remain within them even after they perceive the marriage to be beyond repair (Ball and Wyman, 1978; Roberts, 1984). One way of understanding this behavior is to view it as a means to preserve aspects of an otherwise uncertain self-identity. Because even conflictual relationships provide partners with some level of validation concerning their views of themselves and their social field (G. Neimeyer and R. Neimeyer, 1985), it is *threatening* to leave such relationships. Here threat is viewed as an awareness of an imminent change in one's most central self-constructions (Kelly, 1955). In other words, individuals may prefer to remain within an unhappy or disturbed relationship rather than to jeopardize the meaningful image of themselves which they have forged within it. In this case interpersonal conflict is actually preferred over the alternative of dissolving the relationship since this dissolution would require a major revision of the self-identity (cf. Harré, 1983).

But remaining within a conflictual relationship should affect the partners' constructions of other close relationships as well. For example, it seems likely that women in abusive relationships would gradually come to develop more generalized negative systems for interpreting close relations. Clinical impressions indicate particular sensitivity to 'power issues' (i.e. issues of force, domination or control) in intimate relations in a way that sometimes resolves itself by means of social withdrawal, isolation, or learned helplessness (Ball and Wyman, 1978).

Based on this discussion of marital relationships, the following four hypotheses were developed and tested in the present study. First, more satisfied women should be better able to enact their desired identity images in their marriages than should dissatisfied or abused women. Second, because conflictual marriages are characterized by higher levels of invalidation, dissatisfied and abused women should have more loosely organized interpersonal construct systems. Third, compared to satisfied women, women who remain in abusive or unhappy relationships should experience higher levels of threat associated with leaving their marriages. Here threat is understood as the perceived need to revise one's self-image as a result of dissolving the relationship. Fourth, abused women should be more prone to perceive and anticipate negativity in their close relationships, as reflected in the content of their interpersonal constructs.

Method

Subjects

Thirty-one women from the community were solicited to participate in the study. Volunteers were contacted randomly through (1) university married housing, (2) a local community counseling service for women, and (3) a spouse abuse shelter. Subjects ranged in age from twenty to fifty-two years, (median age = 29.0 years).

All participants had successfully completed high school, although most had also attended college.

The first group consisted of ten women who resided in university married housing (median age = 27.0). The second group consisted of ten women who were receiving counseling for marital dissatisfaction (median age = 27.5) through a community counseling service but who did not report spouse abuse as a presenting problem. The third group consisted of eleven women who were residing in a women's shelter following physical abuse by their husbands (median age = 29.0). These groups were designated as Satisfied, Dissatisfied, and Abused, in that order, and marital-adjustment indices were administered to confirm their differential levels of satisfaction (see results).

Procedure and instrumentation

Subjects were tested individually in their homes or in the shelter home. The female interviewer administered each of the instruments in the following order.

Dyadic adjustment scale (DAS)

The DAS (Spanier, 1976) is a self-administered 32-item questionnaire designed as an index of overall marital adjustment. This measure was chosen for use in the study due to its demonstrated reliability and validity (See Spanier, 1976), ease of administration, and frequent use in clinical and research literatures. The possible range of scores is 0 (low satisfaction) to 151 (high satisfaction).

Repertory grid

The repertory grid was explained to subjects as a structured interview designed as a 'method for exploring your way of understanding some important relationships in your life.' Fifteen constructs were elicited in standard fashion from triadic sorts of intimate friends or relatives (e.g. husband, father, mother, former lover, best friend). The women were then asked to rate each of these people, and the following three self-descriptions, along all fifteen constructs: 'myself in my current marriage,' 'myself as I would be if I were *out* of my current marriage,' and 'myself as I would *like* to be in a marriage.' After all ratings were completed, subjects were instructed to value code each side of their constructs as positive (+) or negative (−). From this matrix of ratings the following three measures were derived: desired identity enactment, organization, and threat. Two construct post-codings were also performed to assess the valence and content of the dimensions.

Desired identity enactment was measured by comparing the construct ratings of 'myself in the current marriage' with 'the way I would *like* to be in a marriage.' The score was calculated by taking the sum of the absolute values of the differences between the two sets of ratings. Higher scores reflect a greater discrepancy between current and desired identity images. Scores could range from 0 (low discrepancy) to 180 (high discrepancy).

Organization was measured by the intensity score (Fransella and Bannister, 1977). The intensity score reflects the overall amount of correlation in the construct system, indicating its degree of organization or structure.

Threat scores were computed by comparing the ratings of 'myself in my current marriage' with 'myself *out* of this marriage.' The threat score was calculated by summing the number of times there was a 'split' in ratings with one rating occurring on one side of the zero point and one occurring on the other, as in previous research (See Rigdon, Epting, Neimeyer, and Krieger, 1979). The rationale for the threat score is that it reflects the number of significant revisions in one's self-image which would be required by dissolving the marital relationship. Scores could range from 0 (no splits) to 15 (all splits), with higher scores indicating a greater degree of threat.

Construct post-codings

Two sets of post-codings were performed on the women's constructs. Both post-codings involved categorizing the *emergent* pole of the constructs. The emergent pole is viewed as the most salient or accessible pole of the construct, operating as figural in a figure-ground relationship with its implicit contrast. The two sets of post-codings involved categorizing the *valence* and the *content* of the constructs.

Valence ratings were performed by the women themselves in

response to instructions to 'value code each side of every construct as either positive (+) or negative (−).' The number of *positive* ratings assigned to the emergent poles was used as an index of construct valence. This score could range from 0 (no positive emergent poles) to 15 (all positive) and was used to test the prediction that less satisfied partners are set to perceive relationships in less positive terms.

Content post-codings were based on Landfield's (1971) post-coding dictionary. Three categories were chosen for consideration due to their relevance to issues of marital adjustment: forcefulness, social activity, and tenderness. Forcefulness is defined as 'any statement denoting energy, overt expressiveness, persistence, intensity' (Landfield, 1971, p. 168, e.g. 'aggressive,' 'dominating,' and 'intolerant'). Social activity is defined as 'any statements in which ongoing or continuing interaction with others is clearly indicated' (p. 167; e.g 'extrovert,' 'leader,' and 'friendly'). Tenderness is regarded as 'any statement denoting susceptibility to softer feelings' (p. 173) such as 'compassion,' 'kindness,' or 'love.'

Using these three categories, two independent raters post-coded all emergent poles of the constructs. Interjudge agreement for forcefulness (83 per cent), social activity (78 per cent), and tenderness (74 per cent) was moderately high. Only post-codings on which both raters agreed were used in the analysis, however.

Results

Prior to testing the predictions of the study, a one-way ANOVA was performed on the DAS scores to confirm that levels of marital satisfaction were in fact different among the satisfied (M = 117.1; sd = 7.97), dissatisfied (M = 85.7; sd = 18.7) and abused (M = 52.8; sd = 9.59) groups. Results confirmed these differences, $F_{(2,82)} = 6.84$, $p \leq 0.01$. Abused women were significantly less satisfied than either of the other two groups, and the dissatisfied women were less satisfied than the satisfied women, $p \leq 0.05$ Tukey's.

To test the predictions of the study, one-way ANOVAS were conducted on each of the five dependent measures. The first ANOVA was performed on the desired identity-enactment scores. The significant result, $F_{(2,28)} = 14.8$, $p \leq 0.001$, revealed that satisfied women reported enacting identities significantly closer to their preferred images (M = 15.5; sd = 13.1) than did dissatisfied (M = 77.2; sd = 46.9) or abused (M = 135.8; sd = 19.3) women.

The one-way ANOVA on intensity scores also showed a significant effect, $F_{(2,28)} = 5.55$, $p \leqslant 0.02$. Abused women showed lower levels of construct system organization (M = 1129.4; sd = 586.8) than did dissatisfied (M = 1444.5; sd = 501.9) or satisfied women (M = 1685.4; sd = 439.9).

The analysis of threat scores also indicated a significant effect, $F_{(2,28)} = 3.82$, $p \leqslant 0.05$. Threat scores from abused (M = 9.5; sd = 3.24) and dissatisfied (M = 8.1; sd = 4.09) women were higher than those for satisfied women (M = 5.01; sd = 4.14). There was no significant difference between the threat scores of abused and dissatisfied women, however.

Finally, in order to test the prediction that less satisfied women are predisposed to anticipate relationships more negatively, two analyses were conducted. First, a one-way ANOVA was conducted on valence scores. Valence scores reflected the number of emergent construct poles which subjects coded as positive (possible range = 0 to 15). The analysis revealed a significant effect, $F_{(2,28)} = 14.42$, $p \leqslant 0.001$, with abused women providing fewer positive codings (M = 6.82, sd = 3.28) than dissatisfied (M = 7.7, sd = 2.4) or satisfied (M = 9.4, sd = 2.22) women.

The content of these emergent poles was further examined through analysis of the personal construct dimensions based on three of Landfield's (1971) post-coding categories: *forcefulness* (e.g. dominates me), *Social activity* (e.g. outgoing), and *tenderness* (e.g. affectionate). Chi-square analyses indicated significant effects along the forcefulness dimension, $X^2_{(2)} = 9.86$, $p \leqslant 0.01$, and the social activity dimension $X^2_{(2)} = 9.94$, $p \leqslant 0.01$, but not along the tenderness dimension. The first effect revealed that abused women more often characterized relationships in forceful terms (61 per cent) than did dissatisfied (21 per cent) or satisfied (18 per cent) women. The second effect indicated that satisfied women construed relationships more frequently in terms of social activity (46.1 per cent) than did dissatisfied (30.1 per cent) or abused women (23.8 per cent).

Discussion

The results of this study provide some insights into possible differences between satisfying and disturbed marital relationships. The finding that satisfied women reported enacting identities closer to their desired self-images supports previous work (Schlenker, 1984) and is consistent with Wright's (1984) position that intimate partnerships provide *self-affirmation* value. From the perspective of personal construct theory this affirmation is understood as validation of the partners' core role constructs, those constructions by which the individual 'maintains his (or her) identity and existence' (Kelly, 1955, p. 482).

The absence of this support leaves partners in unhappy or abusive relationships experiencing repeated invalidation (G. Neimeyer and Hudson, 1985; R. Neimeyer and G. Neimeyer, 1985). As in previous experimental clinical research (Bannister, 1963), the results of this study suggest that the impact of this invalidation is to loosen the correlation among constructs in the system, thereby limiting the usefulness of the system for anticipating interpersonal experience. This effect was especially marked among abused women, leaving them with relatively unstructured and poorly organized construct systems. This disorganization of the interpersonal construct system may help to account for the confusion and ambivalence experienced in highly conflictual but intimate relationships (Roberts, 1984). This confusion follows from a construct system that is not sufficiently structured to permit clear and unvarying predictions. In this case initial clinical interventions might be aimed at providing therapeutic *reassurance*. Kelly (1955) understood reassurance as 'a simplified' superordinate construction placed upon the clinical situation. It is communicated to the client so that his [or her] behavior and ideas will temporarily appear . . . to be consistent, acceptable, and organized' (p. 649).

Without intervention it seems likely that this disorganization would present liabilities not only for understanding current relationships but also for developing future intimate relations. For example, the inability to predict with some certainty that close relationships will be related to feelings of security, sensitivity, and respect, might create interpersonal *anxiety*. The presence of this anxiety reflects an awareness that one's construct system does not adequately predict interpersonal events, an interpretation which helps clarify the interpersonal tentativeness reported by abused women in forming subsequent intimate relationships (Roberts, 1984).

Part of this tentativeness may also be accounted for by the generalized negativity in the interpersonal systems of abused women. Results indicated that positive relationship constructions were less available to dissatisfied and abused women than to their more satisfied counterparts. In contrast to women who were not abused in their relationships, abused women were distinguished by their constructions of close relationships in more forceful, but less socially active ways. These findings would seem to support the clinical literature which emphasizes the prevalence of 'Power' issues (i.e. issues of dominance, control, and force) among abused women, as well as the tendency toward social withdrawal associated with abusive episodes (Ball and Wyman, 1978).

A final factor which was related to abused and dissatisfied women concerns their higher levels of *threat* associated with leaving their marriages. Compared to women who were more satisfied with their relationships, dissatisfied and abused women perceived the need for a greater number of revisions in their self-images upon dissolution of their marriages. This finding is consistent with Kalmus and Strauss's (1982) finding that noted a relationship between 'marital dependency' and wife abuse. Among other important factors (financial dependency, emotional dependency), the current finding suggests the possibility of an 'identity dependency' as one factor contributing to the reluctance to dissolve even highly conflictual relationships. In this case preserving the marriage serves as one means of preserving an otherwise uncertain self-identity. One testable corollary of this reasoning is that abused women who see divorce as requiring fewer revisions in their self-identity should be more likely to subsequently dissolve their marriages. Unfortunately, the limited sample size and the cross-sectional nature of the present study prevented testing this prediction.

In sum, the tentative findings of this study support the intimate interplay between interpersonal relationships and personal identity (cf. Harré, 1983). But the interpretability of these findings is restricted by the exploratory nature of the study. In particular, future efforts to study disturbed relationships could usefully add to these tentative findings by studying *both* partners within the context of larger and better-controlled longitudinal designs. Such efforts will gradually compensate for the imbalance in the interpersonal-relationship literature which has long favored the study of fairly *superficial* and *developing* relationships by contributing to the growing effort to understand *disturbed* but *intimate* relations.

References

Ball, R. G. and Wyman, G. (1978). Battered wives and powerlessness: what can counselors do? *Victimology* 2, 546–52.

Bannister, D. (1963). A genesis of schizophrenic thought disorder: a serial invalidation hypothesis. *British Journal of Psychiatry* 109, 680–7.

Breakwell, G. M. (ed.) (1983). *Threatened Identities*. New York: Wiley.

Doster, J. A. (1985). A personal construct assessment of marital violence: some preliminary findings. In F. R. Epting and A. W. Landfield (eds.), *Anticipating Personal Construct Theory*. Lincoln: University of Nebraska Press.

Duck, S. W. and Gilmour, R. (1981). *Personal Relationships 3: Personal Relationships in Disorder*. London: Academic Press.

Duck, S. W. and Sants, H. (1983). On the origin of the specious: are personal relationships really interpersonal states? *Journal of Social and Clinical Psychology 1*, 27–41.

Finchman, F. and O'Leary, D. (1983). Causal inferences for spouse behavior in maritally distressed and nondistressed couples. *Journal of Social and Clinical Psychology* 1, 42–57.

Fransella, F. and Bannister, D. (1977). *A Manual for Repertory Grid Technique*. New York: Academic.

Harré, R. (1983). Identity projects. In G. M. Breakwell (eds.), *Threatened Identities*. New York: Wiley.

Kalmuss, D. S. and Strauss, M. A. (1982). Wife's marital dependency and wife abuse. *Journal of Marriage and The Family* 44, 277–86.

Kelly, G. A. (1955). *The Psychology of Personal Constructs*, Vols. I and II. New York: Norton.

McCarthy, B. (1981). Studying personal relationships. In S. Duck and R. Gilmour (eds.), *Personal Relationships 1: Studying Personal Relationships*. London: Academic Press.

Neimeyer, G. J. (1984). Cognitive complexity and marital satisfaction. *Journal of Social and Clinical Psychology* 2, 193–8.

Neimeyer, G. J. (1985). Personal constructs in couple's counseling. In F. R. Epting and A. W. Landfield (eds.), *Anticipating Personal Construct Theory.* Lincoln: University of Nebraska Press.

Neimeyer, G. J. and Hudson, J. E. (1985). Couple's constructs: personal systems in marital satisfaction. In D. Bannister (ed.), *Issues and Approaches in Personal Construct Theory.* London: Wiley.

Neimeyer, R. A. and Neimeyer, G. J. (1985). Disturbed relationships: a personal construct view. In E. Button (ed.), *Personal Construct Theory and Mental Health.* Beckenham, Kent: Croom Helm.

Rigdon, M. A., Epting, F. R., Neimeyer, R. A., and Krieger, S. R. (1979). The Threat Index: a research report. *Death Education* 3, 245–70.

Roberts, A. R. (1984). *Battered Women and Their Families: Intervention Strategies and Treatment Programs.* New York: Sprieger.

Schlenker, B. R. (1984). Identities, identifications, and relationships. In V. Derlega (ed.), *Communication, Intimacy, and Close Relationships.* New York: Academic Press.

Spanier, G. B. (1976). Measuring dyadic adjustment: new scales for assessing the quality of marriage and similar dyads. *Journal of Marriage and the Family* 38, 15–28.

Wright, P. H. (1984). Self-referent motivation and the instrinsic quality of friendship. *Journal of Social and Personal Relationships* 1, 115–30.

Chapter 5
Contextual shifts in interpersonal constructions

L. M. Leitner

Repertory grid research may be hampered by assuming that a particular rating of another is the subject's *only* perception of the other and ignoring the possibility that the subject may see the other in markedly different ways in different contexts. This paper attempts to illustrate the importance of understanding such contextual shifts in perception through clinical examples. Further, two theoretical explanations of these contextual shifts will be presented. Some data from a repertory grid study which attempted to measure contextual shifts in perception will be presented. The paper will conclude with a discussion of implications for future research in this area.

Clinical examples of contextual shifts

Clinicians often deal with contextual shifts in the construing process. Crises in relationships often occur in association with different understandings of the other. For example, Jeff entered therapy following a serious suicide attempt. Certain incidents in his past had been used as the basis of a comprehensive core ROLE construct (Leitner, 1985) in his life. First, there was a history of violent assaults by his father. Further, there were many incidents in which his mother abandoned him. For example, she once took him 'for a ride', threw him out of the car and left him alone in a deserted area of the country for several hours before he found help. *Assaulting* versus *abandoning* was the ROLE construct around which Jeff organized his life. When I attempted to understand aspects of his experience, Jeff experienced great distress and saw me as assaulting him. When I 'backed off', Jeff felt abandoned by me. When Jeff saw me as 'assaulting' him, he often experienced psychotic episodes characterized by severe panic, depersonalization, derealization, and the experience of being a 'scrunched up little person' who was 'falling out of the world.' When I was seen as 'abandoning' him, Jeff became suicidal. By understanding contextual shifts on the *assaulting* versus *abandoning* construct, we were able to understand the erratic nature of his experience in a way which led to therapeutic growth.

John was referred to therapy following an episode in which he seriously beat his son. As we struggled to understand his life, it became clear that John's behavior toward his son was tied to John's perception of himself on a construct of *good parent* versus *bad parent*. Being a 'good parent' was important because he loved his son *and* because he was trying to prove to his family of origin that they could be proud of him. Being a 'bad parent' was terrifying in that it validated earlier experiences of being totally inadequate. When his son misbehaved, John became quite threatened due to the implications of the 'bad parent' pole of the construct and violence occurred. If John was less threatened, he saw the child's behavior in other terms. Thus the contextual shifting of the perception of self on the *good parent* versus *bad parent* construct was tightly linked to the problems between John and his son.

Theoretical explanations

The clinical examples given above illustrate the importance of understanding how the construing process shifts in various contexts. In this section, we will explore two PCT approaches to understanding such contextual shifts.

Fragmentation Corollary

Kelly's (1955) Fragmentation Corollary, one way of approaching contextual shifts, implies that people may be experienced through different (and incompatible!) constructs at various points in the relationship. At a higher level, these incompatible constructs may be (but not necessarily are) integrated under certain core structures. However, the experience of the other may shift in marked ways at a less superordinate level.

In this context the same 'verbal words' may assume drastically different implications due to their linkages to various construct subsystems. Alternatively, the same events may be experienced in drastically different ways when various subsystems are in effect. For example, when beginning clinical students are evaluated using a 'student construction subsystem,' certain behaviors may elicit terms like 'intellectually aggressive,' 'critical thinker,' 'always challenging in seminar discussions,' and so on, which are viewed as quite positive perceptions. However, these same behaviors may result in quite critical evaluations when the 'therapist construction subsystem' is employed. The behaviors which had been previously validated by the faculty now may be termed 'intellectualizing,' 'hostile,' 'excessively confrontive and attacking,' and so on. Thus, depending upon which subsystem is dominant, the student may be seen in quite different ways.

Contrast reconstruction

Contrast reconstruction, or *slot-change*, is defined by Kelly as redefining an element on the contrast pole of a construct. While contrast reconstruction may be a relatively superficial form of change, Kelly implies that it may be the basis of many types of contextual shifts in the construction of self and others. 'Sometimes this kind of superficial movement is worth seeking; but, as every clinician should know, it is all too likely to end up in seesaw behavior: the client is 'kindly' as long as things are going well, then he turns to hostility, then back again, ad infinitum' (Kelly, 1955, p. 938).

While relatively superficial, contrast reconstruction may be our most immediate response to the experience of invalidation. By employing contrast reconstruction the person may be able to maintain an organized system with relative ease. The other two forms of change Kelly discussed (reorganizing the ways in which constructs relate to one another and developing totally new ways of experiencing the world) are much more apt to throw the person into a profound experience of personal turmoil. In most relationships, then, contrast reconstruction may be a common experience when times are stressful. Thus, while slot-change itself may be a relatively trivial form of change, the systematic studying of this experience would appear to be quite important in understanding interpersonal relationships.

Contextual shifts: a repertory grid study

In an attempt to understand this aspect of human relationships in more detail, fifty couples agreed to complete a variation of Kelly's (1955) Repertory Grid. These individuals, predominantly undergraduates, had been involved with the partner for time periods ranging from six weeks to several years. Thus relationships of differing durations and levels of intimacy were involved in the study.

Method

Each participant completed a standard 15 × 15 grid for eliciting constructs (Landfield, 1971, 1977). After completing the elicitation, each person rated the elements 'myself,' 'my partner,' 'ideal self,' 'ideal partner,' 'myself as my partner sees me,' and 'my partner as my partner sees herself or himself.' These ratings (termed the general ratings) are the typical ratings employed in most repertory grid studies in the person perception literature.

The couple next discussed a *recent, specific*, incident in which they were relating well. After describing this incident in detail, subjects rated the 'self,' 'partner,' 'myself as my partner saw me,' and 'my partner as my partner saw himself or herself' *as they were experiencing one another at that time* on the fifteen constructs elicited previously.

The couple then described a *recent, specific*, incident in which they did not relate well. After describing it in detail, each subject completed the same four ratings described above *as they were experiencing one another at that time* on the fifteen constructs elicited previously.

Measures

Five measures dealing with aspects of the relationship were computed for the general ratings as well as the two specific incident ratings described above. These measures were (1) *perceived similarity of the self and the partner*, (2) *self/ideal self* discrepancy, (3) *partner/ideal partner* discrepancy, (4) *myself/myself as my partner sees me* discrepancy, and (5) *my partner/my partner as my partner sees him or herself* discrepancy. All of these measures were computed by summing the algebraic differences between the ratings of the elements on the fifteen constructs. All of the ratings were done on thirteen-point scales (ranging from 6 on one pole to −6 on the contrast pole). Thus a higher score indicates a lack of perceived congruence in an important area of the relationship.

Results

The data were separated by sex and are visually presented in Figures D5.1 to D5.5. As can be inferred, main effects were present for context on each of the measures. Greater discrepancies were present on measures derived from the construing of the 'bad' context and lesser discrepancies derived from the construing of the 'good' context with the scores derived from the general ratings occupying a middle position. While these effects make intuitive sense, it is important to note that an investigator would make erroneous inferences about the magnitude of the discrepancies in the specific contexts based upon an analysis of the 'general' construing pattern.

Only one main effect for sex was found. Males felt less well understood by their partners than females (Fig. D5.4). There was also a trend for males to see less similarity (greater discrepancy) between themselves and their partners (Fig. D5.1). In both of these cases the differences between males and females were most pronounced in the 'general' as opposed to the 'contextual' construing. This may imply that sex differences are less important in the construing of specific contexts than when more general rating patterns are used.

Correlations between the measures are summarized in Tables D5.1 to D5.5. Out of twenty correlations between the 'general' and 'contextual' measures (two for the females and two for the

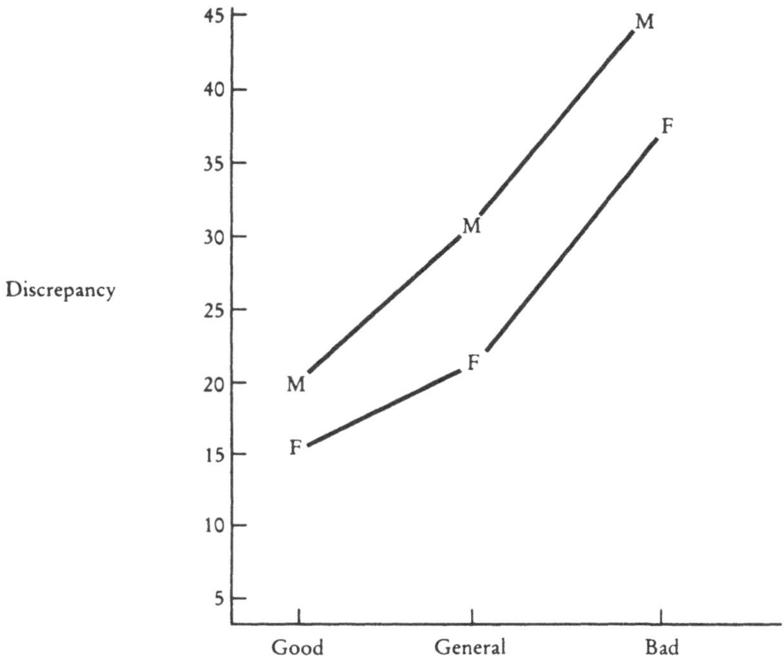

Figure D5.1 Self/partner discrepancy

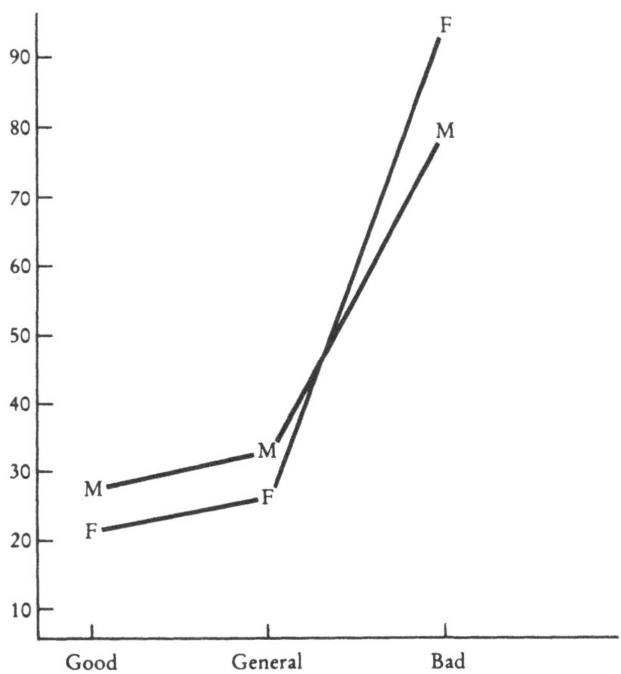

Figure D5.2 Self/ideal self discrepancy

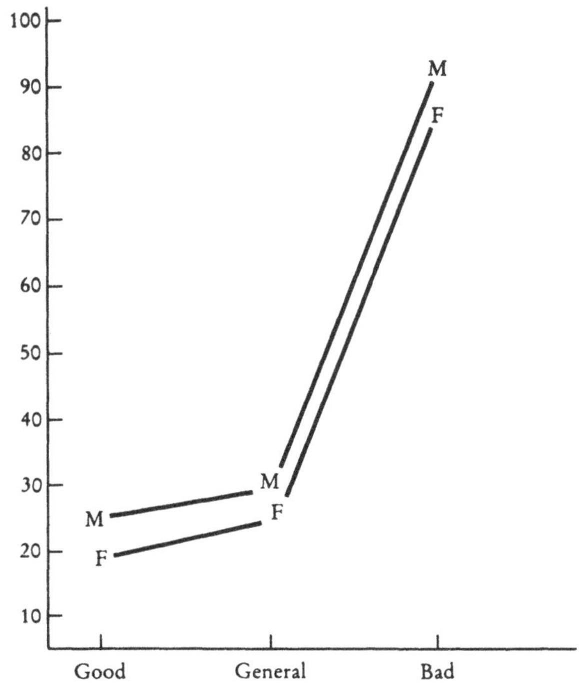

Figure D5.3 Partner/ideal partner discrepancy

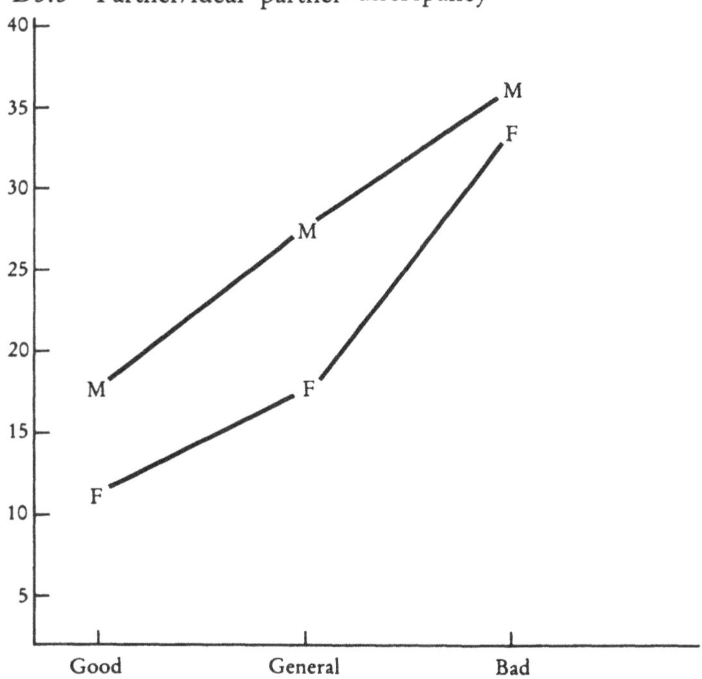

Figure D5.4 Self/myself as my partner sees me discrepancy

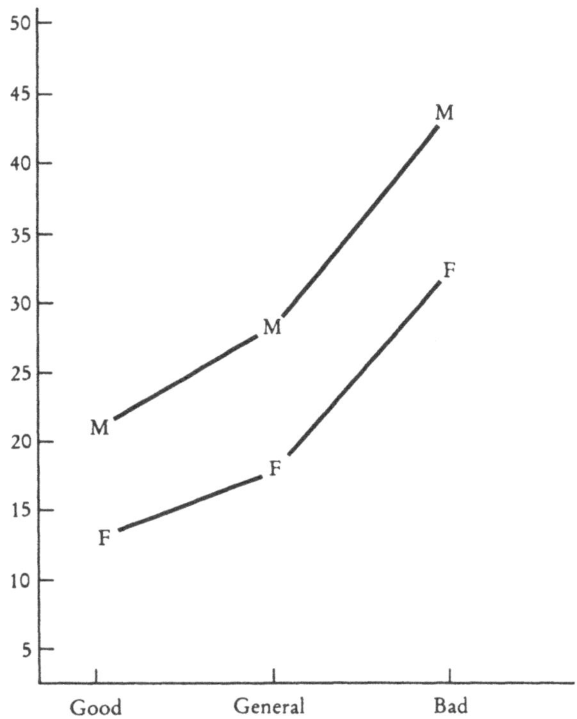

Figure D5.5 Partner/partner as partner sees self discrepancy

males on each of the five measures), only one reached 0.40. This particular score was the correlation between the general rating of *self/myself as my partner sees me* discrepancy and the rating of this discrepancy in the 'good' context for males (Table D5.4). In addition, ten of these twenty correlations are *less* than 0.20! In other words, the general ratings derived from the repertory grid tell the investigator very little about how these ratings may shift in specific contexts. Further, only two of the ten correlations between the 'good' and 'bad' context ratings were above 0.40 (six were less than 0.20). Once again, these data suggest that the investigator must take the time to understand each person's construction of each context.

Table D5.1 Self/partner discrepancy

	FEMALE			MALE		
	General	Good	Bad	General	Good	Bad
General	X	X	X	X	X	X
Good	0.14	X	X	0.34	X	X
Bad	0.39	0.47	X	0.06	0.55	X

Table D5.2 Self/ideal self discrepancy

	FEMALE			MALE		
	General	Good	Bad	General	Good	Bad
General	X	X	X	X	X	X
Good	0.23	X	X	0.33	X	X
Bad	0.01	−0.01	X	−0.04	0.10	X

Table D5.3 Partner/ideal partner discrepancy

	FEMALE			MALE		
	General	Good	Bad	General	Good	Bad
General	X	X	X	X	X	X
Good	0.39	X	X	0.16	X	X
Bad	0.02	−0.11	X	0.27	0.21	X

Table D5.4 Self/myself as my partner sees me discrepancy

	FEMALE			MALE		
	General	Good	Bad	General	Good	Bad
General	X	X	X	X	X	X
Good	0.19	X	X	0.40	X	X
Bad	0.05	0.35	X	0.25	0.32	X

Table D5.5 Partner/partner as partner sees self discrepancy

	FEMALE			MALE		
	General	Good	Bad	General	Good	Bad
General	X	X	X	X	X	X
Good	−0.01	X	X	0.35	X	X
Bad	−0.12	0.14	X	0.34	0.10	X

Implications

These data have implications for our current understandings of the person perception process as well as for future research. However, the study does have some limitations.

Limitations

This study focused only on contrast reconstruction with nothing in the Fragmentation Corollary being investigated. The reason for this focus is the important role contrast reconstruction plays in the construing process of most individuals. Future research should, however, address the implications of the Fragmentation Corollary for understanding the contextual shifts in construing.

This study also relied on recall data. However, *every* repertory grid study involves the use of recall data. There is always a time period between an event and the reporting of the construction of the event. Further, all of our clinical techniques and theories rely on the recall of experiences by the client and the therapist. Finally, the process of this study might be more usefully described as 'relived' – not 'recalled.' My research partners described these events in great detail (in most cases 're-fighting' in the more negative context!)

Current understandings

These data imply that typical repertory grid studies do not tell us much about the construing process in specific situations. Asking our research partners to construe generalized others has been useful, but we are limiting our understanding of others by not focusing on contextually specific construing. In addition, the focus on construing more generalized others may be inconsistent with our theoretical assertions that the person is an evolving, construing organism. These assertions imply that we need to develop techniques which specifically measure the process of construing. Asking participants to tell us how they experienced different situations in their lives may be one such method.

Future research

Future research can investigate the relationship between contextual shifts in construing and the presence of interpersonal problems in those contexts. For example, we are currently exploring the precise nature of the contextual shifts in construing which occur during violent episodes in relationships. Research in this area may empirically validate Walker's (1979) theory of spouse abuse as well as help us better understand the nature of marital violence. Similar studies in many problem areas could be performed.

Another way of measuring contextual shifts in the construction process involves actually *changing* the context. To take one example, a better understanding of the experience of alcoholism may be developed through having individuals complete various repertory grid measures with differing amounts of alcohol in their systems. This may tell us something about the precise ways in which the construction of the self shifts when alcohol is introduced into the system. Such understandings may lead to treatment programs tailored to the specific construing processes of the troubled person as opposed to the tailoring of people to the specific requirements of the treatment program.

References

Kelly, G. A. (1955). *Personal Construct Psychology*, Vols I and II. New York: Norton.

Landfield, A. W. (1971). *Personal Construct Systems in Psychotherapy*. Chicago: Rand McNally.

Landfield, A. W. (1977). Interpretative man: the enlarged self-image. In J. K. Cole and A. W. Landfield (eds.), *The Nebraska Symposium on Motivation 1976*, Vol. 24. Lincoln: University of Nebraska Press.

Leitner, L. M. (1985). The terrors of cognition: on the experiential validity of personal construct theory. In D. Bannister (ed.), *Issues and Approaches in Personal Construct Theory*. Orlando: Academic.

Walker, L. E. (1979). *The Battered Woman*. New York: Harper & Row.

Chapter 6
Phobias: a journey beyond neurosis

Gavin Dunnett

Phobia is a term used to describe a specific type of syndrome. It is defined in its own right, but it is also related to other syndromes in the classification of mental illness. It is regarded as one of the neuroses, a generic term covering 'anxiety related' syndromes. It is itself generic being divided clinically into three main types: agoraphobia, social phobias and simple phobias (Hamilton, 1985). This pattern of classification can be related to the constructs of superordinacy and subordinacy (Kelly, 1955) such that *mental illness* versus *mental health* becomes the most superordinate construct and the emergent poles, as the constructs become more subordinate, include *neurosis*, *phobia* and then the types of *phobia* (i.e. *agora-*, *social* and *simple*).

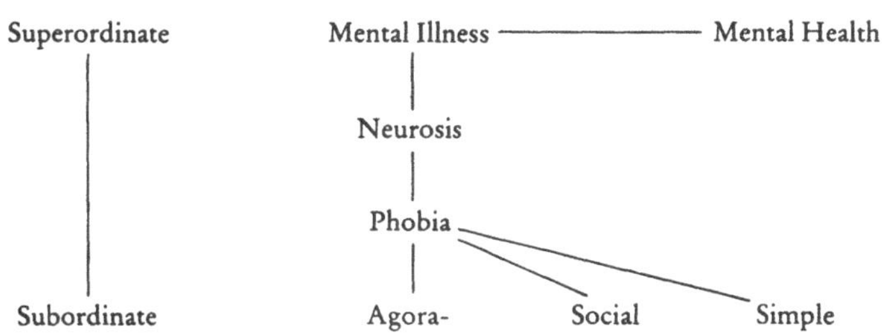

This subsystem is the starting point for this chapter, beginning with the construct of *phobia* versus *non-phobia*. As the exploration develops, the implications of our journey on both superordinate and subordinate constructs will be considered.

Phobia is defined variously in the psychiatric literature. Gelder, Eath and Mayou (1983) quote the *International Classification of*

Disease, 1975 (Ninth) Revision as 'neurotic states with an abnormally intense dread of certain objects or specific situations which do not normally have that effect'. This definition they subsume under a heading of 'phobic anxiety neuroses'. Marks (1969) states that phobias can be defined on the following four criteria:

1 A fear out of proportion to the demands of the situation.
2 The fear cannot be reasoned or explained away.
3 The fear is beyond voluntary control.
4 The fear leads to the avoidance of the feared situation.

Kaplan and Saddock (1981) identify phobia clinically as 'an exaggerated and invariably pathological dread of some specific type of stimulus or situation'.

Gelder, Eath and Mayou (1983) sum up the behavioural model in saying, 'Learning theory attempts to explain agoraphobia as a series of conditioned fear responses with learned avoidance'.

All these definitions refer to a specific phobic stimulus producing a reaction that is out of proportion to that stimulus, and which the patient recognises as being out of proportion. These definitions suffer from the defect inherent in orthodox psychiatric classification of being phenomenologically based. It is an *observed* problem, and the statement that the patient concurs that the feeling is irrational allows a minimal subjective sop to those concerned with the patient's own position. He/she agrees that it is irrational, so what more is to be said?

This type of definition begs a number of questions. What is irrational in this context? What is being said is that the constructs held by a majority of people in this particular culture are similar and agree that the reaction is out-of-proportion to the stimulus. This invocation of Kelly's Commonality Corollary conveniently avoids the need to consider the meaning of the irrationality from the perspective of the individual concerned. After all, he agrees it's irrational. But is this agreement really surprising? Individuals are perfectly capable of mutually contradictory systems of construing in different circumstances (Fragmentation Corollary), and there is no reason to think that this is not happening in this case. There may be good psychological reasons for the patient to choose to agree that the problem is irrational. Were he to deny its irrationality he might be deemed to have lost 'insight' and become subject to a delusion – a much worse fate altogether. PCT encourages us to consider that a construct of *rational* versus *irrational* is not especially useful since by its nature it requires external referencing and ignores internal consistency. In clinical practice the fact that a patient/client may consider the problem irrational is important therapeutically. The view the client has of his own problem dictates what he will do about it. The very fact of construing it as a phobia has brought him to the therapist. But it is important to separate the psychological process that causes the phobia from the constructs about the phobia itself. The PCP clinician must ask himself, '*Why* does this patient act the way he does?'

This leads to the second question these definitions beg. A single specific object/event is said to trigger the response. But this is evidently not true in many cases of agoraphobia, which is perhaps why it is not always regarded as a 'true' phobia. Conversely, simple phobias are thought to be much more specific. In a simple series of experiments to test out this notion I constructed a sample of elements which I presented to a number of spider phobics. The elements provided were:

Bats	Daddy-long-legs
Mice	Wasps
Snakes	Centipedes
Flies	Snails
Spiders	Worms

Elicitation of constructs, using these elements, was then carried out; one example of which is below:

1	Eyes like humans	– Eyes unlike humans
2	Lots of obvious legs	– Has less obvious legs
3	Stays in garden	– Comes into house
4	Cuddly	– Uncuddleable (wriggly)
5	Warm-blooded	– Bloodless
6	Feels horrible on skin	– Doesn't feel horrible on skin
7	Hides in dark corners and leaps out	– Floats around visibly
8	Sticky	– Dry
9	Has controlling force which is not instinct	– Unpredictable
10	Shows that it knows I'm there	– Behaves as though I were a bit of the furniture
11	Can relate to me	– Cold-blooded

This shows the variety of constructs employed to differentiate amongst small animals/insects. In this example, one construct applied solely to spiders – *shows that it knows I'm there* versus *behaves as though I were part of the furniture*. This construct can then be laddered to explore its significance for the individual. Other sufferers, however, reacted differently producing constructs relating to type of movement, shape of legs and creation of webs as descriptive perceptions, and more abstract ones relating to evil, and a perception of the relationship of the spider to the person. It is not the spider itself which is the phobic stimulus, it is a particular quality of the spider; and it is not too far a leap from there to postulate that the important factor is the individual's own construction of that quality. The notion of a single stimulus may still exist, but it has to be faced that this stimulus may be unique to the individual and has meaning only within *their* construct system. This view varies from the widely held standpoint that patients have well-elaborated constructs of the phobic object: varies not so much by contradicting it but by elaborating another part of the fragmented system. The phobic object, construed as irrational and so forth, belongs to the system dictated by Commonality, and it is entirely predictable that the object itself would be well elaborated by a patient desperate to make sense in his cultural context. The unique meaning of the phobic object, however, lies within a different subsystem and deserves separate exploration.

Kelly (1955) does not discuss phobia as an entity but does deal extensively with anxiety. He defines anxiety very precisely as 'the awareness that the events with which one is confronted lie outside the range of convenience of his construct system'. It may seem obvious to state that the anxiety Kelly describes may not correspond with the clinical variety as used in the definitions of phobia. Kelly's anxiety deals with awareness of situations occurring for which one's construct system has no answers, and while this is certainly significant in many instances, it does not provide an explanation for the incredibly powerful reaction which occurs in the severely phobic person.

Work has already been done in the field of neurosis and phobia from a PCT perspective. *Personal Styles in Neurosis* (Caine, Wijesinge and Winter, 1981) has looked at the whole field of neurosis, while individual workers have considered particular areas. Unsurprisingly, most work has been on agoraphobia due to its frequency of clinical presentation.

Winter (1985) notes that phobic avoidance reactions 'can be

considered to represent clear behavioural expressions of a constrictive process, the drawing in of the outer boundaries of the perceptual field to minimise apparent incompatibilities in the construct system'. He goes on, 'Constriction can also be regarded as serving to maintain the client's symptoms, in that continuation of the phobic avoidance . . . prevents invalidation of predictions that cessation of this behaviour is likely to have catastrophic consequences'.

This latter statement seems to accept the underlying assumption that phobic reactions are irrational and unreasonable. Phobic avoidance reactions are about avoiding 'truth' about the phobia and say nothing about the meaning of the phobia itself. The underlying theme of PCT is credulousness in therapy – the uncritical believing that the client actually has a reason *within his own system* for thinking, feeling and acting the way he does. Any assumption of irrationality is a fatal flaw in attempting to make sense of the process occurring. By contrast, why not consider a phobia as understandable and reasonable, even if unpleasant.

Hopkins (1983) regards loss as the initiating problem; the loss being so profound as to cause the disintegration of part of all the social portion of the individual's core role constructs. This leads in turn to anxiety/threat/panic when away from environments that validate the remaining core role constructs. Hence home (or similar) is 'safe' while going out with a family member or taking an object from home with them renders 'outside' also safe.

At least here is an attempt to consider process and meaning. But the range of convenience of the argument is too small. He does not postulate that the same process occurs in other phobias, and indeed his description is defined in relation to the symptoms of agoraphobia.

In his review of some work related to therapy, Winter (1985) states 'these approaches could be regarded as directed towards the invalidation of constructs underlying neurotic symptoms' and appears to support the case that repeated disconfirmation of expectations weakens phobic avoidance behaviour. This is all to do with the client's choice to have these symptoms. It is possible to postulate that people choose phobias and other neuroses as a means of dealing with their worlds, but I do not really believe that many people make *that* active choice. Rather the choices they make are more fundamental, and the 'neurotic' symptomatology follows as a result of that choice. If that is the case then invalidation of the neurotic symptoms may be too superficial a way of dealing with the problem. It may produce the reappearance of the problem under a different guise or dislodge the focus of the problem to another symptom. The 'cured' phobic may become depressed or obsessional, or develop a different phobia or relapse. He may even develop a problem not defined as neurotic, in which case he may be seen as 'cured'. The psychoanalytic notion that one has to delve beneath the surface of the symptom complex to discover the conflicts these signposts direct us to should not be disregarded by personal construct therapists. We may not choose to construe the problems in the same way, but we should be prepared to essay the abstraction needed to investigate them in our own model.

Virtually all the PCT work on phobia is done in the context of the construct of *neurotic* versus *non-neurotic* (a catch-all contrast pole!). But this itself is just another way of construing behaviour, and to remain within it is to be constricted ourselves. The research, although useful, does not seem to reach to the root of the problem.

Let me try to provide an analogy for my meaning. In the world of art, paintings are done in a particular medium. There is a variety of mediums to choose from – oils, watercolours, pastels, pen and ink, and so forth. In human activity these mediums can be seen as the different theoretical models we can use to play with, experiment with. Artistically, these mediums are used to express the artist's perceptions of a subject. Similarly, we attempt to use our medium to make sense of the way people are. But an artist has a number of ways of expressing his perceptions. He may choose a very representational form – an attempt to paint his subject as it is commonly seen. The picture is instantly recognisable and speaks to the viewer in its own context – of landscapes, buildings, still lifes or whatever. Alternatively, he can choose to disregard the accuracy of what he sees and what is commonly accepted, and attempt to convey a deeper meaning as he construes it. So his art becomes less instantly recognisable and depends more for its impact on the non-verbal response of its audience. Ultimately, the work becomes totally abstract: no representation at a subordinate level is visible but it is still conveying something the artist construes in his subject, through his chosen medium to his audience. Further, because he has abandoned strict representation, the perceptions he conveys may no longer be constricted to the original context of the subject – they may have wider significance and be more readily seen to be similar to perceptions produced in apparently vastly different subjects. All this assumes the sincerity of the artist, as it is as possible to blind people with garbage abstraction on canvas as with garbage abstraction in the scientific paper! Many people find abstract painting difficult to deal with, they expect their art to come in packages they can easily comprehend. They don't want their own representations challenged and they dismiss the artist's attempt to do so. It seems to me that the analogy with our work is that much of it is still highly representational. We attempt to express the subject in PCT terms, and in this case the subject is neurosis or phobia. We expect to still be able to recognise we are dealing with these subjects so we restrict our shape and form to the limits these prescribe. But if we are going to be courageous with our medium, we must be prepared to let these structures go in our search for 'inner meaning', 'superordinacy' or aspects which are much harder to verbalise.

If we are prepared to do this, then we begin with the person. We don't begin with neurosis or phobia, except in so far as there is a person who exhibits symptoms that can be described by others as a phobia. But what else can it be described as? How can we represent the personal as being in our chosen medium of personal construct psychology. Let us look at our person and think what is happening to him? What could be happening to him?

The Creativity Cycle, loosening then tightening, gives the direction to follow, as below:

There is an object which precipitates each crisis. There is the crisis itself and there is a not unreasonable attempt to avoid the crisis. A lot of what is happening to the person doesn't make sense to him, at least not in ways he can verbalise. He knows it happens, but he cannot *explain* it to others. He accepts the Commonality explanation. The symbols we use to transfer our constructs from one to another fail him. So perhaps there are pre-verbal constructs in action, or perhaps they are so superordinate and so abstract as not to have any coherent verbal labelling. Along comes this object and does something to our person. What can this object be construed as by him? We know he may have all kinds of constructs about it, and that he may react to it in a personal unique sense. But what does he see it as doing? Whatever it is, it seems fairly fundamental because it provokes quite a reaction. Perhaps he construes it as threat ('the awareness of an imminent comprehensive change in one's core structures', Kelly, 1955). We have agreed this object carries personal meaning with it. The spider phobic saw spiders as *behaving as though I was a bit of the furniture*. The spider therefore becomes the carrier of a construct which acts as a threat. To coin a term, the spider in this instance is a 'threator' rather than a phobic object or stimulus. The threator may be any object or situation, although there are some more common ones. But what is being threatened? The definition of threat relates to core structures, and the reaction is positive and total. Avoidance becomes understandable as an attempt to preserve the core constructs under threat. As such, it may be seen as constriction but only in that singular area – related to the threator. There is a threat, unique, personal. But this cannot be all. Not all threats on core role constructs produce a phobia or even phobic-type response. In phobia, all else diminishes before the phobic situation. It does not matter in what context the threator appears, the reaction is immediate and extreme. He is not in a specific role at the time, the threat always exists. So the core construct under attack must apply all the time in his life: it must have a wide range of convenience. Equally, it must be superordinate partly because of its wide applicability and partly because it is difficult to get hold of to explain what is under attack. Now there is a threat to a superordinate core role construct of wide range of convenience. But the person knows *something* is happening. He doesn't walk into it blindfold. He is aware that this object carries a threat in it even though he cannot verbalise it. There is an awareness of threat to a superordinate core role construct of wide range of convenience. The picture is beginning to develop. But there is another aspect to add to this. Specific objects usually cause this reaction. These have now been called threators. These threators are potentially invalidating an important construct and promising imminent change by themselves, that is as a single invalidational event. Nothing more is needed to have the effect – it is an all-or-none response. So the hypothesis can be refined again to become:

The awareness of threat produced by a single invalidational event upon a superordinate core role construct of wide range of convenience.

Now that this picture is painted, what do we do with it? Well the first thing is to show it to an audience to see whether it carries any meaning for them. It is not a statement of fact, it is a hypothesis for further exploration. There may be many other hypotheses, even within this medium, to attempt to explain this person's activity. Further, it is not a representation of phobia as such. It is related: phobia was where it began, but if you go on to explore this picture, a variety of different relationships come into view. Where, for example, is a construct called 'neurosis'? No longer really applicable, perhaps. What kinds of reactions are produced by multiple invalidational events, or if the superordinate construct has a narrow range of convenience or is more or less permeable? The range of questions is endless, and in amongst the answers there might be found familiar themes such as panic, depression, frustration, anger, despair – some clinical entities, some emotions, some activities, some behaviour – not parcelled up in different contexts to be examined separately, but intimately connected with a process that occurs by changing one or more variables from the process that seems to occur in phobia.

It must be remembered that this is only one possible hypothetical model for phobia (although it has stood up to many attempts endeavouring to discredit it without immediate success). What is important to defend is the need to let go of the restraints we put about ourselves and our work. The theory is there to be played with, experimented with, used and enjoyed. It can even be fun! But play is not aimless – all activity is an attempt to increase our anticipations, elaborate our system. We constrict ourselves perhaps because of our own fears of leaving behind the known in our respective professional worlds. It is not really acceptable to abandon notions of neurosis and mental illness, so we force ourselves to work within them. Neimeyer (1985) suggested a dichotomy of development of PCP between elite and revolutionary, and he contended that PCT workers have chosen the elite rather than revolutionary pole. I suspect for most of us 'elite' is a preferable choice for elaborating our professional systems. But I must contend that to use PCT to its full potential we may have to abandon our constrictive goggles and be prepared to be seen as revolutionary. If we believe that personal construct theory is personal (and the adjective gets left off significantly often these days), then the pictures we paint must always begin *there*, and not with the already created artifacts of others' construing.

References

Caine, T. M., Wijesinge, O. B. A. and Winter, D. A. (1981). *Personal Styles in Neurosis*. London: Routledge & Kegan Paul.

Gelder, M., Eath, D. and Mayou, R. (1983). *Oxford Textbook of Psychiatry*. Oxford: Oxford University Press.

Hamilton, Max. (ed.) (1985). *Fish's Clinical Psychopathology*. 2nd ed. Bristol: Wright.

Hopkins, N. (1983). Causes of agoraphobia. Personal communication.

Kaplan, H. I. and Saddock, B. J. (1981). *Modern Synopsis of Comprehensive Textbook of Psychiatry*. 3rd ed. Baltimore and London: Williams-Wilkins.

Kelly, G. A. (1955). *The Psychology of Personal Constructs*, Vols. I and II. New York: Norton.

Marks, I. M. (1969). *Fears and Phobias*. London: Heinemann.

Neimeyer, G. (1985). *The Development of Personal Construct Psychology*. Lincoln: University of Nebraska Press.

Winter, D. A. (1985). Neurotic disorders: the curse of certainty In E. Button (ed.), *Personal Construct Psychology and Mental Health*. Beckenham, Kent: Croom Helm.

World Health Organisation. (1977, 1978). *Manual of the International Statistical Classification of Disease, Injuries and Causes of Death, 1975 (ninth) Revision*. Geneva: WHO. Vol. 1 (1977) and Vol. 2 (1978).

Chapter 7

Building change in patients with agoraphobic symptoms

Roberto Lorenzini and Sandra Sassaroli

It is common clinical knowledge that agoraphobics have difficulty dealing with vital processes (Sullivan, 1984). In particular, they have a tendency to limit physical activity directed towards the outside world. This is a significant fact as far as differential diagnosis is concerned both in simple anxiety neurosis and obsessive syndromes. Personal construct theory suggests that, from the patient's point of view, the explorative field is the best way to make predictions about themselves and their world (Kelly, 1969; Sullivan, 1984).

We would also like to examine another clinical datum: their difficulty in distinguishing, knowing and constructing emotions. According to PCT, we can define this as a difficulty in constructing variations in the arrangement and hierarchy of one's own construct system (Goldstein and Chambless, 1977; Bowlby, 1979).

In this paper we consider explorative behaviour an important and distinct class of behaviour. It has the biological function of validating or invalidating hypotheses about the outside world and other people, thus creating new situations and making possible continuous change in knowledge of one's position in the world. We consider explorative behaviour to be subordinate to the more general concept of growth of knowledge regarding the outside world, self and one's internal world. We stress the specificity of explorative behaviour so that reference to attachment theories will be more coherent and explicit. The argument is that in the growth of knowledge in general, and in explorative behaviour in particular, we test out our hypothesis about ourselves and the outside world. However validated, the explorative behaviour attains its goal and is reinforced as a whole (i.e. as a behavioural class of acts not each specific act). Explorative behaviour is reduced and inhibited only if the subject's overall predictive ability is decreased as a result, for example when an explorative gesture in the outside world corresponds to a relative decrease of predictability about oneself.

Agoraphobic patients

We will omit a detailed description of the syndrome's various aspects (see Liotti, 1981) in order to report on elements which seem more useful to our interpretative hypothesis.

Often the patient's history is clearly divided into two parts. First, there is a pre-pathological period characterised by a 'compulsive self-reliance' (Bowlby, 1980) where the patient, whose family situation clearly generates anxiety (symptomatic mother, often phobic, fear of illness, always calling for the doctor, tendency to construct everything outside the house as dangerous, confusing and to be avoided as much as possible). This generates constructions of self as 'a lion', 'strong', 'active', 'eager to travel' and aiming to be 'successful in many fields'. Second, the period of discomfort, where the symptomatology is clear, is defined by the crumbling of this myth and an awareness of a scarcity of means and energy, of personal weakness and need of care and protection from others. The onset of agoraphobic symptoms is often linked to situations like 'environmental or existential changes' that require a new adaptation (marriage, greater professional responsibilities, financial problems, separations, mourning).

Even when the symptomatology is structured by complicated avoidance behaviour and versatile variants, it is clearly monotonous and poorly articulated. There is difficulty in constructing emotions coherently and precisely, as well as in elaborating them in the Kellian sense of extension and definition of one's construct system. Often the few available constructs are overworked with implication. These the patient uses for interpreting all the various situations in life.

It is difficult for patients to construe themselves as capable of dealing with transformation situations on their own. This makes it necessary always to have someone, as an attachment figure, who is readily available to telephone, touch or see. This could be an understanding wife or husband who is willing to listen or someone in a general outpatient clinic or regional hospital on the patient's way to and from work.

Development hypothesis

The question to consider now is why explorative movements in the world correspond to an overall reduction of predictive abilities? An interesting fact which has already been noted in the literature (Parker, 1979; Solyom, Silberfeld and Solyom, 1976) is the presence of an over-protective, anxious, worried mother. She often imagines that she is ill, she is tense, phobic, worried about getting ill and in general feels the constant danger of illness. As a rule, a physician is called in, even for the slightest case of flu or for a common cold. The mother tends to keep her children near to her, inhibiting their explorative behaviour in many ways: (1) she becomes unpredictable when faced with the child's explorative behaviour, (2) she fosters the child's construction of self as weak, physically frail, unsuitable for facing the outside world, which is often described as hostile and full of dangers and uncertainties; (3) she tends to decodify the emotions the child shows (crying, fear) as signs of weakness, fostering this construction of self within the child who will soon consider their own emotions as danger signs to avoid, linking them to situations to be avoided. Goldstein and Chambless (1978) reported that in pre-agoraphobics even the internal acknowledgment of an angry feeling can generate anxiety, hence they learn to avoid contacting their own feelings. Marks (1969) has reported on various phobias connected with facing life events.

If we accept Bowlby's assumption (1982) that at the base of an explorative behaviour there is good attachment, in the same way that a theory is the basis of our ability to experiment (i.e. we must have a good theory in order to make good experiments), then we can deduce that children comparing themselves with an attachment figure whose behavioural experiments in the outside world are ineffective, will come to construct the idea that explorative behaviour and attachment are incompatible. In other words, they may have difficulty integrating exploration and the construction of themselves with exploration and construction of the outside world.

To give an example of this dilemma, we could say that such a child is faced with choosing between (1) 'If I explore the outside world actively, I give up attachment' and (2) 'If I maintain good attachment, I give up exploring'. We can make the hypothesis that the first alternative in the example above corresponds to the pre-pathological phase. The subject demonstrates an attachment behaviour which is the opposite of being anxious, which Bowlby describes as 'compulsive self-reliance'. Since these subjects are far from looking for affection and care from others, they tend to show strength of character and do everything alone in almost every circumstance. Many of these patients have had experiences similar to those who develop anxious and tense attachments. However, the pre-agoraphobics react differently in that they inhibit sensations of attachment behaviour and fight off any desire to have close relationships with others (Bowlby, 1969).

These subjects construe themselves as *strong* versus *weak* and as *independent* versus *dependent*. These two constructs are strongly correlated, very polarised and not well articulated. Since they are poorly articulated they are exposed to direct invalidation (without filtering through any subordinate constructs in a hierarchical system). Even though the subjects see themselves at the emergent pole of the superordinate construct as *strong* rather than *weak* and *independent* rather than *dependent*, they also have the tendency to explore and construct emotions awkwardly and with difficulty psychologically and not just in the problem area.

The triggering-off event is construed as a situation that invalidates the self construction of 'being strong'. The event can be quite obvious; the example, a trauma, marriage, the onset of unexpected difficulties, new responsibilities, loss or other life event. These subjects may change their self-placement on the *strong* versus *weak* construct, switching over to the contrast pole. However, this construction of the self as *weak* makes the first alternative in the example above of attachment behaviour unendurable, since the constructs of attachment are primitive (Lorenzini, Mancini and Sassaroli, 1985).

The second alternative outlined above is characteristic of evident agoraphobia. An anxious type of attachment is developed and avoidance substituted for exploration. Avoidance behaviour is the exact opposite of explorative behaviour and it aims at defending the predictive skills of the subject, who gives up predicting any further because he runs the risk of not successfully predicting anything at all. Hence, the person's knowledge does not grow, it decreases and this behaviour transforms that which is known into something less known and new. Avoidance is generalised because the less one explores, the more situations become alien and the boundaries between knowledge and ignorance progressively retreat. Venturing forth from the territory of knowledge gives way to ignorance. To obtain safe predictions, the experimental area is constricted; it is preferable to be sure of a few things than to be uncertain of many. Definition and constriction are chosen rather than extension and dilation. The person as scientist is transformed into a miser as far as experimentation is concerned. Constructs are not permeable and the person is more and more satisfied with narrow hypotheses that explain external reality less well, often creating confusion. A characteristic of the agoraphobic is a severe limitation of experimentation, giving up or reducing attempts to be an active scientist, the withdrawal of knowledge and a lack of ability to construe change that becomes the potential falsifier of the entire theory of self.

The agoraphobic's theory has an ultimate rule of this type: 'If I experiment, I will confuse the theory'. Thus it is a theory that has great difficulty in providing for change and it does not allow itself to undergo the control phase of the C-P-C cycle with the consequent spread of a negative heuristic. In fact, the constructs dealing with change in the construct system are crude or absent altogether in the clinical phase as well. Emotions are viewed in an indistinct manner as 'loss of control, paranoia, disaster and *weakness* versus *serenity*'.

Since the person gives up experimenting on the problematic situation, they gain no validation for their system of construing, hence (1) it does not develop hostility and (2) it is poorly articulated at its base.

Crisis and maintenance

Crisis and maintenance

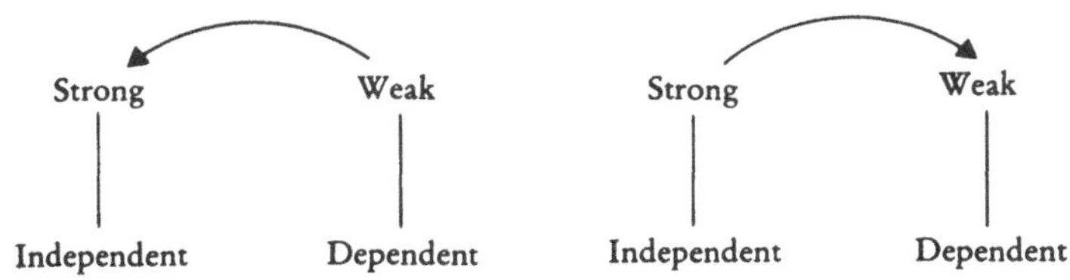

At this point a single crisis of anxiety is sustained by the construction of two activating situations which appear to be different but are essentially analogous. Explorative-type situations concerning both 'out in the open where I am alone' and 'in close spaces where I am constricted' correspond to the two poles of the superordinate construct *independent* versus *dependent*. Once the first episode has occurred, the subject begins actively to avoid all situations with explorative connotations be they constructing or expansive. Therefore maintenance is due to a double vicious circle, on one hand between avoidance, which the subject constructs as a proof of weakness, which requires avoidance; and on the other, between searching for an escort and the construction of self as dependent. The secondary problem begins from the strategies of being accompanied and avoiding, and it uses the same constructs as the primary problem; that is, it is linked directly at the level of the problematic nucleus 'weak' and 'avoidance' and the subordinate construct of 'dependent' with the strategies of being accompanied.

We do not know if this form of construing is shared by all neurotic patients or if it is specific to agoraphobic patients, but it is an evident clinical fact that the construct *loneliness* or *me alone* seems to be superordinate, although extremely primitive and not very well constructed. It seems that all other types of construct, such as *independent* and *autonomous*, are actually subordinate to the *I'm not alone* construct, and the pole *I'm alone* is unexplored and primitive like a dry branch which is not integrated with the rest of the structure.

Research

In our research we wanted to strengthen some of the hypotheses previously explained, specifically the following: the past and present state of attachment in phobic and control subjects; the relationship between 'triggering-off' and attachment situations; and the state of primitiveness, integration, polarisation and articulation of emotional constructs with regard to both phobic and control subjects.

Subjects and instruments

The following tests were given to two groups of seven subjects: (1) a group of phobic patients with evident symptomatology and (2) a group of neurotic non-phobic patients.

1 *Patient Bonding Instrument (PBI)*, which measures the attachment to parents according to a scale of care and control.
2 *Current Attachment Questionnaire* elaborated by the authors, which measures the current attachment on the same scales (Lorenzini, Mancini and Sassaroli, 1985).
3 *Repertory Grid 1* used twelve situations elicited from the subject who answered each of the following questions four times:
   - What makes you understand that another person loves you?
   - What situations make you feel bad?
   - What situations make you face change?

   In this way we obtained four situations of attachment constructed by the subject; four situations that triggered off anxiety constructed by the subject and four explorative situations.

   The constructs were subsequently elicited using the triadic system and concerned the emotions the subject felt in various situations. The rating scale ranged from 1 to 5.
4 *Repertory Grid 2* used the constructs elicited from Grid 1 as elements and six aspects of the self: how am I? how would I like to be? how am I when I'm alone? how am I when I'm in company? how was I before I felt bad? and how am I when I feel bad?

Results

Attachment

Confirming the results of a study that we carried out previously (Lorenzini, Mancini and Sassaroli, 1985), we found that in the phobic group, five subjects have a current anxious type of attachment and two show a lack of attachment, while the control subjects demonstrate a successful type of attachment (Fig. D7.1).

(a) *Current Attachment Questionnaire*

The scale of control
group of phobic patients $\bar{x}$ = 21.71
group of neurotic non-phobic $\bar{x}$ = 6.28

t of Student = 6.15 gl 12 $p<0.001$

(b) *Parental Bonding Instrument*

The scale of control
Father phobic patients $\bar{x}$ = 22.33
neurotic non-phobic $\bar{x}$ = 10

t of Student = 2.764 gl 12 $p<0.01$

mother phobic patients $\bar{x}$ = 21.35
neuotic non-phobic $\bar{x}$ = 12.3

t of Student = 2.326 gl 12 $p<0.5$

(c) *The differentiation of attachment on three levels*
chi square calculations

	Level 1	Level 2	Level 3	Total
phobic	13	11	4	28
non-phobic	3	14	11	28
	16	25	15	56

$\chi^2 = 9.87$ gl 12 $p<0.01$

Figure D7.1 Attachment

Both with PBI and the questionnaire on current attachment, phobic subjects construct relationships with attachment figures that show extensive control. Moreover, the differentiation of attachment on three levels has been hypothesised: from the highest primitive level (of a passive subject) to the highest maturity level (of an active subject). In this way it is also shown that phobic subjects present a more primitive attachment construction.

Situations

The correlations between 'triggering-off' situations and attachment are not statistically significant. However, the correlations between 'triggering-off' situations and explorative situations are statistically significant and relevant. It can be deduced from this that phobic subjects construct 'triggering-off' situations and explorative situations in a more similar way than control subjects do. The correlations between explorative situations and attachment are significant and it can be deduced that phobic subjects' constructions of explorative situations and attachment situations are inversely correlated or opposites. This is something that does not happen with control subjects. When we calculate the average of the correlation coefficients of 'triggering-off' situations it emerges that phobics construct situations which make them feel bad in a much more homogeneous way than do the control group.

Emotions

It emerges that phobic subjects have a tendency to elicit a smaller number of differing emotions. Calculating the average intensity of emotional constructs and comparing these by Student's t, it turns out that there are more connections between emotional constructs in phobics when applied to aspects of self. Having calculated the differentiation, results show that the emotional constructs in phobics are less differentiated than in control subjects.

(a) *Correlations between triggering-off and explorative situations*

r Pearson	−1<−·65	−·64<−·50	−·49< 0	0<·49	·50< ·64	·65<·1	Total
phobic	4	3	12	26	3	37	85
non-phobic	30	14	32	25	5	6	112
	34	17	44	51	8	42	197

$\chi^2 = 57.01$ gl 5 $p<0.001$

(b) *Correlations between explorative and attachment situations*

r Pearson	− 1<−·65	−·64<−·50	−·49<− 0	0<·49	·50<·64	·65<1	Total
phobic	27	6	35	18	6	9	101
non-phobic	6	1	23	30	8	44	112
	33	7	58	48	14	53	213

$\chi^2 = 45.38$ gl 5 $p<0.001$

(c) *Average of the correlation coefficients of triggering-off situations*

phobic $\bar{\chi} = 72.41$

non-phobic $\bar{\chi} = 38.56$

Figure D7.2 Situations

Aspects of self

Sixty-six per cent of the phobics have a negative correlation between 'real self' and 'ideal self' as compared with 14 per cent control subjects. Fifty per cent of the phobics, as compared with 14 per cent of control subjects, present a negative correlation between 'if I'm alone' and 'if I'm in company'. All the phobics

(a) *Intensity* Grid 2 constructs = emotions
elements = aspects of self

phobic $\bar{\chi} = 78.0$ ds = 6.9
non-phobic $\bar{\chi} = 63.42$ ds = 14.03
t of Student = 2.26 gl 12 $p<0{\cdot}05$

(b) *Extreme ratings:* chi-square calculations

Grid 1

Scores	1 and 5	2 – 3 – 4	Total
phobic	212	304	516
non-phobic	227	445	672
	439	749	1188

$\chi^2 = 6.67$ gl 1 $p<0.01$

Grid 2

Scores	1 and 5	2 – 3 – 4	Total
phobic	142	138	280
non-phobic	122	270	392
	264	408	672

$\bar{\chi}^2 = 26.26$ gl 1 $p<0.001$

Figure D7.3 Emotions

present a positive correlation between 'if I'm alone' and 'because of my sickness', while all of the control subjects have a negative correlation.

Conclusions

It is confirmed that phobic subjects show either an anxious type of attachment or lack of attachment; primitive forms of constructs on attachment and a strong correlation between 'triggering-off' situations and explorative situations. An inverse correlation between explorative situations and attachment also emerges. Although our research does not cover a large number of cases, it does confirm the abrupt shift from construction of (1) 'I give up attachment and explore freely', to a phase of (2) 'I give up exploration or I limit it in order to have good attachment'. From an existential point of view this shift is linked to a traumatic fact. Difficulty in exploring and the limited variations within the construct system also imply that there is a poorly articulated or differentiated construction of emotions in subjects with a phobic symptomatology. In conclusion, our research confirms the already known fact that there is a negative correlation in neurotics between 'ideal self' and 'real self' and between 'if I'm alone' and 'if I'm in company', and a very positive correlation between 'if I'm alone' and 'if I'm sick'.

References

Bowlby, J. (1969). *Attachment and Loss. Vol. 1, Attachment.* Hogarth Press: London.

Bowlby, J. (1973). *Attachment and Loss. Vol. 2, Anxiety and Anger.* Hogarth Press: London.

Bowlby, J. (1979). *The Making and Breaking of Affectional Bonds.* Tavistock: London.

Bowlby, J. (1980). *Attachment and Loss. Vol. 3, Sadness and Depression.* Hogarth Press: London.

Chambless, D. L. and Goldstein, A. J. (1977). Anxieties: agoraphobia and hysteria. In A. M. Brodsky and R. Hare-Mustin (eds.), *Women and Psychotherapy.* Guildford Press: New York.

Goldstein, A. J. and Chambless, D. L. (1977). A reanalysis of agoraphobia. *Behavior Therapy* 9, 47–59.

Kelly, G. A. (1955). *The Psychology of Personal Constructs*, Vols. I, II and III. Norton: New York.

Kelly, G. A. (1969). The autobiography of a theory. In *Clinical Psychology and Personality: Selected Papers of G. Kelly.* Wiley: New York.

Liotti, G. (1981). Un modello cognitivo-comportamentale dell'agorafobia. In V. F. Guidano and M. A. Reda (eds.), *Cognitivismo e psicoterapia.* Franco Angeli: Milan.

Lorenzini, R., Mancini, F. and Sassaroli, S. (1985). La costruzione dell'attaccamento. In F. Mancini and A. Semerari (eds.), *La psicologia dei costrutti personali: saggi sulla teoria de G. A. Kelly.* Franco Angeli: Milan.

Marks, I. M. (1969). *Fears and Phobias.* Academic Press: New York.
Parker, S. (1979). Reported parental characteristics of agoraphobia and social phobias. *British Journal of Psychiatry* 135, 550–60.
Solyom, L., Silberfeld, M. and Solyom, C. (1976). Maternal overprotection in the etiology of agoraphobia. *Canadian Psychiatric Association Journal* 21, 109–13.
Sullivan, B. O. (1984). Understanding the experience of agoraphobia. Unpublished PhD thesis, Dept. of Psychology, Trinity College, Dublin.

Chapter 8
Constructions in social skills training

David Winter

Personal construct theory and the cognitive revolution

> The roles of the client and therapist have been compared to those of the research student and his supervisor. The student knows the literature in his field of interest far better than his supervisor ever will, but he lacks the expertise to design a properly controlled experiment. The supervisor . . . is able to help the student to set up hypotheses, test them out and interpret the data. (Mackay, 1984, pp. 276–7)

If this quote has a familiar ring to it for an audience of personal construct theorists, it may be surprising to learn that it derives from a description, containing no reference to Kelly, of the therapeutic relationship in behaviour therapy. Although Kelly (1970) himself acknowledged that some behavioural treatment approaches encourage clients to become better personal scientists, he considered that they generally fail to recognise the client's role as 'principal investigator', and joked that the construct of psychopath is not inapplicable to those behaviour therapists who attempt to modify their clients' behaviour while neglecting the constructions underlying it. Naturally enough, he thought that a book classifying him as a learning theorist was so 'patently ridiculous' as to be highly amusing (Kelly, 1969, p. 216), but an *Introduction to Clinical Psychology* published some twenty years later still includes behaviour therapy and personal construct theory as strange bedfellows in its category of 'learning orientation' (Sundberg, Taplin and Tyler, 1983). Would Kelly have still found this classification so ridiculous given that, following the 'cognitive revolution', the behaviour therapy of today, except as practised by the inappropriately named radical behaviourists, is very different from that with which he was familiar? His insistence that personal construct theory is not a cognitive theory suggests that he would have done.

Nevertheless, the language of schemata, expectancies and attributions does bear at least a superficial resemblance to that of personal construct theory (Neimeyer, 1984; Sheehan, 1981), leading Fransella (1978, p. 6) to assert, when opening the last Personal Construct Psychology Congress held in England, that 'If behaviour therapy is up for grabs – we must be in there doing the grabbing.' But how revolutionary is the cognitive revolution? In some cases (e.g. Boyd and Levis, 1983) it seems that the judicious use of such concepts as internal cues, with a little generalisation and a few chains of secondary reinforcers thrown in, has merely rendered behavioural formulations as incapable of disproof as learning theorists have traditionally accused psychodynamic formulations of being. Such an approach, incorporating cognitive processes into existing paradigms, can be contrasted with the more radical paradigm shift advocated by writers such as Trower (1984). The 'agency approach' which Trower proposes as a radical alternative to the behavioural paradigm 'conceptualizes man as a social agent who actively constructs his own experiences and generates his own goal-directed behaviour on the basis of those constructs' (p. 4). Once again, while not sounding altogether unfamiliar to a group of construct theorists, no reference to Kelly will be found in Trower's chapter outlining the agency approach.

A personal construct theory perspective on models of social skills training

Trower's primary concern is social skills training, which will now be used to illustrate, and to compare with the personal construct theory perspective, trends in the behavioural treatment of neurotic disorders. As originally conceived, and still commonly practised, it involved the teaching of skills assumed to be deficient in clients exhibiting maladaptive social behaviour. Extending Kelly's joke, he might have applied his construct of psychopath not only to practitioners of such a training programme but also to its products, with their newly developed skills in manipulating others, and indeed this criticism has been acknowledged by some of the original proponents of the approach (Trower, Bryant and Argyle, 1978; Yardley, 1979).

Apart from the skill-deficit model, three alternative models of training have been identified by Linehan (1979). One, the 'faulty discrimination model', views the client as unable to discriminate between the skills appropriate in particular situations. Personal construct theory would also, of course, regard the capacity to make appropriate predictions about social situations as central to successful social interaction, its emphasis on construing the constructions of others being shared by some social skills trainers (Argyle, 1981; Trower, Bryant and Argyle, 1978; Wessler, 1984). Research evidence suggests that failures to anticipate others, and consequent difficulties in forming role relationships, may have their basis in structural features of the construct system (Adams-Webber, 1969; Adams-Webber, Schwenker and Barbeau, 1972; Applegate, 1983; Bruch, Heisler and Conroy, 1981; Delia and O'Keefe, 1976; Olson and Partington, 1977). Personal construct psychotherapy for clients with interpersonal difficulties of this nature might therefore include techniques which encourage engagement in cycles of construction (Reid, 1979) or exploration of the constructions of other people (e.g. Bonarius, 1977; Landfield, 1979; Mair, 1970). What it would not involve, unlike therapies based on the faulty discrimination model, would be attempts to instruct clients in how they 'should' construe their social world.

Linehan has also identified the 'response inhibition' model of training, which sees the client as being inhibited in displaying their social skills by conditioned anxiety or maladaptive expectations and self-statements. Essentially, this is the model underlying the methods proposed by Trower to reflect his 'agency approach'. Rational-emotive therapy (Dryden, 1984b), Trower's most favoured method, may share personal construct psychotherapy's concern to facilitate reconstruing, but nevertheless a recent comparative analysis of therapist behaviour in ten different treatment methods indicated that it was the approach most dissimilar to personal construct psychotherapy (Dryden, 1984a). This difference, as anyone who has seen Albert Ellis in action will appreciate, concerned the rational-emotive therapist's greater expressiveness and directiveness, perhaps reflecting their assumption that the client's problems stem from irrational thinking which should be replaced by a set of rational perceptions (Karst and Trexler, 1970). However, their focus tending to be on individual subordinate constructions rather than on hierarchical interrelationships between constructs, rational-emotive and other cognitive therapies may unduly emphasise the client's irrational thinking while overlooking any capacity for resolution of these apparent illogicalities provided by the client's superordinate constructs (Sheehan, 1981; Winter, 1983).

The therapist who considers their client's behaviour and beliefs to be irrational may, therefore, simply not understand the client's construct system sufficiently to appreciate its logic. Such a view would reflect Linehan's 'rational choice' model, which, concerning problems of assertion, states that the unassertive person 'has the skills, is not inhibited, knows when an assertive response is likely to be effective, and chooses to behave in a nonassertive manner' (Linehan, 1979, p. 207). Linehan claims that this model is 'generally held by clients but usually not shared by their therapists'. In fact, it is not dissimilar to the personal construct theory perspective, which will now be elaborated further by considering the constructions of clients undergoing social skills training.

Clients' constructions and social skills training

Repertory grid[1] and questionnaire assessments were carried out pre- and post-treatment on twenty-five neurotic clients accepted for social skills groups basically operating on the skill-deficit model. After every group session, clients also completed the Group Climate Questionnaire (MacKenzie, 1983) to indicate their perceptions of the session; and after the fifth session they completed self-ratings and predicted those of other group members. As in previous research on social skills training, treatment gains appeared modest in that, although therapists rated their clients as improved ($t = 12.11$; $p < 0.001$; 1 tail), no change was evident on clients' own ratings on their constructs of social competence or on questionnaire measures. The extent of the disparity between clients' and therapists' views was indicated by a correlation of −0.35 between their ratings of clients' social inadequacy.

It appeared, then, that the clients and therapists in these groups may have construed social competence somewhat differently.

Construct correlations in clients' pre-treatment grids were therefore examined to identify the implications of constructs concerning social interaction and self-confidence. In 80 per cent of the clients, social competence carried some negative implications in terms of their elicited constructs, over half of these involving Landfield's (1971) construct content categories of 'Low Tenderness', 'High Forcefulness', 'Low Morality', 'Closed to Alternatives' and 'High Egoism'. Thus, confident, assertive extraverts were construed by individual clients as likely to be, amongst other things, uncaring, arrogant, dishonest, pigheaded and bigheaded. It is small wonder, then, that these clients were resistant to social skills training for, given their constructions of social skills, many of them may have construed this form of treatment as involving training in selfishness, contempt and deceit. Indeed, constructions of this type may be validated by assertiveness and social skills training programmes which give clients such homework assignments as driving into a garage and, without buying petrol, asking the attendant to check the oil, water and tyre pressures and wash the windows (e.g. King, Liberman, Roberts and Bryan, 1977).

To test the hypothesis that clients' dilemmas concerning social interaction influenced their construal of the social skills group experience, a grid measure of these dilemmas was derived such that the higher a client's dilemma score, the more the preferred poles (as indicated by ideal self-allocation) of their constructs concerning social interaction were associated with non-preferred poles on other constructs. Correlations with Group Climate Questionnaire scores indicated that, as predicted, clients with higher dilemma scores perceived the group more negatively, seeing it as more characterised by interpersonal conflict ($r = 0.58$; $p < 0.01$; 1 tail) and avoidance of responsibility ($r = 0.71$; $p < 0.001$; 1 tail). Constructs relating to clients' most frequent dilemmas were pooled in a standard grid administered to a further neurotic sample, and a dilemma score derived from this grid correlated very highly with Social Situations Questionnaire (Trower, Bryant and Argyle, 1978) measures of the degree of difficulty and avoidance of such situations ($r = 0.86$ and 0.77; $p < 0.01$; 1 tail), as well as with self-ratings on clients' constructs of social inadequacy ($r = 0.38$; $p < 0.05$; 1 tail). Those clients for whom social competence carried more negative implications were therefore less likely to construe themselves as socially competent, receiving the pay-off of at least being able to see themselves as humane and virtuous, and thereby maintaining some modicum of self-esteem (cf. Tschudi, 1977). That such a strategy is not confined to this client group is suggested by research evidence on construing of the self and the complaint in moderately depressed individuals (Neimeyer, Heath and Strauss, 1985; Rowe, 1971, 1978; Space and Cromwell, 1980; Winter, 1985b).

Two further aspects of construing considered in clients attending the social skills groups were its tightness (as reflected in a small second component from INGRID analysis of the grid) and perceived dissimilarity of self and others.[2] Both these characteristics have been associated with neurotic disorder and the quest for certainty which it involves (Ryle and Breen, 1972; Winter, 1985c), as well as with inaccuracy in construing the constructions of others (Adams-Webber, 1969), and similar results were obtained in the present study.[3] Tight construers also gave more 'don't know' responses on an attitude questionnaire (Wilson, 1975) ($r = 0.39$; $p < 0.05$; 1 tail), perhaps reflecting their use of constriction or, as in Kelly's (1955) definition of anxiety, the inapplicability of their constructs to many events.

The major aim of the research programme of which this study forms a part has been to identify predictors of outcome in different therapies, finding that clients whose construing shows a predominant concern with their internal reality respond better to introspective treatment approaches, and outer-directed clients to more directive, behavioural approaches (Caine, Wijesinghe and Winter, 1981; Winter, 1985a). However, this distinction between treatment approaches was confounded in the research with that between group and individual treatments. Accordingly, group analytic and group behavioural treatments, such as social skills training, are now being compared. Only the social skills group results are currently available, but multiple regression analyses carried out on these indicate that inner-directedness, as measured by high scores on the Direction of Interest Questionnaire (Caine, Smail, Wijesinghe and Winter, 1982), is the best predictor of successful outcome as assessed by therapist ratings and by changes in total neurotic symptomatology, accounting for over 80 per cent and over 60 per cent respectively of the variance in these change scores. This result was contrary to predictions in that outer-directed clients, with their preference for structured, didactic treatment methods, were expected to respond more positively to a skills-training approach. To explain this discrepancy, clients' post-treatment descriptions of their social skills group experience were examined. In fact, none mentioned training in specific social skills as one of the group's therapeutic ingredients, the most commonly stated of which was the opportunity provided for members to appreciate that others experienced similar problems. Yalom (1970) claims that this experience of 'universality' is a major curative factor in group psychotherapy and, indeed, one of the few significant changes observed in the social skills group members during therapy, echoing similar findings with analytic groups (Fielding, 1975; Koch, 1983; Winter and Trippett, 1977), was their greater identification with others ($t = 4.35$; $p < 0.001$; 1 tail). It may be, then, that inner-directedness predicts response to group therapies, regardless of their orientation, because it signifies greater openness to sharing the perspectives of other group members.

An alternative approach: personal construct psychotherapy

One client for whom the social skills group was not a positive experience was Tom, who had previously failed to respond to analytic psychotherapy. Following treatment, he remarked that 'the group didn't help at all. I'm not lacking in social skills. The problem is the feelings behind the social skills.' Although rated by his therapist as somewhat improved, his self-ratings of social inadequacy, perceived distance from his ideal self, and questionnaire scores of neurotic symptomatology, increased markedly during treatment. The Group Climate Questionnaire indicated that he construed the group more negatively than any other client in the sample, but some explanation of this, and of his resistance to social skills training, was provided by his pre-treatment repertory grid. This revealed numerous dilemmas concerning active social interaction, which he associated with such characteristics as being demanding, aggressive and selfish. Given these negative implications of extraversion, it was scarcely surprising that he saw himself as shy and socially isolated.

A six-month follow-up assessment indicated further deterioration in his condition and, following his request for additional help, we commenced personal construct psychotherapy on an individual basis. The major concerns of these sessions, described more fully in Winter (1987), were as follows:

1 Controlled elaboration of his complaints, using Tschudi's (1977) ABC procedure to explore both positive and negative implications of such problems as his difficulties in self-assertion. Having made the connections outlined in Figure D8.1, Tom immediately remarked that they were invalid because he was always unassertive and reasonable but was not perceived as a 'good bloke'. We therefore explored the possibility that being too reasonable could be boring and irritating to others, who would have to embody the 'unreasonable' pole of his construct.

2 The encouragement of propositional construing, attempting to replace his notion of 'right and wrong opinions' with that of alternative constructions of reality which could be appreciated by taking the perspectives of others. This discussion focused particularly on his work situation, where he construed himself as more 'refined' and 'sensitive' than his workmates, whose happiness and extraversion he associated with insensitivity and irresponsibility. The implication that his introversion and depression might belie a superiority to others echoed a theme from his self-characterisation, in which he described how, as a child, his friend would spend pounds on new fishing gear but Tom, with his piece of string on the end of a stick, would catch all the fish.

3 The elaboration of a more assertive self-construction which would provide as much structure as construing himself as socially incompetent afforded him (demonstrated, for example, in his

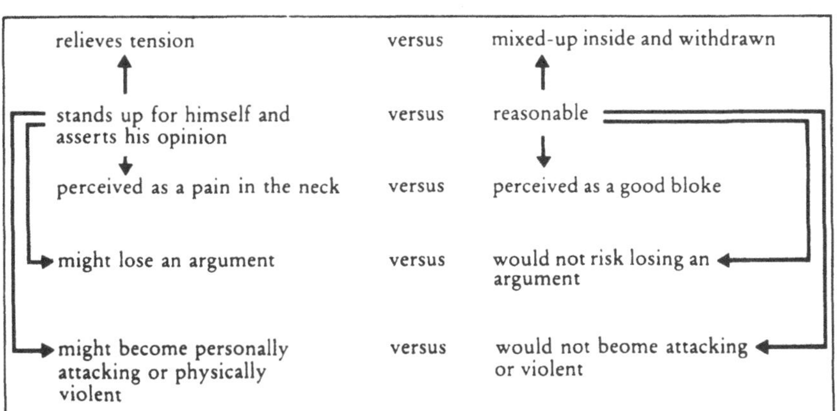

Figure D8.1 Positive and negative implications of assertiveness for Tom

insistence that he was schizophrenic, which he later admitted was because the diagnostic label provided him with some certainty, whereas without it his life would be 'a mystery'.)

4 The use of time-binding (Kelly, 1955), in which I suggested that many of his constructions were anachronisms initially developed to anticipate, and reduce the anxiety occasioned by, the behaviour of a depressive, socially phobic mother who rarely spoke. He construed his mother's silence as unselfish in that she did not burden others with her problems, but after I encouraged him to explore alternative constructions, he asked her directly the reasons for her behaviour. Her lack of response led him to reconstrue her as 'the most boring person in the world' and to decide not to visit his parental home again, seeing this as like 'avoiding the plague' and the possibility of 'catching' a way of construing and of behaving which was inappropriate to other social situations. Although there was an element of constriction and foreshortening of the Circumspection-Pre-emption-Control cycle in this response, and while such a departure from his core role structure inevitably produced some guilt, it at least did not result in the violent consequences which he had anticipated. Instead, its results and those of similar experiments with more assertive behaviour at work were that he increasingly experienced himself as less isolated from others and acknowledged that, rather than being trapped in a schizophrenic personality structure, he was self-creating.

Conclusions

Some of the reconstruing apparent in Tom during personal construct psychotherapy included what the cognitive therapist might regard as the correction of cognitive errors. However, his constructions and resistances to change were not regarded as irrational but rather as serving a definite purpose for him in his attempts to anticipate his world. Similarly, alternative constructions were offered to him in an invitational mood rather than as prescriptions for more rational thinking and correct social behaviour.

Commenting on Trower's proposed radical approach to social skills training, Schroeder and Rakos (1983, p. 125) remark that 'the emphasis on cognitive restructuring suggests an orientation towards conformity' which 'highlights the fact that we must be prepared to confront the ethical and political issues involved in endorsing the status quo'. To label such an approach radical scarcely seems appropriate. By contrast, it is perhaps by its credulous and constructive alternativist stance that personal construct psychotherapy still offers a genuinely radical alternative to the models of social skills training discussed above and, more widely, to other treatment approaches. This is not to deny the possibilities for cross-fertilisation between personal construct theory and other models, or for the incorporation of alternative treatment approaches, including social skills training, in a therapeutic service with an underlying philosophy of constructive alternativism, matching therapies to clients' constructions (Winter, 1985a). Respondents to Neimeyer's (1985) survey on the future of personal construct theory saw integration with the cognitive therapies as a not altogether unlikely prospect, and there have also been calls for a broader integration (Ryle, 1978). However, whether 'in there doing the grabbing' or integrating more gently, personal construct theorists will need to ensure that the result is not a dilution of the radicalism of Kelly's theory and its therapeutic applications.

Notes

I am indebted to Dr Kevin Gournay, Dr Barbara Hedge, Helen Cottee, Mary Sweetman and Bill Drysdale for assistance with data collection.

1 Grids employed ratings on a seven-point scale of sixteen elements, elicited to fit certain role titles, on fourteen elicited constructs together with 'depressed-happy'. They were analysed by Slater's (1972) INGRID computer programme.
2 Measured in terms of the percentage of grid elements allocated to the same construct poles as the self, assuming ratings of 1, 2, 3 and 5, 6, 7 to represent contrasting poles and excluding midpoint ratings from the analysis.
3 Correlations of size of Component 2 with number of anxiety symptoms on Crown–Crisp Experiential Index (CCEI) (Crown and Crisp, 1979), therapist's problem rating, and accuracy in predicting self-ratings of other group members: $r = -0.64$, $p < 0.001$, 1 tail;

−0.40, $p < 0.05$, 1 tail; and 0.52, $p < 0.05$, 1 tail respectively; correlations of percentage of grid elements similar to the self with client self-ratings of social competence and accuracy in predicting other members' ratings: $r = 0.46$, $p < 0.05$, 1 tail and 0.51, $p < 0.05$, 1 tail respectively.

References

Adams-Webber, J. (1969). Cognitive complexity and sociality. *Brit. J. Soc. Clin. Psychol.* 8, 211–16.

Adams-Webber, J. (1979). *Personal Construct Theory: Concepts and Applications.* Chichester: Wiley.

Adams-Webber, J., Schwenker, B. and Barbeau, D. (1972). Personal constructs and the perception of individual differences. *Can. J. Behav. Sci.* 4, 218–24.

Applegate, J. L. (1983). Construct system development, strategic complexity and impression formation in persuasive communication. In J. Adams-Webber and J. Mancuso (eds.), *Applications of Personal Construct Theory.* Toronto: Academic Press.

Argyle, M. (1981). The contribution of social interaction research to social skills training. In J. Wine and M. Smye (eds.), *Social Competence.* New York: Guildford.

Bonarius, H. (1977). The interactional model of communication: through experimental research towards existential relevance. In A. W. Landfield (ed.), *The Nebraska Symposium on Motivation 1976.* Lincoln: University of Nebraska Press.

Boyd, T. L. and Levis, D. J. (1983). Exposure is a necessary condition for fear-reduction: a reply to de Silva and Rachman. *Behav. Res. Ther.* 21 (2), 143–50.

Bruch, M., Heisler, B. and Conroy, C. (1981). Effects of conceptual complexity on assertive behaviour. *J. Counsel. Psychol.* 28, 377–85.

Caine, T. M., Smail, D. J., Wijesinghe, O. B. A. and Winter, D. A. (1982). *The Claybury Selection Battery Manual.* Windsor: NFER-Nelson.

Caine, T. M., Wijesinghe, O. B. A. and Winter, D. A. (1981). *Personal Styles in Neurosis: Implications for Small Group Psychotherapy and Behaviour Therapy.* London: Routledge & Kegan Paul.

Crown, S. and Crisp, A. H. (1979). *Crown–Crisp Experiential Index*. London: Hodder & Stoughton.
Delia, J. G. and O'Keefe, B. J. 1976). The interpersonal constructs of Machiavellians. *Brit. J. Soc. Clin. Psychol.* 15, 435–6.
Dryden, W. (ed.) (1984a). *Individual Therapy in Britain*. London: Harper & Row.
Dryden, W. (1984b). Social skills training from a rational-emotive perspective. In P. Trower (ed.), *Radical Approaches to Social Skills Training*. London: Croom Helm.
Fielding, J. M. (1975). A technique for measuring outcome in group psychotherapy. *Brit. J. Med. Psychol.* 48, 189–98.
Fransella, F. (1978). Personal construct theory or psychology? In F. Fransella (ed.), *Personal Construct Psychology 1977*. London: Academic Press.
Karst, T. O. and Trexler, L. D. (1970). Initial study using fixed role and rational-emotive therapy in treating public speaking anxiety. *J. Consult. Clin. Psychol.* 34, 360–6.
Kelly, G. A. (1955). *The Psychology of Personal Constructs*. New York: Norton.
Kelly, G. A. (1969). The psychotherapeutic relationship. In B. Maher (ed.), *Clinical Psychology and Personality: The Selected Papers* of George Kelly. New York: Wiley.
Kelly, G. A. (1970). Behavior is an experiment. In D. Bannister (ed.), *Perspectives in Personal Construct Theory*. London: Academic Press.
King, L. W., Liberman, R. P., Roberts, J. and Bryan, E. (1977). Personal effectiveness: a structured therapy for improving social and emotional skills. *Behav. Anal. Modif.* 2, 82–91.
Koch, H. C. H. (1983). Changes in personal construing in three psychotherapy groups and a control group. *Brit. J. Med. Psychol.* 56, 245–54.
Landfield, A. W. (1971). *Personal Construct Systems in Psychotherapy*. Chicago: Rand McNally.
Landfield, A. W. (1979). Exploring socialisation through the Interpersonal Transaction Group. In P. Stringer and D. Bannister (eds.), *Constructs of Sociality and Individuality*. London: Academic Press.
Linehan, M. M. (1979). Structured cognitive-behavioral treatment of assertion problems. In P. C. Kendall and S. D. Hollon (eds.),

Cognitive-Behavioral Interventions: Theory, Research and Procedures. New York: Academic Press.

MacKenzie, K. R. (1983). The clinical application of a group climate measure. In R. R. Dies and K. R. MacKenzie (eds.), *Advances in Group Psychotherapy: Integrating Research and Practice.* New York: International Universities Press.

Mackay, D. (1984). Behavioural psychotherapy. In W. Dryden (ed.), *Individual Therapy in Britain.* London: Harper & Row.

Mair, J. M. M. (1970). Psychologists are human too. In D. Bannister (ed.), *Perspectives in Personal Construct Theory.* London: Academic Press.

Neimeyer, R. A. (1984). Toward a personal construct conceptualization of depression and suicide. In F. R. Epting and R. A. Neimeyer (eds.), *Personal Meanings of Death: Applications of Personal Construct Theory to Clinical Practice.* New York: Hemisphere/McGraw-Hill.

Neimeyer, R. A. (1985). The future of personal construct theory: a Delphi poll. Paper presented at Sixth International Congress on Personal Construct Psychology, Cambridge, 5–9 August.

Neimeyer, R. A., Heath, A. E. and Strauss, J. (1985). Personal reconstruction during cognitive therapy for depression. In F. R. Epting and A. W. Landfield (eds.), *Anticipating Personal Construct Theory,* Lincoln: University of Nebraska Press.

Olsen, J. M. and Partington, J. T. (1977). An integrative analysis of two cognitive models of interpersonal effectiveness. *Brit. J. Soc. Clin. Psychol.* 16, 13–14.

Reid, F. (1979). Personal constructs and social competence. In P. Stringer and D. Bannister (eds.), *Constructs of Sociality and Individuality.* London: Academic Press.

Rowe, D. (1971). Poor prognosis in a case of depression as predicted by the repertory grid. *Brit. J. Psychiat.* 118, 297–300.

Rowe, D. (1978). *The Experience of Depression.* London: Wiley.

Ryle, A. (1978). A common language for the psychotherapies? *Brit. J. Psychiat.* 132, 585–94.

Ryle, A. and Breen, D. (1972). Some differences in the personal constructs of neurotic and normal subjects. *Brit. J. Psychiat.* 120, 483–9.

Schroeder, H. E. and Rakos, R. F. (1983). The identification and assessment of social skills. In R. Ellis and D. Whittington (eds.), *New Directions in Social Skills Training.* London: Croom Helm.

Sheehan, M. J. (1981). Constructs and 'conflict' in depression. *Brit. J. Psychol.* 72, 197–209.

Slater, P. (1972). *Notes on INGRID 72.* London: St George's Hospital.

Space, L. G. and Cromwell, R. L. (1980). Personal constructs among depressed patients. *J. Nerv. Ment. Dis* 168, 150–8.

Sundberg, N. D., Taplin, J. R. and Tyler, L. E. (1983). *Introduction to Clinical Psychology: Perspectives, Issues and Contributions to Human Service.* Englewood Cliffs, NJ: Prentice-Hall.

Trower, P. (ed.) (1984), *Radical Approaches to Social Skills Training.* London: Croom Helm.

Trower, P., Bryant, B. and Argyle, M. (1978). *Social Skills and Mental Health.* London: Methuen.

Tschudi, F. (1977). Loaded and honest questions: a construct theory view of symptoms and therapy. In D. Bannister (ed.), *New Perspectives in Personal Construct Theory.* London: Academic Press.

Wessler, R. (1984). Cognitive-social psychological theories and social skills. In P. Trower (ed.), *Radical Approaches to Social Skills Training.* London: Croom Helm.

Wilson, G. D. (1975). *Manual of the Wilson–Patterson Attitude Inventory.* Windsor: NFER-Nelson.

Winter, D. A. (1983). Logical inconsistency in construct relationships: conflict or complexity? *Brit. J. Med. Psychol.* 56, 79–87.

Winter D. A. (1985a). Personal styles, constructive alternativism and the provision of a therapeutic service. *Brit. J. Med. Psychol.* 58, 129–36.

Winter, D. A. (1985b). Group therapy with depressives: a personal construct theory perspective. *Int. J. Ment. Health* 13(3–4), 67–85.

Winter, D. A. (1985c). Neurotic disorders: the curse of certainty. In E. Button (ed.), *Personal Construct Theory and Mental Health.* London: Croom Helm.

Winter, D. A. (1987). Personal construct psychotherapy as a radical alternative to social skills training. In R. A. Neimeyer and G. J. Neimeyer (eds.), *Personal Construct Therapy Casebook.* New York: Springer.

Winter, D. A. and Trippett, C. J. (1977). Serial change in group psychotherapy. *Brit. J. Med. Psychol.* 50, 341–8.

Yalom, I. D. (1970). *The Theory and Practice of Group Psychotherapy.* New York: Basic Books.
Yardley, K. M. (1979). Social skills training: a critique. *Brit. J. Med. Psychol.* 52, 55–62.

E

Methodology

Chapter 1

Construal of events: personal constructs versus personal projects

James Horley

> Events. Man ultimately seeks to anticipate real events. This is where we see psychological processes as tied down to reality. Anticipation is not merely carried on for its own sake; it is carried on so that future reality may be better represented. It is the future which tantalizes man, not the past. Always he reaches to the future through the window of the present. (Kelly, 1955, p. 49)

Personal construct theory is centrally concerned with events. According to Kelly's Fundamental Postulate, a person's processes are psychologically channelized by the way in which he or she anticipates events. What did Kelly mean by 'event'? Although we discover that it is 'real events' that concern man, Kelly's discussion of event leaves the meaning of the construct unclear. Although it could be expected that a more detailed examination of the writings of Kelly and the work of later personal construct theorists could clarify the use of the construct, such an examination only clarifies the extent of confusion surrounding 'event.' Kelly (1955), for example, stated that 'the new outlook which a person gains from experience is itself an event' (p. 79). He also wrote that 'people, too, are events' (p. 175), and one of his students described 'elk' as an event (Hinkle, 1970, p. 95). In just these three examples we have constructs (the new outlook), people, and things referred to as events. Do any of these qualify as events? If so, what is not an event? Further examination and clarification of this construct appear warranted.

The construal of real events

Kelly consistently supported a linear view of time, and it is this view of time that forms the basis of his notion of event. As he wrote, 'The separation of events is what man produces for himself when he decides to chop up time into manageable lengths' (Kelly, 1955, p. 52). That which is 'chopped' has been described as the flux of empirical data (Husain, 1983). An event, therefore, can be described as a segmented portion of the temporal flux of empirical data. We should add, however, that the segmentation is an individual action, because the spatio-temporal chain can seemingly be divided in as many ways as there are individuals. Placing in parentheses the epistemological problem that the reality of events cannot be determined by Kellian man (Hinkle, 1970),[1] 'event' may be defined as an individual's segmented portion of the temporal flux of empirical data. Accepting this tentative definition, the question of the status of constructs, people, and things can be examined.

According to Kelly, an individual can derive a new construct or set of constructs from experiencing a real event, and this new construct(s) is also an event. One must wonder, however, whether the new construct(s) *per se* can be legitimately considered an event. Husain (1983) has argued quite convincingly that an event cannot be a construct, nor can it be derivable from, nor definable in terms of a construct. In the case of Kelly's remark, the process or experience of gaining a 'new outlook' should have been described as the event. Kelly (1955) seems to say as much in more than one discussion, and this understanding is presented more clearly in his later writing (e.g. Kelly, 1970).

Concerning people and things, it is obvious that neither people nor things, in and of themselves, can be described as events given our definition. People and things are entities – aspects or components of time and space. Although we may generally construe people and things, as Kelly (1955) argued, this entitative construal involves an abstraction of object from context. The behavior of entities is that which is construed, not the entities *qua* entities.

From her reading of Kelly's *The Psychology of Personal Constructs*, Husain (1983) has described Kelly as recognizing that we typically interpret the world entitatively but, for purposes of flexibility and an orientation to the future, he felt that we should rather interpret the world as consisting of events. This may be an accurate reading of Kelly. For Kelly, however, the importance of entitative construal, especially the construal of people, cannot be denied. Role titles (i.e. people) were Kelly's elements of choice in his development of the repertory test and, with few exceptions (cf. Easterby-Smith, 1981), people have remained the interpretive focus of the repertory grid to date.

If he is seen as an advocate of the construal of events, why did Kelly not employ events as elements in the repertory test? One possibility is the apparent difficulty in eliciting events. Would assessees understand a request to list personal occurrences of happenings? Would assessors ask for past, present, or future events? Would there be a limit on the event domain, such as a restriction to work-related events? Such may have been the methodological and theoretical roadblocks. Little (1983) has developed an approach that appears to steer around these obstacles. In response to a perceived need for a more adequate unit of analysis in both personality and environmental psychology, Little (1972, 1983) has argued that analysis of an individual's everyday concerns and activities can serve as the basis for a better understanding of the individual and his or her world. To conduct this analysis, he proposed the framework for a theory and a methodology, personal projects analysis (PPA).[2]

Personal projects as analytic units

Provisionally defined as an act or set of interrelated acts extending over time which is intended to attain or maintain a state of affairs foreseen by an individual (Little, 1983), personal project refers, quite simply, to the day-to-day, purposeful, temporally extended activities in which people engage. As such, a personal project places individuals in a physical and social environmental context. As a unit of analysis, the personal project appears to be an analytic unit that must be used in conjunction with, rather than in place of, the personal construct and other established units in the field of personality.

The issue of the choice of an analytic unit in the personality field is a longstanding one (see Allport, 1958), although perhaps one that has not received sufficient attention to date. According to Mancuso and Adams-Webber (1982), the choice of a unit of analysis is one of five issues that must be considered by any clinician or personality researcher. Mancuso and Adams-Webber, and Allport, have pointed to a number of analytic units that have been adopted by personologists. These include traits, dispositions, needs, drives, teleonomic trends, instincts, humors, and personal constructs. Little (1983) would also add the personal project to this list, but the personal project seems to represent a subtly different type of analytic unit. Units like the trait, or personal construct, and the personal project can be seen as apples and oranges, or perhaps Granny Smith and Red Delicious apples – similar yet different. The similarity between, say, the personal construct and the personal project is that both are units or dimensions employable in the enterprise of making sense of human personality; the difference lies in the way in which each is employed in the enterprise. The personal construct – or the trait, or the drive, or the need – is the unit that is used to make sense of personality. 'Personality', however, is a broad construct, and a manifestation or an expression of personality is needed to which these units may be applied. Stimulus behaviors, verbal responses to projective test protocols, the endorsement of objective test items, and the grouping of role construct elements, for example, have in the past been grist for the analytic unit mill. The distinction between these two unit types is that some dimensions are employed as the *subject* of personality study while other dimensions are employed as the *object* of personality study. Henceforth, and not to connote any hierarchical ordering, these units will be referred to as A Units and B Units respectively.

The personal project, therefore, appears to be a B Unit – an expression of personality that is made sense of or analyzed. Little (1983) has developed a technique, the personal projects matrix, for analyzing everyday pursuits using 'project dimensions.' In spite of Palys and Little's (1983) contention that personal constructs have been abandoned by project analysts, constructs do appear in the guise of project dimensions. Little (in press), however, appears to have correctly noted that the examination of personal projects allows trait theorists to use their chosen unit, the personality trait. Indeed, it appears that all A Units and B Units are more or less interchangeable, permitting a 'mix and match' (so long as one unit is chosen from column A and one from column B), although there are perhaps more complementary unit-pairs. The personal project, owing much to the Kellian tradition, and the personal construct appear to be one example of complementary unit-pairs.

Let us return briefly to our definition of events – an individual's segmented portion of the temporal flux of empirical data – to understand how a personal project can qualify as an event. Given Little's definition of personal project, it is evident that a personal project is not necessarily a single event, although it can be. The personal project 'Going to the football match today,' for example, might involve one segment of the temporal flux, or one event. More typically, however, a personal project – for example, 'Becoming a more creative person' – involves numerous segments of the temporal flux, numerous events, perhaps occurring over the time period of several decades. Even a football match project, perceived as a single event by one person, could be seen as several distinct but related events, such as 'Getting the car started' and 'Finding a babysitter for the kids,' by another.

Thinking of a project as an event or set of events also addresses a minor but annoying question: why do we encounter or witness the events that we do? Even accepting that chance is a component in the encounter or witnessing of any event (Bandura, 1982), there is a great degree of nonrandomness in the spatio-temporal location of individuals. According to the projects that they formulate and enact, people choose a time and place to pursue their goals and, hence, select at least a range of possible events with which to deal. A war correspondent with a newspaper, for example, in accepting assignments, selects a set of spatio-temporal locations (current war zones) as arenas to play out the chosen vocational role.

How can personal constructs and personal projects be used together? What are the benefits and implications of combining the two units? These questions will be addressed in the context of a presentation of results from studies involving two slightly different techniques that combine constructs and projects.

Construct–project studies

The first explicit attempt to wed a PCT with a PPA approach was a study conducted by Cameron in 1984. Cameron first developed and piloted a technique that she called a 'personal projects rep grid.' This technique was a 10 × 10 repertory grid with elicited constructs but with personal projects as elements. Respondents were required to rate, from 0 to 10, each of ten listed activities/concerns on each construct pair. The purpose of the main study was to determine the degree of correspondence between the freely elicited constructs of the personal projects repertory grid and the provided 'project dimensions' of the personal projects matrix technique (an identical set of project elements was used for both).

From the seventy-eight undergraduate subjects (thirty-eight males, forty females) who participated in the study, data were obtained indicating substantial representation of all seventeen project dimensions among the personal constructs of the subjects (see Little, 1983, for a description of the seventeen dimensions used). Not only was some support found for the choice of the provided project dimensions, but several new dimensions, such as tedium and self-centredness, were suggested by examination of the elicited constructs. In essence, this study represents another approach to the PCT issue of elicited versus provided constructs. This research has been summarized by Adams-Webber (1979) and Fransella and Bannister (1977), among others. It is not necessary to address the issue here.

The two techniques employed in Cameron's study were very similar. In fact, a 90-degree clockwise rotation of the personal projects matrix yields a repertory grid with provided constructs. Exploring further the use of personal project elements in a repertory grid, and adopting a more idiographic approach, a technique similar to Kelly's (1955) original grid has been developed using projects as elicited elements. Preliminary data from several nonclinical pilot subjects have revealed some interesting and encouraging results. Presented briefly are the results from one study participant.[3]

The respondent in question is a twenty-year-old female who had just completed the second year of a Canadian university program in psychology. Examples of activities/concerns from her list of personal projects include 'Keeping in touch with several friends by writing,' 'Saving money for school,' 'Trying to start taking the dog for a walk daily,' and 'Overcoming a slight feeling of illness.' A nonparametric factor analysis, terminated after two factors, revealed a first factor, comprised of three constructs, that pointed to a 'regular, socially required' versus 'irregular, not socially required' dimension. A second factor, comprised of two constructs, suggested a 'personal' versus 'social' dimension. Following Kelly (1955), project elements were graphed in two-dimensional space. It was found that such project elements as 'Writing to friends,' 'Cleaning the house,' and 'Saving money' were located in the 'regular, required' and 'social' quadrant of the graph; whereas, in the 'irregular, not required and social' quadrant, the only element was 'Walking the dog.' The two projects in the 'regular, required' and 'personal' quadrant were 'Riding my bike to work' and 'Buying necessities,' while 'Seeing my boyfriend at the end of the summer,' 'Going swimming,' and 'Overcoming a feeling of illness' were in the 'irregular, not required' and 'personal' quadrant.

Without exception, the results obtained to date have been sensible to both assessor and assessees. There is no reason to suspect that the use of personal project elements with many of the other varieties of grids described by Fransella and Bannister (1977) would present difficulty. Also, just as Kelly (1955) suggested assessment techniques other than the repertory grid (e.g. self-characterization technique), Little (1983) suggested non-grid techniques (e.g. an 'act-laddering' technique for examining particular behaviors enacted in the pursuit of a project) that may prove to be useful assessment devices.

What are the clinical implications, or what are the potential therapeutic benefits of adopting a construct–project approach? A combination of personal constructs and personal projects opens important systems to the Kellian clinician. Although change in the manner in which clients interpret events might remain the focus of therapy, an important intervention strategy would involve an attempt to change the nature of the events, or at least the probability of encountering certain events. One can think of numerous examples.

Imagine a lower-middle-class male having problems at school and with the criminal justice system. Rather than simply helping the youth to adopt a new set of constructs more likely to lead to school success and noninvolvement with the law, one of his current academic activities/concerns (perhaps only academic project) – say, 'Learning more about dinosaurs' – might become the focus of the intervention. Perhaps shifting the project from the impoverished school library, with its single dinosaur book, to a downtown library with its twenty books, would increase the chances that the project would end successfully and, with some luck and direction, would lead to other similar projects. This is not to say that anti-educational or illegal acts can be eliminated by reading about dinosaurs, but in the case of this youth, educational and prosocial activity is facilitated and rewarded, perhaps for the first time ever, and hence is more likely to recur. This example undoubtedly represents an oversimplification of an intervention; an actual situation would be more complex. In the end, systemic intervention – that is, intervention aimed not only at an individual's thoughts, feelings, and behavior, but also at the social and physical environmental systems in which an individual operates – may involve the analysis of more client data by a clinician, but it would appear to increase the chances of a successful manipulation.

Summary and conclusions

In spite of the centrality of the term 'event' to PCT, the precise meaning of the construct is unclear. It is clear that constructs are not events, nor vice versa. As well, neither people nor things (i.e. entities) are events, although they can certainly be the focus of events. Interpretation of the behavior of entities, entitative construal, appears to be common, but event construal is to be recommended for purposes of flexibility and better anticipation. It can only be surmised that practical considerations and/or methodological difficulties prevented Kelly from developing a repertory grid with events as elements.

One recent methodological development that appears to capture events for use as elements in the repertory grid is PPA. The personal project, the basis of the approach, and the personal construct appear to be complementary units of personality analysis – the personal construct an A Unit, a dimension used to make sense of a presumed manifestation of personality, and the personal project a B Unit, a dimension that is taken as a manifestation of personality. PPA seems to offer potential benefits to those involved in the assessment of subjective well-being (Horley, 1984), and it also seems to offer potential assessment and treatment benefits to Kellian clinicians. Although construct change might remain the focus of Kellian therapy, examination of a client's activities and concerns – how he or she construes them, who is involved in his or her projects, where activities are conducted – should provide, at moderate cost, high yield clinical interventions.

Preliminary examination of repertory grids with personal projects as elements has produced intriguing, if limited, results. Further exploration is necessary. Some non-grid techniques suggested by Little (1983) might also form the basis of subsequent study. It certainly remains to be seen if a construct–project union lives up to its potential, but all the components for a long and fruitful life together appear to be in place.

Notes

The author would like to thank Jan Clarke, Tom Davidson and Martha Husain for their assistance in the preparation of this paper.

1 This difficulty does not necessarily compromise Kelly's position of theoretical reflexivity, as Hinkle (1970) has charged. To do so, Kelly the theorist would have to claim access to the 'knowledge' of real events to which Kelly the layman had no access. This does not seem to be the case.

2 Lest any mistaken impressions be created, personal projects analysis is being suggested as only one possible approach to the problem of event elicitation. One obvious limitation of the approach concerns the many events that fall beyond the boundaries of individuals' purposive behavior. Tidal waves and rainbows (i.e. natural events) and political coups and coronations (i.e. man-made events) are 'construable' events that are not necessarily attributable to purposive activity on the part of the construer.

3 Additional findings and a copy of the assessment booklet are available from the author.

References

Adams-Webber, J. R. (1979). *Personal Construct Theory: Concepts and Applications.* New York: Wiley.

Allport, G. W. (1958). What units shall we employ? In G. Lindzey (ed.), *Assessment of Human Motives.* New York: Holt, Rinehart & Winston.

Bandura, A. (1982). The psychology of chance encounters and life paths. *American Psychologist* 37, 747–55.
Cameron, L. (1984). A personal projects rep grid. Unpublished BA Honors thesis, Carleton University, Ottawa, Canada.
Easterby-Smith, M. (1981). The design, analysis and interpretation of repertory grids. In M. L. G. Shaw (ed.), *Recent Advances in Personal Construct Technology*. London: Academic Press.
Fransella, F. and Bannister, D. (1977). *A Manual for Repertory Grid Technique*. London: Academic Press.
Hinkle, D. N. (1970). The game of personal constructs. In D. Bannister (ed.), *Perspectives in Personal Construct Theory*. London: Academic Press.
Horley, J. (1984). Life satisfaction, happiness, and morale: Two problems with the use of subjective well-being indicators. *The Gerontologist* 24, 124–7.
Husain, M. (1983). To what can one apply a construct? In J. R. Adams-Webber and J. C. Mancuso (eds.), *Applications of Personal Construct Theory*. New York: Praeger.
Kelly, G. A. (1955). *The Psychology of Personal Constructs*, Vol. I. New York: Norton.
Kelly, G. A. (1970). A brief introduction to personal construct theory. In D. Bannister (ed.), *Perspectives in Personal Construct Theory*. London: Academic Press.
Little, B. R. (1972). Psychological man as scientist, humanist, and specialist. *Journal of Experimental Research in Personality* 6, 95–118.
Little, B. R. (1983). Personal projects: a rationale and method for investigation. *Environment and Behavior* 15, 273–309.
Little, B. R. (in press). Personality and the environment. In D. Stokols and I. Altman (eds.), *Handbook of Environmental Psychology*. New York: Wiley.
Mancuso, J. C. and Adams-Webber, J. R. (1982). Personal construct psychology as personality theory: introduction. In J. C. Mancuso and J. R. Adams-Webber (eds.), *The Construing Person*. New York: Praeger.
Palys, T. S. and Little, B. R. (1983). Perceived life satisfaction and the organization of personal project systems. *Journal of Personality and Social Psychology* 44, 1221–30.

Chapter 2
A PCP analysis of data collection in the social sciences

Linda L. Viney

In the social sciences our tools for data collection seem to determine what we study rather than the nature of our subject-matter (Koch, 1981; Hetherington, 1983; Marsh, 1985). The disciplines which have resulted present a limited view of the person who should be the centre of our activities. For those of us who believe that knowledge is both created by people and a function of their interpretations (Polyani, 1958; Cassirer, 1944), personal construct theory may provide the means by which to overcome some of these limitations. This analysis of data collection in the social sciences has been undertaken with this hope.

People are assumed to be construers

'Man meets experience with meaningful conceptions of basic premises and fashions it at least as much as experience fashions him' (Rychlack, 1970, p. 470). It is this picture of people as the active interpreters of their worlds, inherent in personal construct theory, which makes it important to examine our own interpretations. While many social scientists claim to support this view, the extent to which it has influenced the research of psychologists, at least, has not been great. A modest survey I conducted of the 1983 and 1984 volumes of leading journals in the fields of physiological psychology, perception and cognition, learning, personality and social psychology indicate that research psychologists rarely conceive of their so-called 'subject' as construing people. Nor, more surprisingly, do they recall that the same assumption may be made about their 'experimenters', surprising because these 'experimenters' are often the psychologists themselves. It seems that Kelly's (1965) construct of reflexivity is not accepted by them.

Some aspects of the assumption that people are active construers and interpreters need to be drawn out more fully for my purpose. What I am doing, in the phenomenological tradition, is examining my own constructs and interpretations. What does it imply, then, when I refer to you as 'active', or when data collectors view their informants as 'active'? Allport, one of several American psychologists following in the tradition of Brentano, has maintained that people may be productively viewed as the source of acts. This implies that people are active rather than reactive, and not simply mindless responders to stimuli, as neo-behaviourists like Bandura (1977) would now agree. 'Informants' of social scientists can act, as well as react, with their data collectors. This capacity for action also implies that people are makers of choice.

People are assumed, not only to experience, but to construe their experience. People structure meanings within their experience (Heidegger, 1962; Packer, 1985). Orne understood that 'one of the basic characteristics of human beings is that he (or she) will ascribe purpose and meaning, even in the absence of purpose and meaning' (1969, p. 780). This is what led Orne to recognise the importance of the demand characteristics of the experimental situation for the 'subjects' of psychological research. The meanings or interpretations which people choose may be a function not only of their current situation as they perceive it but also of their past experiences and future goals. These interpretations are accessible to social scientists through a variety of tools (Ericsson and Simon, 1984).

Rocks and plants do not, so far as I can tell, construe or interpret. Yet this is not the only way in which people are different from the objects of other sciences. They also differ in their capacity for reflection, their ability to know that they are aware of things. Each person is, of course, particularly aware of himself or herself, and of that self as knower. It is noteworthy that in Harré's (1979) attempt to devise a more viable social psychology, he has argued not only that people follow rules but that they *know* that they do. Personal construct theory takes this one step further: people are regarded as capable of *saying* what they are up to (Bannister and Fransella, 1985). This is an important development in our view of the relationship between experience and behaviour. It, too, assumes people to be capable of reflecting on their experiences.

One of the main questions which we must deal with is about the forms that the relationship between the subjectively construed experience of people and their observed behaviour may take. The latter is, of course, directly available only to social scientists through his or her external senses. The former, in contrast, is internally perceived. It is perceived directly only by the individual involved. It is only indirectly available, therefore, to the social scientists. Both construed experience and observed behaviour are, I believe, important for the social sciences.

What we need as data is a combination of observation (of behaviour) and description (of personal constructs or interpretations) (Manicas and Secord, 1982). That these objective and subjective perspectives complement one another is vividly apparent in this example of learning which Snygg (1941) used to introduce American psychologists to phenomenological concepts. Let us imagine, first, that we are watching a small girl learn how to do a task, say, solve a puzzle. From our external view that task remains the same during the learning period, but the responses of the child change as she successfully solves her puzzle. We are, then, likely to ascribe the process of change to the learner. From the second perspective, the viewpoint of the active child, she, herself is unchanged during learning, and it is the perceived nature of the task which changes. Different interpretations – or, in personal construct terms, alternative constructs – are possible.

The position of personal construct theory in regard to the relationship between the subjective and objective perspectives is that the behaviour of people can best be understood in terms of their interpretations of their worlds, which in turn are a function of their behaviour, which in turn is a function of their interpretations, which in turn are a function of their behaviour, and so on. We cannot, then, arrive at adequate explanations of behaviour until we take the constructs of the behavers seriously (Mancuso and Adams-Webber, 1982). Harré (1978), too, takes this view. Behaviour and experience are part of a total, overriding gestalt, which consists of the person involved in the situation (Giorgi, 1971). This gestalt is sometimes difficult to bring into focus. Romanyshyn (1975) has described the reciprocal nature of the relationship between construed experience and observed behaviour in this way. What *I* call *experience* is your behaviour behaved by you. What *I* call *behaviour* is your experience behaved by me. Conversely, *your experience* is my behaviour behaved by me, while your *behaviour* is my experience behaved by you. This is itself a matter of interpretation, or distinguishing the actor's perspective on events from that of the observer. It also reminds us that the social sciences are about and even part of a social world, a construed world in which there is the constant give and take of interpersonal interaction.

The difficulties in sharing our construed worlds

The social sciences are embedded in the social world in part because of the topic they have chosen for themselves: the person. This means that any collection by a researcher (a person) of social-science data (from another person) must involve interactions, at some level, between construing people. In the simplest of possible psychological paradigms, there is social interaction between the 'experimenter' and the 'subject', tester and client, and questionnaire user and respondent. This involves two-way interaction between people, each with his or her own interpretations of their situation and the capacity to act and react. Psychologists are, in personal construct terms, trying to construe the construction processes of another. They are trying to enter the interpreted world of the other. When that occurs the psychologist comes to 'play a role in a social process involving the other person' (Kelly, 1955, p. 95).

Schütz, (1967, 1972) whose view of the human condition is very similar to that of Kelly, helps us to gain an understanding of the mutual orientation of the social-science researcher and his or her informant (Thomason, 1982). He maintains that people's behaviour is directed towards an end. It involves a plan; otherwise it is simply expressive behaviour. The purpose of their actions constitutes their meaning. Motives may be 'in-order-to' motives leading to the achievement of interim goals or they may be 'because' motives when the situation they are in appears to demand an outcome. Each other person is conceived of as construing just as each construes himself or herself. If they share a situation with another, that other person is assumed to be construing that situation in ways similar to their own. They interpret the experience of others by observing their expressive behaviour, and guessing at their motives by imagining themselves to be behaving in those ways, as well as through their communication acts. The expression of meaning is assumed by Schütz to be the 'in-order-to' motive for a communicative act. Communication often takes place through symbols. This conceptualisation is similar to that of Mead and the symbolic interactionists. It has formed a basis, too, for the work of the ethnomethodologists in their observations of the situational use of symbols.

Interpersonal interaction, then, is normally a spontaneous activity which springs from construed experience and is intentionally directed towards another experiencing self (Schütz, 1967). It is other-oriented, and the 'in-order-to' motive is to bring about certain experiences for the other person. In a fully functioning face-to-face interaction there is mutual orientation. *I* am aware that *you* are aware that *I* am aware . . . and so it goes on. As I understand your plan it becomes part of my definition of the situation that we are in. If I want our relationship to continue, your plan will become my motive for my own action. And as I communicate with you, my 'in-order-to' motive will become my 'because' motive. This interplay of motives is essential if we are to know whether we share the same meanings. There is a sharing of worlds with all their interpretations and values as well as motives. There is a sharing of constructs (Mair, 1970; Salmon, 1978).

Of course not all interpersonal relationships involve such mutual orientation. Observation does not. Behaviours, not purposeful actions, are observed. The constructs which provide a context for these behaviours are available only indirectly. I can suggest much from observing you – by imaginatively putting myself in your place, by using knowledge from our other interactions in which there was an interplay of motives, and by inferring your 'in-order-to' motive from your behaviour. But I can never be sure of understanding your constructs without our mutual orientation as reflective, creative interpreters of our experiences.

Four models of data collection

The evaluation of four models of data collection which now follows is, then, based on the assumption that it is possible for one person to tap into the inner world of another. Indeed, as ourselves construing people, we social scientists have advantages over biologists and physicists when approaching our subject-matter. As people ourselves, we have acquired a set of special constructs for understanding people and how we stand in relation to them. Schütz has shown how such understanding can be established:

> I can constantly check my interpretations of what is going on in other people's minds, due to the fact that in the live relationship I share a common environment with them . . . I can ask you not only about the interpretive schemes you are applying to our common environment. I can also ask you about how you are interpreting your lived experiences, and, in the process, I can correct, expand and enrich my own understanding of you. This becoming aware of the correctness or incorrectness of any understanding of you is a higher level of the We-experience. (Schütz, 1972, p. 171)

Such mutual understanding in the context of another-directed relationship should be a validational criterion for any collection of experience-based data (Richardson, 1984). Other important criteria are the awareness of social scientists of our own interpretations and assumptions, and for us to provide data which are publicly verifiable.

Four models of data collection are suggested by this approach (Viney, 1986). The first, the *Self-Orientation Model*, is employed when the contributions of both data collector and informant to a social-science study are determined predominantly by the private interpretations of each participant. No sharing of interpretations occurs. This type of interaction, if it can be called that, is determined very little by what takes place between them. In an extreme version of this data-collection model, data collector and informant would be relating to the other only to the extent of waiting until the other stops talking. In psychology some laboratory-based studies of memory employ this model. The second, the *Data Collector Orientation Model* is employed most often when data collectors are given a script which they must follow, but the informants are assumed to be free to respond, more or less spontaneously, to the data collectors. Here, the data collectors are governed by their private interpretations while the informants are assumed to be responding to the data collectors more often than to their own private interpretations. Some person-perception studies have used this model. The third, the *Reactive Orientation Model* can be applied when both participants in a study are reacting to what is currently taking place between them in their interaction more than to their own private interpretations. Finally, the *Mutual Orientation Model*, arguably the rarest model of data collection, is applied when both the data collector and the informant contribute something to, and gain something from, the data collection. Their actions are influenced by both their private interpretations and by what takes place publicly between them, as in Schütz's 'We-experience'. Piaget's tests of conservation in children follow this model.

Evaluation of the status of these four models of data collection in the social sciences reveals that they are based on assumptions revealed as questionable by personal construct theory. The Self-Orientation Model appears to invoke the somewhat dubious assumption that informants are passively cooperative and accept the interpretations of others in preference to their own; and it makes similar assumptions about data collectors. Neither of the principal participants in our data collections is viewed as an active construer. Nor are any of the social implications of their interaction fully accepted. Communication is not taking place through shared interpretations. The Data Collector Orientation Model, on the other hand, gives greater scope to data collectors as active construers and as reflective knowers. The informants of this model, however, are permitted none of these capacities. Also, many of the assumptions about the data-collection interaction are debatable. The Reactive Orientation Model gives full recognition to the nature of that interaction, but studies employing it tend to involve questionable assumptions about informants and data collectors. Specifically, this model assumes that the capacities of each of them to construe and to reflect on their resulting constructs are unimportant and tends to ignore them. None of these models is free from distorting assumptions. The only model of data collection which appears to be free from them is the Mutual Orientation Model. This is the model which, I believe, offers the greatest hope for the future methodological developments in the social sciences, especially in psychology.

Many social scientists would argue that the other models have served us well so far; and they have. But we are searching for a model of data collection suited to ourselves and our subject-matter, that is to interpreting the interpreters. Those models which reduce that subject-matter to less than actively construing people do not suit it well. Psychological models, for example, which assume 'subjects' to be less than human and prohibit 'experimenters' from fulfilling their potential as human beings, can only provide a psychology of less than the person. Further, when the relationship between 'subject' and 'experimenter' is not allowed to be fully interactive, then it can bear little resemblance to what people find out about other people when they relate freely to them. Unquestioning acceptance of these assumptions or anticipatory interpretations is unlikely to result in a generally relevant psychology which is acknowledged as being by and about construing people.

The Mutual Orientation Model of data collection avoids most of the questionable assumptions which reduce the viability of the other three models. The Mutual Orientation Model may also be ethically more acceptable to many social scientists. It achieves this goal through a communication process which has five stages. At the first stage the data collector makes a request of the informant. At the second, the informant responds. At the third, the data collector reflects on the response of the informant. At the fourth, the data collector reveals the results of that reflection to the informant. At the fifth, the informant confirms or denies that reflection. Many existing psychological data-collection techniques can be extended to fulfil these requirements of the Mutual Orientation Model. The Role Construct Repertory Technique (Kelly, 1955) was designed to do so, but is most commonly used in a form which does not complete all of its five stages. Some existing tools are not suitable for tapping into the experience of the informant. The psychological test, 'an objective and standardized measure of a sample of behaviour' (Anastasi, 1982, p. 22), is not. We are concerned with the subjective (and objective) meaning as well as measurement, and experience as well as behaviour. Some other psychological tools, however, show more promise for achieving our goals. Many of them complete at least the first three stages of the Mutual Orientation Model of data collection.

Questionnaires, self-rating scales, the focused interview, Q-sorts and the critical-incidents method all do so with an emphasis on the first stage. That is, they put most effort into the preparation of the best requests for the data collector to make of the informant. Association and analysis techniques, self-characterisations and self-observation of behaviour put their emphasis on the second stage of the informant's response. Projective techniques, content analysis and many of the techniques of attribution theory research emphasise the third stage of the data collector's reflections on the response from the informant. A more complete analysis of these existing tools is available in Viney (1986).

Buyer, beware!

I cannot conclude this paper without noting that, in spite of my enthusiasm, there is a need for self-criticism by social scientists who use this personal construct approach; so, 'buyer, beware!' We have defined the field of research for developing social sciences as behaviour *and* experience, a definition not acceptable to all social scientists. The principles which govern the development of our bodies of knowledge – for example, the standards of reliability and validity applied to our assessment tools – assume both us and the people we study to be interpreters. While based on these principles, the products of the social sciences must also be related to the products of common sense. A social science which recognises its own development in a shared construed world and that its so-called 'facts' are socially created and interpersonally agreed on meanings only, must protect itself from solipsism. We social scientists could easily agree among ourselves on a view of 'reality' which might prove to be in conflict with everyday experience. Such conflict must be dealt with. Another possible trap for any of us who are unwary practitioners of this relativistic form of science is the tendency to dualism. It is sometimes easier to over-emphasise experience so as to detach it from behaviour, than to maintain interpretations which integrate experience with behaviour.

Many criticisms will be levelled at this personal construct approach. It will be said the assumptions that people construe, and that their social contexts affect their constructions, are irrelevant. It will also be argued that such assumptions undermine the search for consistencies or reliabilities in behaviour on which laws are based. Such laws have often been expressed in terms of physical processes, mechanics and mathematical models, and not in terms of people's interpretations or intentions. They have been verified through the logic of the experimental method, the controls for which it is much harder to apply effectively with such people. It will be said that by including human experience in the social sciences we have discarded all rational criteria for the acceptance of rejection of the interpretations of theories of social scientists, since there is no independent criterion of validity for assessments of 'my experience'. Some of these criticisms may be countered; others may not. The interpretive social science which I propose does not provide the only solution to our data-collection problems. Yet I believe that it does provide one of what will prove to be a number of equally viable, alternative solutions.

References

Anastasi, A. (1982). *Psychological Testing*. New York: Macmillan.

Bandura, A. (1977). *Social Learning Theory*. Englewood Cliffs, NJ: Prentice-Hall.

Bannister, D. and Fransella, F. (1985). *Inquiring Man*. 3rd edn. Beckenham, Kent: Croom Helm.

Cassirer, E. (1944). *Essay on Man*. New Haven: Yale University Press, 1967.

Ericsson, K. A. and Simon, H. A. (1984). *Protocol Analysis: Verbal Reports as Data*. Cambridge, Mass.: MIT Press.

Giorgi, A. (1971). The experience of the subject as a source of data in a psychological experiment. In A. Giorgi, W. F. Fischer and R. Von Eckartsberg (eds.), *Duquesne Studies in Phenomenological Psychology*. Pittsburgh: Duquesne University Press, Vol. I.

Harré, R. (1978). Accounts, actions and meanings: the practice of participatory psychology. In M. Brenner, P. Marsh and M. Brenner (eds.), *Contexts of Method*. Beckenham, Kent: Croom Helm.

Harré, R. (1979). *Social Being: A Theory for Social Psychology*. Oxford: Blackwell.

Heidegger, M. (1962). *Being and Time*. New York: Harper & Row (1927).
Hetherington, R. (1983). Sacred cows and white elephants. *Bulletin of the British Psychological Society* 36, 273–80.
Kelly, G. A. (1955). *The Psychology of Personal Constructs*. New York: Norton.
Kelly, G. A. (1965). The strategy of psychological research. *Bulletin of the British Psychological Society* 18, 1–15.
Koch, S. (1981). The nature and limits of psychological knowledge. *American Psychologist* 36, 257–69.
Mair, J. M. M. (1970). Experimenting with individuals. *British Journal of Medical Psychology* 43, 245–56.
Mancuso, J. and Adams-Webber, J. (eds.) (1982). *The Construing Person*. New York: Praeger.
Manicas, P. T. and Secord, P. F. (1982). Implications for psychology from the new philosophy of science. *American Psychologist* 38, 399–414.
Marsh, J. L. (1985). Dialectical phenomenology as critical social theory. *Journal of the British Society for Phenomenology* 16, 177–93.
Orne, M. T. (1969). Demand characteristics and the concept of quasi-controls. In R. Rosenthal and R. L. Rosnow (eds.), *Artifact in Behavioural Research*. New York: Academic Press.
Packer, M. J. (1985). Hermeneutic inquiry in the study of human conduct. *American Psychologist* 40, 1081–93.
Polanyi, M. (1958). *Personal Knowledge*. Chicago: University of Chicago Press.
Richardson, A. (1984). *The Experiential Dimension of Psychology*. St Lucia: Queensland University Press.
Romanyshyn, R. D. (1975). Behaviour, experience and expression: the phenomenon of nostalgia. APA Convention, Chicago.
Rychlak, J. F. (1970). The human person in modern psychological science. *British Journal of Medical Psychology* 43, 233–40.
Salmon, P. (1978). Doing psychological research. In F. Fransella (ed.), *Personal Construct Psychology 1977*. London: Academic Press.
Schütz, A. (1967). *The Phenomenology of the Social World*. Chicago: Northwestern University Press.
Schütz, A. (1972). *Phenomenology of the Social World*. London: Heinemann.

Snygg, D. (1941). The need for a phenomenological system of psychology. *Psychological Review* 48, 404–24.
Thomason, B. (1982). *Making Sense of Reification.* London: Macmillan.
Viney, L. L. (1986). *Interpreting the interpreters: strategies for a science of construing people.* Malabar: Krieger.

Chapter 3
Three-dimensional representations of grid-type data

John Kirkland, Robert Lambourne and Stephen Black

In this paper we offer some thoughts about personal space and of how it might be explored. To do so we have divided the presentation into two sections. First we offer some thoughts about space and how it is that some people are attracted to mapping this out. Then, later, we introduce techniques now under development. These techniques are both guided by and are derived from the preceding thoughts. Thus thoughts and techniques are mutually reciprocal.

Kelly and space: some common ground

From our involvement with students, colleagues, clients and others we believe that whilst Kelly's views on how to tackle meaning may be universally applicable they are not always acceptable. His views relate to space exploration. There are other ways of seeing things, and these ways provide consistency and meaning. We don't wish to extend this point here, it is enough to indicate that some people have a preferred style which is other than constructionism. Given the existence of preferences and stylistic differences, the following thoughts are offered as a draft, mapping out our common intellectual territory.

Thought 1: quantitative and qualitative changes

The distinction between quantitative and qualitative changes is an important one. With the latter, small changes or alterations can produce massive shifts in meaning. For example, in psychophysics, that interface between carefully controlled stimulus parameters and how individuals react to these changes, there are many illustrations of jump-like shifts. Consider auditory perception. The speed at which a sound is presented is known as rise-time. In one study (Cutting and Posner, 1974) rise-times were incremented every 10 msec. for the 'same' speech-like sound. These were later played back in a random order to listeners who had been asked to decide if the sound was *ch* (as in chop) or *sh* (as in shop). These labels were easy to apply and the results unequivocal. Between the 40 and 50 msec. rise-times a dramatic shift occurred, the sound appeared to change suddenly from *ch* to *sh*. This is a discontinuous leap.

Another example may be drawn from catastrophe theory, the outcome of a marriage between mathematics and a desire to account for sudden changes (see Zeeman, 1976, for a readable description of catastrophe theory, with some physical and social-science examples). Consider the sudden change which occurs when bending a piece of light card. Take a rectangular piece in your hands, one hand at each of the shorter sides with thumbs underneath and fingers on top. Hold the card about nose level viewing it across a longer side. Bring your hands together to apply compression so the card buckles upwards. Then, keeping your hands equidistant, apply steady load to the top of the card by rotating your hands downwards (just lift your elbows). After some initial resistance the card will suddenly pop downwards. This is the sort of thing catastrophe theory addresses. The one just described is a cusp catastrophe, there is a point beyond which a small change in the state of affairs results in a collapse of stability. There are seven different catastrophes, the higher-order ones are in multi-dimensional space and are visible only as slected sections.

Thought 2: brain hemisphere specialisation

Although there is some controversy in the literature on this topic, it appears that the two halves of our brains engage in different sorts of activities. For those of us who are right handed, the left side seems to be pretty good at mechanical tasks (like logic and speech) while the right half has a bias towards space (music, intuition, shape). Perhaps those of us who do follow Kelly's initiative are good at translating from one hemisphere to the other; the techniques designed for use in PCT are aimed at precisely this purpose, transducing and translating. Thus we explore personal space (right side) and then talk about this (from the left).

Thought 3: individuals

Ordinal changes and individuals are important. In spite of an implicit bias by many researchers who aim only at precision by striving for masses of interval-type data, we believe a relaxing of these constraints can be productive. People's thoughts can move in mysterious ways. Locking onto main effects or interactional models based on group data may be tidy for many types of policy-type research which is intended to have political clout. But it is often at a cost of losing sight of individuals. We think a trade-off between these orientations is worth pursuing.

Thought 4: structure

People move freely in their thinking from making associations to playing with structure (Miller, 1956) and back again. Structure lies beyond and is of a different order from what one is presented with in one-to-one matching tasks. In part, it involves the ways in which what is offered is organised. For instance, skilled chess players are like strategists, aware of the game structure, and tackle their games in quite a different way from novices, who tend to be tacticians, responding to the more immediate situation. As an analogy, computers are like tacticians, they can be programmed to weigh up the odds, balancing in an incremental manner the different consequences of adopting each of the possible moves.

Thus an awareness of structure involves a search for something more than accepting what is happening at the moment: awareness provides motivation to go beyond the present. In the words of the familiar expression, the whole is greater than the sum of the parts.

But we are saying more than this. Namely, one has to be facile in moving in *both* directions: between the association and the structure falls the construct. Our brains work with these complementary forces, evolving intuitions and talking about them.

Thought 5: abstraction

One consequence of our space-walking is exposing those with whom we are more relaxed in our private settings to an abstract sense of humour. This, in all probability, reflects highly divergent-thinking capabilities. Included too is a capacity for both generating and recognising metaphors.

Thought 6: rotating visual images

Space-walking requires agility in rotating visual images. We believe most people can accomplish this task, given appropriate opportunities. For others this capability may have atrophied; they have been persuaded to limit themselves to disconnected keyhole peeping.

From developmental research it is known that recognising consistencies when adopting different views of the same three-dimensional landscape (or object) is one hallmark of advanced cognitive growth. With the advent of sophisticated computer-driven graphics packages, rotating three-dimensional representations have become commonplace in television commercials. A car frame, for instance, is rotated before our very eyes. However, this is different from trying to fathom the shape of something which is almost beyond our grasp. We need to be able to rotate or be rotated in multi-dimensional space and make sense of this.

Here is a more manageable puzzle. We plotted the following four shapes as two-dimensional representations. Now, your task is to interpolate the extra dimension, to generate shapes in your head. We believe you will be able to do this quite easily. How much patience will those of you who can do this have for those who cannot?

Look at the shapes drawn in Figure E3.1. Are these the same or are they different? What do we mean by different? If we mean in an immediate (association) sense then the answer is quite obviously Different. Now, go beyond the immediate; get into

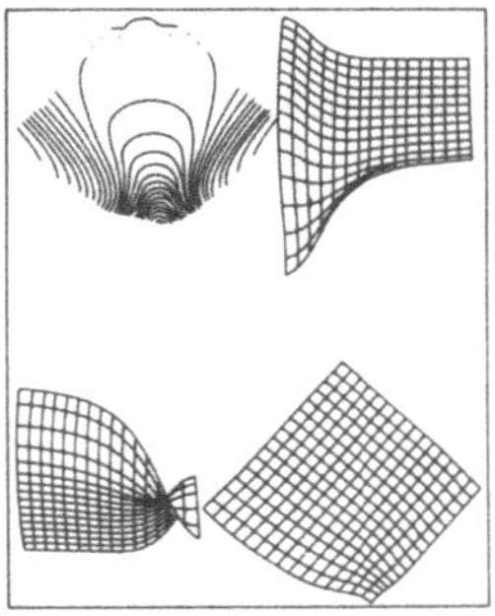

Figure E3.1 A set of computer-drawn figures

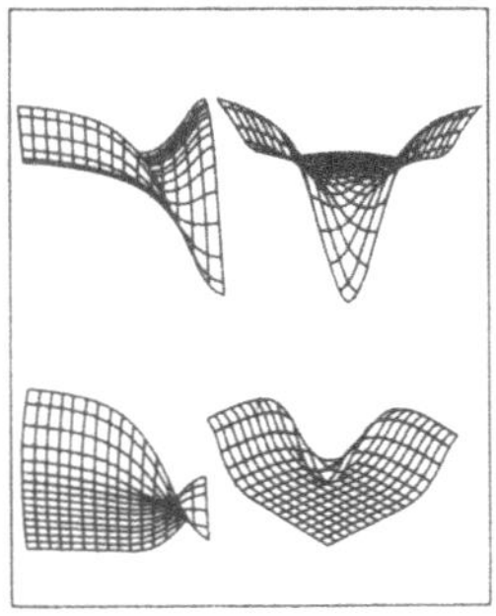

Figure E3.2 Systematic 45-degree rotations on both horizontal and vertical axes

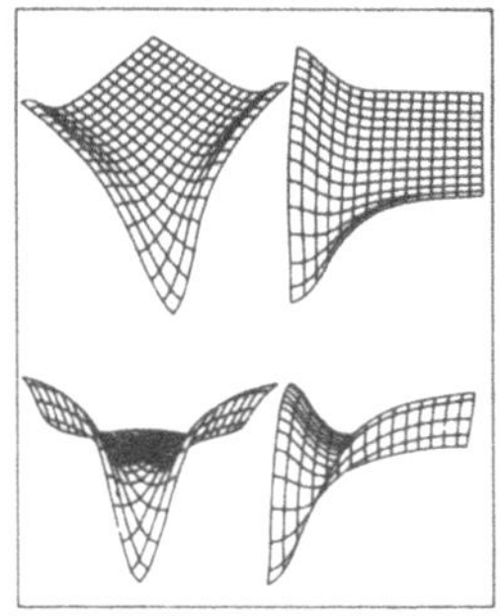

Figure E3.3 Further rotations

your brain, feel the shapes. Are these different views of the same thing, variations on an original theme?

To help unravel the puzzle consider Figure E3.2. Begin with the ram's head at the top right. (We call it a ram's head as the Massey University crest is crowned with a ram's head.) If you stretch your imagination, you can see the winged horns on either side, the nose pointing down and the plateau-like forehead.

For this exercise you now have a decision to make. You can either keep the ram's head stationary and walk around it, much like viewing a piece of sculpture. Or, instead, you can remain where you are and toy with it in your hands, turning it over.

If you look at the original head shape from 45 degrees underneath (rotating it on the horizontal axis) it would appear as the drawing immediately below. So, the bottom and top drawings are rotated by 45 degrees. Apply the same process to the left–right ones; these are displaced 45 degrees on the vertical axis. Hence the diagonally opposite corner ones are shifted on two planes, each by 45 degrees. You'll notice the lower-left drawing is the same as one of those shown in Figure E3.1.

Now, what happens if you look down (tip forward the ram's head) 45 degrees? You'll see the effect of this change on Figure E3.3. Then, if you twist this on the vertical axis, you arrive at the drawing beside it. Thus Figure E3.3 depicts twin 45-degree rotations as well. Hence the upper-right drawing of Figure E3.3 and the lower-left one of Figure E3.2 are 90–90 apart, rotated on both horizontal and vertical planes.

Finally, if you could look down on top of the ram's head you would get the picnic-cloth drawing in the lower left of Figure E3.1. To recognise what is within this criss-cross cloth, to put some shape into it, overlay the topographical contour map shown at the top right. The initial question of whether the shapes are the same or different remains unanswered.

Thought 7: conclusion

What's the point? The point is that the search for structure is a necessary motivational force for those involved in communication about personal constructs. Working in multi-dimensional space can be hazardous; you can get utterly lost without a vehicle. For us Kelly provided a Tardis, a hole-in-the-middle lifebuoy.

Some techniques under development

When supplying grid-type data, people are often requested to show, on several bi-polar construct scales, where elements are located. Taken one at a time these ratings are uni-dimensional. Whenever objects are ordered along a continuum we are dealing with a single dimension. This process can be repeated for any number of elements and constructs. As soon as one tries to make pairwise contrasts between ratings offered on different constructs, another dimension is involved. There may be as many dimensions as there are constructs. One reason for using multi-dimensional scaling techniques is to reduce the myriad of possibilities into a few major ones. The upshot of many techniques is a two-dimensional map. This fits nicely with personal construct theory; meaning is found at the intersection of the ranked positions on the various constructs.

At least two deviations occur during this process. One is the convenient squeezing of several dimensions into two. There are at least a couple of reasons for this constraint. First, clinicians and researchers have adopted two dimensions as a matter of convenience: these are easy to show on paper. The second is that there are few tools available to help people explore multi-dimensional space in a systematic and communicable manner.

The second deviation is more insidious. There is a curious lack of congruence between how constructs are elicited and how they are used when collecting grid-type data. For instance, when using triads, people consider three elements and make a distinction between these. This is largely a two-dimensional activity, as is any pairwise matching task. But once the constructs are elicited, people are required to treat them as unique – a set of uni-dimensional continua, generating data which are subjected to multi-dimensional analyses and two-dimensional representations. There is some slippage here as it appears personal construct theorists wish to have their (invisible) multi-dimensions and to see them as well.

As an analogy, you can view the shadows of a three-dimensional object on a two-dimensional screen by back-projection. You could then take a single narrow view of that image for a uni-dimensional slice. Working backwards, it would take a lot of slices to create the two-dimensional shadow, and lots of rotations of the original object to interpolate from the shadows what the three-dimensional shape was at the outset. If you are in trouble at this stage, consider how much more difficult it is to work in multi-dimensional space which has been collapsed into two dimensions.

By addressing the second deviation (of retaining pairwise distinctions, as in construct elicitation, when obtaining element rating data), we are simultaneously dealing with the first (of collapsing dimensions) as well. We have used semantic differential scales in numerous studies dealing with infant crying (e.g. Brennan and Kirkland, 1985). There, as in many personal construct approaches, people rate objects using end anchors. As we cannot begin with any assumptions about the characteristics of the sounds, we check to see if the sounds are similar or different. This is quite straightforward. People listen to a series of discrete cry signals and indicate the similarity of each to the one which immediately preceded it. As only a few cries generate many pairwise contrasts, this is a tedious, time-consuming task. Yet from personal experience it seems that each and every comparison in the $n \times n$ matrix has to be made, as the multi-dimensional nature of cries does not permit extrapolation. For example, if a listener is presented with a series of cries (A, B, C, D . . .) and asked to rate successive pairs (A with B, B with C, C . . .) using a seven-point scale, with 7 = perfect agreement, then consecutive ratings of, say, 4 do not necessarily provide information on non-pair members in that series (say A and D). A listener may be using pitch on one occasion (A, B). loudness on another (B, C) and number of coughs for a third (C, D). Simply put, coughs and pitch may not be related perceptually.

Of course, you suggest, why not use constructs and then rate each cry against all of these attributes? We did, using semantic-type scales. During this process we realised that the scales could slide, since a listener had to retain a clear idea of just what the scale extremes depicted. Practically, how does one calibrate the anchors; what *is* screaming?

Our current solution is to go back to collecting ordinal rather than interval data. Throw out the idea of 'point' scales and go back to basics, namely pairwise contrasts. Identify the attributes or (constructs) and show how pairs differ from one another (more or less) for each attribute. This conceptual solution is elegant and respects ordinal contrasts. The next task is to get the computers to catch up to our thinking on this matter.

In the meantime we will do what most others do, force people into interval-type decisions on single dimensions and then apply multivariate analyses. There are two reasons for this pursuit. One is to bide time until the difficulty mentioned above has been resolved. The other is to explore means of showing just how small changes can be significant: sculpturing meaningful shapes in space.

As data, we use for the following example parent ratings of several infant behaviours on different 'temperament' dimensions (Kirkland and Brennan, 1984). We wanted to find out the structure of these behaviours, at least so far as the situations and the ways of seeing these are interrelated for a particular parent. In the following example the behavioural situations are as follows: (1) when having a bath, (2) after having a bath, (3) middle of night feeding, (4) after middle of night feeding, (5) 'breakfast' feeding, (6) after 'breakfast' feeding, (7) midday feeding, (8) after midday feeding, (9) early-evening feeding, (10) after early-evening feeding, (11) late-evening feeding, (13) new food offered, (14) having nappies changed (morning), (15) having nappies changed (early evening), (16) when waking at beginning of day, (17) when put down for morning nap, (18) when waking from morning nap, (19) when put down for afternoon nap, (20) when waking from afternoon nap, (23) when playing alone with toys, (24) immediate reaction to strangers.

Stereoscopic views may be plotted (Fig. E3.4) and a standard stereogram used to examine these pairs. In this example we have connected the items and double-circled those which represent clusters (at 92 per cent agreement). One cluster contains items *1* and 10, another the items 2, 8, *11*, 15, 17, and the third consists of 5 and *7*. The additional cluster members were dropped since they cluttered up the picture.

In Figure E3.4 are shown two stereoscopic aspects of a 3-D cube. (To approximate two-dimensional plots of these three separate views, simply look at one side of each pair.) These three-dimensional representations provide an enriched view of the items and their interconnections.

As to the future, we can look towards holograms; walk through the element/construct configurations and see how these are arranged in space by recognising their interdependencies. In the interim we plan to continue unravelling paired-comparison

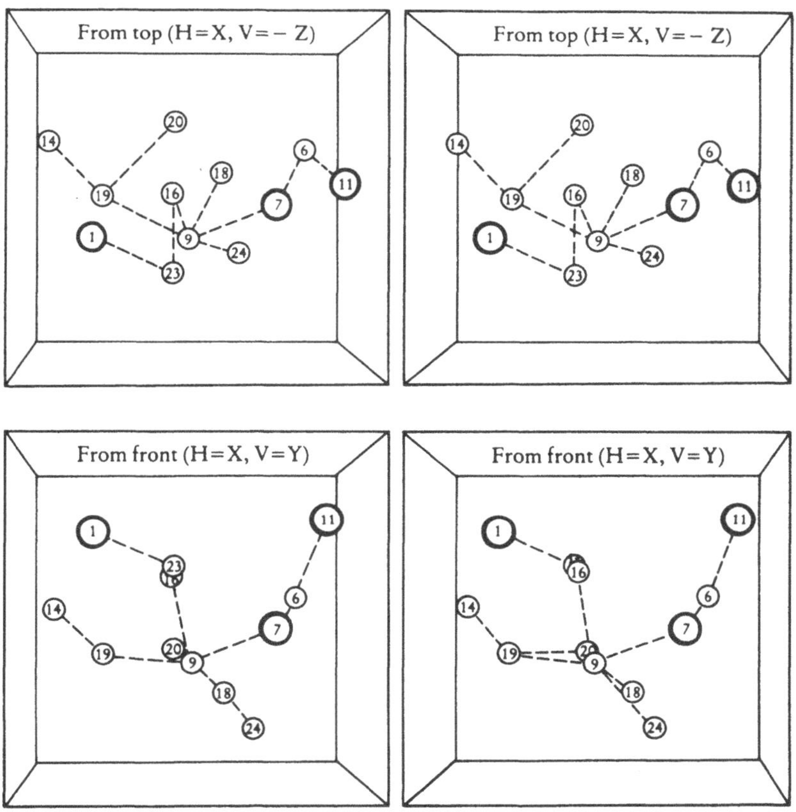

Figure E3.4 Two stereoscopic views

contrasts and display selected aspects of the available multi-dimensional space. One aim is to get a better handle on what this means, how it can be seen, how changes can be recognised and how therapeutic interventions may be implemented. So, for future developments watch this space.

References

Brennan, M. and Kirkland, J. (1985). Comparison of perceptual dimensions uncovered from infant-cry signals using the method of pair-comparisons and semantic differential. *Scandinavian Journal of Psychology* 26, 12–20.

Cutting, J. E. and Posner, B. S. (1974). Categories and boundaries in speech and music. *Perception and Psychophysics* 16(3), 564–70.

Kirkland, J. and Brennan, M. (1984). Profiles obtained from clustering behaviours in situations rated on temperament dimensions. *The Exceptional Child* 32, 31–5.

Miller, G. A. (1956). The magical number seven, plus or minus two. *Psychological Review* 63, 81–97.

Zeeman, E. C. (1976). Catastrophe theory. *Scientific American* 234, 65–83.

Chapter 4
Information loss in grid analysis

J. W. Cary

The use of grids, or repertory grids, in personal construct analysis has two principal functions: the elicitation of constructs and the determination of the cognitive structure pertaining to individuals' use of constructs and perception of elements. There then follows a subsidiary, but no less important, task of establishing a means of interpreting these structures and of communicating the patterns within the structures. In this paper the focus of interest is the process of measurement employed to construct a grid and the implications of the level of measurement in determining the accuracy of the structure of the concepts used in the grid. In examining the impact of the level of measurement, the process of analysis to establish the structure in the measurements taken will also be indirectly considered.

Techniques for collecting grid data are well established (Fransella and Bannister, 1977); considerable attention has also been given to techniques for the analysis of grid data (e.g. Slater, 1972; Pope and Keen, 1981; Shaw, 1981) and to the implication of different forms of analysis on the outcomes of grid analysis (Rathod, 1981). Categorical-, ordinal- and interval-level data are all widely used in texts on grid technology and in published applications of the use of grids. Current preference seems to be for the use of rating scales. While, perhaps, it is implicit that measurement theory is widely understood by grid practitioners, there is a suprising lack of explicit examination of the effect of measurement level on the accuracy of structures derived from grid data. This may be due largely to the use in personal construct theory of a categorical approach to elicit constructs from a set of derived or supplied elements.

There are two main classes of use for grids in personal construct psychology: the psychotherapy situation and the research situation where grids from larger numbers of subjects are obtained. The first situation is characterised by a 'one on one' interaction, with the grid being used as an aid to diagnosis and communication between the therapist and the client. In this situation the outcomes of grid analysis can be modified by communication between the therapist and the client; but misinformation or inadequate analysis may create a false agenda for the therapeutic interaction. In the research use of the grid, particularly where the number of subjects is greater than one, measurement and analysis are more critical to the validity and particularly the reliability of derived cognitive structure.

Information potentially available in a grid can be lost both in the process of measurement and in the process of analysis which establishes the pattern or structure in the measurements taken. Principal-components analysis has been the most enduring and the most popular of the non-classificatory techniques of grid analysis. It will be used in this paper for the analysis of the data sets to be considered. A metric multi-dimensional scaling technique which uses data which has ratio-level characteristics will also be presented. We turn now to a consideration of potential effects of the level of measurement.

An experimental study of country images

To examine the effects of different levels of measurement on grid analysis a study was undertaken of the comparative images of products made in different countries with data collected at varying levels of measurement precision. Comparative image studies have been reported frequently in the marketing and behavioural literature (e.g. Jaffe and Nebenzahl, 1984).

Data were gathered at three levels of measurement exhibiting categorical, interval and ratio characteristics, respectively. Twenty honours-level university students were respondents for the three levels of data-gathering, with three questionnaires being administered to the same subjects over a period of one week. Categorical-level data was collected in standard repertory-grid format with five elements (countries) compared by seven constructs (attributes) using a dichotomous choice. Interval-level data were obtained by rating the country elements on attribute constructs using a seven-point semantic differential scale. Ratio-type data was derived by pairwise comparison of all country elements and attribute constructs. The ratio unit of measurement was established by arbitrarily defining the distance between two relevant concepts as being 100 units. Subjects then used this measurement standard to estimate distances between all elements and concepts: perfect correspondence between two concepts being represented by zero and large differences unconstrained by any upper numerical limit. Pairwise comparison involved collection of sixty-six 'pieces' of information in contrast to thirty-five data observations for the other two levels of data collection. For each of the three questionnaires the same order of presentation was used for all subjects.

The categorical and interval data were analysed using principal-components analysis in Slater's INGRID program. The ratio data were analysed by metric multi-dimensional scaling (MMDS) using the GALILEO program (Woelfel and Fink, 1980) based on Torgerson's (1958) modification of Young and Householder's (1938) procedure for converting inter-point distances to a scalar-products matrix which is then transformed to principal axes (by the same process as principal-components analysis of a covariance matrix). The GALILEO program is designed to accommodate eigenvalues of less than zero, thus giving an indication of the degree of intransitivity between concept comparisons.

The underlying structure of relationships between concepts, both elements and constructs, for each of the data sets is shown in Figure E4.1. The first two dimensions for the three data sets were manually rotated to achieve a best fit. The matrices resulting from the two conventional forms of grid data-gathering are fully resolved in four dimensions with the first two dimensions accounting for 94 per cent of the variance in both cases. The analysis of the ratio data set produced six dimensions in real space and six dimensions in imaginary space (negative eigenvectors), with the first two dimensions accounting for 72 per cent of the real space.

A comparison of the patterns in the three data sets (Fig. E4.1) indicates that the general 'order' of spatial relationship is consistent for the three situations and that the concept locations are spatially

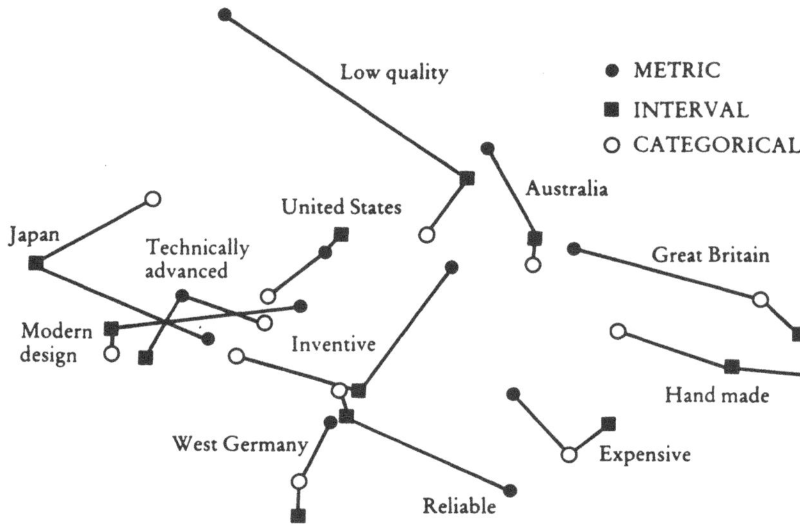

Figure E4.1 First two dimensions for three levels of measurement (dimensions for each set manually rotated for best fit)

closer for the categorical and interval data sets. It is not possible to establish which set and which form of analysis provides the most accurate structure; this problem will be pursued later. If it can be assumed that the metric analysis ought to produce the most accurate result then there are significant discrepancies in the relationships between concepts for the categorical and interval data.

A selective interpretation of the two-dimensional relationships (Fig. E4.2) indicates some differences between the three data sets. For the categorical data, the United States [6] is seen as Technically Advanced [1] and Inventive [12]; and Australia [7] and the United States [6] are associated with Low Quality [11]. This latter association also applies for the interval data but there is no close association between the United States and Technically Advanced. Interpretation discrepancies would be reduced if we adopted Slater's (1972) advice that the constructs be projected onto the circumference of a circle centred on the origin. This seems to be rarely done in practice. But such an approach also reflects that the data are standardised in the analysis, with the constructs having a standard deviation of 1.

For the ratio data, Hand Made [10] and Low Quality [11] are not associated with any country; and all countries are seen as less Reliable [5]. The magnitude of the distance of concepts 10 and 11

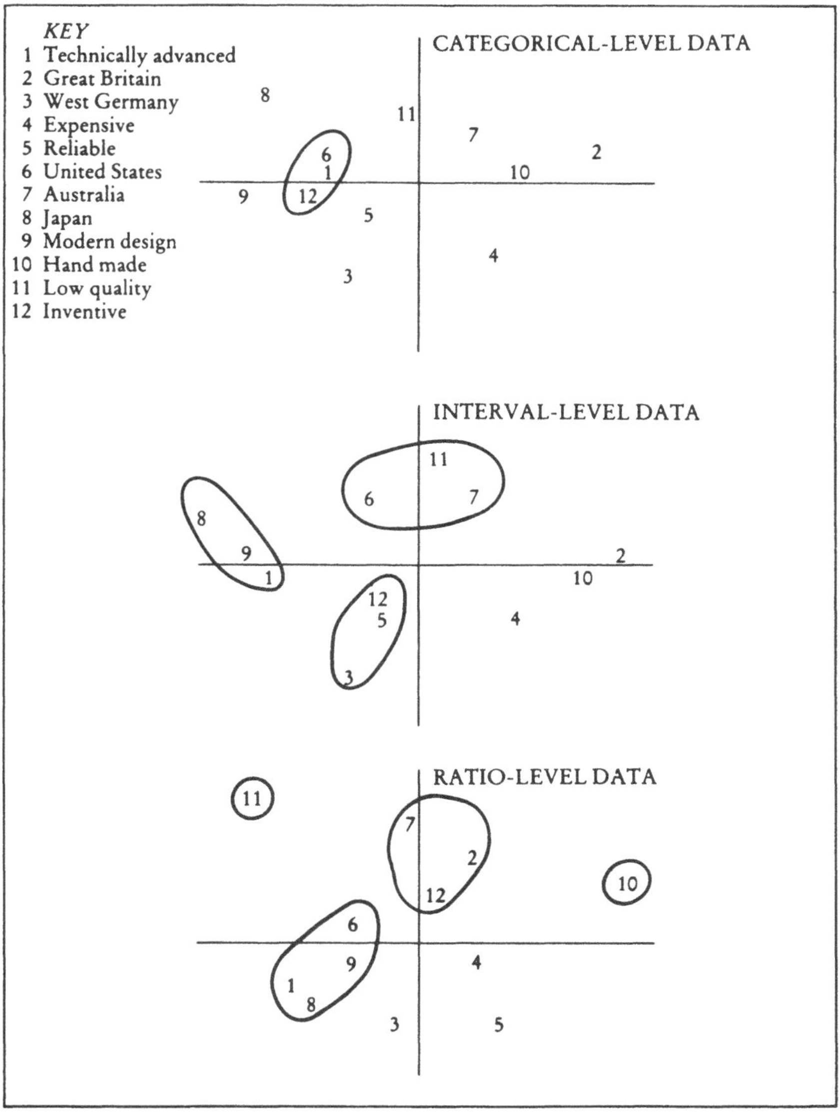

Figure E4.2 Interpreting the concept structures for three levels of data on first two dimensions

from the other concepts in the ratio analysis indicates the potential danger of the natural inclination to assume metric properties exist once we spatially depict categorical and interval data in Cartesian-type plots. The ratio data indicates that these two 'constructs' were not relevant to a consideration of the countries chosen as elements. The 'rule' adopted by personal construct theorists to always operate with elements and constructs within the range of convenience is a wise one to follow, but often we cannot be aware of when this rule is being broken, particularly where predetermined elements and constructs are used with large numbers of subjects. In such cases categorical and interval data are likely to distort the true relationships between concepts. We turn now to a more specific example of potential information loss, or distortion, with different levels of grid measurement.

An analysis of physical structure

There are several limitations to the analysis presented so far. First, each of the data sets used to measure country images comprise matrix cell means for twenty subjects. Thus the categorical analysis is in fact based on data with interval characteristics, having a potential range from zero to one. For any individual subject in the country-image analysis, there is a greater discrepancy between the categorical-data analysis and the analysis based on the other levels of data than occurs when the mean data is used. This reflects the operation of the law of large numbers. Beail (1984) and Cary and Holmes (1982) have highlighted some of the problems of handling variance in consensus grids and the limitations these impose on the analysis of multiple grids. The present analysis suggests that there is a need to be more circumspect about using categorical data, such as the common dichotomous choice, with single-subject grids than with multiple-subject grid sets.

A second, and major, constraint on the assessment of the effect of measurement level in the country-image data sets is the impossibility of determining what is the correct underlying structure of the relationships between the concepts. To overcome this problem we will consider the analysis of relationships of known physical structure. The data base is provided by the Cartesian coordinates of a rectangular pyramid with five points where the planes intersect. The Cartesian coordinates of these points are P1 (−4, 2, −4); P2 (−4, 2, 6); P3 (4, 2, 6); P4 (4, 2, −4); and P5 (0, 8, 1).

Ratio-level data for MMDS analysis were the ten inter-point distances between the five coordinate points. The five Cartesian coordinates were also used as ratio-level data in a grid format for principal-components analysis. Interval-level data were created by rescaling the Cartesian coordinate distances on a seven-point scale. Categorical data were created by categorising the coordinate points as being either above or below the mid-point of the range of coordinate values. The interval and categorical data were analysed in grid format using principal-components analysis. The variance for all data analyses is fully expressed in three dimensions. Comparisons of the resulting structures can thus be observed in three-dimensional plots of the coordinates produced by each analysis (Fig. E4.3).

Analyses of the ratio-level data by both MMDS and principal-components analysis produce true symmetrical representations of the original rectangular pyramid. The interval-level data produce a small distortion of the original structure (after the base of the pyramid is rotated to a horizontal position) and in the case of the categorical-level data there are major distortions of the original structure – the base of the pyramid is not a flat plane and a vertical gravity line from the apex of the pyramid falls outside the base of the pyramid. In the less precise data sets the spatial order and direction may be correct, but the distances between 'concepts' indicate considerable measurement error. Such errors may considerably distort specific interpretations of grids containing larger numbers of concepts.

The accuracy of principal components analysis and metric multi-dimensional scaling in resolving the true structure of the grid sets has not been specifically considered. Both methods appear to give similar results for the two ratio data sets shown in Figure E4.3. However, in a comparative analysis of matrices of inter-city distances, metric multi-dimensional scaling gives a more accurate representation of the spatial relationship between the cities (Woelfel and Fink, 1980).

Concluding comments

It can be concluded that the distances between concepts will be less accurate for less precise levels of measurement. Less precise forms of measurement produce degradation in the 'true' structure of relationships between concepts – both elements and constructs. While this is an obvious concern for research uses of the grid –

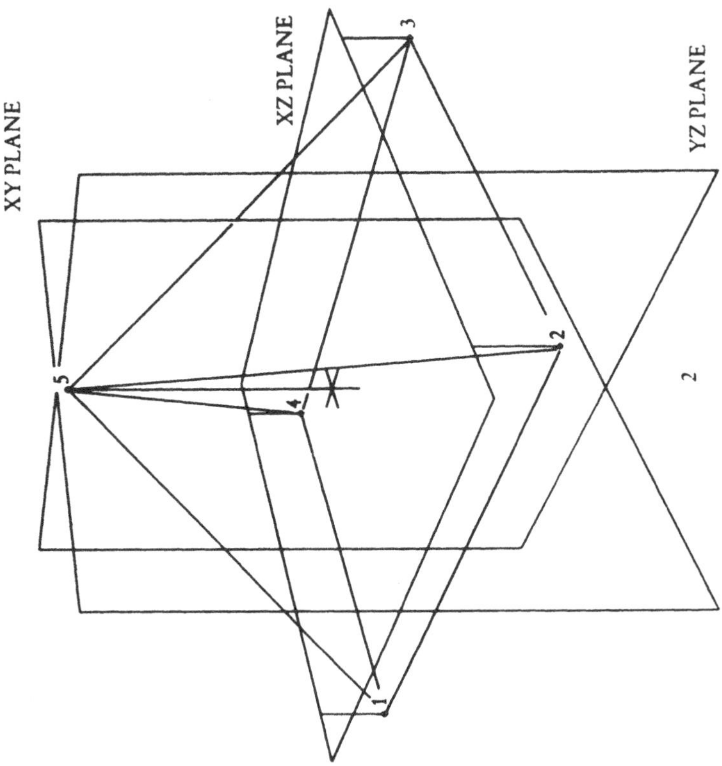
XY PLANE
XZ PLANE
YZ PLANE
3
5
4
2
1
2

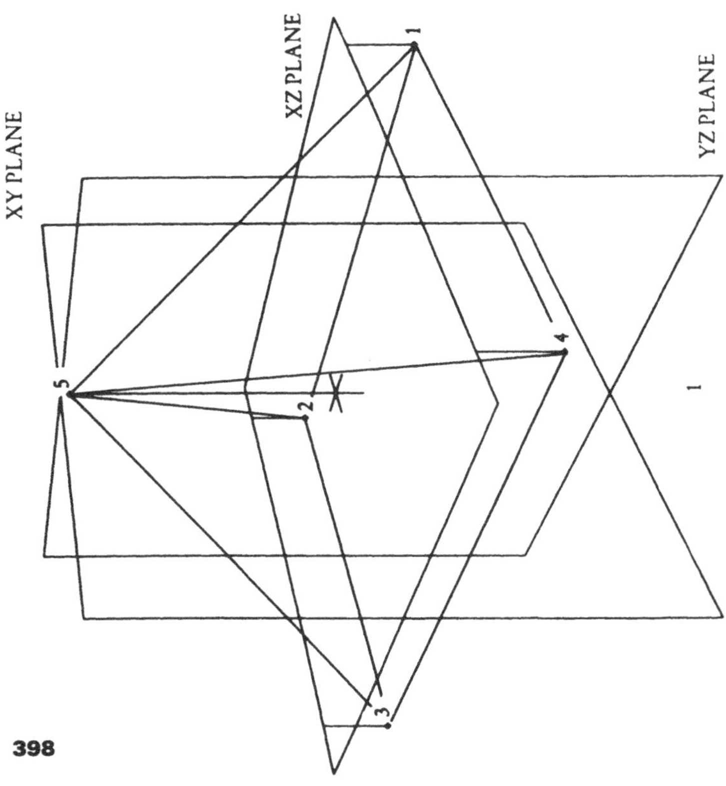
XY PLANE
XZ PLANE
YZ PLANE
1
5
2
4
3
1

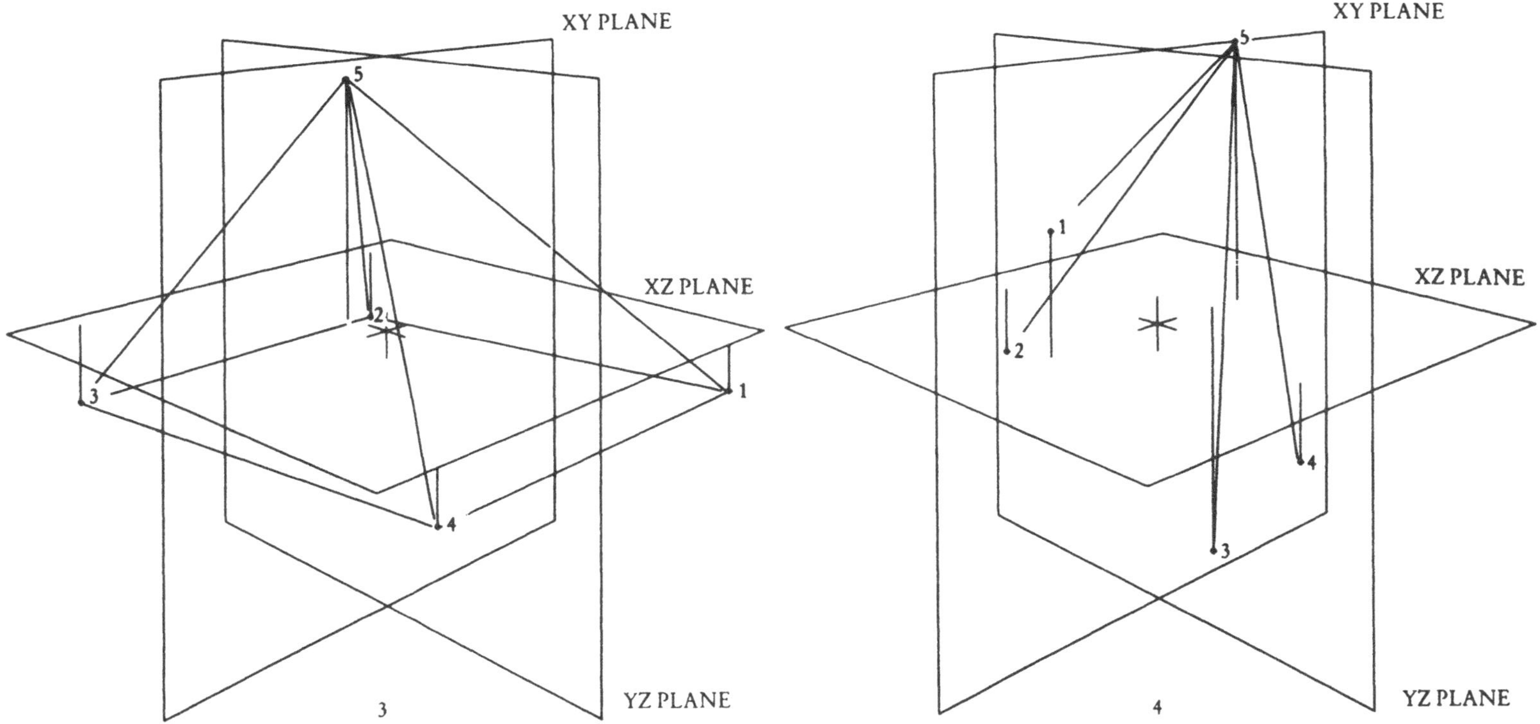

Figure E4.3 Three-dimensional structures for three levels of data measurement: (1) ratio data (MMDS analysis of inter-point distances), (2) ratio data (principal components of Cartesian coordinates), (3) interval data, (4) categorical data where acceptable levels of reliability ought to be desired – in the use of single grids, distortions of the 'true' structure will be potentially quite large when using categorical-level data. The resulting misinterpretation may have serious implications. For aggregate-level categorical data the distortions are likely to be lessened because the data are no longer truly categorical.

When measuring changes in grid structures over time, categorical data are unlikely to give an acceptable level of result because the larger error associated with the location of any concept at different time points will preclude an accurate assessment of true movement over time.

A consideration of measurement theory and the two studies reported here would indicate that larger numbers of observations – more constructs and elements – tend to compensate for deficiencies in categorical data. But the major conclusion to be drawn from the examples presented is the commonsense observation that refined analysis will not adequately substitute for unrefined measurement.

References

Beail, N. (1984). Consensus grids: what about the variance? *British Journal of Medical Psychology* 57, 193–5.

Cary, J. W. and Holmes, W. E. (1982). Relationships between farmers' goals and farm adjustment strategies: some empirics of a multivariate approach. *Australian Journal of Agricultural Economics* 26, 114–30.

Fransella, F. and Bannister, D. (1977). *A Manual for Repertory Grid Technique*. London: Academic Press.

Jaffe, E. D. and Nebenzahl, I. D. (1984). Alternative questionnaire formats for country image studies. *Journal of Marketing Research* 21, 463–71.

Pope, M. L. and Keen, T. R. (1981). *Personal Construct Psychology and Education*. London: Academic Press.

Rathod, P. (1981). Methods of analysis of repgrid data. In H. Bonarius, R. Holland and S. Rosenberg (eds.), *Personal Construct Psychology: Recent Advances in Theory and Practice*. London: Macmillan.

Shaw, M. L. G. (ed.) (1981). *Recent Advances in Personal Construct Technology*. London: Academic Press.

Slater, P. (1972). *The Measurement of Intrapersonal Space by Grid Technique*, Vol. 2: *Dimensions of Intrapersonal Space*. London: Wiley.

Torgerson, W. S. (1958). *Theory and Method of Scaling*. New York: Wiley.

Woelfel, J. and Fink, E. L. (1980). *The Measurement of Communication Processes: Galileo Theory and Method*. New York: Academic Press.

Young, G. and Householder, A. (1938). Discussion of a set of points in terms of their mutual distances. *Psychometrica* 3, 19–22.

F

Industrial Settings

Chapter 1

A range of applications of PCP within business and industry

Fay Fransella, Helen Jones and Joyce Watson

Working with the individual: the development of self-awareness
Helen Jones

Personal construct theory provides an excellent model for helping people become more aware of the situations facing them and the personal problems which are thus implied.

The topic of Philip Boxer's paper 'Regnancy: a shadow over personal construing' (pp. 418–25) is the theme of this particular case study. Kelly describes regnancy as the allocation of constructs on an all-or-none basis, as in Aristotelian logic. The experience of this for an individual is often to have a sense of being stuck, of there being *no* alternatives available. At these times personal-construct counselling can be of considerable help. Kelly pointed out that we are only ever stuck because of our limited range of vision. The integral universe, on which his theory is based, is always out there if only we can reach it.

Dissolving the glue: the case of Frank

It is a rewarding experience for the counsellor to help a person stuck in his regnancy and shadowed by it to dissolve some of the glue. I have recently worked with a manager in the personnel department of a large organisation on such an exercise.

Frank is the husband of Anne, who is described in more detail in my chapter 'Creativity and depression' in Jones (1985) – the short story of a woman who was depressed and whose husband, Frank, had been referred to me for psychotherapy. At the end of that story it was significant that Frank, who usually spent our therapy hour in another room working on papers from his brief-case, joined Anne and me as a person not isolated from his wife's problem any more. For a while the three of us worked together on family issues. Quite soon, however, Frank began to use the time to explore issues relating to his work.

Changing roles

For many years he had been a manager in charge of catering, and this work was familiar to him and the detail it required suited him. His recent opportunity to expand the range of his work in general personnel management was a challenge. It involved a much more personal approach to people in areas such as health and safety, industrial relations and other fields as yet unknown to Frank. He loves paper, dotting 'i's and crossing 't's. He enjoys his briefcase and its contents. The job was indeed an adventure. His deeply held views about adventure are that it should not be undertaken without thorough checking out beforehand, preferably with several appendices attached as cautions and controls. He was stressed by this and found it hard to change. He had to develop better communication skills and to be more flexible with people, and he found he did not easily respond to the everchanging nature of human behaviour. He was unhappy.

During the time we had worked as a family he had begun to understand why Anne had become depressed. Her loose construction of events, her dreamy nature, was constantly blocked by his tight way of needing to see the outcome before he would take risks. His view that you should begin only things that you could complete, otherwise you should never start, was at variance with Anne's – that you should experience the space around you in whatever form and change accordingly, and she felt crushed by his single, pre-emptive view of the world. His regnancy both crowded her out and shadowed his own construing (see Figure F1.1).

Our joint sessions helped Anne to understand Frank's work-world better and we gradually became more propositional in the work experiments we discussed and Frank tested out. She was now able to play a more active part in helping Frank to take risks,

(a) FRANK

Ladder 1

Being a family man ↓ ↔	being isolated, lonely, not belonging
belonging, not isolated →	no point in life, isolation

Ladder 2

Rational ↓ ↔	irrational, silly
Identify, and be positive with ↓ —	difficult to understand at a human level
Something to work on, know what I have to do ↓ →	don't understand
more achievement ↓ →	can't succeed
belonging, not isolated →	no point in life, isolation

(b) ANNE

Being taken over by Frank ↔	being equal ↓
Brings out worst in me ↔	give as good as you get ↓
Makes me quiet, sarcastic, go too far ↔	feel part of what's going on not just an onlooker ↓
Feel constrained and trapped ↔	leads to easy free life, not constrained

Figure F1.1 Examples of Anne's and Frank's ladders

and her depression began to lift as she became more inspirational to her husband and herself in her behaviour. It was not long before she stopped attending the sessions to get on with her life.

Moving into the organisation

Frank wanted to continue his work with me and asked his employers to support a personnel skills training course with me. They agreed. He then had ten sessions with me as a contract to work on his *personal* skills. The words, after all, were similar.

His main problem was his pre-emptive way of construing. His whole educational, personal and work ethic was based on the notion of there being 'right and proper' ways of doing things, and his need to be 'open and honest' about this. He was a perfectionist and *knew* the way things were achieved. He brooked no argument. So when we began to dwell on the nature of constructive alternativism his world dilated in a radical way. He began to discover a Community of Selves (Mair, 1977) within himself, on which he could draw to deal with the many difficult situations which he faced at work.

Action in the therapy room

We used a lot of role play. I became angry nursing sisters, stubborn trade-union leaders, warehousemen unwilling to carry out health and safety checks in areas where lethal chemicals were stored, busy bosses and harassed secretaries, and a whole range of characters who were inclined to drop Frank's memos into the bin without reading them. Gradually, he stopped writing so many. He started to go out and meet people. He began to look healthier, less worried and he smiled more. Oddly his managerial skills seemed to be improving and he began to recount with some delight the conversational enterprises he was now more frequently involved in. He began to see that he did not always have to believe the organisational, personal and regnant constructs he was ingrained with. They could instead be a useful uniform for him to wear in certain contexts. To change his conversational clothes in terms of the person he was working with moved him into a more flexible and creative way of working.

Action in the organisation

He began to be more ambitious and at this point tested out a major experiment by putting together a CV and applying for a senior-management job in another organisation. He thought he had little chance of getting this. However, he was shortlisted and was invited to the final residential interview. He hates parties, and the social chat that goes with them. They are not 'serious living' (another regnant view). But he reported back success in his new 'partygoer' conversational clothes, and a way of in future finding the official party 'interesting'. He was also able to report failure in the final interview without seeing it as personal failure.

Outcome: Frank the father, Helen the briefcase

Until that final interview, when someone else got the job, Frank had held the view that 'all failure is total'. Another regnant view was under threat and it really was time for him to accept invalidation of part of his former view of the world.

He was, after ten sessions of discussion, feeling much more in control of both his personal and personnel skills. In fact, his whole life seemed more balanced. He had become a role player, and fun had crept in somewhere. Frank was always punctual and never missed appointments. One Saturday he took his family out instead. Anne was really pleased as she had begun to wonder if our meetings were another kind of briefcase. I suppose I should be pleased at this – and add the costume of briefcase to my other professional clothes as a therapist!

Addendum (1986)

Frank is now in a new job where he has an 'influential' role (his words). He is enjoying the challenge of introducing human change in a Rambo-style organisation in a subtle and powerful way.

Working with individuals within the organisation
Joyce Watson

Working with people to bring about change within the context of their organisation can often present both the company and the individual with problems. Whether this is a sales representative who is not selling the product, or manager who does not get on with his boss, there can often be a discrepancy between what the referring agency see as the desired outcome and what the individual would choose to do. A company may agree a change in policy at management level, but to actually bring about these changes at all levels within the company also implies a change in behaviour of the individuals concerned. How does a policy change become a behavioural reality?

Kelly's Choice Corollary states that 'a person chooses for himself that alternative in a dichotomized construct through which he anticipates the greater extension and definition of his system' (1955, p. 64). But should an organisation decide that if their sales people were to behave in a more friendly style customer relations and the company image would be improved, this change in policy may not allow for the extension and definition of the system of every individual sales representative. Therefore, for any training programme to be effective, it must to some extent take the individual's system into account.

If the person chooses, at some level, to accept the directions his company has imposed on his job description, training to adapt to this new style may be necessary. Learning new skills will require him to reconstrue facets of his work, and ideally this learning will allow him to elaborate his system. Personal construct psychology can readily deal with such situations as the philosophy of constructive alternativism means that a desired outcome can be attained in an infinite number of ways if one can be creative enough to envisage them. Therefore, a training programme designed for groups must be flexible enough to adapt to individual needs as well as to the groups as a whole.

Not only was Kelly at pains to stress that there is little difference between what goes on in education and therapy, but that 'the functions of group psychotherapy are broadly the same of those of any form of psychotherapy – to assist the person to develop more effective channels through which he and others may anticipate events' (Kelly, 1955, p. 1155). In other words, whether the situation be group or individual, therapy or training, our aim is to help the person achieve, in a manner suitable for them, a more desirable way of operating. In the context of performance-skills training the aim is to achieve more optimal functioning at work and to create more effective channels of anticipation for a designated role. Whether one is carrying out counselling, self-development or performance-skills training, from a PCP perspective the processes involved in bringing about change are the same.

The PCP Centre was involved in the retraining of a group of supervisors to improve their standard of performance. The programme was designed to use a combination of group and individual settings. These arenas can be used in a complementary fashion to allow the testing of new hypotheses and the trying out of new skills. The one-to-one situation provided a more secure environment to allow the individual to focus on some of the more personal implications of the change for them; the group situations provided wider scope for experimentation. This combination can be used very effectively to bring about quite radical change in skills and styles in a relatively short period of time.

Individual setting

Here one can design a mini-course specifically for the individual, concentrating or their issues and problems. The use of laddering (Hinkle, 1965), pyramiding (Landfield, 1971), and ABC networks (Tschudi, 1977) of elicited constructs has proved to be an extremely useful way of exploring the person's system. Using these details to elaborate context at work can clarify issues and allow them to consider new ways of moving towards their goals. Enactment and role play can also be used to aid the transition at a behavioural level.

As Kelly does not separate behaviour from cognition any change in construing will also imply a change in behaviour and vice versa. But it is also important to consider the themes presented. For example, someone who considers that a 'strong style of leadership' is preferable to a 'wishy-washy style' is going to resist changing if they consider the new policy involves them being wishy-washy. This construct may be so strongly held that they will not consider carrying out any of the new role that has been defined. In individual sessions one has the time and space to concentrate on such core issues which may be lost or be too threatening in a group.

Group setting

Here people can test their new ideas on other people who work in the same context as themselves. The design of the group can be such that it allows them to experience a variety of ways of working that they may have not considered themselves, and to see the different interpretations of the new role.

To have the varieties of interpretation of a defined role is valuable in that the person can experience taking on a new role and view others interpretation of it, while being able to retain some of their core structures. Overall, the themes and attitudes of the individual are as important as the skills that they have to attain.

Working with the organisation (Fay Fransella) as the client

The Centre's Idiographic Research Unit (IRU) was set up a year ago to specialise in the carrying out of idiographic research within a business and industrial context.

Focusing on the person

The prevailing stereotypes about research within the business context appear to be of the nomothetic variety. Research is about applying some already well-validated test, questionnaire or procedure to produce results that can at least be understood at *some* level from the experiences of the past.

From the personal construct perspective we do not find it necessary to impose stereotyped theories of human needs and motivations, established questionnaires or off-the-shelf strategies in order to come up with some results that can be of value. We start where the client is, and work from there.

Hinkle (1965) described a way of helping the person climb up and down their own construing ladder. Both of the two preceding sections have given examples of this laddering procedure as we have developed it. We now use this as one of our very basic tools to help us hear more clearly what lies behind the words. It serves many purposes. It enables the person to make explicit the personal values he or she places on things and the everyday contexts within which these operate and to explore conflicts and inconsistencies within their construing systems. It provides insights into why people resist change or do not come up to what is expected of them, and so forth. For instance, laddering quickly showed why it was unacceptable for a manager to change her management style from one of 'organising and being in charge' to one of 'participating and caring'. To be a manager who was 'participating and caring' meant being 'weak and wishy-washy'.

Our specialised interviewing procedures use the methods of standard construct elicitation coupled with laddering, pyramiding (Landfield, 1971), the ABC method (Tschudi, 1977) and several others that have emerged from PCP.

Idiographic work with individuals

While the construing of an individual employee at whatever level in the organisation is of great interest to employee and researcher alike, it seldom answers the questions being posed by the organisation as client. These questions usually concern groups of people – public, management, staff, customers or the entire workforce.

We therefore need to compress the rich language of individuals into a less rich but common language. Let us say that we have collected the ideas, feelings and desires of twenty staff members in each of ten groups within one organisation. We ask one or more representatives of management and staff to sit down with one of us and together construe the language used by that group of staff.

The between 200 and 300 constructs are reduced to ten or twelve groups; each group containing constructs that have similar meanings. One construct is then selected to reflect the overall meaning of that construct group.

It is not surprising that managers, particularly, are sometimes rather overawed by this array of between 200 and 300 small cards each containing a bi-polar construct. But in our experience, once the shock is over, the manager finds it a fascinating task. He is, after all, listening to the ways in which his colleagues and staff talk about themselves, their work and the organisation.

It is of vital importance in our research programme that management becomes personally involved in the research. They will be the recipients of the research results, so it is essential to ensure that they will be able to understand them.

Idiographic work with groups of individuals

Having moved from individuality to commonality, we approach the time to collect some data from a wider sample. Typically, we use two types of repertory grid for this. One consists of the constructs, selected with management and staff to represent those elicited in the individual interviews, used as seven-point rating scales. The other is a resistance-to-change grid. Both are administered to groups of staff, managers, customers, and so on, to yield profiles of meaning. Thus, apart from being able to say what staff think of their customers, their management, their organisation, or whatever, we can indicate where resistance to change is likely to be met.

The analyses

We have the software to analyse these grids in a variety of ways and to include a variety of 'those pesky mislaid variables' (Kelly, 1969, p. 122). For example, we can look at a cross-section of personnel within ten work units and describe similarities and differences in how they see each other, how they see themselves, the organisation itself, management, supervisors and staff (not to mention the customer); we can combine all staff, all supervisors and all management and study similarities and differences in the construing of these groups; we can combine the entire sample and look at the 'corporate image'. There are many other combinations and permutations.

Each of these analyses can include comparisons between men and women, the older and the younger, those who have been in the organisation for a long and a short time, or any other variable thought to be relevant.

Some specific examples

Does the public get what it wants?

Increasing concern is being expressed about whether or not those who train our public servants know what you and I as citizens think they should be like. Do those who train medical general practitioners know what we most want from our GP? What about our teachers, our policemen, our air hostesses or our psychologists?

When we make comparisons between the attitudes of the public towards their servants and the attitudes of public servants towards their customers, we are starting a debate where none was before. Where, as can be the case, considerable discrepancies are found, authorities can act in at least two ways. They can either be hostile and 'make' their customers want what they are given by saying 'we know what is best for you'. Or they can reconsider their entire training programmes. If the enquiry goes further and looks at the *qualities* of personality, attitude, and so on, then our work influences selection procedures.

Selection procedures

At best, psychologists and others can provide techniques, ideas and methods which elicit data about an individual. These data can then be added to other data and so help in selecting the right person for the job. At worst, psychologists and others say they can select the best individual for a certain job on the sole basis of a set of scores on a particular test.

Our forays into the field of selection have been tentative and take place on the understanding that we will never come up with an easy answer. By and large we go to those intimately concerned with the group about whom there are selection issues – let us say senior managers. We may elicit constructs from senior managers about what makes some people good at their work and others poor. Laddering these soon pin-points the evaluative, superordinate constructs considered important. As often as not, there is commonality.

So the next question is: how do you find out whether or not an applicant has those qualities? Probably by the old-fashioned interview. What we do is to make the senior managers spell out their own selection criteria.

Market research

Another aspect of asking the customer what he or she wants comes under the heading of market research. In my experience the repertory grid has often not been used well and has thus come into some disrepute. We believe that any project stands or falls on the quality of the elicitation of constructs. Put meaningless constructs into a grid, you get gibberish out.

Philip Boxer argues strongly that it is vital to be able to link up a persons' construing of a commodity with the here and now. If you like a certain type of product packaging because it is *flamboyant*, we might ask 'when was the last occasion recently in which you remember being attracted by a *flamboyant* article?' 'What was the occasion?' The person may like flamboyant things generally, but, come the crunch, always buys things that are *bland* because that is what her husband likes. As personal construct psychologists we often talk about the importance of context but too seldom do anything about it.

Preparing the ground for retraining programmes

The majority of our research to date has taken place in the context of change. It has been concerned with providing a base-line of 'where staff are now' in their perceptions of their work environment. The creation of a retraining programme or the proposed introduction of new technology takes place against a known background. The data we provide not only yield profiles of staff and management's feelings and fears and needs, but also indicate the areas in which staff will be extremely reluctant to change. The shock-waves from retraining programmes that fail to take account of how those involved construe their work setting can reverberate throughout the whole organisation, adversely affecting staff and management alike.

Obviously, we can also study changes in people's construing over time. Perhaps to find out whether or not the retraining programme has brought about desired changes in ways of viewing work or whether there have just been some changes in behaviour. Personal construct psychologists of course will expect that, if the latter is the case, many people will revert to their previous behaviours and feelings. An example of this process was described in Joyce Watson's sections above (pp. 409–11).

Summary

Virtually all our idiographic research work is based on our skills at eliciting and laddering constructs, in combining and grouping constructs, in designing forms of repertory grid technique that can best provide the data necessary to answer specific questions, analysing these data and interpreting the results, and in ensuring that the clients are involved in the research programme in such a way that they not only can put the results into action, but feel they own them.

References

Boxer, P. (1987). Regnancy: a shadow over personal construing. In F. Fransella and L. Thomas (eds.), *Experimenting with Personal Construct Psychology*. London: Routledge & Kegan Paul.

Hinkle, D. (1965). *The Change of Personal Constructs from the Viewpoint of a Theory of Construct Implications.* Ohio State University. Unpublished PhD thesis.

Jones, H. (1985). Creativity and depression. In F. Epting and A. W. Landfield (eds.), *Anticipating Personal Construct Psychology.* Lincoln: University of Nebraska Press.

Kelly, G. A. (1955). *The Psychology of Personal Constructs.* New York: Norton.

Kelly, G. A. (1969). The strategy of psychological research. In B. Maher (ed.), *Clinical Psychology and Personality.* New York: Wiley.

Landfield, A. W. (1971). *Personal Construct Systems in Psychotherapy.* New York: Rand McNally.

Mair, J. M. M. (1977). The community of self. In D. Bannister (ed.), *New Perspectives in Personal Construct Theory.* London: Academic Press.

Tschudi, F. (1977). Loaded and honest questions. In D. Bannister (ed.), *New Perspectives in Personal Construct Theory.* London: Academic Press.

Chapter 2

Regnancy: a shadow over personal construing

Philip J. Boxer

In 1975 I decided not to take the conventional route out of business school into consultancy or high finance, and instead set up my very own research project on management decision-making. I had remained unconvinced by the solutions to business problems put forward by the business school and wanted to explore the ways in which managers themselves gave structure to what I saw as essentially unstructured problems.

I chose to use personal construct psychology as my reference discipline for this work because I was attracted by Kelly's explanations – he has such a personal way of approaching the person. Also because, looking back on it, it gave me a way of bringing forth into language my sense of *what was really going on*; and of course because, in 1975, I needed a way of holding my academic boundaries. What better than to use a relatively unknown psychology!

To cut a long story short, I now find myself a freelance consultant, helping friends in business to bring about changes in the ways in which they exercise power.

From quite early on, I took PCP seriously. Mindful of those academic boundaries, I began to write serious sounding papers in support of what I thought I was doing. The high point of this phase was a paper entitled 'Supporting Reflective Learning: Towards a Reflexive Theory of Form' – high because I now find myself unable to understand what I wrote. This was the paper which formed the roots of the chapter on the Choice Corollary which I wrote in the Mancuso and Adams-Webber book (1982) – another piece of writing I can't understand! (Incidentally, to have written a paper which it is difficult to understand is a great achievement as long as people think they *ought* to be able to understand it – it creates demand for your explanations. The trick is to get people to take you seriously: Jack Adams-Webber still doesn't understand the paper, but he is sure that there is something of value in it!) Anyway, the point I am getting to is that the suggestion that I write the chapter came out of a conversation with Jack Adams-Webber and Jim Mancuso at the Netherlands Congress in 1979; and it is the conversation which I am getting to.

At that time I was puzzling over the nature of the horizon to my conversations with managers and what the manager's relationship was to that horizon – or to put it another way, I was puzzled about what I could and could not talk about with managers. I had come up with the view that propositional constructs were the person's construction of self-as-context-to the process of construing, and had just finished giving a presentation.

In conversation after my presentation, Jack and Jim's response to my idea was to take it seriously – seriously enough to ask me to write the chapter – but also to suggest that to redefine 'propositional' was unnecessary since it was what Kelly had meant by propositional anyway. At the time, I took it from them because I felt that they were in a better position to know than I was. Looking back on it, however, it was an interesting move. Kelly's explanation remained intact in its essential coherence, and I had been persuaded to contribute to the weight of textual presence the Kellian movement had in the world.

So what?

The incident is interesting because I remember it – it is significant for me. Something of what I was meaning got lost in that move. Somehow I had struck the wrong balance between 'personal' and 'scientist'. It provides me with a way, therefore, of introducing something of the smell of this word 'regnancy' for me. Two things strike me:

1 I bought into an assumption about the coherence of the Kellian thought-form which left me fitting in rather than striking out.
2 The voice with which me-the-scientist had been speaking had not been my own.

In being a personal scientist, these are continuous struggles for me: *to construct explanation for myself*; and *to speak with true voice*.

I will come back to these struggles at the end, but to begin at the end, let me say something of where I want to end up: I am very struck by the fact that the Kellian movement is not more embedded in 'mainstream' academia. Even Bob Neimeyer in his historical analysis concludes that the intellectual and methodological concerns of the Kellian movement map more onto a 1950s social context than the Now. Yet on the surface we look like any other body, with our papers and our practices, with personal construct psychology functioning as a dependable source of academic reference. What is it then that we are doing with PCP?

I think my answer to this question is that for each of us in our different ways, the Kellian movement is a site of resistance – a source of authority for us which we invoke in subverting others' explanations of ourselves. The question that answer raises, however, is whether in invoking the Kellian movement in support of our resistance, we strike the wrong balance between 'personal' and 'scientist'.

Working in organisations

Let me talk about what happens in businesses – how the balance gets struck, and what this leads to.

I think of a business as a tangle of conversations which have formed into a knot. As a consultant, it is very difficult to get a word in edgeways, let alone be listened to, and even if you do get some proposals worked out for changing things – usually proposals which have been around for years, having been put forward by employees – someone else usually pulls at the wrong moment so that the knot re-forms, resulting in an even more tangled knot. As an employee or as a consultant, after years of trying to 'change things for the better', it is very difficult not to become very sceptical, and begin to believe that the people at the top of the management hierarchy don't want things to change, even though they continue to say things to that effect. As my friends have found, it is no surprise that most people seem to prefer to leave the knot alone and live with it in the face of all that history, income and a pension to look forward to – to remain employees.

Developing this metaphor a little further, the knot can be thought of as the particular way in which the conversations come together – they are the history which the business is to those who are in its employ. The knot in this sense is the explanation which governs who can make choices when, where and how about what kinds of things. Don't get me wrong. Such knots are very practical, for once established they coordinate the consensuality of large numbers of people. But problems can arise if they outlive their usefulness. It was in investigating this possibility that I became involved with the PCP Centre's work in British Airways.

I did some work with Fay Fransella in British Airways in 1984. We were doing research designed to give voice to British Airways staff attitudes to management. We were sampling 1,000 staff out of a population of 16,000 spread across nineteen different sub-groupings, and in addition to working directly with each of those nineteen sub-groups' management, we wrote an overarching summary. The following fragment is an extract from it:

> Staff's views of the requirements of their work 'on the ground' appear to differ therefore from those imposed on them by management. How do we account for this incongruence as a research result? We conclude that the attitudes of Staff describe a *mythology*. This mythology about the nature of their work is rooted in history and is not challenged directly by their work experience. Management therefore are experienced as interfering with this myth. (October 1984)

For those of you who are unfamiliar with British Airways, this is an organisation which flies people all over the world, and has a reputation for maintaining very high engineering standards. It is about to be privatised and has been (and still is) going through enormous changes to make it attractive to the private sector, among other things by making it more profitable.

The mythology which we were referring to was no mythology to those who held it – it was their description of what was for them dependable about British Airways, the knot as they saw it. To destroy it would be to destroy their employment. What was the mythology? It was that British Airways staff felt they had a natural and direct access to what was best for British Airways, which was rooted in years of experience of working with aeroplanes; an access which management's actions interfered with, cut across or otherwise revealed a mistrust of. The senior management, however, had different views of the way in which they wanted things to be – the kind of knot which they wanted to be formed – and our research was part of a whole series of moves which they were making to bring this reconstruction of the knot about. The interesting question, however, is whose knot is British Airways, whose knot is it to become by what means, and who cares?

The keepers of the knot are very powerful, because others treat them as *knowing*. In British Airways' case it was the engineers who were the keepers. They knew what made the business work. The engineers' explanations were regnant. Senior management were seeking to cut their regnant knot!

Power can never be taken – only conceded. We concede power to the other when we obey the other. When we obey as employees we concede power to our managers. The British Airways employees had to be persuaded to concede power to different explanations. The name senior management gave to this process was privatisation. How was this change to take place? How were the employees to be persuaded to replace one form of explanation with another? Whose interests were to be served?

And anyway, what has this got to do with us and Kelly?

Going back a bit further

Well, the answers to all these questions have to do with the nature of our dependency needs and the ways in which they are served by the Kellian movement. When we recognise truth in Kelly's explanations we concede power to Kelly. The Boss is he through whom 'what it is necessary to do' is given voice. Equally, the Scientist is he through whom Truth speaks. Let me digress again to talk about being *strategic*, in order to approach this dependency issue from another place.

I was originally drawn to personal construct psychology through an interest in the ways in which managers were decisive – particularly on issues which were seen as strategic. When I started to explore management decision-making, I developed my own use of the repertory grid technique into a reflective analysis. What I was doing was stripping away more and more of the PCP instrumentation and explanation to the point at which I and a manager could engage in no more and no less than a conversation: a conversation about some marks on a piece of paper through which he was re-presenting his experience to himself. In retrospect I was challenging more and more of a regnant PCP: PCP was dropping below the horizon of our conversation. The following comment by a manager on the experience of analysis conveys some of the flavour of what I was doing:

> to discover, by internal examination, what my real emotional response is to those activities and people, and (hardest of all) to express these responses in a way which sheds new light on the expression 'full and frank discussions'! (December 1979)

I was exploring with the managers I was working with, the nature of their dependency needs in relation to their respective knots. I was incidentally also self-employed and trying to make ends meet means: I had the means in the form of micro-NIPPER, a technique for supporting reflective analysis, and the managers had the ends. I was working in support of managers who were trying to change things. To cut a long story short, the managers who I had been conversing with had discovered in our conversations a way of explaining to their own satisfaction 'where they were coming from', or what kind of knot they were not – whatever, these managers were bringing a more personal authority to their decisiveness, being what I like to call self-employed employees. The snag was that others were not always as satisfied as they were, particularly when it came to acting out their explanation. The same manager as quoted above put it as follows:

> The main problem in describing our work is one of labels. What happened was not a 'course', nor was it psychoanalysis. I suppose, if I have to attach a label to it, it was a process of increasing awareness of the emotional culture in which I operate; that culture being one of the most important limiting factors to my performance as an individual and, more important, as a member of a number of groups of people . . . when I get the new team together in Birmingham, you can expect a call. There will be a lot to do! In the meantime, I

> believe that Basil and I can get together to work out a plan for introducing this kind of controlled culture change. . . . The first problem is a label one. If you have no label, how do the uninitiated know what you're talking about? (December 1979)

The result was a situation in which the manager felt he had to either leave, shut up or put up – find ways of taking others along too. I found myself trying to be helpful to some of those who put up; in this manager's case, he never called. The self-employed employees with whom I did work over the next few years became involved in challenging current explanations. That was how I got back into consultancy.

Make it beautiful

Strategic decisions are represented as such in retrospect because they become associated with discontinuities in the way things have been – discontinuities in the knot. When I started I was hoping that I would come up with the philosopher's stone of strategy, the ability to turn a plain and ordinary discontinuity into a strategic discontinuity. Eventually I found a simpler solution: 'strategic' is a quality of the manager's relationship to his own dependency needs. Thus for himself all discontinuities are strategic.

So where does this leave us with all those questions about how to change things? The answer of course is that you can't change things – only your relationship to things. The really difficult bit is realising that there are 'things' there in the first place. Regnancy casts a shadow in which it is difficult to see.

For me, what I take from Kelly's notion of being a *personal* scientist is the quality of *resistance*: resisting others' explanations presented as Science. This strategic relationship to Science comes alive for me when restated as a relationship to Employment: *the self-employed employee*.

Scientific explanation is explanation which holds itself forward as the essence of Truth. Business explanation is explanation which holds itself forward as the essence of Work. We are all employees. Some of us are self-employed employees. We all stand in the shadow of the regnancy of others, particularly the regnancy of employment.

Once seen, a regnant knot simply becomes someone else's explanation, and why make someone else's explanation do when you could have one of your own?! So . . . the struggle for true voice is the struggle for critical relationship. From there explanations can be constructed. All that then remains is that your constructions be beautiful.

References

Boxer, P. J. (1981). Supporting reflective learning: towards a reflexive theory of form. In Bonarius, H., Holland, R. and Rosenberg, S. (eds). *Personal Construct Psychology: Recent Advances in Theory and Practice.* New York: Macmillan.

Mancuso, J. C. and Adams-Webber, J. R. (eds). (1982). *The Construing Person.* New York: Praeger.

Chapter 3

A comparison of the personal constructs of management in new and experienced managers

Cathleen A. Brown and Charles J. Detoy

The effective performance of operating managers is a key ingredient in the success of any business firm. Organizations depend heavily on operating management for their productivity. If the operating managers are not functioning to their maximum capabilities, the chances are excellent that they do not have a clear understanding of the job required of them (Jennings, 1972; Drucker, 1980).

It is the task of the training staff to ensure that managers have a complete understanding of the job. Effective training helps trainees understand and internalize the model of management established by the corporation. If the managers' intuitive model of management is not consonant with the corporate model, effective performance is likely to be limited. If the trainees' model differs markedly from others, co-workers' or supervisors', low productivity, morale problems, and negative performance evaluations are likely to result (Tichy, 1983).

The core of the problem is that the organization and the individual may be operating on the basis of differing constructs of management. The response of the training and development staff of Coldwell Banker (a major commercial real estate brokerage in California) to this problem was to incorporate into the training process an examination of the constructs of their managers, and to utilize this information in the process of changing those constructs which were limiting effective performance.

Related research

Management training traditionally involves the development and presentation of material and the evaluation of how well the material has been learned through various methods of review. Little or no effort is made to ascertain what concepts trainees bring to the learning process. Learning is greatly facilitated if the material to be learned can be related to already existing knowledge (Bruner and Goodman, 1947).

Recently, some management educators have recognized the value of personal construct theory and the use of the Role Construct Repertory Test (Kelly, 1955) in the development of effective training programs. The suitability of personal construct theory to management education is evident if one construes the role of the trainer as that of helping the trainee to explore and reflect upon his models of the world, test them out, and change them when they prove to be inadequate (Beck, 1980).

Management trainers who incorporate PCT in their programs have the advantage of using the Role Construct Repertory Test to elicit constructs of managers and presenting these constructs to them for understanding, clarification, comparing, and change.

Having the constructs available enables both managers and trainers to compare the similarity and dissimilarity of constructs with the corporate models. Another advantage of this technique is the opportunity to examine the effects of experience on the constructs managers.

The Coldwell Banker study

When the training staff of Coldwell Banker was given the task of presenting a new model of management, the Job Competency Model, to both new and experienced managers in the commercial division, we chose to begin the process by administering the Role Construct Repertory Test to our trainees.

The new model places a primary emphasis on power, defined as the ability to get things done through other people. This new emphasis was established to give greater direction to the development of goal setting, market planning, and productivity. We were keenly aware that in past years the emphasis had been to a great extent on the social interaction within the offices, reflecting an affiliative need described by McClelland (1976). It was anticipated that the opportunity to examine and reflect on their constructs of management would create a climate of greater acceptance of the new model.

The questions which we wanted to answer were:

1 How do managers construe the function of management?
2 Do experienced managers construe management in terms of task orientation more than new managers? We hypothesized that their experience would cause them to place a greater emphasis on productivity and task completion than new managers would.
3 Do new managers construe management in terms of social relationships more than task orientation? We hypothesized that new managers would place a greater emphasis on social skills than experienced managers do.

Method

Forty-one *new* managers, assigned to their management positions within the last six months, and thirty-three *experienced* managers, in their management jobs six months or longer, were given the Role Construct Repertory Test at the beginning of a training session at corporate headquarters.

The Role Construct Repertory Test was given by a consulting psychologist who is not a regular member of the training staff.

The role titles used were:

1 The best manager you know
2 The next best manager you know
3 The worst manager you know
4 A manager you would rate as average
5 Self
6 Your father
7 Your mother
8 Your best friend
9 A favorite teacher
10 A person at work with whom you usually feel uncomfortable.

An effort was made to balance the role titles in such a way that an equal number of positive and negative constructs might be elicited.

The test was explained to the groups of managers as an exercise to explore the concepts they held of management. The test was comprised of three sheets of paper: (1) instruction sheet, (2) role-title sheet, and (3) the response sheet. These directions were given:

> *Step 1*: On the role-title sheet ten people are described. Read all the descriptions. From the people you know personally, choose a person to fit each description. On the response sheet write the name of the person who fits each description in the corresponding numbered diagonal space. *Use a person only once.* A good rule to follow is use the first person who comes to your mind. Circle an 'M' for male or an 'F' for female beside each name.
>
> *Step 2*: On the response sheet note that the squares under three names in row 1 have small boxes in them. Think about these three people. Ask yourself this question: *are two of them alike in some important way that is different from the third person?* Put an 'S' (same) in the boxes of the two who are alike. Put a 'D' (different) in the box of the one who differs. Now write a word or short phrase in column 1 that describes the more positive pole of the dimension that differentiates two of the persons from the third. In column 2 write the word that describes the more negative pole of the dimension. Not all dimensions will have a positive and negative quality.
>
> Compare the three people with the boxes in each row in this way. Write the dimensions in the appropriate columns.

The managers were asked to describe their dimensions in positive or negative terms, if these labels were applicable, so that the researchers would know whether the dimension was an admired quality (positive) or a critical one (negative). Most individuals finished the test in less than one hour.

Analysis

The constructs were categorized using Landfield's (1971) categories, with some modification in the classification system. Landfield's twenty-two categories were condensed into six groups. Several of his categories remained intact: Social Interaction, Forcefulness, Organization, Intellective, Morality.

His categories of Self-Sufficiency, Status, Egoism, Emotional

Arousal, and Humor were condensed into one group and given the label Personality Attributes. His remaining categories were not included in this study. The number of constructs fitting these categories was insignificant, and these categories were not immediately relevant to the questions under study.

The six categories used to classify the constructs are given below, along with their definitions and sample constructs which fit them.

1 Social Interaction: 'any statement in which face-to-face, ongoing, continuing interaction (or lack of) with others is clearly indicated.
Positive: friendly, outgoing, puts others at ease.
Negative: cold, isolated, makes others uncomfortable.

2 Forcefulness: any statement denoting energy, overt expressiveness, persistence, intensity or the opposite.
Positive: dynamic, gets things done, takes charge.
Negative: weak, doesn't know what's going on, lets others lead.

3 Organization: any statement denoting either the state of or process of structuring, planning, and organizing or the opposite.
Positive: sets goals, organized, methodical.
Negative: disorganized, erratic.

4 Personality Attributes
Positive: good sense of humor, confident.
Negative: lacks confidence.

5 Intellective: any statement denoting intelligence or intellectual pursuits or the opposite.
Positive: bright, knowledgeable.
Negative: not too bright, uninformed.

6 Morality: any statement denoting moral values or the lack thereof.
Positive: ethical, high standards, fair.
Negative: unethical, unfair.

Six hundred and thirty-seven constructs were sorted into six categories. The sorting was done by an outside judge, who was given the descriptions of the categories but was unaware of the hypotheses under examination.

The two categories which we anticipated would help us determine how the managers looked at social interaction and power were Social Interaction and Forcefulness.

Results

1 Twenty-four percent of the experienced managers' constructs were in the forcefulness category, while only 16 percent of new managers' constructs fit this category. Experienced managers used constructs that involved forcefulness significantly more than new managers.

The expectation that experience contributes to the content of the constructs denoting power was fulfilled.

Here are samples of the constructs of forcefulness:

Experienced managers	*New managers*
effective	authoritative
a doer	demanding
assertive	money motivated
high energy	corporate
dynamic	dominating
decisive	aggressive
motivated	
dedicated	

2 The results also show that 32 percent of the new managers' constructs fit in the Social Interaction category, while only 13 percent of the experienced managers' constructs fit this category. New managers tend to construe management in terms of social behavior to a greater extent than experienced managers do.

Experienced managers	*New managers*
friendly	tactful
patient	diplomatic
outgoing	sensitive
good listener	friendly
empathy/kind	outgoing
supportive	social
understanding	understanding
thoughtful	good with people
considerate	receptive

The percentages of constructs in each of the other four categories was very similar between the two groups.

Here is the percentage of constructs falling into each of the six categories (see p. 430).

The participants were surprised to discover that few of the constructs of both groups fit the Intellective category and that the percentage of constructs in the Morality category was small.

	Experienced managers (%)	*New managers* (%)
Social Interaction	13	32
Forcefulness	24	16
Organization	6	6
Personality Attributes	42	36
Intellective	10	2
Morality	6	8

Another category with few constructs is the Organization category. This category would appear to have less significance than one would expect.

Discussion

The use of the Role Construct Repertory Test for the analysis of constructs and their content was very effective in understanding the models of management which the managers brought to the training sessions. The managers responded with interest to the experience of gaining knowledge of their constructs. Both groups gained awareness of how experience affects their constructions, and how similar or different their models were from the corporate model.

The acceptance of the Job Competency Model was facilitated by the discussions resulting from the study and the findings. The new managers were surprised to find their emphasis on social constructs of management. They discussed the importance of balancing social attributes with the capacity to set goals and to 'get things done.'

The small number of constructs in both the Intellective and Morality categories sparked discussions of the types of individuals who are drawn to sales organizations and the implication of the effects of the sales process on morality. The insignificant role of intellectual capacities in their models provoked discussions of the attitudes toward intelligence in the organization.

Implications

A major implication of the study is that the application of personal construct theory to the training of managers can contribute significantly to the learning process. The sessions which followed were frequently oriented back to the findings by both the training staff and the managers. Collaboration between psychologists and trainers can be productive to organizations in achieving their training goals.

The opportunity for immediate feedback is one of the advantages of the RCRT. Often examination procedures contain an implicit message that the examiners have knowledge about the subjects that is unavailable to the participants. The RCRT technique, used in this way, is an open method of gathering information. The participants get the results along with the researchers. This enables the training situation to convey confidence and build trust between trainers and trainees.

The simplicity of the design of the study allows it to be used in a variety of ways. The ease and value of examining constructs is apparent by the results of this study.

This study suggested that personal construct theory and technique have practical application in other areas of management, such as performance assessment, conflict resolution, labor relations, and career counseling.

References

Beck, J. E. (1980). Changing a manager's construction of reality: the perspective of personal construct theory on the process of management education. In J. Beck and C. Cox (eds.), *Advances in Management Education*, New York: Wiley.

Blake, R. and Mouton, J. S. (1964). *The Managerial Grid.* New York: Gulf.

Bruner, J. S. and Goodman, C. C. (1947). Value and need as organizing factors in perception. *Journal of Abnormal and Social Psychology* 42, 33–44.

Drucker, P. F. (1980). *Managing in Turbulent Times.* New York: Harper – Row.

Jennings, E. (1972). *An Anatomy of Leadership.* New York: McGraw-Hill.

Kelly, G. A. (1955). *The Psychology of Personal Constructs*, Vols. I and II. New York: Norton.

Landfield, A. W. (1971). *Personal Construct Systems in Psychotherapy.* Chicago: Rand McNally.

McClelland, D. C. (1976). Power: the great motivator. *Harvard Business Review*. March–April.
McGregor, D. V. (1960) *The Human Side of Enterprise*. New York: McGraw-Hill.
Robey, D. and Taggart, W. (1981). Measuring managers' minds: the assessment of style in human information processing. *Academy of Management Review*, April.
Tichy, N. (1983). *Managing Strategic Change: Technical, Political, and Cultural Dynamics*. New York: Wiley-Interscience.

Chapter 4

Developing a learning culture in a bank

Maurice Randall and Laurie Thomas

It is sometimes argued that the language we use is a primary influence on the shaping of our perception of reality. It is thus of pressing importance that we reach out for terminological precision. Coffey (1977) has contributed significantly in this respect by offering a view of open learning as something which seeks to remove both educational and administrative constraints on the learner. This paper deals with open learning from an educational design viewpoint, namely an attempt at helping people achieve greater levels of learning competence. It sets out how a person can be helped at work to learn how to learn, and thereby attain a greater degree of self-organisation of learning. It thus deals with that most fundamental aspect of learning – empowering an individual to take charge of and direct his or her learning process.

The concept of self-organisation of learning has been formulated theoretically and experimentally at the Centre for the Study of Human Learning, London, over the last twenty years. This paper describes the pursuit of such a skill by a group of trainers over a period of about three years. This opportunity arose in the TSB when two of its Constituent Banks (now part of the Birmingham Region of TSB England and Wales) amalgamated and, in so doing, set up the education and training department to meet the needs of the newly formed organisation. Seven staff were recruited to the department from within the bank and all except one were inexperienced in training. For the department to be able to offer broad-based and sophisticated education, training and development services called for this group to learn a considerable amount, preferably quickly and without inordinate cost. As a result of the limitations of 'training' as conventionally defined (i.e. instructionally based), it seemed entirely appropriate in the circumstances to combine the learning-to-learn ideology of the Centre for the Study of Human Learning with the authors' managerial ethos in an experiment about acquiring improved learning competence of individuals whilst optimising productivity of the group. This paper describes that enterprise, namely what was being sought as a learning-to-learn outcome, how the leader of the group worked with his team to that end, and the effect of that approach as seen through the eyes of the participants.

But what is self-organised learning?

First a definition of learning itself. The Centre for the Study of Human Learning defines it as the construction, negotiation and exchange of personally relevant and viable meanings. But what is meaning? It is the personalising of knowledge of the world to particular purposes accomplished in a way that satisfies the person concerned. It is idiosyncratic understanding, a set of convictions combining values, beliefs and publicly shared knowledge and on which personal action is based.

So self-organised learning is about getting in touch with personal meaning and how it is constructed and rearranged, and with doing this in a well-directed way. If the structure of learning process is considered as that shown in Figure F4.1, then the self-organised

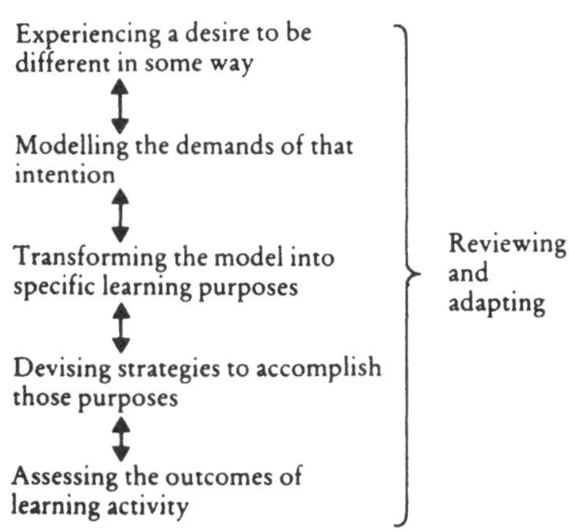

Figure F4.1 The structure of learning process

learner is able to converse with himself about that framework and the relationships and activities within it. Self-organised learning, is to do with being clear about intentions, devising and effectively operating ways of pursuing them and successfully adapting according to a review of the effectiveness of decisions and actions taken.

The need to keep things in perspective

This chapter is to do with bringing about self-organised learning. But that task was not carried out *in vacuo*. It occurred during the operation of a department. As Hayes, Fonde and Anderson (1984) have pointed out, having excellent vocational education and training does not guarantee effective, economic performance of an organisation, even though organisations cannot be successful without effective education and training. The overriding objective for the bank's Education and Training Department was to establish itself successfully. By this is meant creating capacity for dealing with management at all levels about the contribution required of the department to the business of the bank and backing that up with whatever services were called for. In short, the main concern was maximising output.

But in the end, other things being equal, output depends upon individual performances, which in turn depend upon the person's relationships with whom they work and with what they are called upon to do. Integrating productivity and learning at work for a given organisational design is therefore about providing situations from which people draw satisfying personal conclusions. These situational influences – the learning culture – derive from the enactment of a philosophy of human behaviour at work embracing the components shown in Figure F4.2.

But why term it so? Lorenz (1977) expressed the view that 'living is learning'. What he meant by that was that living fully could only arise by seeking to see the world, and hence ourselves, in a new way, regularly building new meanings by which to live, and thus regularly learning. Such living accepts no artificial, unreflected-upon limits, but attempts to define them by a redefinition of self. Such relentless exploration represents a creative urge borne of curiosity. The way of organising, leading and motivating

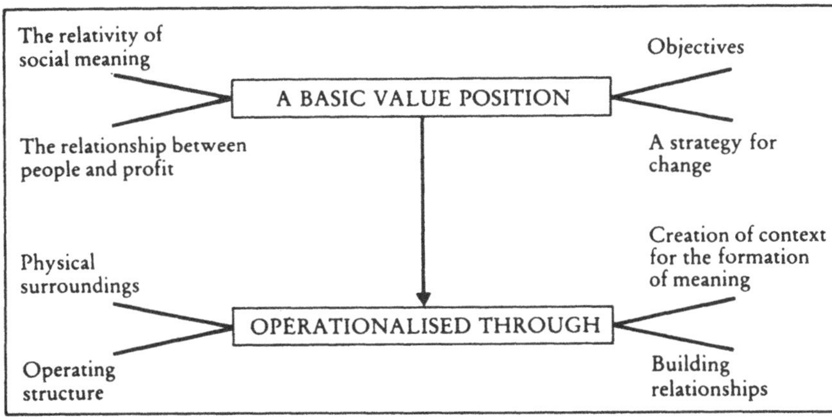

Figure F4.2 Components of learning culture

people inherent in the framework shown in Figure F4.2 is an attempt to secure a commercial parallel to 'living is learning'. It represents a way of working, so aptly described by Harvey-Jones (1985), that is satisfying to participants, that seeks the release of their full potential, energy and imagination, in harmony with the needs of productivity via the pursuit of effectiveness. Accordingly, it seemed appropriate that such a mixture of intentions and methods be termed a 'learning culture', what Ouchi (1981) has called 'theory Z culture' and Peters and Waterman (1982) the 'search for excellence'.

The effect of the approach: personal evaluations of change

From the seven staff involved, the following two examples illustrate how people felt they had changed.

K

> I am more aware of what I am doing and why. I am now much more active in my own development. Sometimes one's superior is narrow in approach and that makes development difficult, but I now believe that it can still be done despite that obstacle. I believe now that my development doesn't depend upon the

whims of a superior. I have realised since being here that I don't need to be encouraged by my superior to get on; and this is an important change for me. Before, if a manager said 'No' to me about my development, I would have delayed dealing with it. I would have taken his lead and backed down in the face of that opposition. And that is why I say that as a result of being here my positiveness has increased in relation to what I want and why I want it . . . I am more analytical about purpose and about reviewing. This is out of accepting the idea of it being possible always to seek improvements, to get things better. I have always wanted to develop on a broad basis rather than being narrow. But before coming here, I hadn't done anything about it. I didn't have a purpose then, I was more haphazard. Now I can see things more clearly and tend to think more deeply. Take studying, for example. Before here I didn't really explore purpose. I didn't think through properly why I as doing what I was doing. Also, if I failed, whilst it was disappointing, I shrugged it off, saying: 'Better luck next time'. I didn't review things properly. I didn't examine what I was doing, where I might have gone wrong. I was too accepting. Now I don't accept things quite so readily . . . I am much more likely to help myself with difficulties. Before asking other people, I will try to find out for myself. I decide now on what I need to know, I don't wait for others to tell me what my needs are. For example, in developing my skills as a supervisor, I decided on how to go about it, whether or not to use the library, or observe others, or talk with people to get feedback, or practise different ways of supervising, or to ask to go on a course, and so on. . . . I feel better as a result of the experience. I am more appreciative of the wholeness of things, that there are different aspects to be considered, that there are other people involved too, not just me. Before, I was working for me. Now I'm more appreciative of the need for working for a team.

G

An important change for me was realising that there is more to learning than I had imagined. It is very much related to emotions. I find now I am more able to overcome obstacles or setbacks or fear (of speaking out, putting ideas into practice in public), to cope with other people who can do things well, to find enjoyment and excitement in what I do, to seek out purposes and be more self-disciplined in pursuing them . . . I now place more importance on creativity and reasoning together. Before I felt that work should be measured in concrete, specific actions and knowledge, but have now realised that creativity is needed at work too. . . . I have realised that interpersonal processes are things that can be learned. Previously, I felt that it was only me who needed to learn about these. I didn't treat it as a legitimate thing for people generally to learn and considered it to be something other people either did well, or if they didn't it was right that they accepted themselves the way they were. . . . With regard to more particular aspects, I feel I now spend more time assessing the requirements of the thing to be learned, have more confidence that I can achieve what I want to achieve, am more engrossed in learning and associate it more closely with my job, am more systematic about how I learn and that I treat learning more as a task; I am more aware of a wide range of resources available to me and of using resources well, I think through purposes more clearly, and am more prepared than I was to admit that I don't know something and accept that this is legitimate to do; I reflect much more on my performance, and feel I face up squarely to my power to influence my learning effectiveness.

Using the learning culture to meet learning-to-learn needs

There are three aspects of this which can be described as: confrontation; support; and preservation of the integrity of the personal learning enterprise.

Confrontation

In seeking to help people develop their ability to learn, sight was not lost of the fact that ultimately the manager's chief concern is productivity. The group had to function effectively about what was expected of it. The appeal of a learning-culture approach to getting results is that it fully recognises that that accomplishment is more likely to come about if people are fully involved in their work, and uses that idea centrally in its methodology. But a learning-culture approach is not a soft option, rather it is a mutual-interest group which seeks to satisfy all of the parties concerned. In doing this, the first and major aspect of confrontation is a demand for effective performance in jobs, the response to which is built around (1) a detailed, personal ownership and understanding of what is required (2) criteria of effectiveness, and (3) sustained attention to seeking improvements. The keys to eliciting such a response are (1) an acted upon belief in the willingness and ability of people to do well, (2) the setting of high expectations for achievement, (3) openness and trust, (4) freedom to assume responsibility for the way in which objectives were pursued, (5) insistence upon the operationalisation of an intellectual understanding of the contribution expected of a job role, (6) challenges to personal myths about learning – personal convictions about what we are, what is possible for us and the processes and conditions underlying personal change, and (7) raising awareness of what Wilson (1967) called the 'robots within' – habitual routines non-consciously operated.

Support

It cannot be stressed too highly, regarding the nurturing of the individual, that a learning culture depends upon a respect for the uniqueness and wholeness of the individual. Whilst the environment is described necessarily by reference to its parts, it nevertheless operates organismically. Similarly, working with the individual needs to respect the integrity of the interconnectedness of the different aspect of our being in the world. This holistic theme is echoed when supporting the individual. Support is embedded in a framework of learning conversations ranging over life, tutorial and learning-to-learn goals. The involvement with the individual must be caring and genuine, a legitimate and probing concern for the other's well-being. Reassurance during the uncertainty of learning is essential. Avoidance of punishment is crucial when mistakes are made in pursuit of better ways. Relationships must be built around a willing collaboration, a conspiracy to find solutions wherever they may lay. There must be a willingness to acknowledge one's own shortcomings and to respond positively to the ideas of others. And perhaps above all is the support provided by the preparedness to listen at any time to the concerns of others.

Preserving the integrity of the personal learning enterprise

This begins with a framework of objectives for personal communications as the basis for developing performance dialogues on which learning conversations depend. These deal particularly with how personal, group and organisational objectives interrelate. Making available opportunities for learning can be an overwhelming experience for the learner. It is important that the tutorial system – in the widest sense of that expression – is subsumed within the circumstances of the individual and his/her workplace. The individual must be able to make sense of things and such conclusions hinge upon (1) being faced with and accepting a demand for learning, (2) possessing a plan of action that takes in the whole of the learning task, and (3) an ability to deal with obstacles to progress. In taking action there is a need to reconcile competing demands about how best to learn and what is most urgent as the content of learning. The role of the manager is pressingly important at this stage. As mentor and guide for the individual he must work to create context for appropriate personal meanings to be established. The varied concerns of the need for results, the insistences of the tutorial system and the needs of the individual must be integrated. In regard to specific learning opportunities, he does this by dealing with the environment that immediately surrounds the intended learning through the mechanism of performance development dialogue.

Implications for managers of the learning-culture approach

Essentially, there are three consequences of employing these ideas that a manager must face. First, the approach calls for a particular managing ethic – a set of values, a code of conduct as it were, that may appear threatening to those unsure of themselves and their ability to work with people. Second, learning-to-learn methodology, applied managerially, calls for a leadership style that emphasises personal communication, with all the demands upon the leader that that entails. Finally, there is perhaps the most difficult aspect of all. Whenever we are engaged in learning it is likely that we have been provided with models, exemplars or recommendations about what is being sought. A model of effectiveness is created, a source of inspiration for the learner. But where is the model self-organised learner to be found? The manager himself must take on this mantle, for where else is the example to be found? It is incontrovertible that the manager's behaviour is enormously influential in eliciting responses from his staff, both desired and unintended. It is an essential part of good managerial practice to match words and actions. If the manager wishes his staff to be self-organised learners, he must provide the referents against which they can gauge their purposes and performances. If he seeks productivity through people, building this on the ability of his staff to teach themselves, he must accept that his staff will look to him to demonstrate what is required. But there is a way out of the predicament. The manager can join with his staff in exploring learning process as equal partners and without relinquishing any of his managerial prerogatives. As Kelly (1955) advocated to researchers of the human experiment that they invite their subjects to join them as co-researchers, so the manager can ally himself with his staff in the pursuit of productivity through learning with and from each other. In so doing, the uniqueness of each individual can be cherished, not as a goal in itself, but as a means of enabling the group to reach for what it values, and having grasped it, to hold on to it firmly.

Note

Maurice Randall is presently Training Development Manager for TSB Group. This paper describes work undertaken by him between 1979 and 1983 when he was Head of Education and Training for the TSB Birmingham and the Midlands. The opinions expressed are a personal viewpoint and do not necessarily reflect TSB's management practice.

References

Coffey, J. (1977). Open learning opportunities for mature students. In T. C. Davies (ed.), *Open Learning Systems for Mature Students*. CET Working Paper 14.

Hayes, C. F., Fonda, N. and Anderson, A. (1984). *Competence and Competition: Training and Education in the Federal Republic of Germany, the United States and Japan.* NEDO: London.

Lorenz, K. (1977). *Behind the Mirror: A Search for a Natural History of Human Knowledge.* Methuen: London.

Harvey-Jones, J. (1985). Switching on – not off. *Management News* 17 (May), BIM.

Ouchi, W. (1981). Theory Z: *How American Business Can Meet the Japanese Challenge.* Addison-Wesley: London.

Peters, T. J. and Waterman, R. H. (1982). *In Search of Excellence: Lessons from America's Best-Run Companies.* Harper & Row: New York.

Wilson, C. (1967). Existential psychology: a novelist's approach. In J. Bugental (ed.), *Challenges of Humanistic Psychology*, McGraw-Hill: New York.

Kelly, G. A. (1955). *The Psychology of Personal Constructs.* Norton: New York.

Chapter 5
A PCP model of decision-making and planning

Annabel Jackson

The word 'planning' is given a bewildering variety of meanings. To some people, it means controlling the future. To others, it means resolving conflicts. To yet others, it means reducing uncertainty. I am going to examine a particular kind of planning: British town planning. I shall show how personal construct theory provides us with a unique insight into the complicated decision-making processes of town planning.

First, I am going to say a word or two about British town planning.[1] Then I shall describe the three basic models of decision-making which have been employed by planners: the rational comprehensive model, disjointed incrementalism and mixed scanning. Lastly, I shall suggest some characteristics of a personal construct theory model of decision-making, and compare this model to the other three.

British town planning

The town planning system of Britain is particularly sophisticated. To be lawful, development requires the permission of the local government authority. By 'development' I mean anything from erecting a house extension to building a residential estate. The local planning authorities judge each application for planning permission on its merits, within the context of broader objectives. These broader objectives include the policies recorded in their development plans. Local authorities produce two types of development plan: structure and local plans. The first sets out the general strategy for the county as a whole. It may consider housing, employment, transport, shopping, recreation and even education. Local plans are less abstract than structure plans and relate to individual areas and sites. In other countries, planning is more narrowly defined. For example, in much of North America the development plan is a zoning map, and planning permission is only necessary for development which contravenes the development plan. My point is that, relative to such systems, British planning is unusually comprehensive. Decision-making is guided by a framework of law, policy and central government advice. These indicate the factors relevant to a particular issue but rarely predetermine the decision, which means that the planner must use his personal judgment to weigh the factors and come to a conclusion.

Rational comprehensive planning

I shall now move on to discuss the three main models of decision-making which have been applied to town planning.[2] The first, and arguably the most influential, is rational comprehensive planning.[3] This is more accurately described as a set of models rather than one model. Its underlying characteristic is an admiration for the methods of natural science. As one United States senator said in 1965, 'Why cannot the engineers who can move a rocket to Mars, figure out a way to move people through our cities without the horrors of modern traffic?' (Nelson, 1965).

The rational component of the model is the act of deducing concrete decisions from abstract objectives. The comprehensive component of the model is the attempt to incorporate all values, opportunities and consequences. In its pure form the rational comprehensive model envisages five stages to decision-making:

1 Establishment of a set of general, agreed values expressed as goals and objectives.
2 Generation and examination of all alternatives open for achieving the goals.
3 Prediction of all consequences which would follow from the adoption of each alternative.

4 Comparison of the consequences in terms of the agreed set of goals and objectives.
5 Selection of that alternative whose consequences rate most highly on the agreed values.

There are many variations on this pure model. For instance, some workers have argued that decision-making can be circular rather than linear, and have subsequently added a sixth stage – feedback and monitoring. Other workers have interpreted the model as automatically excluding alternatives which are unfeasible and outcomes which are unlikely.

Even with these amendments, the rational comprehensive model is seriously flawed. It ascribes to the decision-maker faculties which he just does not have. We do not operate in a state of certainty. Our diagnosis of the present is often wrong: our prediction of the future is virtually always wrong. Then there is the matter of resources. Town planners have neither the time nor the money to explore all options. This is especially true at the moment, when central government is preoccupied with cost-effectiveness. Rationalism has also been criticised for its emphasis on mathematical measurement. The model assumes that the decision-maker can rate alternative strategies according to their contribution to the policy goal. In reality many variables cannot be quantified. Lastly, and of particular concern to personal construct theorists, is the way the model presumes that there is only one construction of reality. The model envisages one central decision-making body operating in circumstances of consensus. Debate about values precedes the rational comprehensive planning process and is, in effect, disregarded.

So there are four deficiencies in the rational comprehensive model, as regards town planning: its treatment of uncertainty, resources, utility and values. The next model which we are going to consider, disjointed incrementalism, directly addresses these problems.

Disjointed incrementalism

Disjointed incrementalism (Braybrooke and Lindblom, 1963; Lindblom, 1965) is based on a complete contradiction of the principles of rational comprehensive planning. Thus incrementalism is problem-oriented rather than goal-oriented. Goals are not specified in advance but are continually evolving in the light of experience. Analysis is not comprehensive. Incrementalism limits its attention to policy alternatives which differ but slightly from current practice. And only the most obvious outcomes of these policies are examined. Policies are not selected because they best serve particular objectives. Rather, the test of a good policy is 'typically that various analysts find themselves agreeing' on it. Decision-making is dispersed and coordination is effected through a process of 'partisan mutual adjustment'. The approach is called incrementalism because problems are not solved all at once but are attacked repeatedly. Policy is formed through a long chain of such small steps.

The incrementalists have overcome some of the problems of rational comprehensive planning. Their method is clearly less demanding. Furthermore, through emphasising the processes rather than the products of decision-making, they allow us to live with uncertainty. Yet these advances have been won at substantial cost. Disjointed incrementalism is less impractical than rational comprehensive planning but it is also less visionary. Through minimising risk, it inhibits change. Through ignoring those people who are presently outside of the decision-making process, it reinforces existing power relations. Incrementalism is inherently conservative. Furthermore, there is good reason for supposing that disjointed incrementalism would be infeasible in subject areas as complicated as town planning. It is most suited to situations where present policies are operating successfully, and there is continuity in the problems addressed.

I have now described two models of decision-making: the first, impractical but inspiring; the second, undemanding but unenlightening. The third method, mixed scanning, combines elements of rationalism and incrementalism.

Mixed scanning

Mixed scanning (Etzioni, 1968) distinguishes between two types of decision:

1 Contextual or fundamental decisions set the basic direction. All possible strategies are briefly examined and one is selected.

2 Incremental or bit decisions prepare for and revise fundamental decisions. The chosen route is analysed in detail.

As the name implies, mixed scanning involves switching between these two levels of analysis as the circumstances dictate.

The creator of mixed scanning, Amitae Etzioni, wanted to combine the advantages of rationalism and incrementalism. In reality, his approach is much closer to rationalism. Etzioni sides with the rationalists on most of the important issues. He assumes that values and goals can be defined and ranked. And he expects all relevant alternatives to be examined, albeit in varying detail. Thus mixed scanning suffers from many of the flaws of rational comprehensive planning.

So, I have now summarised the two main models of decision-making: rationalism and incrementalism. I have also shown how mixed scanning has attempted to bridge the gap between these two approaches. Can personal construct theory help us break out of this bi-polarity between rationalism and incrementalism? What can personal construct theory contribute to decision-making science? There are really two components to this question: how can personal construct theory help us to (1) understand and (2) improve present practice? These are different issues, and it is possible that we need separate models for each. Yet existing work has failed to distinguish between normative and factual statements. The authors of disjointed incrementalism are particularly lax. They seem to be saying that the model of incrementalism describes how decision-makers actually behave and therefore prescribes how they should behave. Kelly himself sometimes makes this sort of mistake, and we should be careful not to do the same.[4]

Personal construct theory

I shall separate descriptive and normative aspects of decision-making through deriving two Kellian models.[5] Table F5.1 summarises these models and compares them to rational comprehensive planning and disjointed incrementalism. The following sections expand on this table by considering the nature of values and objectives, and the examination of alternatives, analysis and the act of choice. My account will of necessity be rather generalised, since personal construct theory is formulated at a high level

Table F5.1 Four models of decision-making

	Rational comprehensive planning	Disjointed incrementalism	Personal construct theory models	
			Descriptive model	Prescriptive model
Direction	Goal-oriented	Problem-oriented	Conventional	Exploratory
Decision-making unit	Centralised unit	Fragmented units	The person	The person
Nature of values/ objectives	Universal, definable	Evolving, integral	Superordinate construction	Superordinate construction
Examination of alternatives	All-encompassing	Unadventurous	Tight construction	Loose construction
Scope of analysis	Systematic	Selective	Pre-emptive	Constellatory or propositional
Choice	Predetermined by goals	Predetermined by status quo	Predetermined by alternatives examined	Creative, adventurous
Strengths of the model	Clear, visionary	Undemanding, process oriented	Fundamental, self-conscious	Flexible, progressive
Weaknesses of the model	Unrealistic	Conservative	Anecdotal	Utopian

of abstraction. Kelly is more interested in telling us where to look in our investigations of human psychology rather than in telling us what we shall see.

Nature of values/objectives

From the Organisation Corollary we can infer that the personal construct theorist would not agree with the rationalist as regards values and goals. We would not see objectives, values and goals as separate from perception and choice. Rather we would say that all are units in the construct hierarchy. Objectives may be more superordinate than perceptions, but the two are closely interrelated. The personal construct theorist would not describe people as selecting a policy in order to further a particular objective. In personal construct theory terms, the policy symbolises the objective.

There is also a normative statement here. The personal construct theorist would say that we can better understand a person if we examine his more superordinate constructs as well as his subordinate ones. Thus my model would not overlook high-level value-judgments, as the other three decision-making models do. On the contrary, it would say that the analyst, and the planner too, should be aware of these abstract constructs.

Examination of alternatives

Kelly would not agree with the rationalist that all alternatives are considered: the planner considers only those alternatives that he can construe. 'Alternative' is defined in the planner's language. An option might have to be seen as practical and politically acceptable to qualify as 'an alternative'. And, as the Range Corollary tells us, the range of convenience of a policy might be narrowly defined. The planner might assume that he needs a 'transport' solution for the problem and would therefore disregard policies which are not within his class of 'transport' solutions. All of this means that usually few alternatives are considered.

And what does personal construct theory say about how planners should act? Well, according to constructive alternativism, planners should be adventurous and creative in their thought. They should include as possible policies, alternatives which are novel and untested. That is to say, they should loosen construction, so that the more superordinate constructions, representing goals, are not automatically linked to particular subordinate actions.

Analysis

In personal construct theory terms, analysis constitutes the process of exploring and articulating implications in the construct hierarchy. Analysis is usually pre-emptive: the planner is fairly rigid in his assumptions about the effects of the policy alternatives.

The normative model of decision-making commands more propositional or constellatory construction. Analysis should consider the range of possible outcomes: the by-products and the side-effects.

Choice

Now I have come to the final stage of my model, in which the planner selects a course of action. If, as I have suggested, few alternatives have been examined, the planner will reach this stage with little room for manoeuvre. To quote Kelly, 'We usually do things the way we have done them before or the way others appear to do them' (1970, p. 3). At this stage, personal construct theory adds little to the views of the incrementalists.

But personal construct theory has some very interesting implications for a normative theory of policy choice. A Kellian approach would see policy not as a means to an end but as a learning process. When we want to deepen our understanding of existing conditions, we should proceed via 'definition'; that is to say, we should choose policies which are little different to those currently operating. When we want to broaden our understanding, we should opt for new strategies, and our choice is described as one of 'extension'. According to this view, a good policy would be one which helps us to predict aspects of the environment.

I have now covered the four stages of my model of decision-making: goal selection, examination of alternatives, analysis and choice. It should be clear that this model differs substantially from the three described earlier. Rationalism, incrementalism and mixed scanning attempt to explain decision-making from the outside.

Personal construct theory focuses on the decision-maker's own interpretation of his actions.

This personal construct theory model of decision-making is useful in town planning for four reasons. First, the Kellian model provides a more basic picture of decision-making. Most existing approaches oversimplify decision-making because they ignore the human element. It is usual to distinguish between the systematic or factual aspect of decision-making and the random or subjective aspect. The latter is normally dismissed as too complicated for analysis. Through acknowledging this random element, the personal construct theory model takes us one stage closer to understanding and improving decision-making. It could be developed to analyse the way in which different people interact during decision-making.

The second contribution of personal construct theory follows on from the first. I have said that most models only mention those elements of decision-making which they see as constant between decision-makers. The problem with this partial view is that it creates a myth about decision-making: a myth that decision-making itself does not vary between decision-makers. This myth is clearly evident in town planning. Planners have long acknowledged that their work is political, yet, in practice, planning is preoccupied with technical processes. Personal construct theory, however, highlights the subjectivity in decision-making and therefore allows us to treat planning as a political activity.

The third contribution of personal construct theory is a practical one. It paves the way for a model of decision-making which is linked to a model of implementation. Rational comprehensive planning and disjointed incrementalism both leave us once a policy has been selected. As one critic has complained, these models treat decisions as commands. Besides, a mechanistic model like rational comprehensive planning could only describe policy execution in terms of the assembly of resources. It would have little to say about the reasons for policy outcomes. Personal construct theory acknowledges the human element and could be developed to interpret implementation processes: processes of consultation and negotiation, consensus-building and commitment-generation.

These three advantages which I have mentioned come from the descriptive model of decision-making. What does my normative model add through its emphasis on learning? The basic contribution is an appreciation of uncertainty. Decision-makers are told that uncertainty should be delineated and addressed, rather than put to one side. Planning becomes an experiment instead of a manoeuvre.

The Kellian models extend our understanding of decision-making. They do not exclude the human or political dimensions of planning. Neither do they underestimate the problem of uncertainty. The models are more complex, but are they also more difficult to use? They demand a degree of openness which could render decision-making awkward. Then there is the matter of acceptability. Many elements of the normative model would be familiar to planners, but its overall message is radical. It is not just refining our theory of decision-making; it is contradicting our present definition of town planning, a definition which underpins established mores. I wonder if there is room for alternative construction!

Notes

1 The statutory framework of town planning is fully described in planning law textbooks, notably Grant (1982), Telling (1982) and Cullingworth (1964).
2 For a more detailed critique of these models, consult Camhiz (1979), Faludi (1973) or Hogwood and Gunn (1984).
3 Rationalist ideas are advanced by Simon (1957) and Dror (1968).
4 Kelly describes the focus of convenience of his theory as the psychological reconstruction of life, which would suggest that personal construct theory is as much prescriptive as descriptive. Yet Kelly often writes as if he is discussing actual rather than ideal behaviour.
5 My models are broadly consistent with Kelly's CPC cycle: circumspection corresponds to examination of alternatives, pre-emption is one way of analysing alternatives, and control is what planners would call choice.

References

Braybrooke, D. and Lindblom, C. E. (1963). *A Strategy of Decision*. New York: Free Press.

Camhiz, M. (1979). *Planning Theory and Philosophy*. London: Tavistock.

Cullingworth, J. B. (1964). *Town and Country Planning in England and Wales*. London: Allen & Unwin.

Dror, Y. (1968). *Public Policymaking Reexamined*. Scranton, Pa: Chandler.

Etzioni, A. (1968). *The Active Society*. London: Collier-Macmillan; New York: Free Press.

Faludi, A. (1973). *A Reader in Planning Theory*. Oxford: Pergamon.

Grant, M. (1982). *Urban Planning Law*. London: Sweet & Maxwell.

Hogwood, B. W. and Gunn, L. A. (1984). *Policy Analysis for the Real World*. Oxford: Oxford University Press.

Jones, S., Eden, C. and Sims, D. (1979). Subjectivity and Organisational Politics in Policy Analysis. In *Policy and Politics* 7(2), 145–63.

Kelly, G. A. (1970). A brief introduction to personal construct theory. In D. Bannister (ed.), *Perspectives in Personal Construct Theory*. London: Academic Press.

Lindblom, C. E. (1965). *The Intelligence of Democracy*. New York: Free Press.

Lindblom, C. E. (1973). The Science of Muddling Through. In A. Faludi (ed.), *A Reader in Planning Theory*. Oxford: Pergamon.

Nelson, G. P. (1965). *US Congressional Record*, 18 October.

Simon, H. A. (1957). *Administrative Behaviour*. 2nd ed. London: Macmillan.

Telling, A. E. (1982). *Planning Law and Procedure*. 6th ed. London: Butterworths.

G

Attitudes and Beliefs

Chapter 1
Feminism and PCT

Bernadette O'Sullivan

Why ask the question?

Personal construct theory, and therapy, and women's issues have been two parallel personal interests for a number of years now. Active consideration of their interrelationship is long overdue.

These dual interests, in feminism and in an exploration of Kelly's ideas, highlighted in the past the undeniable similarity between myself and women clients. However, I also at times experienced a commonality with some of the constructs, regarding women, which were prevalent in the psychiatric service where I worked. Such commonality I frequently found to be personally unacceptable, particularly where it related to the labelling process embedded in stereotypic notions of women and psychological distress. The question, which I then believed I should address, referred to the nature of my role as therapist but especially with clients who were women. This unequivocally self-reflexive paper is a part of that continuing quest. It is an elaboration through the process of definition rather than extension.

I think it is true to say that, as I explored the adoption of a PCT orientation in therapy, I had suspended consciously attending to the implications for therapy of my personal constructions of women's issues. But more recent therapeutic transactions have provoked me into examining these again. Simultaneously, contact with a number of women family-therapists (in a support-group of therapists) drew my notice to *their* attempts to consider feminists' criticisms of family therapy – part of the question I identified as present for me. Conversations with these therapists have been very important in elucidating my ideas.

It is relevant here to mention briefly those clients who acted as catalysts, albeit unwittingly, for the ideas I discuss in this paper. More specifically, there were two clients who, whilst deliberately seeking a female therapist, indicated, at an early stage of contact, the need to be reassured that they were not going to be led towards a radical feminist resolution of their problems. I was disconcerted at the possibility that I might have presented myself in a pre-emptive rather than facilitative role. It was unclear whether either, or both, of them had subsumed me accurately or whether their apprehensions largely derived from their own concerns. However, it seemed important that I no longer suspend an elaboration of feminism and PCT therapy. Both of these clients, once reassurance was given that there could be no question of a feminist resolution being presented as the only reasonable avenue of movement, went on themselves to an understanding of, and an acting on, their problems which I believe would not dissatisfy feminists.

A construction of feminism versus sexism

For me feminism is an attempt not just to add women on to accounts of men's experiences but rather to re-embrace, to make visible, women's experiencing and creating as part of the human enterprise. It is a view on the social world today which recognises women's exclusion, on the basis of gender, from that domain where knowledge, power, and decisions about what constitutes knowledge, are defined. It is concerned in particular with the differentiation of societal roles on the basis of sex.

I will identify some of my superordinate constructs with respect to feminism and to taking a perspective on the world 'as if' I were a feminist. Whilst I think very few feminists would violently disagree with the themes that I shall delineate as important for me, treating such themes as bi-polar constructs will possibly indicate some points of contrast with other constructions of feminism.

Feminism as a construction of social reality *versus* a dogma

To say that feminism is a construction is, of course, to suggest that it is a *way of looking* at the world of social relations rather than to state that it is the *only* way of doing so. This need to spell out its status as a construction rather than as a fixed, complete theory hints at the unease which I, and indeed others too, have expressed about some recent feminist thinking. From time to time I have had a sense of feminist consciousness being portrayed as something which, as Stanley and Wise (1983) comment 'should be experienced in the same way by all women who call themselves feminists'. But not only has feminism to be recognised as different for each individual, it is changing by virtue of being engaged in.

Although feminism does not always imply a constructivist view of knowledge, it does stress the 'personal' in experiencing and knowing. The very occurrence of feminism, in this century especially, has profoundly challenged well-established ways of organising society and of thinking about human development, capacities and ventures. Feminism has, I would argue, drawn particular attention to the constructivist nature of our knowledge because of the razing of the old order and because of respected beliefs about the sexes.

Society is primarily: a patriarchy which is sexist in its construction of social relations *versus* person-oriented and not discriminative on the basis of sex, race or socio-economic status

The personal implication of such a viewpoint is that I recognise authority (i.e. legitimating power) as vested in one group of society by birthright. I would not deny that women have power too, but it is of a different kind. More importantly, perhaps, the limits of women's power is, by and large, defined for them by the dominant male group. There is thus an emphasis on the 'dominated group' learning to play a role (in a Kellian sense) with the 'dominant group'; and with members of the latter group doing things to the dominated (female) group but not necessarily playing a role with them. The result has been a commonality of construing about our world which is derived largely from one (the male) group's constructions with marginal input from the other (female) group. The effects of this have been evident in many major psychological theories, purportedly about the person but actually about the male perspective. This has been cogently argued by others (e.g. Gilligan, 1982). It is a diminution of the human experience for both men and women and reveals objectification of another rather than recognition of a like-being.

The personal is political *versus* private and public worlds are separate entities

This proposition is the one which continues to cause me most challenge. 'The personal is political' has become something of an catchphrase, if not a cliché, in feminists' discussions. It suggests that all political acts (i.e. acts of societal power and organisation) are given realisation in the personal domain. Although it is usual to regard relationships between individuals as purely personal, 'this overlooks the fact', argue two sociologists, that relationships between individuals 'are social as well, that is structured in part by factors that exist outside the immediate relationships' (Brittain and Maynard, 1984). I am forcibly reminded here of Kelly's conviction of the integrity of the universe, which he highlighted by the juxtaposing of apparently unrelated events – the motion of his fingers, the action of the typewriter-keys and the price of yak milk in Tibet (Kelly, 1955).

In conclusion, I am suggesting that there is a coherence of view between the feminists' recognition of the mutual implications of the personal and the political, and the argument which recognises an inevitable political statement in the personal stance taken in psychology, and therapy, whether such statements are made public or are just implicit.

These three themes which I have identified as central to my view of feminism (*a construction* versus *a dogma*; *society as patriarchal and sexist* versus *society as person-oriented*; and *the personal is political* versus *private and public worlds are separate*) match with my constructions, as of now, on the therapeutic venture. This will, I hope, become clearer in the following paragraphs.

Personal superordinate constructs on therapy

Adjustments *versus* reconstruction

Many feminists, conscious of the view of women traditionally portrayed within psychiatry, warn women against therapy. 'The proper aim of therapy', says Ann Oakley (1981), 'is to breed adjustment (with a leader and the led)'. Indeed, it suggests, claim two other feminist writers, 'male therapists telling women they are sick; it suggests a process aimed at adjusting women to conventional and restrictive roles; it suggests drug treatment to passify us, shock treatment to frighten and silence us' (Ernst and Goodison, 1981). The validity of such a construction may be questioned, but its occurrence indicates, at the least, a serious public-relations problem for therapists and a clear reminder of the now famous Broverman (Broverman *et al.*, 1970) findings on health professionals' stereotypic views of healthy women and men.

Kelly's vision of what therapy might be is sufficiently different, to a view of therapy as adjustment-seeking, to have special relevance here. Kelly's theory indicates that successful psychotherapy will lead to 'the movement and release of ongoing processes' (Epting, 1981). It is to assist the client in the pursuit of what possibilities may be ahead in life; an invitation to reconstrue rather than simply to cope 'more effectively with the stresses and strains of everyday life'. And Kelly (1955) is quite explicit in not confining the term 'to construe' to a solely cognitive activity, so that it means a great deal more than a mental or verbal interpretation. Thus reconstruing, as aimed for in PCT therapy, can hardly be confused with adjustment. The latter may be described as seeing things in a better light, although the situation has not varied. In contrast, constructs are acted upon and action brings its own changes.

Therapist as an agent for particular social changes or social maintenance *versus* therapist aware of an image-making role

Connected with the issue of what therapy sets out to do is the problem of whether one is, as a therapist, an agent for social change, and if so, what sort of social change?

Here difficulties await. There is surely a difference between (a) assuming that one's own constructions of Utopia, and therefore of the *best* direction for social change, should be proposed as a blueprint for others and more particularly for one's clients; and (b) believing that all people generate their *own* questions and actions. If one is persuaded by the latter view, as I am, then a more appropriate role for the therapist must be that of facilitating a client to engage in life for *their* ends or ventures, and not for those prescribed by the therapist, according to the latter's lights. This is not to deny that as a therapist (a) one is transmitting a view of the person with inevitable political implications and that (b) one can have *a* role of arguing for particular social changes – but not, I am suggesting, through therapy unless it is also sought, reached out for, by the client(s).

Choices available to a therapist with a feminist perspective

The most obvious alternatives for a therapist who espouses a personal feminist perspective is that between non-sexist and feminist therapy. In the final analysis, neither choice necessarily involves a *particular* therapeutic orientation, technique or 'school of therapy'.

Non-sexist therapy

Non-sexist therapy is described as such when there is an explicit decision to actively avoid working with men and women differently on the basis of their sex. The aim of such an approach can be seen as an endorsement of a move towards androgyny with maybe even egalitarianism as a characteristic of the therapeutic relationship, but on humanist rather than political grounds. Professional associations in a number of countries have formally adopted the principles of non-sexist therapy. I believe it is, however, unrealistic not to admit the political import of non-sexist therapy. Such therapy, rather than colluding with the social norms of a patriarchal society, can be described as actually promoting a change in the status quo and is thus political in consequence if not in intent.

Feminist therapy

Feminist therapy, of which there are many varieties, is more explicit about its political role, that is about its aim to change the patriarchal and sexist nature of the power-structures in our society. Such an aim is justified by feminist therapists since much of the psychological distress described by women, in therapy, is seen as related to the position of women in society. Because the personal is political, an awareness and active consideration of the social system is viewed as central to effective therapy for women by such therapists. They adopt the notion 'that no model of healthy womanhood exists and that it is incumbent upon the therapist to facilitate the development of such a model in individual change' (Forisha, 1981). There is, indeed, the aim of an eventual 'establishment of a social structure consistent with the feminist ideology of egalitarianism' (Gilbert, 1980). Thus the common themes within feminist therapies are the changing of the experience of power and dependence for women; the sharing of uniquely female experiences with other women; and the changing of the political and social environment (Rohrburgh, 1980).

A choice taken

Choosing to take either of the stances described above poses problems, I believe, for the therapist. However, viewing feminism as a construction rather than a dogma, as well as recognising the capacity of each person to make their own choices and their own form of exploration, rules out a prescriptive approach in therapy whether it be non-sexist or feminist in form. The perspective to be taken in therapy becomes an outcome of negotiation with the client. Within this framework, PCT continues to present itself as an appropriate standpoint from which to engage in therapy with women as a therapist with a personal feminist persepctive. I hope to demonstrate the validity of this conclusion below.

PCT therapy as an alternative for feminists

There are some aspects to PCT which might make it seem a potentially uneasy bedfellow with feminism. I shall touch on these aspects below.

1 PCT, and the structuralising approach to therapy construed within it, is content-free and therefore neither presumptive nor prescriptive interpretations are made about the person. Nevertheless, it is *redolent of the socio-historical period* within which it was written. It is not difficult to find, in Kelly's writings, example after example of an apparent acceptance of the status quo by a man who, in many other instances, can be seen as being deeply humane and forever alert to the nuances of another's experiences. Inevitably, linguistic exemplifications of such acceptance of the relationship between the sexes (e.g. 'man the scientist', 'man's personal quest', etc.) can be argued as simply an adoption of the literary conventions of his time. However, there is sometimes a portrayal of women in Kelly's writings which is less than sympathetic. I consider a noteworthy example to be an extract, quoted in the next paragraph, from the otherwise stimulating article entitled 'Sin and Psychotherapy' (in Maher, 1969).

> A woman screams at her husband from 10'clock to midnight, and raises goose pimples on her neighbour's necks; that is sinful; apply the crime model and punish her. But if she has read anything at all in the women's magazines about psychiatry lately, she will realise that midnight is no time to stop. She should keep it up until 6.00 a.m., if the lungs will hold out. No one will punish her for that. They will take her to a place where there is a bed with crisp linen sheets, the same neighbours will send flowers, and the nicest man will come and talk to her! And the really ecstatic thing about it is that her husband – *her husband*, mind you – will have to pay that man fifty dollars an hour! All this, and heaven too!

I hesitate to be critical. The written word is always in danger of being reified and treated as a final statement when, as surely any construct theorist will claim, one's comments are propositional, being tested out and open to change since one is a process, a *being*, rather than a finite, completed figure. Thus written material should only be used as evidence with care, and perhaps more particularly, with regard to the context. I choose to believe that Kelly might have had some things to say about the changing view of the social world that feminists' perspectives have provoked and that such things would not have been dissonant with a feminist standpoint. Kelly did say, 'a client who is genuinely understood should never be confined to the stereotype of the culture' (1955).

Nevertheless, the view of women which one might derive from George Kelly's writings does raise the question of what else might be at odds, within PCT, with a feminist perspective. Indeed, to what extent can a person rise above their biography? I think that Kelly has himself demonstrated (as in the excerpt quoted above) how very difficult it is in practice to do so, despite his proposition that 'No one needs to paint himself into a corner; no one needs to be completely hemmed in by circumstances; no one need be a victim of his biography' (1955).

2 The idea that '*no one need be a victim of their biography*' rings of a denial of the impact of social circumstances as well as the degree to which one may be constrained in one's actions, if not also in one's vision, by the socio-economic and psychological events of one's time and place. It could even be interpreted by feminists as implying that women, and other equally oppressed groups in our society, need not have been as hemmed in by circumstances as they have been, and continue to be. However, I understand Kelly to be drawing our attention to the possibility of alternatives, the possibility of reconstruction rather than of adjustment. This is something which feminists have embodied through their very actions. One can say that they have lived the philosophy of constructive alternativism. Women have challenged constructions of the feminine role and of women as subordinate helpmates or as weaker shadows of men. In posing alternative constructions, feminists have demonstrated implicitly the constructivist nature of our engagements with, and understanding of, reality. Thus, if one may draw from Kelly the notion that there are always alternative perspectives-cum-actions, and that this only means such alternatives are *possible* with no statement of *probability*, then the optimistic nature of such a construction cannot be open to the charge of being a naïve denial of the 'real' world. Furthermore, Kelly did stress that there are, in his opinion, limitations on change and movement when he proposed the Choice and Modulation corollaries. Such limitations might not

make it impossible, for example, to transcend our circumstances but certainly could mean that it would be less likely to be always effected.

3 The seeming *emphasis on the individual* might equally be identified in Kelly's writings as indicative of the unsuitability of his theory for the understanding of women, whose primary experiences are those of connectedness and interdependence rather than separateness and independence. However, Kelly suggests in his discussion of people cooperating in constructive enterprises, that we need not 'so much construe things as the other person does' but we 'must effectively construe the other person's outlook' (i.e. subsume another) in order to engage in constructive enterprises.

This hardly seems like the philosophy of an individualist with elitist tendencies but rather that of somebody keenly aware of the transactional and constructivist nature possible in our participation in the social world. Kelly is thus also giving stress to the egalitarian nature of construing, which is not an argument that one construction is as good as another but that the perspective of one is as right for that person as another's is for them. Echoes of the feminists' emphasis on the validity of each particular woman's experience must be clear, I think, as well as the coherence with the push towards the empowering of the individual, the rightful agency of each person. It is to stress subjectivity rather than objectivity or objectification without an evaluation on a better sort of, a more informed sort of, agency which some people have and others have not yet achieved.

4 The scientist model of the person, proposed by Kelly, implies a *concentration on the rational* and the cognitive, and indeed it is in this light that PCT has been viewed by many commentators. But Kelly counters this idea by discussing in some detail both the pre-verbal and non-verbal nature of construing and, as relevantly, by suggesting that construing must not be treated as solely a cognitive or behavioural or emotional activity. Feminists have given much time to redressing the balance that they have identified as necessary in our world. This relates to the untoward and even unreal emphasis traditionally given to the verbally communicable and the rational. Such an emphasis is seen as unreal because, by objectification, it denies the validity of the subjective and claims a value-free characteristic about one's actions, and thought, which feminists as well as others propose to be not possible. It would seem a pity, therefore, if PCT was disregarded by feminists

because of its unfortunate appearance of high rationality and linear thinking when Kelly was clearly appreciative of the many modes of knowing and experiencing, and of their centrality to the human enterprise.

Are PCT therapy and feminism compatible?

Given the above discussion it is not difficult to see that I do not find PCT therapy and feminism incompatible even if there are some notes of discord.

Whether a feminist construction of social reality leads to non-sexist or to feminist therapy will not, I suggest, matter in the doing of therapy, since both approaches have political implications. I am arguing that a value-free state, a neutrality, is impossible rather than impractical. It is not important from a PCT perspective that a client and therapist hold the same views. But, while the clinician need not adopt the client's view of psychotherapy, 'it does mean that he', and I presume *she* equally, 'must be able to utilize' the client's view (1955). Thus the decision to adopt a non-sexist or a feminist approach in therapy will rest with the client, which does not preclude the proferring of a feminist analysis if that is considered appropriate. The decision to use it or explore it belongs to the client.

In my opinion there are some particular features to PCT and PCT therapy which have especial relevance for female therapists and clients regardless of the extent of their conscious identification with feminism. I will detail some of these below.

1 *Constructive alternativism*, pinpointing the importance and validity of *personal* constructions, can be seen as very meaningful to women recognising their own power and encouraging other women to do likewise.

2 *Credulous listening* to the other is fundamental to PCT therapy. There is recognition of the need for negotiation and transaction rather than defeat by a better, more correct, perspective. The approach resonates with the notion of the importance of the subjective and contributes to the co-experimenter roles, of the supervisor and research student, more characteristic of PCT therapy than of most other therapies (Bannister, 1983). Egalitarian roles in therapy are a central facet to the demands made by feminists about therapy with women.

3 *Anticipation* is a theme running through PCT. This reminds me of Oakley's comment (1981) that it is more important for women 'to know where we're going to than how we got there'. PCT suggests that we are in the business of seeking what we may become rather than what we now are. One could say that that is what the women's movement is about for men as well as for women. To quote Kelly again, 'It is the future which tantalizes man, not the past' (1955).
4 Kelly specifies the *many levels of awareness* within which we construe our experiencing. This connects with the feminist argument stressing the need to recognise as valid intuitive knowing as well as rational knowing. They are both aspects, necessary and integral, of the human experience and need to be reclaimed as such.
5 PCT therapy is in the business of *reconstruction and recreation* rather than adjustment to the status quo. It is this that feminists have sought in their analyses of therapies.

Conclusion

Finally, to say that PCT therapy may be all of those things referred to above is no guarantee, in my experience, that it will be. But that is the *invitation*, the possibility if not the probability, of any venture conceptualised within PCT. The outcome can be severely limited by us the invitees. As I have suggested above, particularly with that excerpt from 'Sin and Psychotherapy', Kelly too found it difficult to rise above his biography. Personally, I find that failure enheartening!

References

Bannister, D. (1983). Internal politics of psychotherapy. In D. Pilgrim (ed.), *Psychology and Psychotherapy*. London: Routledge & Kegan Paul.
Brittain, A. and Maynard, M. (1984). *Sexism, Racism and Oppression*. Oxford: Blackwell.
Broverman, I. K. *et al.* (1970). Sex-role stereotypes and clinical judgements. *Journal of Consulting and Clinical Psychology* 34, 1–70.

Epting, F. (1981). Personal construct psychotherapy. In R. J. Corsini (ed.), *Handbook of Innovative Psychotherapies.* New York: Wiley.

Ernst, S. and Goodison, L. (1981). *In Our Own Hands.* London: Women's Press.

Forisha, B. (1981). Feminist therapy II. In R. J. Corsini (ed.), *Handbook of Innovative Psychotherapies.* New York: Wiley.

Gilbert, L. A. (1980). Feminist therapy. In A. M. Brodsky and R. T. Hare-Mustin (eds.), *Women and Psychotherapy.* New York: Guildford Press.

Gilligan, C. (1982). *In a Different Voice.* Cambridge, Mass.: Harvard University Press.

Kelly, G. A. (1955). *The Psychology of Personal Constructs*, Vols. I and II. New York: Norton.

Kelly, G. A. (1969). Sin and psychotherapy. In B. Maher (ed.), *Clinical Psychology and Personality.* New York: Wiley.

Oakley, A. (1981). *Subject Women.* Oxford: Martin Robertson.

Rohrburgh, J. B. (1980). *Women: Psychology's Puzzle.* Brighton: Harvester Press.

Stanley, L. and Wise, S. (1983). *Breaking Out.* London: Routledge & Kegan Paul.

Chapter 2

What might psychologists tell politicians about intergroup conflict?

Peter du Preez

From time to time it is suggested that there is some single strategy which is better than any other for solving intergroup conflicts. The proposed strategy might be GRIT (graduated reciprocation in tension reduction), pacifism, hawkishness, first strike, unilateral disarmament, conciliation, strong deterrence, immediate retribution, a search for common goals, or some modified version of these. The contention of this paper is that these are all good strategies at the right time but that, just as there is no single good therapeutic strategy for all clients so there is no single conflict-resolving strategy for all occasions. The psychologist should, if this is correct, become skilled at diagnosing conflicts and at suggesting strategies for alleviating them. What might we contribute?

First, we might contribute a therapeutic attitude, which implies that we search for resolutions which are less costly than those presently achieved. It seems to me that we have a good technique for demystifying dishonest and loaded questions, in Tschudi's (1977) ABC method.

Second, PCP makes available a range of diagnostic techniques for probing the ways in which participants to a conflict construe it. Is it total conflict? Does it threaten core or peripheral constructs? Why is so much importance attached in some cases to apparently minor concessions? When we study the implications (a minor concession here may mean that one is perceived as weak, for example), we often know what is at stake, and we can focus on these, rather than continuing to hammer away at the concession itself.

Third, PCP psychologists have devised some techniques, such as fixed-role therapy, reflect (Boxer, 1978) and interactive elicitation programmes (Thomas and Harri-Augstein, 1985) for investigating and changing strategies. However, our range of strategies is not as great as it might be, and should be extended to deal with intergroup conflicts (Deutsch, 1973; Fogg, 1985).

Fourth, PCP psychologists might extend their analysis of social and political traps, drawing on the work of Kaplowitz (1984) and Platt (1973).

Now that I have listed some of the contributions of psychologists – especially PCP psychologists – to conflict resolution, it is worth listing some of our failings. There is, first, our tendency to become too attached to a limited range of strategies. Second, we tend to be rather poor at conceptualising groups and intergroup conflict, as opposed to intrapersonal conflict. Third, we usually fail to grasp the significance of historical processes in shaping intergroup relations, and intergroup relations in shaping historical processes. We must avoid attempts to understand intergroup conflicts as though they have no history. A thin time-slice of a construct system will usually be grossly misleading unless there has been a total break leading to repudiation of the past. And even then, history is significant because the new paths of movement are usually reversals of the repudiated past rather than reconstructions (Kelly, 1962). The point is that historically enduring groups have many ways of perpetuating particular constructions of events and hence we find that many images, myths and characteristic responses survive even major catastrophes.

Let us now try to imagine what sort of advice the psychologist might give if consulted.

Diagnostic procedure

When we attempt to diagnose opponents or potential opponents, what should we attend to? We should

1 take what decision-makers say literally, as a first hypothesis
2 confirm this hypothesis (or reject it) on the basis of what decision-makers do
3 look for historical continuities

4 look at the context in which things are said and done to evaluate their 'rationality' or 'normality'
5 attempt to detect images of the self, core constructs or primal myths.

Before we examine these in greater detail, here are some of the things we should avoid when we are attempting to understand others. We should avoid

1 believing that they understand our benevolent intentions
2 believing that they are mirror images of ourselves
3 understanding others in terms of our own primal myths or self-images
4 listening only to those we like and resemble
5 listening only to those who confirm our hypotheses
6 taking too much advice from either Hawks or Doves.

Turning to the first point of what we *should* do – listening to what leaders say and taking it literally – we should get to know what decision-makers have written and what they have said, in major speeches and at the dinner table, if possible. We should look for symbolic inflation such as military rallies, parades, decorations, bombast, grandiose speeches which create a flow towards war. We should look particularly for conspiracy theories, such as those characterising fascists (Billig, 1978) and doctrinaire Marxists (Cohn, 1985; Leites, 1953). Of course, there *are* conspiracies, but the full-blown conspiracy theorist will see the hidden hand of the enemy in every ill, and will use language to describe the conspirators which leads to their natural liquidation.

Actions confirm or weaken our diagnosis; they must be interpreted in context. When an insult seems gratuitous, or interference is in an area which is thought to be outside the domain of interest of the actor, we are likely to diagnose it as particularly serious, calling for a deep construal of its significance. As an example, we may cite the Kruger Telegram, sent by Kaiser Willhelm to President Kruger in 1896, in which he congratulated him on his successful action against the Jameson Raid. Since South Africa was regarded as a peculiarly British zone of influence at the time, the gesture was regarded as signifying distinctly hawkish intentions. The Kaiser's grandmother, Queen Victoria, sent him a letter of reprimand and received his abject apologies, as well as the explanation that he had been 'totally misunderstood by the British press' (Geen, 1946, p. 131).

We should look for historical continuity, unless we have good reason to suppose that there is a break with the past. Thus Kennan analysed Russian responses in 1944: 'Behind Russia's stubborn expansion lies only the age-old insecurity of a sedentary people reared on an exposed plain in the neighbourhood of fierce nomadic peoples.' And when we attempt to anticipate South African responses to pressure we might bear in mind that Afrikaners have usually preferred war to loss of independence, even against hopeless odds. In 1880 they fought and won against Great Britain; in 1902 they were defeated; in 1910 the Union of South Africa was formed, and in 1960 they regained their republic.

We should look at the primal myths of those we are confronting. Primal myths are images of historic conflicts with others, images which may be activated in subsequent relations. The Holocaust, the Siege of Leningrad in the Great Patriotic War, Soweto 1976 and other images may be revived in present relations. We should study the use which is made of these primal myths in different contexts, collecting series of them to discover trends.

A careful analysis of cognitive style (Kelman, 1983) and of imagery in speeches will also tell us a great deal about the core constructs and myths which decision-makers are likely to bring to bear in negotiations. Particularly important are those referring to body: virulent anti-semitism and anti-black imagery take a physical form. Physical imagery is particularly potent in sweeping up emotions. This sort of analysis was applied to Smuts' speeches. Thus, in his 1917 speech at a Savoy Hotel dinner given in his honour, he advanced the axiom, 'No intermixture of blood between the two colours.'

> It is probably true that earlier civilisations have largely failed because that principle was never recognised, civilising races being rapidly submerged in the quicksands of African blood. (Smuts, 1940, p. 16)

This image of the consequences of intermixture of blood was probably widely accepted at the time (du Preez, 1984).

What the psychologist should do is to study the significance and vitality of a particular myth in a current conflict. Surveys will show how widespread and important particular primal myths are, as well as the extent to which followers are likely to respond to decision-makers' use of a particular myth. We may conjecture that if a myth is widely shared and if decision-makers can plug into its implications, they can gain widespread support for appropriate activities. Studies of primal myths in a population should thus go beyond the checking of frequency and rated importance, to studies of networks of meaning.

Now we turn to the mistakes we commonly make in assessing our opponents, actual or potential. I exclude, for the purposes of this paper, estimates of their military strength. The first major mistake is to assume that others understand our benevolent intentions. John Foster Dulles said, 'Kruschev does not need to be convinced of our good intentions. He knows we are not aggressors' (cited in Jervis, 1976, p. 76).

The point is that we see our own preparations and manoeuvres as defensive, whereas the measures which other people take strengthen them for attack. There is asymmetry of understanding which leads to arms races.

A second danger is that we tend to think that others are like us, in spite of good evidence that they construe matters rather differently. When Nazi Germany began to rearm in the 1930s, many people interpreted it as a reasonable response to the humiliation of Versailles and continued to see it as such till late in the day, making concessions to what they believed were reasonable claims (Taylor, 1961). This means we are not prepared when demands exceed what we think is reasonable.

When we enter into intense relations of hate and fear with others (or with powerfully evoked media images of them) we respond in terms of our own primal myths and may fail to see that theirs are different. Racists may interpret class struggle in racial terms. United States decision-makers tend to respond to South Africa in terms of the civil war between the American North and South and their own civil rights campaign of the 1960s. European powers responded to South Africa in terms of the myth of colonial conquest (and the white man's burden) in the early part of this century – which is why the South Africa Act was approved – and then later in terms of the myths of equality and decolonisation. Our own history myths must affect our reading of other situations, but every therapist knows how misleading this can be and how it can get in the way of understanding a real situation.

A common danger is that we listen to those we like and understand rather than to those who will make the decisions. The corollary is that often we listen to those who confirm our hypotheses and enable us to achieve cognitive closure. Signals may be present and yet ignored. Often there are good reasons to avoid keeping an open mind – decisions have to be made – but there are occasions when we can afford to delay in the interests of making a better decision. Was the British Parliament of 1909 right to ignore the appeals of the 'Coloured and Native' delegation protesting colour restricted franchise in the draft South Africa Act – and clause 35, which would permit subsequent disenfranchisement of black voters? It had the power of refusal, but progressive myths prevailed and were read into the South African situation, without appreciating that real social relations in that country were utterly different from those in Great Britain. It was assumed that things would improve as the twentieth century advanced. The result was the passing of the South Africa Act without amendment – and without division in the House of Commons. Mr Asquith, Liberal prime minister at the time, expressed regret at racial restrictions in the Act, but hoped that the South African Parliament would modify these provisions. Most speakers were against the colour bar but did not wish to endanger union or to interfere in such a way as to retard the spread of liberal opinion in South Africa (Odendaal, 1984). In this, they ignored both the repeatedly expressed racist views of delegates to the National Convention in South Africa, where the bill was drafted, and the social structure of the country. They listened too easily to those delegates who sounded like themselves while in London.

British leaders wished to be liberal, to promote independence, to be rid of colonies, especially white colonies which could be rebellious, and to see themselves as doing a good thing. They were not prepared to listen to troublesome objections, especially when these went against barely concealed theories. The Archbishop of Canterbury declared in the House of Lords that, since the overwhelming majority of blacks would for generations not be fit to share equal citizenship with whites, it was reasonable to impose limitations and restrictions on them of the sort which we impose on our children (Odendaal, 1984, p. 221). Archbishops have said other fashionable things since then. Like most of us, they are often merely captives of their time and place.

Strategy

We now turn to the role of psychologists in reducing conflict, bearing in mind that all interventions should be related to a careful diagnosis of the core constructs of those in conflict, as well as to an analysis of the situation in which they find themselves.

Since most social problems are 'wicked problems' (Rittel and Webber, 1973), in which every solution is costly, the best we can hope to do is to reduce the cost of current solutions (see also Tschudi, 1977). In particular, we aim at converting conflict into competition. This defines our overall socio-therapeutic aim.

Whereas conflict is modelled on war, in which parties may attempt to inflict the costliest defeat on each other by whatever means available, competition is modelled on games, at the heart of which is a cooperative enterprise in which 'each player cooperates in bringing out the skills of the other' (Minogue, 1984, p. 32), thus enjoying the activity of the game as well as the prospect of winning. The important thing here is that one cherishes and nurtures good opponents even when competing to win. Relations between friendly states and between rivals within the well-regulated state take this form, and such relations are characterised by many conventions and institutions for changing these conventions. Two tactics follow from the strategic construct defined by the contrast between conflict and competition. The first is to institutionalise change wherever possible, and the second is to promote conventions wherever possible. Even in war there are many conventions, such as the 1925 Geneva Protocol on the use of gas and bacteriological weapons and the 1972 convention on biological warfare. What is urgently needed is a convention on the use of atomic weapons, making their manufacture and use criminal actions.

We should make it clear that the institutionalisation of change is not just 'one reform among others, it is a profound change in political climate, which would make subsequent reforms unperilous, but which itself is very perilous indeed' (Gellner, 1979, p. 331). All social arrangements are provisional and must be revised either by conflict or institutionalised competition. The institutionalisation of competition is, therefore, the principal strategic aim of the psychologist applying therapeutic skills to conflict.

Given that competition has so many advantages over conflict, why do we often enter into the traps of escalating violence and the futile cycles of violence and repression which characterise political stalemates? A stalemate is a situation in which the status quo is a scandal and yet change is impossible; and we find stalemates on every hand. One of the most striking is the stalemate of nuclear deterrence; but there are also many examples of states characterised by 'structural violence', which means that they survive by inflicting harm and misery on many and yet are too powerful to be overthrown.

In general, we find ourselves in social traps because

1 the rewards of one group are obtained by exploiting others
2 social structures change and make old institutions inappropriate
3 we chase rapidly diminishing returns
4 the alternatives to current solutions seem inconceivably costly to those in power
5 we cannot go beyond the horizons of the immediate future
6 we provoke hostility to which we respond with hostility
7 one or other party believes in ultimate victory
8 we believe that any concession will lead to escalating demands.

As a result of a received history and an interested misrepresentation of alternatives, people often ask their questions in a loaded and dishonest way (Tschudi, 1977), suggesting that the struggle is really a matter of maintaining free enterprise, civilisation or liberty, rather than of retaining privilege. This impedes resolution of the problem. Psychologists can, by facilitating group discussions, clear up dishonest questions.

There are many possible strategies for intervening, each depending upon available resources and on an accurate diagnosis of the situation. We might introduce peacekeeping forces, if the situation is right (Nelson, 1984/5), or use threats and rewards, or attempt to construe the situation in a new way. Conflicts do not disappear unless the causes of conflict are dealt with, and it is here that we return to our overarching strategy. Our goal must be to create the instruments for competitively institutionalised change, using the term 'competition' in the sense in which it has been defined above.

Finally, disintegration of an association of parties and the growth of conflict is usually marked by the absence of a positive ideal, an ideal which is realistic in its recognition of interests, agencies and constellations of power, and active in its transformation of these into a national purpose. When our ideas are shabby and second rate, they are not worth defending and few can be recruited to defend them.

Conclusion

Just as there is no recipe for therapy, so there is no recipe for resolving intergroup conflict, though valuable summaries of possible techniques exist (Fogg, 1985; Hare and Blumberg, 1968). To develop tactical skills, we should study historical cases, sharpen our diagnosis of situations and the personal constructs of leaders and their followers, and relate tactics to diagnosis.

It is suggested that we be guided by the overall aim of converting conflict into competition. This requires us to explore the poles of this superordinate construct and elaborate on its implications, continually clearing up the confusions and deceptions associated with the choices we make between them.

If this appears to be a modest goal, then we should remind ourselves that modesty becomes our ignorance.

References

Billig, M. (1978). *Fascists: A social Psychological View of the National Front.* London: Academic Press.

Boxer, P. (1978). Supporting a reflexive theory of form. *Human Relations* 33, 1–22.

Cohn, W. (1985). 'A clear provocation': esoteric elements in communist language. *Encounter* 64, 75–8.

Davenport, R. H. T. (1978). *South Africa: A Modern History.* Braamfontein: Macmillan.

Deutsch, M. (1973). *The Resolution of Conflict.* New Haven: Yale University Press.

du Preez, P. (1984). Myths and social individuals. Paper presented at the International Conference on Self and Identity, Cardiff.

Fogg, R. W. (1985). Dealing with conflict; a repertoire of creative, peaceful approaches. *Journal of Conflict Resolution* 29, 830–58.

Geen, M. S. (1946). *The Making of the Union of South Africa.* London: Longmans.

Gellner, E. (1979). *Spectacles and Predicaments.* Cambridge: Cambridge University Press.
Hare, A. P. and Blumberg, H. H. (1968). *Non-violent Direct Action.* Washington: Corpus Books.
Jervis, R. (1976). *Perception and Misperception in International Politics.* Princeton: Princeton University Press.
Kaplowitz, N. (1984). Psychopolitical dimensions of international relations: the reciprocal effects of conflict strategies. *International Studies Quarterly* 28, 373–406.
Kelman, H. C. (1983). Conversations with Arafat. *American Psychologist* 38, 203–16.
Kelly, G. A. (1962). Europe's matrix of decision. In M. R. Jones (ed.), *Nebraska Symposium on Motivation.* Lincoln: University of Nebraska Press.
Kelman, H. C. (1983). Conversations with Arafat. *American Psychologist* 38, 203–15.
Leites, N. (1953). *A Study of Bolshevism.* Glencoe, Ill.: Free Press.
Maynard Smith J. (1974). Game theory and the evolution of behaviour. *Proceedings of the Royal Society of London* B205, 475–88.
Minogue, R. (1984). How critical is the 'crisis' of liberalism? *Encounter* 63, 30–5.
Nelson, R. W. (1984/5). Multinational peacekeeping in the Middle East and the United Nations model. *International Affairs* 61, 67–90.
Odendaal, A. (1984). *Vukani Bantu!* Braamfontein: Ravan Press.
Osgood, C. E. (1962). *An Alternative to War or Surrender.* Urbana: University of Illinois Press.
Platt, J. (1973). Social traps. *American Psychologist* 28, 641–51.
Rittell, H. W. J. and Webber, M. M. (1973). Dilemmas in a general theory of planning. *Policy Sciences* 4, 328–36.
Smuts, J. C. (1940). Greater South Africa: plans for a better world. *The Speeches of General the Rt. Honourable J. C. Smuts.* Johannesburg: The Truth Legion.
Taylor, A. J. P. (1961). *The Origins of the Second World War.* London: Hamish Hamilton.
Thomas, L. F. and Harri-Augstein, E. S. (1985). *Self-organised Learning: Foundations of a Conversational Science for Psychology.* London: Routledge & Kegan Paul.

Thompson, L. M. (1985). *The Political Mythology of Apartheid.* New Haven: Yale University Press.
Tschudi, F. (1977). Loaded and honest questions. In D. Bannister (ed.), *New Perspectives in Personal Construct Theory.* London: Academic Press.
Wason, P. C. and Johnson-Laird, P. N. (1972). *Psychology of Reasoning: Structure and Content.* London: Batsford.

Chapter 3
Religious belief and PCT

Norman Todd

Most people are familiar with the process of secularization, the loss by the religious establishment of more and more parts of life – law, education, health – until the state, in one form or another, is quite separate from the religious establishment of which it was originally an indistinguishable part. In terms of the sociology of knowledge (Berger and Luckmann, 1966) it is described as the breakdown of the plausibility structure. The official, traditional religious structures of thought and behaviour are no longer strong enough to contain the living experience of individuals and groups. People say, 'That I can no longer believe'. The official custodians of the plausibility structure are rejected and there is, at least for a time, a privatization of these structures of understanding and belief.

Within the history of religions there is always a rhythm of prophecy and reform, usually in the form of a recall to fundamentals, to the true spirit and away from the all too human accretions which are felt to have gathered round it. It is felt from the inside that traditional ways are being abandoned (the Christians were accused of atheism by the Roman state religion), but we seem to be in a new situation today. Berger (1980) believes that other world religions are bound to enter the same situation as we are experiencing in the West. Religious belief is confronted by three possibilities: an extreme fundamentalism; a watered down humanistic version; or a rediscovery of its experienced reality expressed in renewed or newly invented language.

We all know people intimately who may be indistinguishable in their professional work and in their attitude to their fellow beings, yet one will claim to gain his commitment from religious belief while another will regard all religion as an epiphenomenon. He may be neutral to religion while yet another may be strongly hostile to what is to him a reactionary or regressive influence.

The situation can be described hypothetically in terms of two orthogonal continua (Fig. G3.1).

The easier continuum to describe is the horizontal of religious language and behaviour. The vertical is harder and is provisionally labelled 'commitment to life, to neighbour and to self in these'.

We can imagine four people, one in each quadrant. They could all be teachers or bank managers or psychologists.

Quadrant I Competent and conscientious in her job, committed to people beyond the recognized limits of duty, concerned about the way they are affected by the pressures of society. Finding satisfaction in work and in private life. Has rejected all traditional and private religion as at best superfluous and at worst harmful.
Quadrant II Equally competent, conscientious and committed, but experiencing her work and private life as an expression of her religious faith for which traditional language and practice provide a framework and inner resource.
Quadrant III Though competent, she does not have a caring approach to her clients, treating them more as existing for her benefit than she for theirs. Her apparently sincere membership of a traditional religious organization does not seem to have any effect on her life or the way she does her work.

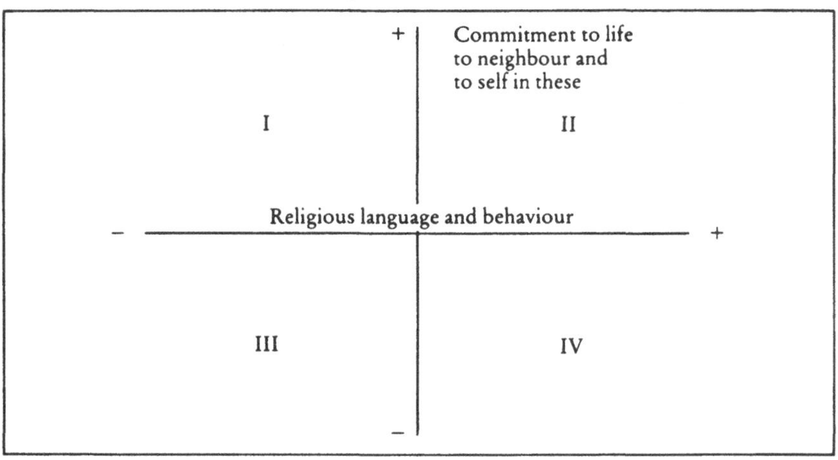

Figure G3.1

Quadrant IV She is neither committed to her work and to others, nor to any involvement in religious belief or practice.

An example of movement from one quadrant to another is provided by a theological student who lost his faith, left college and became a probation officer. While working as a probation officer he discovered in a new way that the springs of his motivation originated in religious exploration. He joined his local church. He then undertook part-time training for ordination and became a worker-priest while continuing full-time as a probation officer. Finally, he resigned from the Probation Service and became a full-time parish priest.

It seems likely that, starting in quadrant III, he moved first to I and then to II.

Other disciplines

So far I have been describing some of my constructions of my own religious belief and the way I construe my observation of that of others. The continua, however, correspond closely with the conclusions of a number of other observers of religious belief.

When a large number of definitions of religion were factor-analysed (Yinger, 1969) they showed two main factors similar to the continua I have described. An eminent theologian (Tillich, 1965, p. 10) defines religion as our ultimate concern but then attempts to describe it (the ground of our being) by linking it to his reinterpretation of traditional Christian language. He recognizes the situation described by the two continua. It is similarly described with an approving quotation from Merleau-Ponty, 'At this point religion ceases to be a conceptual construct or an ideology and once more becomes part of the experience of human life' (cited in Batson, Becker and Clark, 1973, p. 5). A philosopher (Masterman, 1971) gives another description of the same situation, and Kee in a recently reissued book says, 'I do not think that a case can be made out for saying that a man who takes the way of transcendence as his ultimate concern lacks anything because he does not believe in God' (1971, p. 218).

Especially helpful and well-informed is Cantwell Smith, who writes:

> The proposal that I am putting forward can, at one level, be formulated quite simply. It is that what men have tended to conceive as religion and especially as a religion, can more rewardingly, more truly, be conceived in terms of two factors, different in kind, both dynamic: an historical 'cumulative tradition', and the personal faith of men and women. (1978, p. 194)

Starting from Cantwell Smith's ideas, Fowler (1981) gives an account of an examination of 'the psychology of human development and the quest for meaning' under the general title 'Stages of Faith', and has attempted to correlate his findings with those of developmental psychology.

I return to psychology with a quotation from (if I am permitted the expression) that high priest of personality factors, Cattell. He is quite prepared to accept revealed religion as a good, though provisional, guide for life (1972, p. 125). He quotes the tetragrammaton revealed to Moses as beautifully expressing the core of science: 'It is our task to discover the nature of the cosmos – the glory of God – and increasingly to understand its message, but not to pretend that it will adjust to us' (p. 257).

PCP and religion

My own research (Todd, 1975) uses PCP to ask people what they believe and to help them reflect upon it. Normal grids can be developed from suitable lists of elements which focus on religious experience. Laddering elicits more superordinate constructs which can express or point towards our ultimate concern. A Resistance to Change Grid can indicate those constructs on which we are most reluctant to change our preferred positions. We can begin to see how we construe what is most important to us and whether we do this in the language of any traditional or private religion. If our constructs of religious belief form a constellation with few outside implications and quite apart from our superordinate constructs, then they play little part in our ultimate concern.

Kelly's constructive alternativism enabled him to reinterpret phenomena usually described in religious terminology (sin, forgiveness, conversion) in personal construct terminology. This he attempted in his paper 'Sin and Psychotherapy' (Kelly, 1969). PCP enables us to examine our beliefs systematically and experimentally in the form of the way we construe raw experience in order to anticipate the future. In some ways it is similar to the normal processes of traditional Judaeo-Christian religion. A footnote to Ecclesiastes 3:11 in the *Jerusalem Bible* reads:

> Or 'God has set eternity in their heart'. This phrase, however, is not to be taken in the Christian sense; it means simply; God has given the human heart (mind) awareness of duration, he has endowed him with the power of reflecting on the sequence of events and thus of controlling the present. But the author adds, this awareness is deceptive; it does not reveal the meaning of life. (1966, p. 983)

Similarity is also apparent with Underhill's presentation of mysticism. She writes of the mystic life:

> What we have been looking at is a life process, the establishment of a certain harmony between the created self and that Reality whose invitation it has heard: and we have discussed this life process rather as if it contained no elements which are not referable to natural and spontaneous growth, to the involuntary adjustments of the organism to that extended or transcendental universe of which it gradually becomes aware. But side by side with this organic growth there goes a specific kind of activity which is characteristic of the mystic: an education which he is called to undertake, that his consciousness of the Infinite may be stabilized, enriched and defined. (1911, p. 298)

To the general idea of decision-making on the basis of past experience, Kelly adds the structure and precision of his theory and the increased opportunity which these bring for analysing growth in belief, as in other aspects of the total life of people – and to compare it with the findings of a growing body of research.

Against this background of understanding I have used PCP with individuals directly and indirectly, and have also compared the consensus grids of various groups (theological students, members of an ashram, businessmen). Ingrid analysis has been used to produce graphs of a person's constructs of religion and of ultimate concern. This has proved useful as an aid to learning conversation in the in-service training of clergy. As in other types of counselling and therapy PCP is used indirectly as a resource for the mutual learning of counsellor and client in spiritual direction – helping identify direction for development rather than prescribing the direction in which the client should go.

Superordinate constructs

In a preliminary study of two people, eliciting constructs from a prepared list of elements, adding the construct 'religious and its opposite', and then laddering the constructs, a list of about twenty ordinary and superordinate constructs was obtained. These were used in an Implications Grid. The procedure is described later.

Jean was a trained social worker, thirty years old, who chose to work in voluntary and fringe projects. She was from a Free Church Evangelical background and had given up all practice of religion. Her chosen opposite pole to 'religious' was 'bound'. Some of the implications of this construct were as follows:

religious	*bound*
positive within	hatred within
contenting	discontenting
producing social stability	producing chaos

John was a business executive, twenty-one years old, who subsequently left his job 'to avoid getting in a rut'. He was from a Church of England background and had given up all practice of religion. His chosen opposite pole to 'religious' was 'free'. Some of the implications were as follow:

free	*religious*
part of greater activity	lives in space of loneliness
moves towards a greater state of consciousness	stagnates
right view of right	wrong view of right

Clearly Jean was in quadrant II of the original diagram and John was in quadrant I.

As part of continuing research, a series of PCP 'tests' lasting about three hours was given to eight people separately. The object was to measure superordinacy and religious constructs.

Starting with a self-characterization, each subject selected people and events significant in his life and to his religious beliefs, if any. Using these as elements, constructs were elicited from triads in the usual way. Each construct was laddered using Hinkle's (1965) technique. The bi-polar constructs on each rung of the ladders were examined with the subject and a comprehensive list of about twelve superordinate constructs was prepared. Together with about twelve of the constructs first elicited and similarly selected, the total of twenty-four constructs were written on cards. With the subject's agreement that they were of some meaning to him, three more constructs were supplied.

like me	not like me
like I'd like to be	not like I'd like to be
religious	the opposite of religious

All the construct cards with preferred poles marked were used in three tests to measure superordinacy.

1 The subject sorted the cards in order of their importance in his life.
2 Resistance to Change Grid as devised by Hinkle (1965). The grids were scored by counting the number of times each construct resisted change.
3 Bipolar Implications Grid (Hinkle, 1965) modified by Fransella (1972). The grids were scored by counting the number of implications for each construct.

Details of the procedures are also given in Fransella and Bannister (1977).

The results of these tests on two of the subjects are sufficient in the context of this paper. Each column gives the order of superordinacy according to that test.

First, let us look at the results of Jim, an Anglican parish priest:

Rank order	*Resistance to change*	*Implications*
1 Christian	1 Christian	1 Open to ideas
2 Fully human	Fully human	Religious
Like I'd like to be	3 Religious	3 Like I'd like to be
4 Religious	4 Have key to whole of life	4 Related to whole personality
Have key to whole of life	5 Open to greater truth	5 Revealing
6 Open to greater truth	6 Has basic structure	6 Fully human

Although 'Christian' heads the first two columns it is twelfth in the Implications column, whereas 'Religious' is first.

Here are the results of Beryl, the wife of an Anglican priest, a housewife and part-time teacher, who continues in the Church set-up but with difficulty:

Rank order	*Resistance to change*	*Implications*
1 Can control self	1 Makes the world more colourful	1 Mature
2 Enjoy being a person	2 Frightening	2 Terrors of death
3 Live more fully	Can understand them	3 Live more fully
4 Life-giving	4 Concerned for me	4 Makes the world more colourful
5 Have more respect	5 Open to new possibilities	5 Welcomes exposure
6 Makes the world more colourful	Powerful	6 Can control self and cope

For Beryl, 'Religious', of which her opposite was 'Open' came sixteenth, fifteenth and twenty-first in each of the columns respectively.

A number of interesting points are raised by the interpretation of these lists and by the use of them to aid the subject's own reflection. The main point here is the way they illustrate and give detail about the position of the subject on the belief-commitment quadrants with which I started. While both Jim and Beryl are together on commitment, they are separated by the belief language they use to express their commitment. If they were married (they are not) they might be in trouble. The 'What' is similar, the 'How' is different.

Many questions are left unanswered. There is scope for more research. But the research, of which this paper is a partial description, shows the value of using PCP in the area of religion, ideological belief and personal commitment.

Further reflection

The original quadrant diagram can be developed speculatively by rotating the belief (x) axis round the commitment (y) axis (Fig. G3.2).

Each of the x planes represents a person's belief system appropriate to his y axis of commitment. It should therefore be possible to compare the different belief systems analysed into constructs. This could provide precision for inter-faith dialogue.

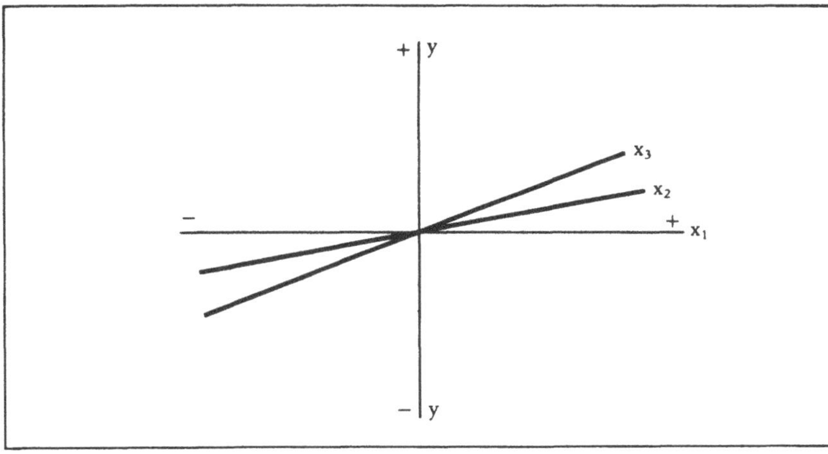

Figure G3.2

It is not proved that the two continua are completely orthogonal. There may be some connection which could lead to a person changing from *x*1 to *x*2 because it is seen as more adequately expressing his *y* continuum.

It may be that with an individual person as the *x* increases it reaches a point where it curves either towards the full wordless faith of apophatic mysticism or towards the awful silence of some kind of hell.

Here we move into the area of super-superordinate or of meta-superordinate constructs, and the metaphorical nature of superordinate construct labels. I hope to have demonstrated the usefulness of PCP methodology in what is a notoriously difficult area of

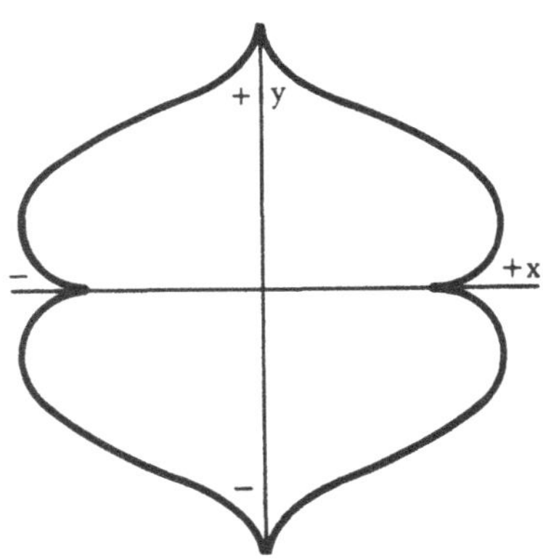

Figure G3.3

research. Perhaps it will help forward mutual understanding between the many warring champions of 'right' and 'wrong'.

Notes and References

Batson, C. D., Becker, J. C. and Clark, W. M. (1973). *Commitment without Ideology.* SCM Press: London.

Berger, P. L. (1980). *The Heretical Imperative.* Collins: London.

Berger, P. L. and Luckmann, T. (1966). *The Social Construction of Reality.* Penguin: Harmondsworth.

Bible (1966). *Jerusalem Bible.* Darton, Longman & Todd: London.

Cantwell Smith, W. (1978). *The Meaning and End of Religion.* SPCK: London.

Cattell, R. B. (1972). *A New morality from Science: Beyondism.* Pergamon: Oxford.

Fowler, J. W. (1981). *Stages of Faith.* Harper and Row: London.

Fransella, F. (1972). *Personal Change and Reconstruction.* Academic Press: London.

Fransella, F. and Bannister, D. (1977). *A Manual for Repertory Grid Technique.* Academic Press: London.

Hinkle, D. N. (1965). The change of personal constructs from the viewpoint of a theory of implications. Unpublished PhD thesis, Ohio State University.

Kee, A. (1971). *The Way of Transcendence.* Penguin: Harmondsworth.

Kelly, G. A. (1969). Sin and psychotherapy. In B. Maher (ed.), *Clinical Psychology and Personality.* Wiley: New York.

Masterson, P. (1971). *Atheism and Alienation.* Penguin: Harmondsworth.

Tillich, P. (1965). *Systematic Theology II.* Nisbet: Welwyn Garden City.

Todd, N. H. (1975). Religious belief and personal construct theory. Unpublished PhD thesis, Nottingham University.

Underhill, E. (1911). *Mysticism: A study in the Nature and Development of Man's Spiritual Consciousness.* Methuen: London.

Yinger, J. M. (1969). A structural examination of religion. *Journal for the Scientific Study of Religion* 8(1), 88–9.

Chapter 4

Psychological investigation of offending behaviour

Adrian Needs

The study of offenders and offending represents a rather neglected field in personal construct psychology. This is rather ironic since one of the earliest papers describing the use of repertory grids in clinical assessment was a case study of an arsonist (Fransella and Adams, 1966). It is also perhaps surprising, given the key role assigned to subjective factors in recent work in related areas such as proneness to anger (e.g. Novaco 1978), 'psychopathy' (Blackburn, 1984; Blackburn and Lee-Evans, 1985) and episodes of violence (e.g. Dobash and Dobash 1984). The possibility arises that much of this could be usefully integrated and extended using a Kellian framework. This paper, however, merely seeks to cultivate an awareness of some applications of grid techniques in this field.

The fact that 'deviant' individuals may hold highly idiosyncratic models of reality is shown in the case studies described by Fransella and Adams (1966) and Howells (1978). In the former, a series of grids was elicited from the fire-raising client which permitted examination of stages of offending and other emotionally loaded facets of the individual's experience. The crucial stage of offending appeared to be associated with feelings of power and retribution, and the client did not see himself as an arsonist but rather as a punisher of wrongdoing. Howells presented the example of a poisoner who saw himself as deliberately setting himself apart from society in general, and his parents in particular, by his offending.

A grid investigation by Kelly and Taylor (1981) found evidence that teenagers who illegally borrow cars, if successful once, tend to see their behaviour as exercising a desired self-image. Miller and Treacher (1981) found in delinquents a tendency to identification with television heroes who embody the ideal of direct and forceful action; real-life adults were seen as less adequate role models. An investigation of changes in construing over a two-month period in a Detention Centre by Norris (1977) indicated that trainees often 'emerged with both lowered self-respect and lowered aspirations' (p. 135). Lewis (1973) noted changes in self-esteem and identification of self as criminal in samples of long-term prisoners, although the effect was not unidirectional. In this study, valued aspects of people and activities in the prison environment were also investigated.

A study of interpersonal perception in emotionally disturbed boys by Hayden, Nasby and Davids (1977) found lack of differentiation of construing to be associated with poor social adjustment and a limited ability to predict in an interpersonal context. Testing the hypothesis of a role-taking deficiency in 'psychopaths', Widom (1976) found that primary psychopaths erroneously believe that other people view situations as they do. Howells (1979) found that paedophiles tend to construe adults in terms of dominance versus submission. This suggested the possibility that, seeing adult relationships as difficult to control, one source of attraction of children for paedophiles is the child's passivity and, in some cases, perceived innocence. Cognitive processes relevant to the performance of a violent act were inferred by Howells (see Howells, 1983) in a repertory grid investigation of Megargee's (1966, 1971) hypothesis of the 'overcontrolled offender'. Howells suggested that the pattern of grid results of individuals who had carried out an apparently 'out of character' offence of extreme violence, typically within a close relationship, indicated a positively biased view of other people which was prone to a sudden, massive, reversal when unpleasant events made such a simple scheme of things untenable. A grid study by Howells and Steadman-Allen (1977) found that some rapists see anger following from feelings of inadequacy or failure as a major precursor of offending.

From the limited amount of work published so far it would appear that grid techniques can aid in identifying, formulating and testing issues relevant to offending and the offender. In passing, it may be noted that grid-related techniques also appear to have an important role in explicating how various groups in society (e.g. those who administer the law) think about offences, as in the atheoretical multi-dimensional scaling study of perception of aggressive episodes of Forgas, Brown and Menyhart (1980). This line of investigation may be of considerable importance in, for example, the area of sexual offences (see Howells, 1980).

Cultural myths apart, sex offenders can be rather difficult to construe. The use of different levels of analysis and approaches in the literature (from the socio-political to the biological) and different research techniques (from questionnaires to penile plethysmographs) can make the field appear rather fragmented. There is also considerable heterogeneity within broad categories such as 'rapist' and 'child molester' (e.g. Quinsey, 1977; Howells, 1981). Largely because of this diversity, some authors have advocated a 'broad-based' approach in the individual case (e.g. Crawford, 1981; Perkins, 1983). Yet even when a contextual, developmental formulation going beyond a mere checklist of relevant problems is attempted (Perkins, 1983) it might appear that detailed identification and integration of relevant factors can be problematic if one maintains an external, deterministic, 'organism' (see Trower, 1984) approach. For example, it has been noted fairly frequently (e.g. Pacht and Cowden, 1974) that sex offenders often seem to have difficulty in relating successfully. 'Social skill' has proved extremely difficult to adequately conceptualise in itself (e.g. McFall, 1982), especially when the frame of reference of the individual himself is neglected (c.f. Trower, 1984). It may also be remembered that Howells (1979) found possible evidence of a subjective continuity between social difficulty and attraction to children in some paedophiles. It remains a possibility that some of the fragmentation which can be a product of an external perspective is open to integration within the implicit frame of reference of the subject himself.

In using grids with sex offenders an important aim of mine has been facilitation of communication and understanding in the course of clinical work. From a research perspective I have been comparing grids in a way similar to the 'serial deviant case analysis' approach to formulation and revision of hypotheses described by Kelly and Taylor (1981): description and hypothesis generation should precede more preemptive hypothesis-testing (McGuire, 1973).

The most obvious explanation of sexual offending is that it is perpetrated in order to gratify sexual arousal. This would appear to be true in, for example, many incest cases (e.g. Frude, 1983).

Yet I would follow Plummer (1984) in making the point that sexual behaviour in general can include many purposes. It can involve, for example, the affirmation of attractiveness, maturity and gender role, the endorsement of commitment to a relationship or to a life-style, and can be used in the course of material gain or to relieve tension. Discussion will initially focus on rape.

Groth (1981) writes that the rapist is 'no more raping to satisfy a sexual need than an alcoholic is drinking because he is thirsty' (p. 466). Desire to humiliate or dominate, compensating for feelings of having been wronged, or for feelings of inadequacy and failure, are seen as central (see also Osborne, 1982). Some rapes have been regarded by other researchers also as primarily aggressive acts (Cohen et al 1971; Gibbens, Garotalo, Boucher and Seghorn, 1977; Wright 1980).

Studies of attitudes of rapists (see Hegeman and Meikle, 1980) suggest that some rapists do not regard themselves as guilty of a criminal act (Clark and Lewis, 1977), are frequently conservative in their attitudes toward sex roles and tend to have negative or sharply polarised attitudes towards women. It would seem important to clarify the nature of the possible interactions between these kinds of attitudes and the concerns with humiliation and dominance described by Groth.

Some might argue that such simplistic or resentful attitudes reflect a general tendency among rapists to have difficulty in interacting with women. Unfortunately, this broad assumption, to the extent that it has been tested rigorously at all, has been investigated in terms of a rather narrow, behavioural, 'social skills' paradigm (not always noted for discriminating power; e.g. Leary, 1983), and recent evidence is not particularly supportive (Alexander and Johnson, 1980; Segal and Marshall, 1985). Another possible interpretation is that the existence of such limited attitudes towards women in generally conformist individuals signifies a literal adherence to a common cultural orientation toward male–female relationships. The rape act itself has been seen (e.g. Brownmiller, 1975) as the extreme of pervasive aggressive and demeaning male attitudes. In a similar vein, Plummer (1984) writes that rape 'could be seen as the epitome of the male role for the man who takes his role just too seriously' (p. 43). The way some processes (of maybe wider relevance) appeared to operate in one individual (a repeated rapist) was suggested by the grid results described below.

It was apparent from a principal-components analysis of the

grid (representing construing of other people and self) that one main dimension predominated. This was identified as being 'selfish', 'resorting to violence' and 'blaming others', along with 'unfairness', 'insincerity' and 'going to any lengths not to be seen as a failure' versus being 'unselfish', 'thinking things through', 'not blaming others', 'fair', 'straight' and 'not hurting anybody for anything'. The second component was interpreted as reflecting weakness and inadequacy versus being strong and ruthless. Women in the grid were seen as either weak and selfish, or strong and ruthless and selfish, although a minority (mother, previous psychologist and the heroine of a novel he was writing) were seen in highly idealised terms. 'Self when depressed' (a typical antecedent of offending) was described as 'weak', 'selfish' and 'going to any lengths to avoid being seen as a failure'. 'Ideal self' and to a lesser extent 'self now' were seen as 'unselfish' and 'thinking things through'. In addition, there was a correlation of 0.72 between 'looking for sincerity in a relationship' and 'would fall for a con'.

Interviews based on grid results suggested a preoccupation with personal failures and a desperate need for validation of core constructs relating to inadequacy, maturity and coping; the latter was seen as having to come from a successful relationship with a woman. These ideas appeared to have a cultural basis: while personal difficulties (including feeling that he had failed to reach culturally desirable standards) made these issues salient, culturally available ideas of endorsing a mature male role through a relationship with a woman suggested the solution. He idealised having a relationship, its conduct and, initially, his partners. The result was minimal assessment of compatibility, and a style of relating more characterised by lavishing gifts than by negotiating mutual adjustments. Unfortunately, when relationships failed, as was arguably likely, he was faced with the very implications he had tried to negate, and an extra bitterness was introduced by the fact that he felt he had been very generous and therefore cheated. Seeing himself as wronged, and blind to the aspects of his behaviour which contributed to this state of affairs, he would, it seemed, abandon attempts at worthiness and 'slot-change' (c.f. Space and Cromwell, 1980) to experimenting with being selfish, prepared to use violence and insincere. If women did their worst, why should he not 'drag them down' with him (as he expressed it)? It is important to recognise that his construing acted as the precipitator rather than just predictor of situations (Radley 1977). In fact, Stefan's (1977) comment that 'if a person relies upon an exclusive core construct system, he is vulnerable to recurring crises' (p. 228) seems especially pertinent and suggests that implications for treatment would go beyond conventional 'heterosocial skills training' (e.g. Hayes, Brownell and Barlow, 1983).

Several authors (e.g. Groth, 1978; Howells, 1979, 1981) have commented on the possible operation of personal and social concerns, not reducible to sexual arousal alone, in sexual offences against children. Grid investigation has suggested that some themes may be replicated in part in both rapists and paedophiles. For example, one repeated child molester expressed some rather similar concerns to those of the rapist above. He had engaged in several disastrous relationships (indicated on his grid by negative construing of previous partners) usually meeting partners through 'lonely hearts' columns. Laddering revealed that he was 'terrified' of being alone and that without female companionship he felt 'a failure and a nothing'. In addition, conducting the grid investigation in itself seemed to facilitate the overcoming of what had been a great deal of confusion regarding personal offence patterns (cf. Bancroft, 1979; Crawford, 1981). Especially useful was the indication of a clear identification of himself when depressed with himself when he was eight years old. Exploration of this topic with the benefit of a more mature construct system (cf. Morrison and Cometa, 1982) raised the topic of his own being sexually interfered with as a child (as had the rapist above, something apparently not uncommon among sex offenders; e.g. Petrovich and Templer, 1984).

Another factor to emerge in one paedophile's grid was a failure to identify either self or ideal self with any adults in his social environment. In his self-characterisation he wrote that he 'has never had what he would call a true friend as almost everybody he has ever met has fallen short of the qualities he thinks a real friend should display'. This pattern seemed related to the depression, feeling of alienation and lack of direction in life, which in turn was related to drug-taking, in the course of which he sometimes felt the urge to indecently assault a female child. In fact, his 'self-identity plot' (Norris and Makhlouf-Norris, 1976) showed a tentative identification of only children with ideal and actual self. Further related to both this alienation and his drug-taking is the picture implied by the component graph of his grid.

This showed a tendency to see the alternative to a hedonic lifestyle as being conventional and rather dull. This implicit disadvantage (see Ryle, 1979) of giving up the drugs which contributed to his offending might have severely undermined the effectiveness of other interventions had it not been made explicit and questioned.

Grid-based investigations can permit identification of important yet otherwise elusive factors in individuals given to explosive anger, a problem of particular relevance to prison populations. A first step can be to identify situations in which anger or related feelings occur, usually through a combination of interview and diary information. Comparing situations (either in triads or in pairs) to elicit constructs can then give an idea of what is at stake in relevant situations for the individual – especially if 'laddering' (e.g. Fransella and Bannister, 1977) is used. Thus, in one individual, feeling angry was correlated highly with feelings of unfairness, humiliation, being 'pushed around' and thinking of past problems. In addition, a central construct concerned 'not knowing where I stand with the other people', which seemed to involve anxiety regarding the intentions of others toward him. In Blackburn's (e.g. 1984) characterisation of the so-called 'psychopath', distrust is seen as a pervasive tendency.

In clarifying what has been presented as an 'anger problem', important facets to explore include the degree of justification an individual sees in his anger, and (as with the paedophile drug-user above), how he sees the alternatives. One individual argued that the only alternative, in his terms, to being 'wild' was being 'soft'. To give up being 'wild' would result in 'being taken advantage of'. There was of course an element of truth in this, bearing in mind the prison setting and his previous antagonistic conduct. He had spent much of his life tightly defining core constructs of being 'tough', forthright and the victim of a devious and uncaring world. To give up his sustaining 'hostility' (defined in both the Kellian and conventional senses) would be threatening indeed. Aggressiveness can play an important role in validating an individual's core constructs (e.g. Toch, 1969), which is one important reason why 'assertiveness training' procedures may be rejected by offenders (Kirchner, Kennedy and Draguns, 1979). Interestingly, he described his anger as being a response to being 'tested out' (see McCoy, 1977).

In attempting to gain understanding of offences such as some murders where reasons underlying actions (and reactions) are obscure, there can be advantages in applying grid techniques to the study of offences as situations. Offences and related situations are identified and presented in a comparison task. Various methods for construct elicitation are being tested, such as presenting pairs and asking for similarities and/or differences, or asking for groupings then presenting elements within groupings in triads to try and overcome 'range of convenience' problems. The latter can make a full grid inappropriate, even when laddering (an integral part of the elicitation strategy) has yielded more superordinate constructs. In fact, sensitive use of laddering can in this context make a full grid partly redundant.

This mode of investigation permits study of the construing process in its situational, sequential context. This appears to hold the promise of enriching both our understanding of construing and of potentially important processes which contribute to offending, possibly enabling us to go beyond stereotyped and superficial suggestions of 'motive'. As McGuire and Priestley (1985) point out, owing to an emphasis on the psychology of the offender, the study of offences themselves is largely 'virgin territory'. The approach can, in addition, through asking questions in unfamiliar yet structured ways, help in developing understanding beyond the 'scripted' interview response or the (not necessarily merely evasive) 'don't know'. At the same time, the structured yet flexible nature of the approach means that the method used can be stated explicitly (see Wright, 1970).

The approach, like any other, is not without difficulties. Many of these are common to all modes of interviewing (e.g. see Linehan, 1977) – for example, forgetting, social desirability, inarticulacy and rationalisation. Some would argue that offenders are especially prone to dissimulation, unwillingness or rationalisation (e.g. Matthews, 1980; Linehan, 1977). A full-blown approach is perhaps best reserved for the cooperative, although cooperation can be negotiable, and setting up a brief comparison task (e.g. how is *x* similar or different to *y*) and clarifying answers through pyramiding and laddering (e.g. 'What else is that like?' 'Why is that important?') can in any case increase the effectiveness of more conventional interviewing practice. The probing nature of these techniques, especially laddering, dictates a need for sensitivity (c.f. Rowe, 1983). It is not always easy to assess when an approximation of constructions which actually operated at the time has been gained. Also, while it is possible to cross-reference some concerns, and to seem to identify some changes in anticipation as an offence developed, one should be prepared to tolerate some uncertainty in the course of investigation.

A major source of this hinges upon a fundamental aspect of construing in action. Radley (1977) writes that there are many occasions when the goal or end point which we seek is not 'readily specifiable, and sometimes most difficult to make explicit' (p. 223). This arises from the fact that 'Our behaviour is not merely a means of verifying what we can already predict, but is the way in which we grasp the world and thereby precipitate a new situation' (p. 231). This transactional nature of construing is an important reason why 'intent' within an offence may fluctuate, be confused and multifaceted, or difficult to specify (Briscoe, 1976). This is not to say that there are not many offences which are almost entirely premeditated: I would just make the point that 'intent' *can* be complex.

Grid techniques (and the theoretical vantage points of personal construct psychology) might enable us to glimpse something of this complexity.

Addendum

Since completing this paper a further relevant grid paper has appeared in the literature, which is of especial interest in that it uses grids to monitor changes in a rapist's construing over a four-year period in a forensic unit (Shorts, 1985). In addition, a particularly imaginative set of elements is used.

Note

The views expressed in this paper are the author's and do not necessarily represent those of the Home Office.

The grids referred to above were analysed using programmes devised for the Medical Research Council Service for analysing grids, under Dr Patrick Slater.

References

Alexander, B. B. and Johnson, S. B. (1980). Reliability of hetero-social skills measurement with sex offenders. *Journal of Behavioral Assessment* 2(3), 225–37.

Bancroft, J. (1979). Treatment of deviant sexual behaviour. In R. Gains and B. Hudson (eds.), *Current Themes in Psychiatry* 2. Macmillan: London.

Brownmiller, S. (1975). *Against Our Will: Men, Women and Rape*. Secker & Warburg: London.

Blackburn, R. (1984). Cognition and antisocial personality: implications for theory and therapy. Paper presented at conference on 'The Mentally Disordered Offender: Issues in Treatment and Rehabilitation', Park Lane Hospital, Liverpool.

Blackburn, R. and Lee-Evans, J. M. (1985). Reactions of primary and secondary psychopaths to anger-evoking situations. *British Journal of Clinical Psychology* 24, 93–100.

Briscoe, O. V. (1975). Assessment of intent: an approach to the preparation of court reports. *British Journal of Psychiatry* 127, 461–5.

Clark, L. and Lewis, P. (1977). *Rape: The Price of Coercive Sexuality*. The Women's Press: Toronto.

Cohen, M., Garotalo, R., Boucher, R. and Seghorn, T. (1971). The psychology of rapists. *Seminars in Psychiatry* 3, 307–27.

Crawford, D. (1981). Treatment approaches with paedophiles. In M. Cook and K. Howells (eds.), *Adult Sexual Interest in Children*. Academic Press: London.

Dobash, R. E. and Dobash, R. P. (1984). The nature and antecedents of violent events. *British Journal of Criminology* 24(3), 269–88.

Forgas, J. P., Brown, L. B. and Menyhart, J. (1980). Dimensions of aggression: the perception of aggressive episodes. *British Journal of Social and Clinical Psychology* 19, 215–27.

Fransella, F. and Adams, B. (1966). An illustration of the use of repertory grid technique in a clinical setting. *British Journal of Social and Clinical Psychology* 5, 51–62.

Fransella, F. and Bannister, D. (1977). *A Manual for Repertory Grid Technique*. Academic Press: London.

Frude, N. (1982). The sexual nature of sexual abuse. *Childe Abuse and Neglect* 6, 211–23.

Gibbens, T. C. N., Way, C. and Soothill, K. L. (1977). Behavioural types of rape. *British Journal of Psychiatry* 130, 32–42.
Groth, A. N. (1978). Patterns of sexual assault against children and adolescents. In A. W. Burgess, A. N. Groth, L. L. Holmstrom and S. M. Sgroi. *The Sexual Assault of Children and Adolescents.* Lexington Books: Lexington, Mass.
Groth, A. N. (1981). Rape: The sexual expression of aggression. In P. F. Brain and D. Benton (eds.), *Multidisciplinary Approaches to Aggression Research.* Elsevier/Marsh/Holland Biomedical Press: New York.
Hayden, N., Nasby, W. and Davids, A. (1977). Interpersonal conceptual structures, predictive accuracy, and social adjustment of emotionally disturbed boys. *Journal of Abnormal Psychology* 86, 315–20.
Hayes, S. C., Brownell, K. D. and Barlow, D. H. (1983). Heterosocial skills training and covert sensitization: effects on social skills and sexual arousal in sexual deviants. *Behavior Research and Therapy* 21(4), 383–92.
Hegeman, N. and Meikle, S. (1980). Motives and attitudes of rapists. *Canadian Journal of Behavioral Science* 12(4), 359–72.
Howells, K. (1978). The meaning of poisoning to a person diagnosed as a psychopath. *Medicine, Science and the Law* 8, 179–84.
Howells, K. (1979). Some meanings of children for paedophiles. In M. Cook and G. Wilson (eds.), *Love and Attraction.* Pergamon: London.
Howells, K. (1980). Social reactions to sexual deviance. In D. J. West (ed.), *Sex Offenders in the Criminal Justice System.* Cropwood: Cambridge.
Howells, K. (1981). Adult sexual interest in children: Considerations relevant to theories of aetiology. In M. Cook and K. Howells (eds.), *Adult Sexual Interest in Children.* Academic Press, London.
Howells, K. (1983). Social construing and violent behaviour in mentally abnormal offenders. In J. Hinton (ed.), *Dangerousness: Problems of Assessment and Prediction.* Allen & Unwin: London.
Howells, K. and Steadman-Allen, R. (1977). The emotional mediation of sexual offenders. Paper presented at the Annual Conference of the British Psychological Society, Exeter.
Kelly, D. and Taylor, H. (1981). Take and escape: a personal

construct study of car 'theft'. In H. Bonarius, R. Holland and S. Roseberg (eds.), *Personal Construct Psychology: Recent Advances in Theory and Practice*. Macmillan: London.

Kirchner, E. P., Kennedy, R. E. and Draguns, J. G. (1979). Assertion and aggression in adult offenders. *Behavior Therapy* 10(14), 452–71.

Leary, M. R. (1983). *Social Anxiety: Social, Personality and Clinical Perspectives*, Sage Library of Social Research: London, vol. 153.

Lewis, P. S. (1973). The prisoner's perception of himself and his world. Unpublished PhD thesis, University of London.

Linehan, M. M. (1977). Issues in behavioral interviewing. In J. D. Cone and R. P. Hawkins (eds.), *Behavioral Assessment: New Directions in Clinical Psychology*. Brunner/Mazel: New York.

McCoy, M. (1977). A reconstruction of emotion. In D. Bannister (ed.), *New Perspectives in Personal Construct Theory*. Academic Press: London.

McFall, R. M. (1982). A review and reformulation of the concept of social skills. *Behavioral Assessment* 4, 1–33.

McGuire, W. J. (1973). The yin and yang of progress in social psychology: seven koan. *Journal of Personality and Social Psychology* 26, 446–56.

McGuire, J. and Priestley, P. (1985). *Offending Behaviour: Skills and Stratagems for Going Straight*. Batsford Academic: London.

Matthews, R. (1980). Assessment of sexual offenders at Wormwood Scrubs. In D. J. West (ed.), *Sex Offenders in the Criminal Justice System*. Cropwood: Cambridge.

Megargee, E. I. (1966). Undercontrolled and overcontrolled personality types in extreme antisocial aggression. *Psychological Monographs* 80(611), whole issue.

Megargee, E. I. (1971). The role of inhibition in the assessment and understanding of violence. In J. E. Singer (ed.), *The Control of Aggression and Violence: Cognitive and Psychological Factors*. Academic Press: London.

Miller, K. and Treacher, A. (1981). Delinquency: a personal construct theory approach. In H. Bonarius, R. Holland and S. Rosenberg (eds.), *Personal Construct Psychology: Recent Advances in Theory and Practice*. Macmillan: London.

Morrison, J. and Cometa, M. C. (1982). The experience corollary.

In J. C. Mancuso and J. R. Adams-Webber (eds.), *The Construing Person.* Praeger Scientific: New York.

Norris, H. and Makhlouf-Norris, F. (1976). The measurement of self-identity. In P. Slater (ed.), *The Measurement of Intrapersonal Space by Grid Technique, Vol. 1: Explorations of Intrapersonal Space.* Wiley: London.

Norris, M. (1977). Construing in a detention centre. In D. Bannister (ed.), *New Perspectives in Personal Construct Theory.* Academic Press: London.

Novaco, R. (1978). Anger and coping with stress. In J. P. Foreyt and D. P. Rathjen (eds.), *Cognitive Behaviour Therapy.* Plenum: New York.

Osborne, K. (1982). Sexual violence. In P. Feldman (ed.), *Developments in the Study of Criminal Behaviour, Vol. 2: Violence.* Wiley: London.

Pacht, A. R. and Cowden, J. E. (1974). An exploratory study of five hundred sex offenders. *Criminal Justice and Behavior* 1(1), 13–20.

Perkins, D. (1983). Assessment and treatment of dangerous sexual offenders. In J. Hinton (ed.), *Dangerousness: Problems of Assessment and Prediction.* Allen & Unwin: London.

Petrovich, M. and Templer, D. I. (1984). Heterosexual molestation of children who later become rapists. *Psychological Reports* 54, 810.

Plummer, K. (1984). The social uses of sexuality: symbolic interaction, power and rape. In J. Hopkins (ed.), *Perspectives on Rape and Sexual Assault.* Harper & Row: London.

Quinsey, V. (1977). The assessment and treatment of child molesters: a review. *Canadian Psychological Review* 18(3), 204–20.

Radley, A. (1977). Living on the horizon. In D. Bannister (ed.), *New Perspectives in Personal Construct Theory.* Academic Press: London.

Rowe, D. (1983). *Depression: The Way out of Your Prison.* Routledge & Kegan Paul: London.

Ryle, A. (1979). The focus in brief interpretive psychotherapy: dilemmas, traps and snags as target problems. *British Journal of Psychiatry* 134, 46–54.

Segal, Z. V. and Marshall, W. L. (1985). Heterosexual social skills in a population of rapists and child molesters. *Journal of Consulting and Clinical Psychology* 53, 55–63.

Shorts, I. D. (1875). Treatment of a sex offender in a maximum security forensic hospital: detecting changes in personality and interpersonal construing. *International Journal of Offender Therapy and Comparative Criminology* 29(3), 237–50.

Space, L. G. and Cromwell, R. L. (1980). Personal constructs among depressed patients. *The Journal of Nervous and Mental Disease* 168, 150–8.

Stefan, C. (1977). Core role theory and implications. In D. Bannister (ed.), *New Perspectives in Personal Construct Theory.* Academic Press: London.

Toch, H. (1969). *Violent Men.* Aldine: Chicago.

Trower, P. (ed.) (1984). *Radical Approaches to Social Skills Training.* Croom Helm: Beckenham, Kent.

Widom, C. S. (1976). Interpersonal and personal construct systems in psychopaths. *Journal of Consulting and Clinical Psychology* 44, 614–23.

Wright, K. J. T. (1970). Exploring the uniqueness of common complaints. *British Journal of Medical Psychology* 43, 221–32.

Wright, R. (1980). Rape and physical violence. In D. J. West (ed.), *Sex Offenders in the Criminal Justice System.* Cropwood: Cambridge.

H

The Arts

Chapter 1
A PCT view of novel writing and reading

Don Bannister

Novel reading is an exercise in continuous anticipation. As you turn the pages, on the basis of your elaborating understanding, you anticipate what will happen next. 'Happen next' refers not only to events and narrative turns of plot but also to the unfolding over time of what the people in the story are saying and experiencing, the way in which the nature of the context reveals itself, the way in which the harmonics of the novel's world are developing. You may be only intermittently and partially aware that you are predicting, and (as in daily life) it is often misprediction that brings the process into conscious focus.

If the act of novel reading is truly an act of constructive anticipation, then the reader is constantly subject to validation or invalidation or to experiencing the unfolding events as being outside the range of convenience of his or her construing. In swift sequence, a novel packages for us those confrontations which Kelly thought basic to life, in which we find our forecasts right or wrong or totally irrelevant.

Perhaps most markedly, in our novel reading, we crave validation. We have the experience of having our anticipations confirmed, of seeing the significance of what is presently portrayed, verified by outcome. Children grasp at narrative validation in a very direct way when they demand to have the same story read to them over and over again. Familiarity deepens their understanding and endows them with a sense of anticipative control. Adults often achieve the same guarantee of validation not by re-reading the same story but by reading endlessly the same kind of story. Thus much popular fiction caters to our craving for validation by working out, in varying detail, unvarying sequences, such as that of the heroic hero triumphing over the villainous villain. Detail may vary, but the essential landmarks are where we expect them to be, signposts are clear and the landscape is broadly familiar. So the most successful popular fiction is that which offers us comforting superordinate validation while, in its colourful detail, it invites us to widen (not too uncomfortably) the range of convenience of our construing. Thus the historical romance depicts for us a world in which the physical paraphernalia and customs are curious and unfamiliar, while the central psychology and metaphysic is conventional and of our time.

Nevertheless, novel reading is not a risk-free occupation. The story may, in some essential way, run contrary to our expectations and we may be invalidated. When this happens we may see the story as untrue, badly written and misleading. Alternatively, we may come to see it as true and revise our initial construing. This is the most powerful effect that a novel can have, in that it provides us with the kind of puzzlement and dismay which becomes insight and enables us to elaborate our understanding.

Equally, a novel can take us to the frontiers of our range of convenience, not comfortably (as on a tourist excursion to well-ordered foreign parts) but so that we find ourselves in a threatening and confusing landscape. At such times we may simply abandon the novel as a literal nonsense. Alternatively, we may find enough points of contact between worlds we have lived in and the world we are exploring in the novel, contact by analogy, metaphor, through a scatter of small but significant clues, to encourage us to complete the journey and learn.

Novel writing

Novel writing is an exercise in the controlled elaboration of an author's construct system.

Whatever the formal working system of the author, a novel stems from some personal intersect of elements and constructs which has vast implicative mass. As, for example, from a childhood memory of seeing miners drinking at night time in a town square, I found myself drawn outwards into unfolding reflections and themes to do with the colliery on which my village centred, the texture of the village and its manner of life, the *mores* of childhood, unchosen life paths, and so forth (Bannister, 1979).

True, the starting point can be pre-empted into the form of a plan, and the novel be constructed to fulfil that plan rather than having its form evolve from the detail of exploration. These two processes represent varying forms of the creativity cycle, described by Kelly (1955) as a cycle which starts with loosened construction and terminates with tightened and readily validatable construction. Many novels (such as the classic 'whodunnit' mystery, which is not at all mysterious) seem written by rapidly tightening their vague and speculative origins into specific superordinate constructions from which a mass of subordinate detail can be mechanically read off. Then the cycle is worked through (in major form) once only, from loose to tight. Contrastingly, a novel can involve a perpetual cycling from loose to tight to loose construing. Thus its total shape and meaning is generated in play with its detail, rather than acting as dictator of specific content.

If a novel is thus unfolded by (for and from) the author, then just as readers may have their anticipations of what is forthcoming denied, so the author may experience invalidation. Authors may recognise that what they have written is, in an essential sense, false. That is to say, that it is untrue in the light of the construct system of the author, it is false to that total way of understanding of the world from which the particular narrative is derived. The author realises that the people on the pages could not have done or said or experienced at this point and in this context what he or she has set them down as doing, saying, experiencing. Then comes a moral choice: whether or not to consign eminently plausible pages of narrative to the wastepaper basket.

Kelly depicts the act of construing as partaking of both invention and discovery. We invent the terms in which we will view the word and thereby discover what is to be seen by taking such a view. This inextricable mixing of what we create with what we are confronted by, is most manifest in novel writing. I have grown used to working on a novel spurred on by the thought that now I shall find out what happens next. Perhaps the very length of novels emphasises this quality of 'finding through making' in our construing. We *construe* through *constructs.* Novels remind us that elaborative construing takes time, that it is a long search for what is hidden, not a simple detailing of what is manifest.

Central to elaborative construing is the movement between

subordinate and superordinate construing (and back and forth again) already referred to in relation to the creativity cycle. At the heart of novel writing is exactly this deriving, working out, of the subordinate (the detail and content of the novel) from the superordinate (the theme of the novel). Equally, new aspects of the superordinate theme are generated by subordinate exploration. I had written a substantial part of the novel already referred to (Bannister, 1979) convinced that its sole theme concerned the nature of the pit village community before I realised that the specific events adumbrated an alternative autobiography – a superordinate which then I consciously articulated into yet further narrative. But in novels, as in life, we sometimes fail to listen to the new melodic lines implicit in the notes we are playing. Thus it is that the novel *Walden II* did little for Skinner's abstractions except to illustrate them.

Writers and readers

The relationship of novel writer to novel reader is precious but mysterious. It is intimate without being conversational. Letters are written to someone, but novels are written to whom it may concern. Kelly's Sociality Corollary asserts that it is by construing the construction processes of others that we enter into a social role with them. We might conclude that novelists are essentially construing not the construction processes of their readers but the construction processes of the characters in the novel. In the final analysis, perhaps our genius for standing in angled relationships to aspects of ourselves and others is such that the novelist is construing his or her own construction processes and re-presenting this construction through the figures in the novel. The reader, it is, who provides sociality by construing the construction processes of the author. True, many novelists annotate their narrative, they tell the reader what to think, but in so doing they are essentially writing for a 'typical' reader. Thereby, they restrict themselves to some easily accessible and mundane part of their own construing, which is taken to represent the 'typical' reader.

This is not any kind of injunction to novelists to disregard their readers. It is the reading of a novel that ultimately gives it life. Rather, it is argued that novelists must respect readers and acknowledge both their right and their ability independently, to read significance *into* the novel. In chess there is the notion of playing the board rather than playing the man. It is argued that the best kind of chess is played when you do not try to capitalise on what you imagine to be the particular weaknesses or foibles of your opponent but play each move as if your opponent were a perfect chess player who will make the perfect reply. Thus it is that novels might be written. Novelists should struggle to represent their experience as truthfully and as vividly as they can, resting secure in the belief that, through our common humanity, the novel will have its significance affirmed and properly transmuted by the construct system into which it passes.

The novel, in PCT terms, is not unique. It is a special case of the anecdote, the poem, the play, the daydream. Indeed, Kelly argues it is close kin to that other great public enterprise in make-believe, Science. He set out the relationship thus:

> But there are two differences between him [the novelist] and the scientist; he is more willing to confide his make-believe – even publish it – and he is willing to postpone the accumulation of factual evidence to support the generality of characters and themes he has narrated.
>
> But neither of these differences between the novelist and the scientist is very fundamental. Both men employ nonetheless typically human tactics. The fact that the scientist is ashamed to admit his fantasy probably accomplishes little more than to make it appear that he fits a popular notion of the way scientists think. And the fact that a novelist does not continue his project to the point of collecting data in support of his portrayals and generalizations suggests only that he hopes that the experiences of man will, in the end, prove him right without anyone's resorting to formal proof.
>
> But the brilliant scientist and the brilliant writer are pretty likely to end up saying the same thing – given, of course, a lot of time to converge upon each other. The poor scientist and the poor writer, moreover, fail in much the same way – neither of them is able to transcend the obvious. Both fail in their make-believe. (Kelly, 1979, p. 150)

References

Bannister, D. (1979). *Sam Chard.* Routledge & Kegan Paul. London.
Kelly, G. A. (1955). *The Psychology of Personal Constructs*, Vols. I and II. Norton: New York.
Kelly, G. A. (1979). *Clinical Psychology and Personality: The Selected Essays of George Kelly.* Ed. B. A. Maher. Krieger: New York.

Chapter 2

Applying PCP to constructs related to music

Miriam Ben-Peretz and Devorah Kalekin-Fishman

We will analyze the applicability of personal construct theory to the construal of music. Then we will point out some problems of data collection and discuss difficulties that arise in interpreting reactions to music from the perspective of personal constructs. In this connection we will cite some tentative solutions that are suggested by our research. Finally, we will claim that by exploring constructs in relation to music, we can provide material for extending the range of convenience of PCT and for eventually reconstructing our understanding of the theory.

Applicability of PCT to the construal of music

Downs (1976, p. 79) presents six of Kelly's major claims and applies them to the study of environmental knowing. He focuses on:

'1 The underlying philosophical assumption: constructive alternativism.
2 The central role of anticipation.
3 The nature of constructs.
4 Systems of constructs.
5 The role of time.
6 The *personal* nature of constructs.'

We will discuss these points in relation to an analysis of constructs derived from listening to music. The first five will underline the importance of a research project on music in describing individuals. The sixth, to our mind, can and should be formulated more flexibly, and we will elaborate on this further on.

1 The underlying philosophical assumption: constructive alternativism

In line with an ongoing discussion in the psychological and sociological literature about the influences of the 'higher' processes of cognition, affect, and sociation on perception (cf. Gibson, 1966; Hebb, 1949; Hilgard, 1951; Kaplan, 1978; Sekuler and Blake, 1985), Kelly holds that 'perceptions are anchored in cognitive constructs.' But constructs are designed to match a recalcitrant reality and therefore 'some constructions serve us better than others' (Kelly, 1977, p. 6).

Because PCT was elaborated in relation to the concerns of therapy, it is usually taken for granted that the events that may turn out to be recalcitrant and in need of reconstruction are those that arise in symmetric relations with others.

Since the construction of *intra*personal perceptual experience, however, guides the individual in coping with daily living, it makes sense to examine how constructs of perception function when, as in the aesthetic realm, the *perceptual experience* itself is the focus.

An awareness of such construals can contribute to an understanding of the self (Bannister, 1983), but the experience of aesthetic objects, and especially of music, is dependent on the content of a group reality (Lomax, 1968). Thus an awareness of constructs related to experiencing aesthetic objects can help the individual to understand the relation of his self and his group to that reality.

2 The central place of anticipation

Since a construct 'invariably expresses anticipation' (Kelly, 1955, p. 1089), it commits us 'to see fresh possibilities of relationships' (Kelly, 1977, p. 11). People are constrained to revise constructs when the fresh possibilities are not in tune with anticipations, even though there is a vested interest in having been accurate. For the tension between the inclination to preserve inappropriate constructs and the constraint of reality on infelicitous anticipations may induce a painful misreading of crucial life situations and generate a need for therapy.

The same kind of tension exists in music as gaps between the styles of sounding one has evolved constructs for and those styles of sounding that defy one's anticipations. Research (Jenne, 1977) and the everyday experience of the mass media transmitting music, bear witness to the degree to which the perception of music may arouse total involvement.

3 The nature of constructs

Constructs can only be understood if the discriminations a person makes and what is being 'grouped together as similar' are known (Downs, 1976, pp. 82–3). The emphasis on personal choice constitutes a call for openness and acceptance on the cognitive and the affective plane – a banner for education as well as therapy. The traditional view that aesthetic reactions are governed by interpretations of self is included. Although the congruence between PCT and common sense is not an overriding argument for its application to a study of the understanding of music, it is intuitively satisfying.

4 Systems of constructs

A further argument in favor of studying people's grasp of music with the help of PCT can be derived from the commonality, organization and the range of convenience corollaries of the Fundamental Postulate.[1]

There are grounds for asserting that an objective reality influences the organization and range of convenience of constructs of *all* the members of a given society. Sociological wisdom has it, moreover, that this reality is the product of collective human effort and skill. If we define aesthetic phenomena as variously organized resources combined into products that are designated for 'perceptual consumption', we can see that works of art are part of the recalcitrant reality that constrains constructs and behavior.

The hierarchical organization of music is a conscious common artifact of composers, players and adept listeners. Constructs generated on the basis of musical elements can, therefore, be expected to have a range of convenience that reflects the actual uses of music in a group's culture.

Socio-cultural change is reflected in beliefs, modes of production, and structures of interpersonal relationships. An issue of importance, then, is the question of whether such changes lead to changes in music and its construal (cf. McCoy, 1983), in the range of convenience of constructs related to music, and in their organization.

Empirical study can help determine whether constructs derived from relating to music are organized, and if so, whether they are related systematically to constructs used (a) in the interpretation of other experiences in the aesthetic realm or (b) in the systematic interpretation of interpersonal events.

5 The role of time

On the basis of an experimental study of the constancy of systems of constructs over time, Bannister and Mair (1968, p. 170) state tentatively that people have more stable systems through which to view objects than those through which to view people. They imply that modes of construing and perceiving correlate with inclinations towards a people- or an object-oriented vocation.

As an art that is perceivable only in performance, music has an ambiguous status. It is not clear *a priori* whether music is perceived as an 'object' or as a 'people' event. Can we, in other words, expect the construal of music to be more or less stable in the course of a lifetime?

Furthermore, what differences can be discerned between professionals and amateurs in their constructions of the experience of music. On the one hand, it is possible that professional musicians have a more stable system of constructs in regard to music (Sekuler and Blake, 1985). On the other hand, among non-professionals, constant selective exposure to music that is well known and known to be pleasurable may provide reinforcement and confirmation for some basic system of constructs that replication is never allowed to challenge.

6 The personal nature of the constructs

The Individuality Corollary is of major importance to a constructivist therapy. We think, however, that the axiom of the exclusively personal nature of constructs requires re-examination. For one thing, Kelly emphasized introspection and reflection to lead students to an understanding of the ways in which other people construe their conditions (Adams-Webber and Mancuso, 1985). There is evidence that PCT practitioners do, in fact, accept the assumption that constructs are likely to be common to groups (Duck, 1983) if only because researchers, therapists, and patients all inhabit similar worlds (Bannister, 1970).

Another problem is methodological. The Individuality Corollary is an assumption that involves researchers in a theoretical paradox. Whereas the use of PCT commits researchers to the holistic study of individuals, that is to a study of the entire person functioning in a socio-cultural milieu, the methodological stance of investigating constructs as purely 'individual' leads to general conclusions based on the rightly disdained *accumulative fragmentalism*.

Investigations of group constructs show that results of the grid test may usefully be interpreted in order to help groups clarify the problems that face them in the 'external' world (Honikman, 1976). Some researchers have discovered that constructs evolve in interaction (cf. O'Reilly, 1977; Salmon, 1970; Shotter, 1970). Findings cited relate to constructs of the external world. If, however, people inhabit similar internal cultural worlds as well, the exploration of these issues must be extended.[2]

Only a few researchers have used the repertory grid to characterize cultures. McCoy (1983) presents findings from a study of the constructs of one individual who has migrated. Orley (1976) describes 'the use of grid technique' in an anthropological study of supernatural beliefs, where a modified semantic differential was based on observations. Ben-Peretz has studied constructs that characterize the 'culture of teaching' (Ben-Peretz, 1984; Ben-Peretz and Katz, 1983).

Applying PCT to the study of groups

Basing ourselves on the view that interaction is the source of constructs, we will argue that construal is inevitably a social process.

By definition (Kelly, 1955), construal is a recurring *process* in which replication evokes re-examination of anticipations. This implies a re-evaluation of existing constructs and of the system as a whole. The Commonality Corollary (Bannister and Mair, 1968) acknowledges that people may be similar in their 'construction of experience', or identification of an event as a replication. Whether the 'construction' is identical with the verbal construct remains open. Yet even if we take similar verbal constructs to be only part of the construction, the labeling signals that there are social sources of the process of construal.

Labels for constructs are possible because people use language to constitute groups.[3] The mechanisms that make revisions of construct systems possible can be identified with a mechanism of lifelong socialization – sharing meanings. Investigations of constructs derived from relating to music can be seen as a means to demonstrate the viability of this interpretation.

Symbolic interaction: the mechanism of sharing meanings

Mead's (1934) theory of symbolic interaction describes how the self is formed and maintained. His model of socialization proposes a biologically shaped, but unavoidably social, mechanism for generating consensus. The theory also explains the constant re-evaluation of the components of a system of constructs.

In Mead's view, a physiologically based community of feeling makes interpersonal encounters *and* the development of mind possible. People participate in interaction by making 'gestures' – signals that can function in communication because they call out the same responses in the sender as in the receiver. The signaller plans a gesture and anticipates a probable reaction to it in her own mind. But the instinctive foundation of human behavior, which is beyond awareness, shapes the actual response and the actual message that the signal conveys.

Plans and anticipations are expressions of the 'me', the internalized gestures that accumulate in interaction with others. But in performance they are modified by the spontaneous, uncontrollable intervention of the 'I'. Throughout life the 'I' provides novel behaviors which are reinterpreted in interaction. Mutual gesturing is, therefore, both the means for preserving agreed-upon interpretations of reality, and the spur to introducing and sharing novel conceptions in a range of social situations.

Mead's theory of symbolic interaction explains how data elicited by the repertory test, or any other methodological translation of PCT, represent the range of constructs for the group reality in a determinable socio-cultural context. This has important implications for explicating aesthetic phenomena, which are cultural products.

Construal of music

Interpreting – thinking and feeling about – music is not independent of a group's shared language. Music is created for use by groups in religious ceremonies, at work, and as an expression of institutionalized beliefs (Blacking, 1970; Durkheim, 1965; Lomax, 1968). Modern media have revolutionized the amount of exposure to music and effected a homogenization of tastes (Adorno, 1981; Lowenthal, 1949; Silbermann, 1963). The big business of musical performances (Denisoff and Peterson, 1972) has a major impact on styles of living and the contents of thinking of people all over the world (Bontinck, 1974).

At the outset of our discussion, we underlined the importance of exploring the construal of *intra*personal events. On the basis of Mead's theory of symbolic interaction, we can claim that together with the characteristic sounds of music, the habitual signals of performance and response are gestures that construct *both* musical reality *and* the minds of the people who participate in it. Perceiving music is indeed an intrapersonal experience, but it derives from and contributes to the formation of a consensus of gesture, the essence of a communicated culture.

Studies of music have a variety of objectives. Much research focuses on its emotional meanings.[4] Recently, researchers adopting a cognitive view of meaning have paid increasing attention to the kinds of thinking that are important to musical composition and performance (Jackendoff and Lerdahl, 1983; Serafine, 1983). In these analyses, the focus is on rules of preference employed in listening rather than on didactic criteria (Jackendoff and Lerdahl, 1983, pp. 307–8). Using the repertory grid to study how people construe music would allow the layman/woman to express rules of preference directly and thus to instruct the researcher in the shared meanings of music in a given socio-cultural milieu.

It can be seen that PCT is eminently suitable for exploring the ways in which music is grasped. Yet to date, it has not been used to elicit constructs related to the experience of music or to music education.[5]

Difficulties in preparing repertory grid tests for musical elements

Among the difficulties that attend the choice of elements for a grid based on music are (1) the transience of music, (2) the fusion of elements in music, (3) limitations on eliciting verbal responses, (4) interpretation and validity of respondents' constructs, and (5) the degree to which responses can be constrained or encouraged.

1 The transience of music

It is a banal but decisive fact that having sounded, music disappears before a considered judgment can be made. This, of course, is true of any sound, including spoken language. Graphic representations of speech are, however, equivalent to the sound that is no longer heard when presented to adolescent and adult respondents. This is not the case with musical notation. Even those who know how to read music are not necessarily able to conjure up the sounds that the notes represent unless they have some mechanical prop at hand.

In deciding on what elements to include in the triads, therefore, the researcher must consider the fact that respondents will be required to be highly attentive in order to sort elements while listening. This is not 'natural' – for music often serves as an unobtrusive background.

2 The fusion of elements in music and compiling triads

Triads are compiled of elements that are categorized by a generally recognizable scheme. With music, the characteristics of such a scheme and its components are not yet known.

Music is identified holistically by pitches and durations, meter and rhythm, the quality (timbre) of required voices or instruments, speed and dynamics, as well as harmonic organization, accompaniment and distribution of voices. Which technical similarities are most significant is the issue and the object of the research. Moreover, defensible criteria for isolating dimensions of the performance (i.e. for deciding what features are construed as being heard) are elusive.

3 Limitations on eliciting verbal responses

Eliciting verbal responses to musical elements is problematic. Music may be construed with the aid of pre-verbal constructs, or grasped as an experience that does not require verbalization. So the request for a response in words may be embarrassing or inappropriate for some respondents.

Attempting to elicit constructs creates an anomalous situation. Constructs are usually elicited for elements that belong to the language of interpersonal gestures. There would seem to be a basic incompatibility, an organic mismatch, so to speak, between the community of intrapersonal 'gestures' relevant to the construing of music and that of language.

4 Interpretation and the validity of constructs

In dealing with constructs derived from relating to musical elements, the grid researcher must decide not only how to interpret the elicited constructs but also how to define their bias and validate an interpretation. Laymen's reactions are likely to be free of aspirations to meet criteria of social desirability. This has the advantage of indicating that any ambiguity disclosed is probably part of the respondent's repertoire of constructs.

It has disadvantages as well. At performances of music audiences move expressively and engage in ritualistic collective reactions: applause and, for some types of performances, shouting or sighing. Elicited constructs may thus be biased in the direction of ultra-conformity because of the perceived situation.

The professional musician, on the other hand, has a vocabulary designed to enable participation in the technical discourse of a community. Constructs deriving from such respondents may be biased toward demonstrating expertise.

5 The degree to which the instrument constrains/encourages responses

A grid based on musical elements must encourage respondents to find words, on the one hand, and prevent them from falling into the easy rut of phatic clichés, on the other. The area of the socio-cultural construction of the experience of music provides an opportunity to test repertory grids as a research tool.

Tentative solutions to the problems of research on the construal of music: some possible extensions of PCT

In this section we will note some tentative solutions that we have experimented with, and cite how we think this line of inquiry may lead to additional insights.

For probing systems of constructs shared by groups, school frameworks are a strategic point of departure. Society as a whole has a hand in constructing the school experience and in influencing the systems of constructs it fosters, not least by defining how students are to be allocated to educational organizations. Students who share classes are likely to develop group commonalities. The characteristics of shared commonalities are the research issue.

1 Cardinal questions are the optimal length of elements included in triads, the number of hearings needed, and the number of triads to include for sorting. In pre-tests it turned out that respondents (adults and adolescents) could easily sort a triad with elements that are 50 to 60 seconds in length after a single hearing. Sorting one triad at a time, respondents were attentive and efficient in sorting up to eight triads. Beyond that number, strain was sometimes evident.[6]
2 To define elements suitable for inclusion in the triads, we used

two different approaches. In one study, elements were defined in terms of the mode of performance of vocal music that was found in preliminary interviews to be popular and frequently heard on radio and television. In a study conducted among students in elementary and in secondary schools, elements were defined in terms of goals and topics of the music curriculum (Bruen, Ben-Peretz, Kalekin-Fishman and Radouan, in progress).

3 The problems associated with putting reactions to music into words were explored by varying the preparation for the repertory test. Some groups were simply handed the grid with written instructions for listening and sorting triads by number. Others were supplied with a written introduction in which sensory experiences of various kinds were described and a list of the titles of the songs included in the triads. We also studied the effects of oral preparation.
4 Our tentative solution for problems of interpretation was to correlate the elicited constructs with the uses of music on the media in the one study, and to school procedures in the other.

Findings demonstrated (a) that music is an event that can be construed and (b) that there are systems of constructs that characterize variously constituted groups (cf. Kalekin-Fishman, Bruen, and Ben-Peretz, 1986).

The general empirical aim of these studies has been to delineate the types of groups who share systems of constructs in relating to musical elements and who can thus be shown to share a communicable culture. A further aim is to discover relationships between group culture and 'idiosyncratic' personal constructs in the aesthetic realm. We also hope to be able to describe the developmental 'career' of constructs related to music. Beyond the specific questions lurks the general issue of whether systems of constructs related to music imply a specific way of constructing sound (Kalekin-Fishman, 1986).

Studies such as these can make a contribution to education. Recent debates on the content of the music curriculum have dealt with issues of hegemony and class on a level far removed from the concerns of students (Swanwick, 1984; Vulliamy and Shepherd, 1984). The application of PCT to the construal of music can help put these discussions in perspective by providing educators with information about the ways in which music is heard and interpreted by different student populations. Such information may also have wider educational applications. In clarifying the differences and the commonalities of the constructions that different social groups put on the experience of music, we may be shedding light on sources of mutual (mis)understanding below the levels of awareness (cf. Duck, 1982, p. 233).

In this paper, we have attempted to demonstrate that there is justification for taking the methodological and analytical risks that are necessary to carry forward our work on interpretations of music shared by groups. In a sense, this is a challenge to some of the basic orientations of PCT. Yet the confrontation of PCT with its own logic is, to our minds, part of the heritage of Kelly. We are obliged to construe and reconstrue PCT in the light of changes in reality and in our modes of perception. It is our hope that studies of how socio-cultural constructs related to music are shared by culturally defined groups, will make a modest contribution to the future development of personal construct theory.

Notes

1 The Commonality Corollary states, 'to the extent that one person employs a construction of experience which is similar to that employed by another, his psychological processes are similar to those of the other person' (quoted by Duck, 1982, p. 222). The Organization Corollary states, 'each person characteristically evolves, for his or her convenience in anticipating events, a construction system embracing ordinal relationships between constructs' (Kelly, 1955). The elaborated organization of constructs in hierarchical typifications enables people to anticipate experiences effectively. The Range of Convenience Corollary states, 'a construct is convenient for the anticipation of a finite range of events only' (Downs, 1976, p. 78).

2 Internal and external worlds have been examined for the most part among groups suffering from a social or a psychological pathology (Barton, Walton, and Rowe, 1976; Dingemans, Space, and Cromwell, 1983; Landfield, 1976; Space, Dingemans, and Cromwell, 1983).

3 Individual differences in the formation and the interpretation of construct systems do not account for the entire range of conceptual consensus that characterizes a language community. Saussure (1959) analyzed 'la langue', which is the normative language of the group, and 'la parole', the individual deviations in speech which are the key to the evolution of language.

4 Davitz (1964) carried out a series of experiments in order to test the capacities of people to recognize the intended mood of a musical piece. This type of research was in line with theories of emotion in music that were developed by Meyer (1957, 1973). It could also be justified by the philosophical view that music was a form of 'symbolic communication' (Langer, 1953; Goodman, 1968).
5 In the realm of aesthetics, the repertory test has been applied to elicit personal constructs related to the graphic arts. Cf. Benjafield, 1976; Benjafield and Adams-Webber, 1976; O'Hare and Gordon, 1976; Salmon, 1976.
6 This was true of one entire class – an oblique validation of our interpretation that constructions of the experience of music are shared.

References

Adams-Webber, J. and Mancuso, J. C. (eds.) (1985). *Applications of Personal Construct Theory.* New York: Academic Press.

Adorno, T. (1981). *Prisms.* Cambridge, MA: MIT Press.

Bannister, D. (1970). The logic of passion. In D. Bannister (ed.), *Perspectives of Personal Construct Theory.* London: Academic Press.

Bannister, D. (1983). Self in personal construct theory. In J. Adams-Webber and J. C. Mancuso (eds.), *Applications of Personal Construct Theory.* New York: Academic Press.

Bannister, D. and Mair, J. (eds.) (1968). *The Psychology of Personal Constructs.*

Barton, E. S., Walton, T. and Rowe, D. (1976). Using grid technique with the mentally handicapped. In P. Slater (ed.), *Explorations of Interpersonal Space*, Vol. 1. London: Wiley.

Benjafield, J. (1976). The 'golden rectangle': some new data. *American Journal of Psychology* 89(4), 737–43.

Benjafield, J. and Adams-Webber, J. (1976). The golden section hypothesis. *British Journal of Psychology* 67(1), 11–15.

Ben-Peretz, M. (1984). Kelly's theory of personal constructs as a paradigm for investigating teacher thinking. In R. Halkes and J. K. Olsen, (eds.), *Teacher Thinking.* Lisse: Swets & Zeitlinger.

Ben-Peretz, M. and Katz, S. (1983). From simplicity to complexity: differences in the construct systems of student teachers. Paper presented at the Fifth International Congress on Personal Construct Psychology, Boston.

Blacking, J. (1976). *How Musical is Man?* London: Faber.
Bontinck, I. (ed.) (1974). *New Patterns of Musical Behaviour*. Vienna:
Bruen, H., Ben-Peretz, M., Kalekin-Fishman, D. and Radouan, S. (in progress). Perception and interpretation of vocal music: constructs of students in Israeli-Jewish and Israeli-Arab schools.
Davitz, J. R. (1964). The communication of emotional meaning. In A. G. Smith (ed.), *Communication and Culture*. New York: Holt, Rinehart & Winston.
Denisoff, R. S. and Peterson, R. A. (eds) (1972). *The Sound of Social Change*. New York:
Dingemans, P. M., Space, L. G. and Cromwell, R. L. (1983). How general is the inconsistency in schizophrenic behavior? In J. Adams-Webber and A. C. Mancuso (eds.), *Applications of Personal Construct Theory*. New York: Academic Press.
Downs, R. M. (1976). Personal constructions of personal construct theory. In G. T. Moore and R. G. Golledge (eds.), *Environmental Knowing*. Stroudsberg, PA: Dowden, Hutchinson, & Ross.
Duck, S. (1983). The commonality corollary. In J. C. Mancuso and J. R. Adams-Webber (eds), *The Construing Person*. New York: Praeger.
Durkheim, E. (1965). *Elementary Forms of the Religious Life*. New York: Free Press.
Gibson, J. J. (1966). *The Senses Considered as Perceptual Systems*. Boston: Houghton Mifflin.
Goodman, N. (1968). *Languages of Art*. New York: Harper & Row.
Hebb, D. O. (1949). *The Organization of Behavior*. New York: Wiley.
Hilgard, E. R. (1951). The goals of perception. In R. R. Blake and G. V. Ramsey (eds.), *Perception: An approach to Personality*. New York: Ronald.
Honikman, B. (1976). Personal construct theory and environmental meaning: applications to urban design. In G. T. Moore and R. G. Golledge (eds.), *Environmental Knowing*. Stroudsberg, PA: Dowden, Hutchinson, & Ross.
Jackendoff, R. and Lerdahl, F. (1983). *A Generative Theory of Tonal Music*. Cambridge, MA: MIT Press.
Jenne, M. (1977). *Musik, Kommunikation, Ideologie*. Stuttgart: Klett.

Kalekin-Fishman, D. (1986). From the perspective of sound: towards an explication of the social construction of meaning, *Sociologia Internationalis* 24, Band, H.2, 171–95.
Kalekin-Fishman, D., Bruen, H., and Ben-Peretz, M. (1985). Perception and interpretation of vocal music: constructs of social groups, *International Review of Aesthetic and Sociology of Music* 17(1), 53–72.
Kaplan, S. (1978). Perception of an uncertain environment. In S. Kaplan and R. Kaplan (eds.), *Humanscape*. MA: Duxbury R.M.
Kelly, G. A. (1955). *The Psychology of Personal Constructs*, Vols. I and II. New York: Norton.
Kelly, G. A. (1977). The psychology of the unknown. In D. Bannister (ed.), *New Perspectives in Personal Construct Theory.* London: Academic Press.
Langer, S. (1953). *Feeling and Form: A Theory of Art.* New York: Knopf.
Lomax, A. (1968). *Folk Song Style and Culture.* Washington, DC: AAAS.
Lowenthal, L. (ed.) (1949). *Popular Culture.* New York: Knopf.
McCoy, M. M. (1983). Personal construct theory and methodology in intercultural research. In J. Adams-Webber and J. C. Mancuso (eds.), *Applications of Personal Construct Theory.* New York: Academic Press.
Mead, G. H. (1934). *On Social Psychology.* Chicago: University of Chicago Press.
Meyer, L. (1957). *Emotion and Meaning in Music.* Chicago: University of Chicago Press.
Meyer, L. (1973). *Explaining Music.* Berkeley: University of California Press.
O'Hare, D. and Gordon, I. E. (1976). An application of repertory grid technique to aesthetic measurement. *Perceptual and Motor Skills* 42, 1183–92.
O'Hare, D. (1981). Cognition, categorisation and aesthetic responses. In H. Bonarius, R. Holland, and S. Rosenberg (eds.), *Personal Construct Psychology.* London: Macmillan.
O'Reilly, J. (1977). The interplay between mothers and their children: a construct theory viewpoint. In D. Bannister (ed.), *New Perspectives in Personal Construct Theory.* London: Academic Press.
Orley, J. (1976). The use of grid technique in social anthropology.

In P. Slater (ed.), *Explorations of Intrapersonal Space*. London: Wiley.

Salmon, P. (1970). A psychology of personal growth. In D. Bannister (ed.), *Perspectives of Personal Construct Theory*. London: Academic Press.

Saussure, F. de (1959). *Course in General Linguistics*. New York: Philosophical Library.

Sekuler, R. and Blake, R. (1985). *Perception*. New York: Knopf.

Serafine, M. L. (1983). Cognition in music. *Cognition* 14, 119–183.

Shotter, J. (1970). Men, the man-makers: George Kelly and the psychology of personal constructs. In D. Bannister (ed.), *Perspectives of Personal Construct Theory*. London: Academic Press.

Silbermann, A. (1963). *The Sociology of Music*. London: Routledge & Kegan Paul.

Space, L. G., Dingemans, P. M., and Cromwell, R. L. (1983). Self-construing and alienation in depressives, schizophrenics, and normals. In J. Adams-Webber and A. C. Mancuso (eds), *Applications of Personal Construct Theory*. New York: Academic Press, 365–78.

Swanwick, K. (1984). Problems of a sociological approach to pop music. *British Journal of Sociology of Education* 5, 1, 49–56.

Vulliamy, G., and Shepherd, J. (1984). Sociology and music education: A response to Swanwick. *British Journal of Sociology of Education* 5, 1, 57–76.

Chapter 3

Music and personal constructs

Eric Button

To set the scene for this paper I feel I need to explain how it has come about. For some years I have had regrets over not choosing to pursue music as a career. I would often say to myself and others, 'I wish I had carried on with music'. Eventually, I came to recognise that I didn't need to go on *wishing* and that I wasn't too old to start *doing* something now. I have thus begun to 'elaborate' on the musical pole of my psychologist–musician construct in the here and now. This is taking me in interesting directions, one of which is to explore ways of combining psychology and music. In fact, I am excited at possibilities for making more use of the arts in general, but I would particularly like to share with you my thoughts about links between music and that other interest of mine, personal construct theory.

To my knowledge there is no existing construct theory literature on music. Nor have I yet found any references to personal construct theory in the literature on music, but on delving in the latter one finds many echoes of a constructivist position. A major theme which runs through such writings is the importance of *form* in our appreciation of music. For example, Joseph Machlis (1979) states:

> A basic principle of musical form is repetition and contrast, which achieves both unity and variety. The one ministers to man's joy in the familiar and to his need for reassurance. The other satisfies his equally strong craving for the challenge of the unfamiliar. (p. 47)

The business of construing is thus clearly at work in the musical context and presumably playing its customary role in our anticipatory processes. When a person listens to music he or she will thus be looking for similarity and contrast. One common way in which composers achieve this melodically is by the use of 'ternary form', which embraces Kelly's affinity for triads. Typically, there is an A–B–A or A–A–B–A structure in which a fairly short phrase (A) is heard with a pause, typically followed by its repetition (more or less identical). Next, a contrasting phrase (B) is heard, and finally there is a return to the original. Such forms are so familiar to most of us that we easily recognise the musical 'constructs', although, of course, we don't necessarily share the same meanings. In contemporary 'serious' music, however, perhaps because of it's very newness, the form is not thrust at the listener and the music requires more active construction on the part of the listener. Repetition–contrast remains as a basic principle, but it is less obvious and predictable, with irregularity of the essence, so much so that many people find it unpalatable. But art moves on with time and it would not truly reflect life if it only presented us with forms (or constructs) which we already know.

Musical experience, like all experience, can lead to what Kelly called 'elaboration', either through increasing *definition* or *extension*. From a musical point of view we may see choice exercised in a definitive way by the repetition of themes, rhythms, harmonies, and so on. Some repetition is indeed necessary for us to identify the theme, but typically in music, repetition is not identical. The basic musical idea is presented in a number of guises. In the development section in sonata form, for example, the principle themes are presented in a number of different keys, but there are a variety of other techniques of varied repetition, like differing pitch, rhythm, instrument, and so on. In all these cases, however, underlying features recur. Furthermore, in the case of sonata form this development is followed by the 'recapitulation' in which the basic theme is returned to in more or less its original form. This repetition with a difference can be seen to be analogous to non-musical action. For example, someone seeking to present a sporting image may engage in a variety of energetic or competitive pursuits, but which all seek to confirm the common theme of 'sporting'. I am suggesting, therefore, that a major role for much musical activity is in the *confirmation*, mainly of identity, but also of beliefs, values, moods, achievements, and so on; for example,

'I appreciate Bach', 'This is a sad day', 'I'm a jazz person'. Such confirmation is not just individualism but also has a social role in establishing or confirming what a group of people have in common. This is vividly demonstrated by national anthems, which remind us that our country still exists, what it stand for and that we are part of it.

But we would soon get bored with music that was entirely predictable. John Booth-Davies (1978), although making no explicit reference to personal construct theory, makes the point that 'It is this process of confirmation or disconfirmation of expectancies which is at the centre of musical experience' (p. 68). He goes on to assert, 'Listening to a tune is therefore not a passive process of mere reception, but one of active construction' (p. 82). Booth-Davies suggests that our musical preferences tend towards intermediate degrees of predictability or what he refers to in information theory terms as 'complexity'. In other words, music which is either too familiar or too unfamiliar will not be appealing – with the emphasis on personal interpretation as determining what is meant by familiar. This accords with our experience of even our favourite piece of music becoming less appealing if repeated too much. If we are not just trying to stand still in life, we will need some contrast: fast music may lead to the slower; sad songs at concerts are often followed by something cheerful; highly rhythmic music may be followed by more freely flowing music.

It seems to me, therefore, that there may be two broad kinds of way in which people use music. One is as a kind of confirmation: here we know what to expect, in fact we deliberately look for it – we dig out the record, we sing the song, we whistle the tune. In a sense there is a kind of reaching *back* – validating something we've been through before. In contrast, we may also wish to reach *forward* with the exciting prospect of 'extension' or broadening of our horizons. The pleasure perhaps comes from the anticipation of going somewhere new, something just beyond. So, are these two aspects as different as they seem? Perhaps not, since it is feasible that both alternatives are dependent on our degree of certainty/uncertainty: when faced with too much certainty we may look for something new from music, but following much uncertainty we may go back or stay with familiar music.

I suggest that such musical choices don't just stand in isolation and may reflect our efforts to make sense of things at a more general level. A healthy balance may be reflected by the ability to go back *and* forward with music at different times. In addition, he or she may be able to tolerate a range of different types of music. A person who has severely constricted his or her world, however, may opt for only one kind of music, perhaps reflecting a particular mood. One of my patients seemed to have chosen this kind of course: for her it was important to be *serious* and she steadfastly rejected any music which could be regarded as *frivolous*. I don't imply here that there is anything unhealthy about having musical preferences. To the contrary. At any point in time a person will be seeking to 'elaborate' or express some particular theme. Muscially, this will mean that right now we may have a favourite song, composer, mood or style of music. At the same time, however, what we are receptive to musically now may not be the same tonight, tomorrow morning or next year.

This leads me on to the point that an essential ingredient of music is movement. Music is always going somewhere. This is most powerfully revealed in relation to the movement towards a climax. We often know what's coming but, much as in sex, it's the build-up that makes it all worthwhile. The musical content at the peak would have little effect without that which precedes it. Similarly, the musical climax needs to be followed by a coming down, and this may be in pitch, loudness or speed. Just as in life in general, of course, the climax forms just one small part of a piece of music, and we see continuous movement in a much more general and variable way. It is in melody that movement is most obvious with its succession of rises and falls, usually with some degree of pattern, so that one is often able to roughly anticipate where the music is going, although we are sometimes surprised, if not teased, by delays and diversions, all of which add to the experience of the music.

In emphasising movement we are inevitably drawn towards Kelly's 'Dimensions of Transition' and the question of emotion. Emotion is a controversial issue in music. Although there has never been a question about the emotional potential of music, there have been changing fashions in the extent to which composers seek to elicit it, as opposed to a more intellectual approach. Most current authorities on music, however, are at pains to emphasise that good music is not just about the evocation of 'the passions'. Not that emotion is unimportant in music but that it is a by-product of *form*:

Great music is great because of its beauty of form and because of the emotions experienced by listening to it, which are largely a function of its beauty of form. A piece of music by Mozart may pass through a variety of moods which will be reflected in the listener but his delight and excitement will be mainly derived from Mozart's masterly handling of the form. This is what makes Mozart a greater composer than Tchaikowsky.' (Bacharach and Pearce, 1977, p. 21)

This rapprochement of the cognitive and emotional aspects of music is, of course, consistent with a construct theory approach. Furthermore, it is also known that although there is a certain amount of agreement about broad musical parameters influencing emotion (especially speed and pitch), wide individual differences in emotional response have been reported to the same music. Thus it is reasonable to suppose that the emotional impact of a piece of music is a reflection of how the listener construes it. The Kellian position, elaborated by Mancuso and Hunter (1983), is that emotion occurs when we fail to anticipate. I must confess to not being entirely happy with this position, since it seems to me that we often feel things when we anticipate having an expectation fulfilled. McCoy (1981) touches on this when she states 'positive emotions are those which follow validation of construing. Negative emotions follow unsuccessful construing' (p. 97). To my mind, however, each of these authors overemphasise the role of validation *after* an event is construed. What seems to me to be the crucial aspect is a degree of *uncertainty* as we *anticipate* some change in what we can expect. Take, for example, the lover (or potential lover) who carefully selects a record to set the scene for what he or she hopes to follow. I argue that it is because there is an element of doubt surrounding this situation that these preliminaries are gone through: I wonder if we all take this amount of trouble once the relationship appears to be confirmed.

A comment that has been made repeatedly about the emotional aspect of music is its link with associations from the past. When music from the past evokes some sort of emotion in us, I suggest this is because the events which surrounded this music were associated with a degree of uncertainty. It is also possible that musical past can create an emotional response in the present because of the doubts it casts on our present construing. Like me, I'm sure you've sometimes had an uneasy feeling when listening to music of the past which perhaps creates 'threat' by reminding us of constructs we thought we'd outgrown.

Another way of looking at such uncertainty is in terms of *transition*, a concept central to Kelly's view of emotion. Within a piece of music there will be a number of points of change, where the music moves from one set of expectations to another. At these points, such as the junction between movements of a symphony, the listener is in a state of transition requiring a change of expectations. Sometimes the change is extremely abrupt and startling if not disturbing, but more commonly the composer eases the listener into the new mood or theme. It could be argued that it is at times of transition that the vulnerabilities of a person's construct system are most exposed, and there may be therapeutic potential in using music as an indirect way of tackling such difficulties. By experimenting with the experience of changes in musical key, speed, loudness, and so on, a person may become more prepared for transitions in his or her life in general.

Much of what has been discussed so far has revolved around the personal, individual act of listening, performing or composing music. At the social level, I have already referred to the way in which anthems have a role to play in validating a national identity, values, and so on. But music does not just symbolise a nation: take, for example the protest songs of Joan Baez, rugby songs, *Auld Lang Syne*. There are numerous instances of this kind, all of which perhaps illustrate Kelly's Commonality Corollary. Like individual behaviour, we can regard group music as forming an elaborative choice – to extend or to define. A group may be emerging or expanding, and in such circumstances music seems to suggest where the group is going or it may be that the group is wishing to remind itself and others what it is. This was dramatically expressed in the recent British miner's strike by the theme tune *Here We Go*. It is my contention that there is an audience for much of our behaviour and the group which sings together seems to be both defining the group but also stating who is *not* part of the group, so that music can be at the forefront of conflict between groups, as vividly evidenced in war.

It can be argued, however, that the most fundamental feature of being social is the ability to enter other people's worlds – to construe their construction processes in Kellian terms. Therapeutic interventions such as Landfield and Rivers' (1975) Interpersonal Transaction Group, explicitly attempt to improve this aspect of a person's construing in their use of techniques like 'rotating dyads'. Music could easily be utilised in this kind of context by inviting the participants to find out about each others' musical experience. For example, the persons in a dyad could be asked to share with the other their favourite song or some other piece of music. Later, they could move on to more differentiated features like each being asked to give an example of a sad, frightening or exciting piece of music. This could be extended to 'music that most represents the way you feel right now' or 'the way you hope to feel by the end of the session'. Both the experience of similarity and difference of musical construction could contribute to an improved ability to understand other people. In the experimental workshop I ran with about twenty people at Cambridge, we began with dyadic experience and later moved on to group exercises, and I shall never forget our ending with a group Amen, which I think demonstrated that we had been able to come together as a group through music.

Having reached Amen I should probably stop, but I would like to add a final comment. I have tried to demonstrate ways in which our musical experience reflects our construing processes in general. It seems to me that we may learn a lot about psychological processes by exploring how people relate to music. I would also like to encourage those involved in helping relationships to experiment with music. It could help . . . it could also be fun!

References

Bacharach, A. L. and Pearce, J. R. (eds.) (1977). *The Musical Companion*. Rev ed. Gollancz: London.

Booth-Davies, J. (1978). *The Psychology of Music*. Hutchinson: London.

Landfield, A. W. and Rivers, P. C. (1975). An introduction to interpersonal transaction and rotating dyads. *Psychotherapy: Theory, Research and Practice* 12, 366–74.

McCoy, M. (1981). Positive and negative emotion: a personal construct theory interpretation. In H. Bonarius, R. Holland and S. Rosenberg (eds.), *Personal Construct Psychology: Recent Advances in Theory and Research*. Macmillan: London.

Machlis, J. (1979). *Introduction to Contemporary Music*. 2nd ed. Dent: London.

Mancuso, J. and Hunter, K. (1983). Anticipation, motivation, or emotion: the Fundamental Postulate after twenty-five years. In J. Adams-Webber and J. C. Mancuso (eds.), *Applications of Personal Construct Theory.* Academic Press: Toronto.

Chapter 4

A repertory grid study of response to poetry

David Miall

I have been working on two problems. First, what are the processes by which a reader comes to understand a poem. Second, what does it mean to say, as Kelly puts it in the Fundamental Postulate, that we anticipate events. These concerns may appear at first sight to be rather far apart, but I shall try to show that an examination of the first leads to some interesting problems in relation to the second. The type of anticipation which I have observed to be most dominant in readers of poems is emotional anticipation. When a reader is trying to understand a poem which is unfamiliar to her, the emotions tend to take over and direct the cognitive processes of response. Thus one major (but largely unconsidered) way in which we anticipate is through the emotions.

There are two problems here, then, with a common research focus on the emotions. In personal construct theory Kelly deliberately abandoned emotion as a distinct construct and has since been erroneously criticized for offering an exclusively cognitive theory of man, as Bannister (1977, p. 26) showed. But ambiguities remain, and several views of the place of emotion in PCP have since been proposed. McCoy (1977) categorized each emotion by its relation to the individual's core and non-core construct systems, showing how each major emotion can be seen as a consequence of a validation or invalidation of these systems. Katz (1984) has argued that an emotion is the psychophysiological effect of invoking a 'primitive' construct – that is, one of the biologically given constructs that Katz sees as precursors of the personal construct system. Another role for emotion is that proposed by Mancuso and Hunter (1980), who assert that 'Emotional enactments are overt declarations of failure to anticipate'. To trace the process of construing a poem, however, is to emerge with a more constructive view of emotion in which emotion is neither the effect of an act of construal, nor the result of a failure in construing. In the context of response to poetry, emotion is the sign of a construct system in transition, but emotion also anticipates and helps determine the direction of transition. In this sense emotion is productive, a form of thinking.

Emotion appears to direct response to a text under conditions of uncertainty. In some cases this is obviously true. Readers sometimes balk at a new poem, overcome by a negative emotion that causes them to jump outside the domain of the poem, such as resistance, anxiety or dislike. Here the emotion may well be explained as a consequence of construct invalidation – a construct such as 'I am a successful reader of poems'. Emotional blocking may also occur more generally in learning experiences, when learners fail or opt out. Such emotion is associated with constructs outside the new domain. More interesting would be to show that such learners are unable to cope with uncertainty because they cannot develop constructive emotions specific to the new domain. I shall be arguing, therefore, that emotion is not just appropriate or inappropriate to reading a poem or learning in a new domain: where response is successful in conditions of uncertainty, it is emotions that take the primary role in cognitive functioning. The emotions are domain-specific, and they provide the vehicle of anticipation for the construct system which is to be developed.

I begin by describing some studies I have done with readers of poetry which show such effects. These have taken place within the framework of personal construct psychology; some have made use of repertory grid technique. I then look briefly at some implications of seeing emotions as anticipatory and constructive, and point to the significance of this for methods of teaching and learning.

Response to poetry

There are two main ways of using construct theory to study readers' responses to literary works. One can compare responses to whole texts or make a detailed examination of the intrinsic structure of one text. In the first category, O'Hare (1981), for example, has used grid technique to examine the effect on response of stylistic modifications to a number of poems. Grid technique also offers a method of exploring the extent to which individuals agree or differ in their experience of literary texts. Applebee (1976), in research on children's responses to a range of stories, found an increasing measure of agreement with age on construing stories.

But my concern has been with the second type of study, where one looks in detail at one text. I wanted to trace the structure of a text in the responses of readers, and at the same time to track the experiential components of such responses. If literary texts have a determinate structure, this should be apparent in the responses of a group of readers; on the other hand, readers vary in the extent to which a text calls on their own experiences and memories. If we knew more about the relationship between these two aspects, we should be able to teach literature more effectively; our findings might also assist in developing a general model of discourse processing. Poetry offers a particularly interesting challenge because of the density and ambiguity of most poems. Poetry is thus an important test case for any model of response one might wish to propose.

Construct theory suggests that we see a poem first as a small-scale construct system. An analysis of a poem can be made in terms of the constructs out of which it is built, showing the relationships between subordinate and superordinate constructs. Poems often take particular ideas and develop them in an argument: this can be seen, for example, as the permeability of a construct applying to a progressively wider range of material across a poem. In various ways poems mirror the structure in our own thought and the kind of discoveries we make in it: that is why we read them.

Poems, of course, do not exist without readers, but as a teacher of literature I am aware that poems are often understood poorly or inappropriately. The extent to which a reader grasps the structure and argument of a poem then becomes a question about the reader's construct system. Do the reader's constructs adequately match those that the poem appears to offer? Or, more interestingly, when the poem presents difficulties and the reader is uncertain about its meaning, what processes take place in her construct system as she progressively comes to understand the poem?

I have some evidence on this from students' written accounts. I have given students an unfamiliar poem and asked them to write down all the thoughts they have as they begin to formulate ideas about the poem's meaning. It is possible to analyse this material for its systematic features. In one sample of sixteen written responses to several poems, for example, the number of references to emotion terms, constructs and direct quotations from the poem, were counted in each third of a student's writing. An analysis of variance yielded a significant interaction effect between type of reference and stage of response, $F(2,60) = 3.74$, $p < 0.05$. Comparing the first and last thirds of the responses, emotion terms decreased by 49 per cent, and quotations by 31 per cent, but constructs increased by 28 per cent. Thus there are more references to emotion at first by comparison with later stages, suggesting that emotion constructs prepare for the conceptual constructs, which tend to take over the response. There are also signs of a progressive emergence of superordinate constructs during the response, and a moving away from the immediate surface details of the poem.

Something about the general processes of individual response can be learned through this method. It is less fitted, however, to detecting the systematic features of a poem itself – in so far as these exist. Poems are intrinsically powerful texts: they probably possess a structure to which all readers will be sensitive to some degree. I can take a poem and form specific hypotheses about what this structure is; but I then need to elicit readings of the poem from a number of readers in such a way that the hypotheses can be tested. For this purpose the repertory grid is well suited. Students are asked to read the poem and work on their understanding of it for a week or two. They are then given a set of specific features in the poem and asked to elicit the constructs they are using to understand and distinguish between those features. The parts of the poem are the elements for a repertory grid; the students provide their own constructs. A commonality among the readings is obtained in this way so that data from a number of grids can be compared to see what regularities there are in line with the hypotheses.

A grid used in this way facilitates the individuality of response, since each student applies her own constructs to understanding the poem. It is possible to follow up interesting clues in this respect by interviewing students and tracking constructs back to their experiential basis – the grid helps to bring to light some of the less conscious determinants of response, the half-forgotten memories and feelings which the poem has drawn upon. A map of the unique features of each individual response can be sketched in this way through a semi-structured conversational technique, focusing on the analysed grid.

Second, a group of grids on one poem can capture some of the common features of response, those due to the intrinsic structure of the poem itself. For example, in one study (Miall, 1985) twenty-one grids on one poem, Coleridge's 'Frost at Midnight', were elicited. Each student was given eight elements from the poem (words or phrases) and completed a grid with eight constructs. A dyadic method of elicitation was used, with a five-point rating scale. In choosing the elements, I nominated eight which I felt were related in significant ways in terms of the argument of the poem, and of which I expected four would be judged as negative and four as positive. When students had completed the grids they were asked to indicate whether there was a negative–positive valency in their constructs: from their replies it was clear that almost all their constructs could be seen in this way. Thus an overall measure of the ratings they provided for each element could be computed, indicating where each element came on a negative–positive scale. An analysis of variance showed that there were consistent differences between the element ratings, $F(7,140) = 10.1$, $p < 0.001$, and a significant difference in particular between the ratings for the negative and positive groups of elements, $t(19) = 4.5$, $p < 0.001$.

I also expected that students who noticed a certain negative quality implicit in one element in the second line of the poem would be more likely to recognize this quality in another element halfway through the poem. I saw the relationship between these two elements as one of the key aspects of the poem's structure. This prediction was also confirmed: a significant correlation between the ratings for these elements was obtained, $r(19) = 0.67$, $p < 0.001$. This meant that students varied consistently in the judgments they made about the two elements. Some of the students were able to tell me about the relationship they noticed in these elements during the interviews.

There was thus a measurable commonality in this group of responses. By commonality, however, is meant not that the students were arriving at the same judgments about the elements of the poem. There is more than one way to read a poem. As the correlation data suggested, it is in the systematic relationship between its elements that the structure of a poem becomes apparent. The poem, as it were, determines that two or more of its elements shall be seen as related; but the reader brings her own experience to colour in the nature of that relationship.

Kelly's Commonality Corollary anticipates this finding (Kelly, 1955, p. 90). Commonality, said Kelly, lies in the similarity of the psychological processes not the experiences as such. In terms of a poem, this means that the structure of the poem channellizes the reading process in ways that are superordinate to the interpretative constructs applied by readers. The commonality I have been describing emerged at the level of emotional structuring, since it was the evaluative negative–positive discriminations that enabled this structure to be identified. But I suspect that this commonality is usually an emotional one in the case of literary response, and that what we mean by literary structure reflects an emotional process in which relationships between parts of a text are first established and then subjected to cognitive verification. The data from the protocol analysis I mentioned earlier, in which emotion appeared to prepare for cognitive constructs, points to a process of this kind. In this context it seems to make sense to say that emotions are the anticipatory aspect of constructs.

Emotions: anticipatory constructs

All mental life consists of constructs, but as Kelly was the first to note, some constructs are more conscious and verbalizable than others. The readers of poetry I have studied tended, at an early stage in response, to operate with the less conscious and more emotional types of construct. Similarly, in the grid responses to the Coleridge poem, the structural relationship between the elements of the poem was emotional rather than cognitive. While the grid itself appears to offer a type of static cross-section of the response process, the grid can be used to recover something of the dynamic processes involved in response; in fact, the elicitation and subsequent discussion of a grid appears to reflect aspects of the normal response process, in which intuitions about meaning are made increasingly articulate and conscious.

What does it mean to say, then, that emotions are the anticipatory aspect of constructs? As I have a special context in mind a distinction is necessary here. When Kelly spoke of anticipation he primarily meant the anticipation of events. Construing is carried on, he said, 'so that future reality may be better represented' (Kelly, 1955, p. 49). We anticipate an event through those features of the event that have been experienced before; that is, we abstract from events features which are likely to recur. Thus anticipation is a cognitive activity which builds on features of existing experience:

> When one abstracts replicated properties in the events he has already experienced, it becomes possible for him to chart events to come in terms of these same properties. . . . What one predicts is not a fully fleshed-out event, but simply the common intersect of a certain set of properties. If an event comes along in which all the properties intersect in the prescribed way, one identifies it as the event he expected. (Kelly, 1955, p. 121)

Now, understanding a poem is not an event in these terms. What is being anticipated is the elaboration of a construct system – that is, a set of constructs that will be sufficient to grasp the main structure and meaning of the poem. Readers who do this successfully appear to follow a strategy, directed by the first emotions of response. The strategy is not often a very articulate or conscious one; rather, the reader begins to elicit constructs closely related to those details of the poem that have an immediate emotional resonance, and in this way she obtains a first intuitive sense of what the poem may be about. Those emotions, as the grid study suggests, are likely to capture important aspects of the poem's structure, even though the reader at this stage has no conscious grasp on structure. Put another way, the poem, through its effects on the emotions, is organizing those aspects of the reader's construct system which it requires for its interpretation. In a sense, as Auden used to say, it is not we that read a poem so much as the poem that reads us.

To understand a poem, then, is to expect that some significant part of one's construct system will be reorganized under the influence of the poem. This process is directed by the first emotions of response, through which the structure of the poem is anticipated. We should thus see emotions as emergent constructs that direct the construing process in conditions of uncertainty. Such emotions organize response in advance of conscious understanding and provide a strategy for keeping cognitive processes on line. Emotions in this context also tend to be holistic, relating constructs across domains in service of the unity of the poem, although the extent to which this happens will obviously depend on the quality of the poem.

The view of response to poetry I have developed here implies a reconsideration of the learning process in literature classes (and perhaps in other contexts). In the conventional learning situation, the lecture or seminar, it is the teacher's constructs about the text which are likely to dominate the discussion. This is to offer the student a goal for her response before she has developed a strategy of her own for reaching it; in addition, it is the first emotions of response which are most likely to be swamped or distorted by the teacher's more powerful construct system (Miall, 1986). This does not mean that we must abolish teaching, but it suggests that when a student first encounters a poem we should enable her to develop the anticipatory implications of her response independently of the teacher. Our aim should be to provide the reader, drawing on her emotional resources, with an earlier and more efficient grasp on poetic structure during the comprehension process; this would also enable her to become more aware of the experiential source of her responses to a poem.

In conclusion, personal construct theory provides a powerful set of heuristics for studying responses to poetry and poetic structure. In this report I have sketched out my main working hypothesis and some of the first tentative findings that support it. A more detailed and searching test of the anticipatory role of emotions in relation to the constructs of literary response will now be required.

References

Applebee, A. N. (1976). Children's construal of stories and related genres as measured with repertory grid techniques. *Research in the Teaching of English* 10, 226–38.

Bannister, D. (1977). The logic of passion. In D. Bannister (ed.), *New Perspectives in Personal Construct Theory*. London: Academic Press.

Katz, J. O. (1984). Personal construct theory and the emotions: an interpretation in terms of primitive constructs. *British Journal of Psychology* 75, 315–27.

Kelly, G. A. (1955). *The Psychology of Personal Constructs.* New York: Norton.

Mancuso, J. C. and Hunter, K. V. (1983). Anticipation, motivation, or emotion: the fundamental postulate after twenty-five years. In J. Adams-Webber and J. C. Mancuso (eds.), *Applications of Personal Construct Theory.* Toronto: Academic Press.

McCoy, M. M. (1977). A reconstruction of emotion. In D. Bannister (ed.), *New Perspectives in Personal Construct Theory.* London: Academic Press.

Miall, D. S. (1985). The structure of response: a repertory grid study of a poem. *Research in the Teaching of English* 19, 254–68.

Miall, D. S. (1986). Authorizing the reader. *English Quarterly* 19, 186–95.

O'Hare, D. (1981). Cognition, categorization and aesthetic response. In H. Bonarius, R. Holland, and S. Rosenberg (eds.) (1981). *Personal Construct Psychology: Recent Advances in Theory and Practice.* London: Macmillan.

Chapter 5
Fragmentation

Peter Stringer

This paper was delivered as part of a symposium, 'Thirty Years On', to acknowledge that people were still offering their own personal experiences and reactions to PCP thirty years after the publication of Kelly's original two volumes. It is therefore offered in the form of a personal biography.

For various reasons I was unable to prepare a proper paper for the Cambridge congress. The best that I could manage was to assemble some fragments of other texts. They did, at least, go some way to showing where I stood, between social psychology and personal construct psychology. They were intended to point to an intersection of interests. I cannot vouch for their authenticity. Anyway, they are for readers to use for their own purposes. Because they are fragments, I regret that all the references are missing.

I

The first fragment is allegedly a part of a paper given by me in 1984, at a conference in the Netherlands – 'allegedly' because the theme of the conference was 'The Unity of Psychology' – as unconvincing a theme as one could hope to find. What follows is a free translation from the Dutch, in which several small errors in the original have been corrected.

A good beginning is the tradition of action research, which Lewin is usually taken as having initiated. In its less manipulative forms it has often entailed a conscious and willing commitment on the part of subjects to the action goals of the research. More recently, a rather different path has been illustrated by Toch and the Rapoports. Toch's (1960) study *Violent Men* adopted a 'peer interview' technique. Important elements of the Rapoports' *Dual Career Families* were the development of a more fully interactive relationship than usual between members of the research group and the family being studied, and an ultimate collaborative search for consensus between parties in the analysis and presentation of research results.

In 1972 Harré and Secord introduced their anthropocentric approach to social psychology. Ethogenics shares with personal construct psychology a considerable respect for ethnographic material. Later, in 1978, Harré made a brief proposal for a 'participatory psychology' for which he would explicitly use 'the kind of explorations of creative cognitive activity proposed by Kelly'.

Developments such as these in the late 1960s and early 1970s were, I believe, a part of the *Zeitgeist* which included the student movement, a growth in participatory politics, and a wish to demythologise professional expertise. My own ideas were stimulated in part by doing research on participatory politics. In 1974, and later in *New Perspectives in Personal Construct Psychology*, I suggested a more participatory approach to research as well, which was to have advantages not only socio-political but also methodological and moral.

At the same time one of my PhD students, Susan Wilkinson, decided to extend her research on the initiation and development of dyadic relationships to include herself as a part of the relationship pattern under study. More recently (in 1978), Perry has also expressed some general ideas towards a triadic psychology. Both Wilkinson and Perry were working within personal construct psychology.

In a series of papers written during the 1970s the Rumanian psychologist Mamali outlined the possibilities of a democratised form of research, in which the subject may actively participate in the choice of research question and of research approach, and in data collection, analysis and interpretation. One of Mamali's influences was Galtung.

In 1981 the source book of so-called 'new paradigm research', *Human Inquiry*, edited by Reason and Rowan, included a number of examples of a changed relationship between researcher and researched – though in its totality the book gives an unnecessarily humanistic flavour to this enterprise, and offers rather few concrete examples of research.

Perhaps a better source of inspiration as to how to develop new relations between psychologists and non-psychologists can be found outside the discipline in the 'participatory research network'. This movement works, for example, through such organisations as the International Council for Adult Education in Toronto or the United Nations Research Institute for Social Development in Geneva. It is active particularly in the Third World.

These few academic examples – and it is academic values which especially bedevil the researcher–researched relation – could no doubt be added to by people here today, not least from clinical and other forms of practice. The point to be made now is only that there has been a distinct growth of interest in recent years in permitting non-psychologists to determine the psychological agenda; in treating the social relation between professional and lay psychologists as, in different ways, of the essence.

Such an endeavour will, of course, meet accusations that it turns its back on objectivity. The interests of the lay psychologist are not properly scientific. They are more immediate and temporary than the permanent, ahistorical framework of reality which science claims to establish. A determined effort to unify the interests of professional and lay person can lead to relativism.

This may not be so serious an outcome. The debate between objectivism and relativism has a long tradition in Western culture. Psychology has been stubbornly single-minded in refusing to explore the possible advantages of relativism. The difficulty increases when relativism becomes radical. This happens, for example, when the content of psychology is localised in the constructions achieved by a professional and lay psychologist through transactions which serve their particular interests as a dyad. This is liable to happen in a thorough practice of personal construct psychology. The focus of meeting is the construction of one another's construct systems. The unified aspect of psychological knowledge achieved is limited to what these two people achieve in their particular context. This is radical relativism.

Any attempt to generalise one's way out of the situation will involve a superordination of the interests of one party. Typically, it will be the psychologist who will attempt to generalise his knowledge, for the purposes of scientific communication. In doing so he appropriates the psychological world of the other for his own purposes. Two allegedly distinct forms of psychological discourse are thus constructed, with quite different status and power attributed to them. This is a reflexive problem for social psychology.

I believe that many personal construct psychologists are radical relativists – that is, those who work outside the universities and work more practically. The pity is that they do not seem to feel free to communicate their relativistic knowledge to others. Objectivist norms dominate our attitudes towards making knowledge public. As a result we have had far too few opportunities for closely and systematically examining the achievements of relativistic psychology.

It is clear that the opposition between objectivism and relativism is a common factor in the splits which disunify psychology. A way *Beyond Objectivism and Relativism* has recently been suggested by Bernstein. He sees in the writings of Gadamer, Habermas, Rorty and Arendt, 'central themes of dialogue, conversation . . . and communal judgement . . . that can take place when individuals confront each other as equals and participants'. The 'way beyond' lies in 'cultivating the types of dialogical communities in which phronesis, judgement and practical discourse become concretely embedded in our everyday practices'. In these two sentences lie seeds of a more unified psychology. And personal construct psychology can be a part of that growth. Kelly, as I suggested earlier, was neither an objectivist nor a relativist. And some recent developments in personal construct psychology – Miller Mair's 'community', Laurie Thomas on 'conversation', my own claims for construct psychology as social psychology, Don Bannister's novels – are all moving in the way beyond which Bernstein indicates.

II

The second fragment comes from a paper given at the 1987 Memphis Seventh International Congress on Personal Construct Psychology, by Professor Bernie O'Merearty.

One of the distinctive characteristics of self-critical reflexivity is that at the personal level construct theorists might be encouraged to interpret their own theoretical shortcomings in terms of their theory. Stringer's paper at the Cambridge congress illustrates this well, in reverse. His failure to build the comprehensive social psychology that he and his theory group argue for was a result of the individualistic focus of convenience of their theoretical constructs.

The completion of my socio-historical study affords me an opportunity to reflect upon the publication of Stringer's intellectual materials. At the end of the 1960s he was gaining visibility by studying personality change with a group of architecture students. The three papers that emerged from this period (1968–72) were salient for a cognitive complexity mold that ignored markedly the social, small-group context of these students' education under the late Jane Abercrombie. Three further papers that looked at architecture from the vantage point of PCT were equally foolish. 'Architecture, psychology: the game's the same' (Stringer, 1970) is an anti-social attempt to sabotage the new discipline of architectural psychology before it reached its network stage. It is not a purist Kellian argument that creative social relations will occur only if role, disciplinary or professional demarcations are displaced.

In 1973 Stringer was hired by a competing group at Surrey, where a specialty in environmental psychology was congealing. Seven articles on environmental perception emerged generated from just one repertory grid study of 200 women's construal of plans for the redevelopment of their neighbourhood shopping center. Stringer assumes for this study: an interesting use of the repertory grid in the field with a large random sample; the explicit socio-political context where the grid was administered; the relation of grid measures to other behavior; and the study's attention to women as a social group. But it was catalyzed more by human geographers than environmental or social psychologists. One of the papers (Stringer, 1973) was published in *The Cartographic Journal.* He was thus seeking a niche in elite journals.

Stringer evolved during the second half of his stay at Surrey into studies on travel-mode choice, tourism, and citizen participation. He claimed for this the germinal status of 'applied social psychology'. More likely influences are the social, economic and political factors operative in the late 1960s and early 1970s. These he merely and artfully transpositioned into 'applied social psychology' at a time when relevance and government research contracts were growing in visibility. Although the centers of gravity of this stage of his research development all involved anticipatory construing and were considered in a social (family, politics) context, this is not enough to make it truly significant either as purist PCT or as social psychology.

Stringer believed that he was escaping from the lack of psychometric soundness that, despite my own basic enthusiasm for grid technique, I should admit it suffers from. Travel-mode choice was examined in terms of constructs only – 3,000 elicited from a sample of 480 Manchester citizens. One of the tourism studies was a PCT analysis of Australian travellers' tales. But PCT was just tagged on to quite superordinate concerns outside its range of convenience.

A serious student of social psychology would at this point in time have been catalyzing a truly social psychological approach to PCT. The ingrown volume *Constructs of Sociality and Individuality* came nowhere near achieving that. Stringer's own problematic and abstruse chapter in that publication shows just how wholly irrelevant his focus was. He stated flatly that he saw 'no relation here'.

In the latter phase from 1980 to 1985, although he occupied a chair of social psychology, his publicly advertized disdain for theory-building efforts was notorious. His cute jokes in *Issues and Approaches to Personal Construct Theory* and in the volume *The Construction of Social Scientific Talk* (admittedly analyses of a PCT workshop transcript) are caricatures of earlier literary studies. Stringer claimed that PCT badly needed to broaden its data-base and to pay attention to what he called 'texts' – novels, newspapers, everyday talk, conversations. He argued – unfairly I think – that these 'texts' were essentially social psychological constructions. We need not agree that this all might have been more convincing if he had elaborated his points in further empirical studies. But his tricks of presentation format – in the *Issues and Approaches* chapter and in his 1985 Cambridge congress paper – merely mask the congealing into emptiness of his nascent textual interests. It was no surprise in the end that in the Fall of 1985 he apparently abandoned psychology.

It may be that there is other evidence behind the published intellectual materials. But sociological observation must discount hearsay and speculative interpretations. The judgment of history is harsh. Stringer has never been a PCT purist and hardly even a social psychologist. As a college student he only took psychology for one year. Though he worked in London in the late 1960s he did not share in the communicative cohesiveness of the rapidly expanding wing of PCT researchers that was thickening there during that period. He began teaching social psychology only in 1975 in Surrey. While there he had no contact with that university's 'personal construction of knowledge' center. There is no trace in Holland of colleagueship with the Bonarius group. In only one of his papers did he cement any social ties by co-authorship, and that with an outsider to PCT. He belonged to no cluster or network; his specialty was to have no specialty; he never had a normal period of scientific development. He was an intellectual isolationist, with none of the adaptiveness of the isolationist stance.

The critical upshot is that Stringer's writing has not really matched the complexity and diversity of his own published literature, which meshes with numerous specialties in the social sciences, with a comparably complex social communication structure that would link it more firmly with other theory groups.

III

The third fragment has also been translated from a Dutch original. It was given to me by a very dear friend. It is an 'other-characterisation', rather than the more usual PCP self-characterisation. Being construed by another gives us our social psychological existence. It is difficult to utter; but it suggests very well, both formally and through its content, much of what I should have liked to say about social psychology and PCP. It is a small part of a social relation.

Peter is a person who realises that the Sociality Corollary precedes the individual. Through construing the constructs of others – of persons, books, films, the newspaper – he becomes Peter, through using them selectively to mark out and extend his construct system. He is aggressive in testing his construct system. If experiences are invalidating, he does not become hostile, but searches the social environment for constructs which make a new and better choice possible.

In his peripheral-construct system this produces a good deal of change. But his core constructs, those which are important, highly valued, remain the same. These imply dealing with one another in a respectful manner, a readiness for cooperation, seeing the social rather than the individual in society, and a rejection of hostility and refusal to change.

In social contexts there is not one Peter but several, dependent on those contexts. The stereotype hung on him is of a quiet, silent, 'soft' man. However, this is only the case in those contexts in which Peter is construing the others' constructs while they are not construing his. Then he is quiet, seeing a validation of his construing of those others who find themselves important and who are only interested in putting forward their own social self. This circular self-esteem-boosting process is easy for a social psychologist to understand.

There is no 'soft' person. He simply isn't continually shouting how important he is, how marvellous everything is which he does. He listens to you, doesn't deny you. 'If you want to know something of Peter, you must ask him.'

In social contexts where people try to construe Peter's construct system, the quiet, silent man gives way to a lively, aggressive man who knows what is important in life and what to strive for, both as a person and as an academic. That person Peter we can also find in his work, as an academic and as a teacher.

In contrast to the general practice of teachers, Peter does not tell students how something ought to be. He is not interested in transferring his own construct system to others – he is more interested in the constructs of his students, while encouraging them to be logical, interesting, and to say something new. He guides students in the definition and extension of their construct systems. Using a metaphor from the countryside, he will tell them that young, green grass is tastier and healthier, and he will help them to look for green grass; but he will not tell them how to eat or digest it. Or, as he once wrote on the lecture-room board, 'Less teaching, more learning'.

Peter is quiet in the classroom, too. It is the students who talk and struggle with the literature which he has put in front of them. Only if asked will he say something. A further approach to his construct system is offered through what he has written. His teaching method is to use as many social situations as possible in which students can define and extend their construct systems in interaction. These vary through plenary discussions of the texts, looking at videos, working in small groups, role-playing, and so on.

His examinations are also different from the usual way of testing knowledge. Exam questions are answered at home, so that you can use all kinds of literature or other people to come to a definition of your construct system in a logical and interesting extension of the work done on the course. An oral discussion of the answers rounds off their evaluation.

Unlike the normal academic, Peter has a career which is consistent with his personal philosophy.

If constructs are invalidated he goes in search of social experience which makes a fresh choice possible, to extend his system and forestall hostility. This means that instead of keeping himself occupied for the whole of his academic career with the same topic, it has followed a very variable, changing course. Change is not only to forestall hostility, but also comes about from construing other construct systems – what Peter comes in contact with he wants to elaborate and experience further. This all implies a belief in constructive alternativism.

A change in his work situation mostly came about when nobody took the trouble to construe his construct system, and his core constructs did not agree with those of the people with whom he had to work. 'He is strange, different.' Being open to such a different person, being willing and able to experience is the only basis for respectful and cooperative dealings with one another in whatever sort of productive organisation. Peter would be told to adapt to an unrespectful, egocentric, greedy way of working and producing. Because this clashed with his constructs, he could do nothing else than invalidate his work situation, and move on.

His academic work is directed towards a critical science. Every product in society for him is the result of a social and not an individual process. A chair made by a joiner, for example, stands apart from the joiner and those who find it beautiful. It is a societal product with a varying societal value. Not everyone will find it equally beautiful. The joiner does not put his name on it. In art and science the contrary is often the case. The product is not valued for itself: more attention is paid to the maker than to what he produces. However, this evaluation is also a social process – the maker is made.

The product of science is a text which can be seen as independent of its maker. This text consists of a collection of others' texts, and is thus social and not individual. It is also independent of its reader – everyone interprets a text in their own manner. Peter's critique is directed first at the great emphasis which is placed on the individuality of the text-maker. Second, at the hostility which exists in the academic readership – people who will read a text only in the way which they have learned and which has long ago been invalidated.

IV

The fragmentation corollary of personal construct theory proposes that 'a person may successively employ a variety of construction subsystems which are inferentially incompatible with each other'.

Index